Beyond Istanbul
Pages 138–151

Excursions from Istanbul
Pages 152–179

BEYOĞLU

BOSPHORUS

Beyoğlu
Pages 102–109

SERAGLIO
POINT

0 metres   500
0 yards   500

Seraglio Point
Pages 52–69

Sultanahmet
Pages 70–85

EYEWITNESS TRAVEL

ISTANBUL

EYEWITNESS TRAVEL

ISTANBUL

DK

DK

LONDON, NEW YORK,
MELBOURNE, MUNICH AND DELHI
www.dk.com

Project Editor Nick Inman
Art Editor Kate Poole
Editors Claire Folkard, Jane Oliver, Christine Stroyan
Designers Jo Doran, Paul Jackson
Visualizer Joy Fitzsimmons

Main Contributors Rosie Ayliffe, Rose Baring,
Barnaby Rogerson, Canan Sılay

Maps Paul Bates, Anne Rayski, Glyn Rozier
(Esr Cartography Ltd); Neil Cook, Maria Donnelly,
Ewan Watson (Colourmap Scanning Ltd)

Photographers Anthony Souter, Linda Whitwam,
Francesca Yorke

Illustrators Richard Bonson, Stephen Conlin, Gary
Cross, Richard Draper, Paul Guest, Maltings Partnership,
Chris Orr & Associates, Paul Weston, John Woodcock

Printed and bound in China by Leo Paper Products Ltd

First published in Great Britain in 1998
by Dorling Kindersley Limited
80 Strand, London WC2R 0RL

14 15 16 17 10 9 8 7 6 5 4 3 2

Reprinted with revisions 1999, 2000, 2001, 2002, 2004,
2007, 2009, 2011, 2013, 2014

Copyright 1998, 2014 © Dorling Kindersley Limited, London
A Penguin Random House Company

A CIP catalogue record is available from the British Library.

ISBN 978-1-40932-925-1

Floors are referred to throughout in accordance with
European usage; ie the "first floor" is the floor above ground level.

MIX
Paper from
responsible sources
FSC™ C018179
www.fsc.org

Front cover main image: The Blue Mosque, Istanbul's most famous religious building

◀ The stunning interior of the Blue Mosque in Sultanahmet Square

Contents

How to Use this Guide **6**

Madonna mosaic in the Church of
St Saviour in Chora

Introducing Istanbul

Tile panel in the Paired Pavilions of Topkapı
Palace's Harem

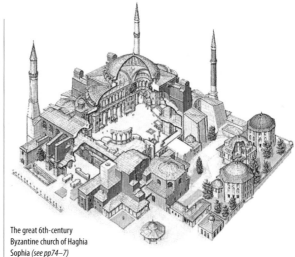

The great 6th-century
Byzantine church of Haghia
Sophia *(see pp74–7)*

Men smoking bubble pipes in Çorlulu Ali
Paşa Courtyard

Ferry passing the busy Karaköy waterfront
below the Galata Tower

Simit seller

Dolmabahçe Mosque with the skyline of Sultanahmet in the distance

HOW TO USE THIS GUIDE

This guide helps you to get the most from your stay in Istanbul. It provides both expert recommendations and detailed practical advice. Introducing Istanbul locates the city geographically, sets Istanbul in its historical and cultural context and gives an overview of the main attractions. Istanbul Area by Area is the main sightseeing section, giving detailed information on all the major sights plus three recommended walks, with photographs, maps and illustrations throughout. Greater Istanbul looks at sights outside the city centre. The Bosphorus guides you through a trip up the straits, and Excursions from Istanbul explores other places within easy reach of the city. Tips for restaurants, hotels, entertainment and shopping are found in Travellers' Needs, while the Survival Guide contains useful advice on everything from personal security to public transport.

Finding your way around Istanbul

The centre of Istanbul has been divided into four sightseeing areas, each with its own chapter, colour-coded for easy reference. All sights are numbered and plotted on an area map for each chapter. The major sights are covered in more detail.

1 Area Introduction This describes the history and character of the area and has a map on which the sights have been plotted. Other key information is also given.

Each area has colour-coded thumb tabs.

Locator Map

The area shaded pink is shown in greater detail on the Street-by-Street map on the following pages.

2 Street-by-Street Map This gives a bird's-eye view of the heart of each sightseeing area. Interesting features are labelled. There is also a list of "star sights" that no visitor should miss.

A suggested route takes in the most interesting and attractive streets in the area.

3 Detailed information All the important sights are described individually. They are listed in order, following the numbering on the area map, with practical information about each.

Istanbul Area Map

The coloured areas shown on this map *(see inside front cover)* are the four main sightseeing areas used in this guide. Each is covered in a full chapter in *Istanbul Area by Area (pp50–109)*. They are highlighted on other maps throughout the book. In *Istanbul at a Glance (see pp36–45)*, they help you to locate the top sights. The introduction to the *Street Finder (see pp246–263)* shows on which detailed street map you will find each area.

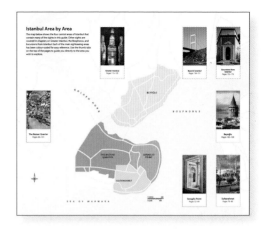

Introductory text gives an overview of the main sights in the Greater Istanbul area.

A map of the city shows Greater Istanbul and the areas covered in the chapter's sub-divisions.

4 **Introduction to Greater Istanbul** Greater Istanbul has its own introduction, outlining what the city suburbs have to offer the sightseer. It is divided into five districts, shown on a map.

Practical information is provided in an information block. The key to the symbols used is on the back flap.

5 **Introduction to Greater Istanbul areas** An introduction places the area in its historical context and provides a map showing the numbered sights.

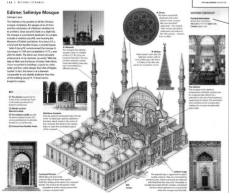

The Visitors' Checklist provides detailed practical information.

6 **Istanbul's major sights** These are given two or more full pages. Historic buildings are dissected to reveal their interiors. Where necessary, sights are colour-coded to help you locate the most interesting areas.

INTRODUCING ISTANBUL

GREAT DAYS IN ISTANBUL

Istanbul is a frenetic city with a wealth of culture, history and nightlife. Split in two by the Bosphorous Strait, it is the only city in the world to straddle two continents, Europe and Asia, and thus has two contrasting atmospheres. These itineraries are designed to provide a flavour of the city as a whole.

Some of the city's best attractions are arranged first thematically and then by duration of stay. All the sights are cross-referenced to the rest of the guide, so it is possible to look up more information and tailor the day to suit your needs. Price guides include meals, transport and admission fees.

A range of exotic spices for sale in the Spice Bazaar

Shopping and Seafood

Two Adults allow at least $105

- Refresh your senses in the Spice Bazaar
- Shop for antiques in Çukurcuma
- Haggle in the unmissable Grand Bazaar
- Enjoy the buzz on Nevizade Sokak

Morning

Start the day with a riot of colour, stalls and smells at the **Spice Bazaar** (see p90). Shop for exotic food items, including handmade Turkish delight and creamy goats' cheese here. Next, head up to the bustling **Grand Bazaar** (see pp100–101), a labyrinthine Ottoman shopping complex housing thousands of leather, rug, ceramics and jewellery shops. Be sure to bargain as prices are mostly inflated and price tags are often absent altogether. All this shopping is bound to whet your appetite, so head for the waterfront district of

Kumkapı. Savour delicious seafood from any of the 50 fish restaurants located here. Again, many outlets do not display prices, so inquire before placing your order.

Afternoon

After lunch, take a taxi to the Galata Bridge. Stroll over to trendy Tünel and **Beyoğlu** (see pp102–9), and enjoy the lovely view enroute. Take time out to browse around the cosy cafés and bars in Tünel, before making your way up **İstiklâl Caddesi** (see pp104–5) to shop for clothes, shoes, books and music. Further up is the district of **Çukurcuma** (see p109), which is famous as a hunting ground for antique furniture and ornaments. Nevizade Sokak, just off İstiklâl Caddesi, is a narrow street lined with dozens of traditional meyhanes or taverns (see p191). The area comes alive at night, when hundreds of locals flock here and passers-by are serenaded by traditional musicians playing fasil, a local form of gypsy music.

A Family Day Out

Family of four allow $120

- See Istanbul in miniature
- A boat trip to Büyükada
- A horse-drawn carriage ride around Büyükada

Morning

Catch a bus from Taksim Square to **Miniatürk** (see pp222–3) in Sütlüce on the northern shore of the **Golden Horn** (see p91). The park displays miniatures of the city's most famous sights, such as **Haghia Sophia** (see pp74–7), as well as other treasures from around the country that reflect Turkey's rich heritage. There is also a children's park and a museum showcasing photographs of Atatürk, the great Turkish leader of the early 20th century, and the wars in Gallipoli. After such a busy morning, head to **Miniatürk's** attractive café-restaurant that overlooks the Golden Horn.

The busy, bustling dock at Eminönü

◄ Mosaic depicting the infancy of Christ, Church of St Saviour in Chora

Afternoon

Head back to Istanbul after lunch and hop on a boat bound for Büyükada, one of the nine islands that make up the **Princes' Islands** (see p161). It is a one-and-a-half hour trip from Kabataş pier (one hour and ten minutes from Kadiköy pier), so there is plenty of time to admire the pretty view and watch as Istanbul recedes on the horizon. On arrival, stroll around the main square of Saat Meydanı or take a horse-drawn carriage ride around the island. Climb the hill to St George's Monastery for panoramic views and enjoy a meal at the hilltop restaurant.

Mosques, Museums and Hamams

Two Adults allow at least $140

- Byzantine iconography at Haghia Sophia
- Get a glimpse of the past at the Museum of Turkish and Islamic Arts
- An awe-inspiring visit to Topkapı Palace

Morning

Begin the day with a visit to the iconic **Blue Mosque** (see pp80–81), perhaps Istanbul's most elegant Islamic sight, famous for its slender minarets and blue Iznik tiles. Stroll through the well-tended garden at the front before making your way to the imposing **Haghia Sophia** (see pp74–7), another of Istanbul's most renowned mosques. Inside is a marvellous array of Byzantine mosaics, friezes and Iznik blue tile decorations, as well as a huge domed ceiling. Next, head to the nearby **Museum of Turkish and Islamic Arts** (see p79), which has a wonderful collection of glass and metalwork, carpets and manuscripts from down the centuries, as well as modern art from Turkey and overseas. For lunch, head to Divanyolu Caddesi, which is lined with several fantastic traditional restaurants with prices to suit all budgets.

The Fortress of Europe overlooking the Bosphorus

Afternoon

Devote at least three hours for exploring **Topkapı Palace** (see pp56–61), a sprawling complex of courtyards, gardens, fountains, a harem and a collection of priceless antiques. Then, at the end of a long day, indulge in that most Turkish of pleasures, a visit to a Turkish bath (see p69). **Çemberlitaş Baths** (see p83) in Sultanahmet is one of the finest.

Decorative blue tiles in the Haghia Sophia mosque

Up the Bosphorus

Two Adults allow at least $95

- Take a boat up the Bosphorus
- Soak up the views at the Fortress of Europe
- Stroll through the pretty village of Bebek

Morning

Catch a bus from Taksim Square or Eminönü bus terminus to Sarıyer or Emirgan and get off at Arnavutköy on the Bosphorus (see p146–7 for details of excursions and boat cruises). There are some lovingly restored Ottoman houses and mansions to admire here, most of them painted in pastel shades and trimmed with intricate wooden fretwork. Cafés line the back streets, so relax and unwind over a coffee and a pastry. From Arnavutköy, continue walking northwards, past the fishing boats and pleasure cruisers bobbing on the water, until you reach **Bebek** (see p140 & p148), one of Istanbul's most affluent villages. There are more than enough chic clothes and antiques shops here to tempt visitors to part with their cash and work up an appetite for lunch. Dine in style at the well-reviewed **Poseidon** (see p206). Sip an aperitif and enjoy the splendid view here before savouring the menu of fresh fish.

Afternoon

Delve into history at the imposing **Fortress of Europe** (see pp142–3), built in the 15th century as part of the Muslim conquest of Constantinople. There is also a fantastic view of the Bosphorus from here. Afterwards, walk around the delightful 19th-century pavilions of nearby **Emirgan Park** (see p143) with its many pine, fir and cypress trees and an ornamental lake. This attractive park is the venue for the Tulip Festival, which is held in April every year.

2 days in Istanbul

- Gaze in awe at the soaring dome of the Haghia Sophia
- Enjoy a steamed bath in the Ottoman Çemberlitaş Baths
- Cruise the Bosphorus, the ribbon of water separating Europe and Asia

Day 1
Morning
Start at the monumental **Haghia Sophia** (see pp74–7), one of the world's truly iconic buildings. Cross the tramline to the **Milion** (see p73), a marble fragment once part of a mighty triumphal arch. Beneath your feet lies the atmospherically-lit **Basilica Cistern** (see p78). Resurface onto Divanyolu Caddesi, an historic thoroughfare lined with traditional Turkish lunch spots.

Afternoon
Cross Divanyolu to the **Blue Mosque** (see pp80–81), a cascade of tumbling domes and slender minarets. Exit onto the **Hippodrome** (see p82), the central barrier of the chariot racing track marked by the Egyptian Obelisk. Then ride the tram to the **Grand Bazaar** (see pp100–101), a centuries old mall selling everything from fake Louis Vuitton bags to antique Turkish rugs. Exit to **Constantine's Column** (see p83) before crossing an alley to relax in the steam of Ottoman-era **Çemberlitaş Baths** (see p83).

Day 2
Morning
Begin the day with a trip to the 15th-century **Topkapı Palace** (see pp56–61), standing in splendid isolation on a hilltop overlooking the Bosphorus and Sea of Marmara. Don't miss the labyrinthine and exotic **Harem** (see pp60–61) before catching the tram to the peaceful grounds of the Süleymaniye Mosque complex.

Afternoon
Explore the **Süleymaniye Mosque** (see pp90–91) complex, presiding majestically over the third of Istanbul's seven hills. Then walk down to **Rüstem Paşa Mosque** (see pp90–91), famed for its İznik tiles, before wandering through the exotically-scented **Spice Bazaar** (see p90). Exit onto the Eminönü waterfront, clustered around the historic **Galata Bridge** (see p91), before finishing with the **Bosphorus Cruise** (see pp146–51) up the famous strait.

3 days in Istanbul

- Delve into the eerie underground world of the Basilica Cistern
- Haggle for a Turkish carpet in the Grand Bazaar
- Follow in the footsteps of Ottoman sultans through the Topkapı Palace

Day 1
Morning
Get to know Istanbul's history at the maze-like **Archaeological Museums** (see pp64–7) before strolling through **Gülhane Park** (see p63) to tea gardens overlooking the Bosphorus. Exit the park and head up pretty **Soğukçeşme Sokağı** (see p63), lined with period houses, to lunch in **Cafer Ağa Courtyard** (see p63).

Afternoon
Explore the city's Byzantine past in the sunken **Basilica Cistern** (see p78), famed for its Medusa-head carvings. Emerge at street level by the **Milion** (see p73), a scrap of a once magnificent triumphal arch, before crossing the tramway to **Haghia Sophia** (see pp74–7), with its soaring dome and glittering mosaics.

Day 2
Morning
Visit the **Blue Mosque** (see pp80–81), its vast interior spangled with predominantly blue İznik tiles. Head out onto the **Hippodrome**, a pleasant square once a chariot racing circuit rivalling Rome's Circus Maximus. Flanking it is the **Museum of Turkish and Islamic Arts** (see p79), which is home to superb carpets. Tread downhill to the beautiful **Sokullu Mehmet Paşa Mosque** (see p84) and the nearby Byzantine **SS Sergius and Bacchus' Church** (see pp84–5).

Afternoon
Weave through the crowds to explore the wonderful **Topkapı Palace** (see pp56–61), home to artifacts as varied as the 86 carat Spoonmaker's diamond and the mantle of the Prophet Mohammed. After exiting the intriguing suite of rooms that comprise the palace's women's quarters, the **Harem** (see pp60–61), catch a tram to the **Çemberlitaş Baths** (see p83) and ease those aching limbs. Opposite the baths rises **Constantine's Column** (see p83), erected in AD 330.

Day 3
Morning
Start with the short version of the **Bosphorus Cruise** (see pp146–51), which takes visitors up to the first continent-spanning bridge and back again. Cross the square to the Ottoman **Spice Bazaar** (see p90) and try your hand at haggling. Head back to the vibrant Eminönü waterfront for a fish sandwich and watch the anglers massed on the **Galata Bridge** (see p91).

The majestic Haghia Sophia, Istanbul's most famous monument

Afternoon

After lunch, head to the **Rüstem Paşa Mosque** *(see pp90–91)*, an intimate place of worship in the heart of the bazaar, before visiting the **Süleymaniye Mosque** *(see pp90–91)* complex to soak up fine views from its grounds. Next, stop at the **Grand Bazaar** *(see pp100–101)*, where a cornucopia of wares await eager buyers.

The colourful Grand Bazaar teeming with shoppers

5 days in Istanbul

- **Get to grips with Turkey's fascinating history in the Archaeological Museums**

- **Enjoy impressive views of the old city from the landmark Galata Tower**

- **Admire the glittering Byzantine mosaics at the Church of St Saviour**

Day 1
Morning

The sprawling administrative heart of the Ottoman Empire and the opulent residence of its sultans, the **Topkapı Palace** *(see pp56–61)*, makes for an engrossing start to the day, especially when combined with the "forbidden" women's quarters, the **Harem** *(see pp60–61)*.

Afternoon

Catch the tram to the **Grand Bazaar** *(see pp100–101)*, a 500-year-old mall, and lunch in one of its myriad tradesmen's cafes before exploring its maze of alleys and thousands of shops. Exit by the Nuruosmaniye Gate and head to **Constantine's Column** *(see p83)*, a late-Roman marvel. Opposite is the **Çemberlitaş Baths** *(see p83)*, ideal to relax after a day's sightseeing.

Day 2
Morning

Take the tram to the city's imposing land walls, walk to the **Church of St Saviour in Chora** *(see pp120–21)* and admire its splendid mosaics. Stroll north alongside the walls, past the remnants of the Byzantine **Palace of the Porphyrogenitus** *(see p119)* and drop down to Golden Horn and catch a ferry to Eminönü.

Afternoon

Head uphill to the **Archaeological Museums** *(see pp64–7)* and immerse yourself in Turkey's long history before relaxing with tea in **Gülhane Park** *(see p63)* and enjoying the views to Asia. Finish with a short stroll up period **Soğukçeşme Sokaği** *(see p63)*.

Day 3
Morning

Weave your way down to the Sea of Marmara to view the **SS Sergius and Bacchus' Church** *(see pp84–5)*, then up to Istanbul's finest small mosque, **Sokullu Mehmet Paşa** *(see p84)*. Housed in a former Grand Vizier's residence above is the engaging **Museum of Turkish and Islamic Arts** *(see p79)*. Outside the museum is the **Hippodrome** *(see p82)*, where chariots once raced. Walk across it to the spectacular **Blue Mosque** *(see pp80–81)*.

Afternoon

Spare a quick glance for the sole surviving piece of a monumental triumphal arch, the **Milion** *(see p73)*, then head down into the beautiful **Basilica Cistern** *(see p78)*. Emerge from its depths and cross the tramway to explore

Detail on a mosaic in the Church of St Saviour in Chora

Istanbul's signature building, **Haghia Sophia** *(see pp74–7)*.

Day 4
Morning

Begin atop the city's third hill and explore its 'crown', the wonderful **Süleymaniye Mosque** *(see pp90–91)* complex. Wind down through a bustling bazaar to **Rüstem Paşa Mosque** *(see pp90–91)*, an Ottoman gem, then stroll to the domed splendours of the **Spice Bazaar** *(see p90)*. Weave through the Eminönü waterfront crowds, cross the **Galata Bridge** *(see p91)* to the Tünel underground funicular and ride up to İstiklal Caddesi.

Afternoon

Start the afternoon at the **Mevlevi Lodge** *(see pp106–7)*, home of the mystical whirling dervishes, then wander along Istanbul's main shopping street, **İstiklal Caddesi** *(see pp104–5)*. Walk down cobbled lanes to the Genoese **Galata Tower** *(see p107)* for panoramic views of the old city.

Day 5

Escape the inevitable foot-slogging around the sites and relax on the full-day **Bosphorus Cruise** *(see pp146–51)*, starting near the Galata Bridge. The cruise passes two suspension bridges, various waterfront mansions and palaces and a couple of Ottoman fortresses - and there's a lunch stop in a fishing village. Alternatively, take a ferry from Kabataş to explore one or more of the picturesque, traffic-free **Princes' Islands** *(see p161)* in the Sea of Marmara, where you can explore on foot, hire a bicycle or opt for a horse-drawn carriage.

Putting Istanbul on the Map

Istanbul stands astride the straits of the Bosphorus,
straddling the European and Asian parts of Turkey and
bordered to the south by the Sea of Marmara. The city is
divided not only by the Bosphorus but also by the Golden
Horn, an inlet forming a natural harbour. Although no
longer the capital of Turkey *(see p33)*, Istanbul is still the
country's largest and most monumental city.

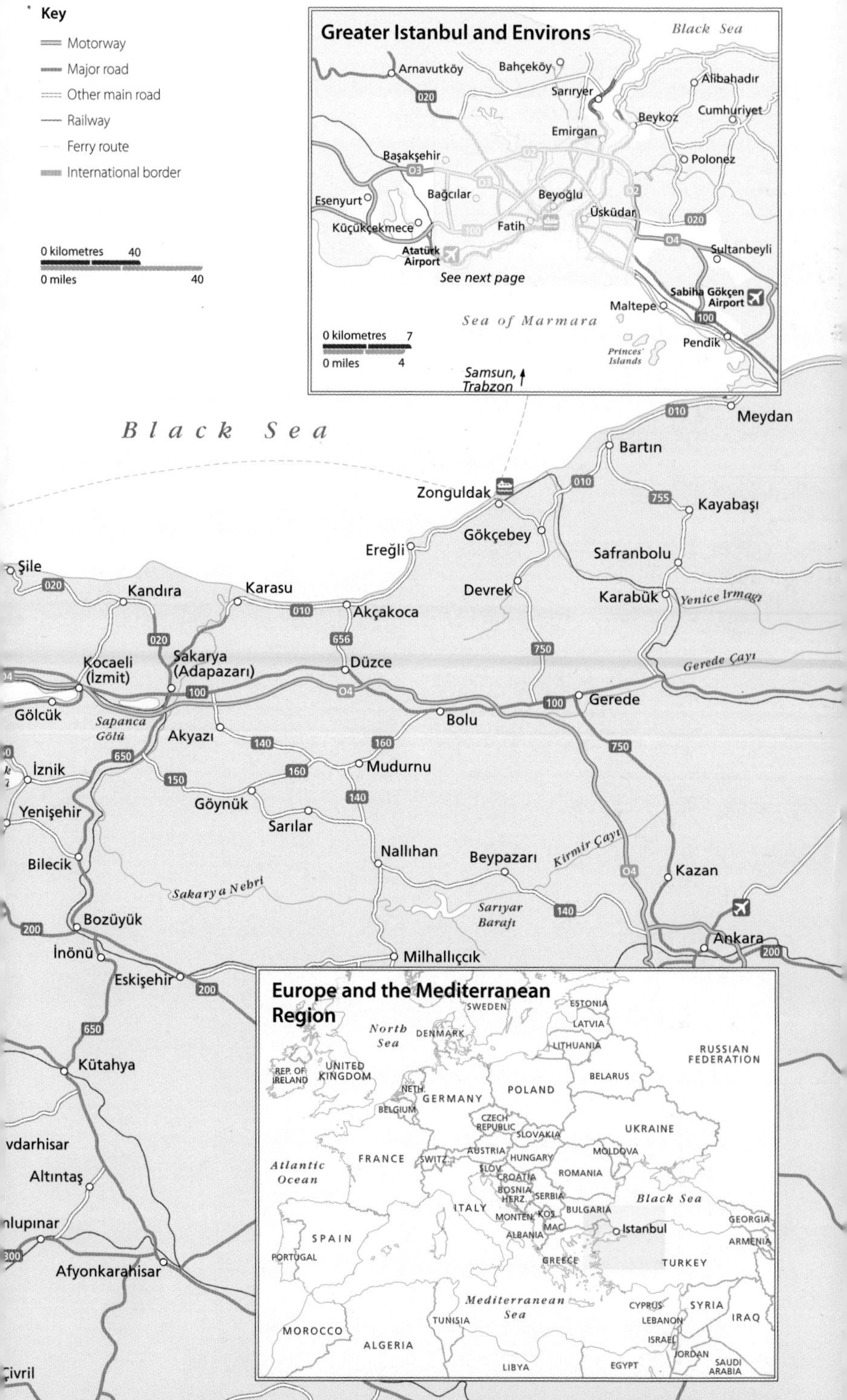

Key

- Motorway
- Major road
- Other main road
- Railway
- Ferry route
- International border

0 kilometres 40
0 miles 40

Greater Istanbul and Environs

Black Sea

Arnavutköy
Bahçeköy
Sarıyer
Alibahadır
Beykoz
Cumhuriyet
Emirgan
Polonez
Başakşehir
Esenyurt
Bağcılar
Beyoğlu
Üsküdar
Küçükçekmece
Fatih
Sultanbeyli
Atatürk
Airport
See next page
Şabiha Gökçen
Airport
Maltepe
Pendik

Sea of Marmara

*Princes'
Islands*

0 kilometres 7
0 miles 4

*Samsun,
Trabzon*

Black Sea

Meydan
Bartın
Zonguldak
Kayabaşı
Gökçebey
Safranbolu
Ereğli
Devrek
Karabük *Yenice Irmağı*
Şile
Kandıra
Karasu
Akçakoca
Kocaeli
(İzmit)
Sakarya
(Adapazarı)
Düzce
Gerede
Gerede Çayı
Gölcük
*Sapanca
Gölü*
Bolu
Akyazı
İznik
Mudurnu
Yenişehir
Göynük
Sarılar
Bilecik
Nallıhan
Beypazarı
Kirmir Çayı
Sakarya Nehri
Kazan
Bozüyük
*Sarıyar
Barajı*
İnönü
Milhallıçık
Ankara
Eskişehir

Europe and the Mediterranean Region

*North
Sea*
SWEDEN
ESTONIA
LATVIA
DENMARK
LITHUANIA
REP. OF
IRELAND
UNITED
KINGDOM
RUSSIAN
FEDERATION
BELARUS
NETH.
GERMANY
POLAND
BELGIUM
*Atlantic
Ocean*
CZECH
REPUBLIC
UKRAINE
FRANCE
SWITZ.
AUSTRIA
SLOVAKIA
HUNGARY
MOLDOVA
SLOV.
ROMANIA
CROATIA
ITALY
BOSNIA
HERZ.
SERBIA
Black Sea
MONTEN.
KOS.
BULGARIA
GEORGIA
SPAIN
ALBANIA
MAC.
Istanbul
ARMENIA
PORTUGAL
GREECE
TURKEY
CYPRUS
SYRIA
*Mediterranean
Sea*
LEBANON
IRAQ
MOROCCO
TUNISIA
ISRAEL
JORDAN
SAUDI
ARABIA
ALGERIA
LIBYA
EGYPT

Kütahya
vdarhisar
Altıntaş
nlupınar
Afyonkarahisar
Çivril

For map symbols see back flap

Greater Istanbul

The expanding metropolis of Istanbul spreads along the Bosphorus to the north, beyond the airport to the west, and inland from the Asian shore in the east. Its official population is put at just under 14 million but the actual population is probably much higher. Transport improvements are being made to make getting around this vast urban area easier. Most visitors, however, stay in the historical central parts where the major sights are located.

0 kilometres 2

0 miles 2

Sea of Marmara

Marmara, Bandirma, Bursa

Key

- ▪ Central Istanbul
- ▪ Greater Istanbul
- ▬ Motorway
- ▬ Main road
- ▬ Other road
- ▬ Railway
- ⋯ Ferry route
- ⦵ Metro / light rail station
- ⦵ Tram station

Central Istanbul

This guide divides central Istanbul into four distinct areas, each with its own chapter. Three areas lie on the southern side of the Golden Horn. Seraglio Point is a raised promontory on which stands the sumptuous Topkapı Palace. Two architectural masterpieces, Haghia Sophia and the Blue Mosque, dominate the area of Sultanahmet. The pace of life is quite different in the Bazaar Quarter, a maze of narrow streets filled with frenetic commerce. North of the Golden Horn is Beyoğlu, which for centuries was the preferred place of residence of Istanbul's foreign communities, and is still markedly cosmopolitan in atmosphere.

İstiklâl Caddesi, Beyoğlu
Old-fashioned trams shuttle up and down the pedestrianized street that forms the backbone of this area
(see pp102–109).

The Grand Bazaar, Bazaar Quarter
This quaint former coffee house stands at a junction in the labyrinthine old shopping complex at the heart of the city's Bazaar Quarter *(see pp86–101).*

Key

◾ Major sight

0 metres   500
0 yards   500

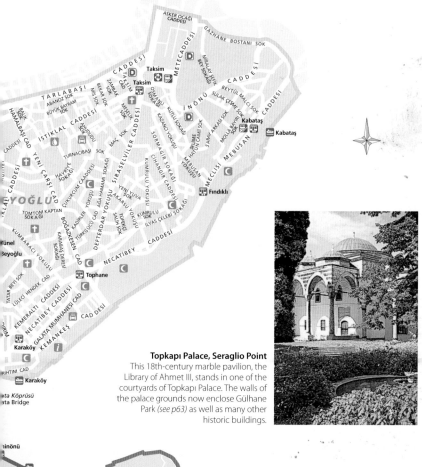

Topkapı Palace, Seraglio Point
This 18th-century marble pavilion, the Library of Ahmet III, stands in one of the courtyards of Topkapı Palace. The walls of the palace grounds now enclose Gülhane Park (see p63) as well as many other historic buildings.

View across Sultanahmet
The six slender minarets of the Mosque of Sultan Ahmet I, better known as the Blue Mosque, soar above the spacious square in the middle of Sultanahmet (see pp70–85), Istanbul's most historical district.

THE HISTORY OF ISTANBUL

Istanbul was founded in the 7th century BC on a naturally defensive site from which trade along the Bosphorus could be controlled. For 16 centuries it was a great imperial capital, first of the Byzantine Empire and then of the Ottoman sultans. Some knowledge of the histories of these two civilizations helps the visitor to appreciate the magnificent monuments found throughout the city.

The topography of Istanbul was formed at the end of the last Ice Age, when meltwaters created the Bosphorus. The Stone Age cultures in the area were replaced by Copper Age villages and walled Bronze Age towns (notably Troy, *see p173*). The Bosphorus was an important trade route in the ancient world along which ships carried wine and olive oil north from the Mediterranean, and grain, skins, wool, timber, wax, honey, salted meat and salted fish south from regions around the Black Sea.

The area around the Bosphorus was subjugated by a series of peoples, starting with the Mycenaeans (1400–1200 BC). Between 800 and 680 BC the region was controlled by the kingdom of Phrygia. Later, in 676 BC, Greek expeditionaries founded the city of Chalcedon (on the site where modern Kadıköy now stands).

The Foundation of Byzantion

The foundation of Istanbul is usually dated to 667 BC when, according to legend, a Greek colonist, Byzas, led an expedition from the overcrowded cities of Athens and Megara to establish a colony on the European side of the Bosphorus. This colony, known as Byzantion, grew to be a successful independent city-state, or *polis*, one of the 40 most important such states throughout the Ancient Greek world. During the next few centuries, Byzantion worked in partnership with Chalcedon, using the same coinage and sharing the tolls exacted from passing sea trade.

But Byzantion had to struggle to maintain its independence in the mercurial politics of the ancient world. It endured Lydian (560–546 BC), Persian (546–478 BC), Athenian (478–411 BC) and Macedonian (334–281 BC) rule before briefly regaining its autonomy. In 64 BC it was subsumed into the Roman Empire as Byzantium. The city was almost destroyed in AD 195 by Septimius Severus because of its support for his rival for the imperial throne, Pescennius Niger. It survived the Goths' devastation of Chalcedon in AD 258 but trade in the region dramatically declined in the following years.

c.676 BC Chalcedon, a Greek settlement, founded on the Asian shore	**340 BC** Philip II of Macedonia unsuccessfully besieges city	*Alexander the Great*	**AD 195** Roman emperor Septimius Severus destroys Byzantium but later rebuilds it and creates the Hippodrome
600 BC	**400 BC**	**200 BC**	**AD 1** **AD 200**
c.667 BC Byzantion reputedly founded by Greek colonists from Athens and Megara, led by Byzas	**334 BC** Alexander the Great crosses the Hellespont (Dardanelles) and conquers Anatolia	**64 BC** Pompey brings Byzantion into the Roman Empire, renaming it Byzantium	**AD 258** Goths destroy Chalcedon

◀ The Byzantine emperor Justinian the Great shown with one of his prefects in a mosaic

Constantine the Great

In AD 324, after defeating his co-emperor Licinius, Constantine the Great (324–37) became sole ruler of the Roman Empire. One of his greatest achievements was to move the capital of the empire from Rome to Byzantium. Initially, Constantine preferred the site of Troy (see p173) for his capital, but was persuaded by advisers that Byzantium held a superior position for both defence and trade.

Gold aureus of Constantine

Constantine's city was officially styled the "New Rome" but became widely known as Constantinople. The emperor quickly started on an ambitious programme of construction work, which included the Great Palace (see pp84–5) and various public buildings.

Constantine was also instrumental in the spread of Christianity. According to legend, he saw a vision of the cross before a battle in 312. Although not actually baptized until just before his death, he worked hard to create a coherent system of Christian belief out of the variant practices of the day. All the early church councils took place in the city or nearby, the first being held in Nicaea (modern-day İznik, see p162), and the second in Constantinople itself.

A successor of Constantine, Theodosius I (379–95), divided the Empire between his two sons, Honorius and Arcadius. When the Latin-speaking Western Empire fell to barbarian armies during the 5th century, the Greek-speaking Eastern Empire, thereafter known as the Byzantine Empire, survived.

The Age of Justinian

The 6th century was dominated by the extraordinary genius of Justinian (527–65), who developed Constantinople into a thriving city and almost succeeded in reconquering the lost provinces of the Western Empire from the barbarians. At the time of his death the empire had expanded to its greatest size, and covered Syria, Palestine, Asia Minor, Greece, the Balkans, Italy, southern Spain and many territories in northern Africa, including Egypt.

Empress Theodora, wife of Justinian

Justinian's formidable wife, the ex-courtesan Theodora, had a great deal of influence over him. In 532 she persuaded the emperor to use mercenaries to put down an angry mob in the most notorious event of his reign, the Nika Revolt. In the carnage that followed, 30,000 were killed inside the Hippodrome (see p82).

Justinian was also responsible for much of the city's great architecture, including Haghia Sophia (see pp74–7), Haghia Eirene (see p62) and parts of the Great Palace.

Relief from the Egyptian Obelisk (see p82), showing Theodosius I and his courtiers

324 Constantine becomes ruler of the Roman Empire	**330** Inauguration of Constantinople	**395** On the death of Theodosius I, the empire is divided into two	**476** The Western Roman Empire falls to barbarians	**674** Five-year-long siege of Constantinople initiated by the Saracens
			532 Nika Revolt is put down by mercenaries; 30,000 are killed	
300		**400**	**500**	**600** **700**
325 First church council meets at Nicaea	**337** Constantine is baptized a Christian on his deathbed	**412** Construction work begins on the Walls of Theodosius II (see p24)	**537** Emperor Justinian dedicates the new Haghia Sophia	**726** Leo III issues a decree denouncing idolatry, and many icons are destroyed

Walls of Theodosius II

The Byzantines at War

The Byzantine Empire never again attained the splendour of the reign of Justinian, but throughout the first millennium it remained rich and powerful. During the early Middle Ages, Constantinople was an oasis of learning, law, art and culture at a time when Europe was plunged into a dark age of ignorance and illiteracy. Considering themselves to be the leaders of Christianity, the Byzantine rulers dispatched missionaries to spread their religion and culture among the Slavic nations, especially Russia.

During this period, Constantinople produced some capable emperors, in particular Heraclius (610–41), Basil the Macedonian (867–86), Leo the Wise (886–912) and Basil the Bulgar-Slayer (976–1025). Between them these rulers contributed a number of buildings to the city and recaptured lost provinces.

Never without enemies greedy for a share of the prodigious riches that had been amassed in the city, Constantinople was besieged by Slavs, Arabs, Avars, Bulgars, Persians and Russians, all without success because of the protection of the land walls. The surrounding seas, meanwhile, were under the control of Constantinople's powerful navy. Its main ship was the dromon, an oared vessel which could ram another ship but above all deliver the dreaded "Greek fire", an early form of napalm.

"Greek fire", used by the Byzantines against the Arabs

A 6th-century ivory carving of a Byzantine emperor, possibly Anastasius I (491–518)

In 1059 Constantine X, the first of the Dukas dynasty of emperors, ascended to the throne. The state over which the dynasty presided was a weakened one, divided between the over-privileged bureaucracy in the capital and the feudal landlords of the provinces. At the same time increasing dependency on foreign mercenaries placed the empire's defence in the hands of its most aggressive neighbours. These included the Normans from southern Italy, the Venetians and Turkic nomads from the east. The Byzantine imperial army was totally destroyed at the Battle of Manzikert (1071) and again, a century later, at the Battle of Myriocephalon (1176) by the Seljuk Turks from the east. These losses effectively ended Byzantine rule of Anatolia, which had for so long been the backbone of the empire. The remarkable Comnenus dynasty (1081–1185) ruled for a century after the Dukas emperors, between these two defeats. Their main achievement was to succeed in holding the rest of the empire together.

843 Icons are permitted again by seventh church council at Haghia Sophia

1071 The Byzantine army is destroyed by the Seljuk Turks at the Battle of Manzikert. Emperor Romanus Diogenes is disgraced and deposed

1138 John II Comnenus recovers Serbia

1176 The Seljuk Turks defeat the Byzantine forces at the Battle of Myriocephalon

| 800 | 900 | 1000 | 1100 | 1200 |

Haghia Sophia mosaic

1054 The Orthodox and Catholic churches break away from each other because of differences over dogma

1096 The armies of the First Crusade pass through Constantinople and assist Alexius I Comnenus to retake the Anatolian seaboard from the Seljuk Turks

The City of Constantinople

For almost a thousand years Constantinople was the richest city in Christendom. It radiated out from three great buildings: the church of Haghia Sophia *(see pp74–7)*, the Hippodrome *(see p82)* and the Great Palace *(see pp84–5)*. The city also had a great many other fine churches and palaces, filled with exquisite works of art. Daily life for the populace centred on the four market squares, or *fora*. Meanwhile, their need for fresh water was met by an advanced network of aqueducts and underground water cisterns.

Walls of Theodosius
Theodosius II's great chain of land walls *(see p116)* withstood countless sieges until the Ottoman conquest of the city in 1453 *(see p28)*.

The City in 1200

At its height, the magnificent city of Constantinople probably had about 400,000 inhabitants. The population density was relatively low though, and there was space within the city walls for fields and orchards.

Mocius Cistern

The Golden Gate was a ceremonial gate through the city's ramparts.

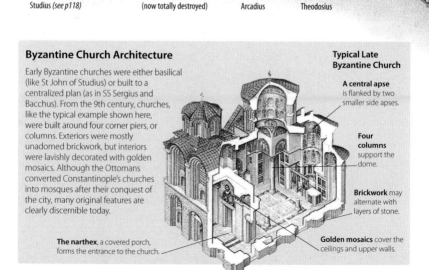

Church of St John of Studius *(see p118)*

Walls of Constantine (now totally destroyed)

Forum of Arcadius

Harbour of Theodosius

Byzantine Church Architecture

Typical Late Byzantine Church

Early Byzantine churches were either basilical (like St John of Studius) or built to a centralized plan (as in SS Sergius and Bacchus). From the 9th century, churches, like the typical example shown here, were built around four corner piers, or columns. Exteriors were mostly unadorned brickwork, but interiors were lavishly decorated with golden mosaics. Although the Ottomans converted Constantinople's churches into mosques after their conquest of the city, many original features are clearly discernible today.

A central apse is flanked by two smaller side apses.

Four columns support the dome.

Brickwork may alternate with layers of stone.

The narthex, a covered porch, forms the entrance to the church.

Golden mosaics cover the ceilings and upper walls.

Church of the Holy Apostles
The domes of what was one of the city's most important churches *(see p115)* are shown in this 12th-century image of the Ascension.

Aetius Cistern

St Saviour in Chora
(see pp120–21)

Blachernae Palace
(see p119)

Monastery of the
Pantocrator *(see p115)*

Valens Aqueduct
Water from the Belgrade Forest *(see p160)* and the mountains west of the city was brought into Constantinople on this great structure *(see p91).*

Forum of Theodosius
(see p95)

Forum of
Constantine *(see p83)*

Basilica Cistern
This cavernous cistern *(see p78)* represented a great feat of engineering when it was built in the 6th century.

Chain across Golden
Horn *(see p91)*

Church of
SS Sergius
and Bacchus
(see p84)

Hippodrome
(see p82)

Great Palace
(see pp84–5)

Haghia Eirene
(see p62)

Haghia Sophia
The great church of Constantinople *(see pp74–7)* was filled with mosaics, including this one showing the Virgin and Child with the emperors Constantine and Justinian.

Milion, Hippodrome
This stone pillar *(see p73)* is all that remains of a Byzantine triumphal arch from which road distances to all corners of the empire were once measured.

The capture of Constantinople during the Fourth Crusade of 1202–4

The Fourth Crusade

In 1202, an army of 34,000 responded to an appeal from Pope Innocent III for a new crusade to the Holy Land. This unruly force of Christians lacked the funds to get beyond Venice, where it needed to hire ships. It consequently fell under the influence of Enrico Dandolo, the manipulative Doge of Venice. With his backing, the crusaders were soon diverted to Constantinople, where they helped the young Alexius IV take the throne.

However, six months later, when they realized they were unlikely to receive their promised financial reward from the emperor, the crusaders lost patience and launched a new attack, ousting Alexius in favour of one their own, Baldwin I,

Icon of St Michael, now in Venice, an example of the fine Byzantine art plundered by the Venetians during the Fourth Crusade

Count of Flanders. Through the dark years that followed, known as the Latin Empire, the once great city was reduced by pillage, misrule and emigration to a scattering of disconnected villages grouped behind the city walls. Outside Constantinople, the exiled Byzantine emperors survived the turmoil, biding their time as the rulers of the Empire of Nicaea, just to the south, which included modern-day İznik (see p162).

Constantinople in decline

In 1261, Constantinople was recaptured for Byzantium by Michael VIII Palaeologus (1258–82), who met almost no resistance in the process. He did this with the aid of the Italian city of Genoa,

1202 An army assembles in Venice to launch the Fourth Crusade

1204 Alexius IV is deposed and Baldwin I is crowned emperor of a new Latin Empire

1261 Michael VIII Palaeologus recaptures Constantinople from the Venetians

1331 Ottomans capture Nicaea (modern İznik)

1326 Prusa (Bursa) is taken and becomes the Ottoman capital

| 1200 | 1225 | 1250 | 1275 | 1300 | 1325 |

1203 Dandolo, Doge of Venice, diverts the Fourth Crusade to Constantinople. He cuts the chain across the Golden Horn (see p91) and storms the city

Bronze horses taken by Dandolo from the Hippodrome (see p82) to Venice

1299 Osman I founds the Ottoman Empire

1321 Outbreak of the disastrous 33-year-long Byzantine civil war

which was naturally disposed to fight against her rival Venice. Yet she still exacted a crippling price for her assistance. The Genoese established the colony of Pera across the Golden Horn from Constantinople, and effectively took control of the city's trade.

Constantinople's recapture and reconstruction caused a flowering of scholarship and artistic activity, known as the Palaeologue Renaissance after the family of emperors. An example of the many beautiful buildings dating from this period is the Church of St Saviour in Chora *(see pp120–21)*.

During this period the double-headed eagle was adopted as the imperial crest, with the two heads symbolizing the western and eastern halves of the empire. Yet, within a few decades there was further discord in Constantinople, when a quarrel arose between Andronicus II (1282–1328) and his grandson Andronicus III

Two-headed Byzantine eagle

(1328–41) over the succession. This led to the disastrous civil war of 1321–54.

The Rise of the Ottomans

The Ottoman state was born in 1299 when Osman I, a leader of warriors who were fighting for the Muslim faith on the eastern frontier of the Byzantine Empire, declared his independence. The new state quickly expanded and in 1326 captured Prusa (modern-day Bursa, *see pp164–70*), which became its capital. The judicious piety of the Ottomans soon won them the support of the general population of their territories, and even of some Christian brotherhoods. Meanwhile, a professional core of Janissaries *(see p129)* was created to add stability to an army which was otherwise too dependent on Turkic and renegade volunteer cavalry.

By 1362, with the Ottoman capture of Adrianople (Edirne, *see pp156–9*), Byzantium had been reduced to the city-state of Constantinople and a few minor outposts, isolated within Ottoman domains. In 1391 the Ottoman army made its first attack on the city's colossal land walls. Only a Mongol incursion in 1402 delayed the invasion of Constantinople itself. As the threat increased, the Byzantine emperor made a last-ditch effort to win the support of the Latin West in 1439. The Hungarians alone answered his call for help, forming a 25,000-strong crusade. However, in 1444 they were defeated en route by the Ottomans at the Battle of Varna on the Black Sea.

Mosaic of the Virgin Mother and Child in St Saviour in Chora

1362 Murat I conquers Adrianople (Edirne), which then becomes the Ottoman capital. Byzantium is reduced to the city of Constantinople

1451 Mehmet II succeeds to the Ottoman throne and orders the construction of the Fortress of Europe *(see p142)* to seal the Bosphorus

| 1350 | 1375 | 1400 | 1425 | 1450 |

1348 The Galata Tower is built by the Genoese inhabitants of the city as a watchtower over the Pera quarter

Galata Tower

1391 First Ottoman siege of Constantinople by Yıldırım Beyazıt (Beyazıt I)

1444 A Hungarian army on its way to help Constantinople is destroyed by the Ottomans at Varna on the Black Sea. Constantinople's last hope of survival is lost

The Conquest of Constantinople

On 29 May 1453 Sultan Mehmet II (1432–81), known as "the Conqueror", entered Constantinople after a 54-day siege during which his cannon had torn a huge hole in the Walls of Theodosius II *(see p116)*. Mehmet's first task was to rebuild the wrecked city,

Sultan Mehmet II, "the Conqueror"

which would later become known as Istanbul. The Grand Bazaar *(see pp100–1)* and Topkapı Palace *(see pp56–9)* were erected in the years following the Muslim conquest. Religious foundations were endowed to fund the building of mosques such as the Fatih *(see p115)* and their associated schools and baths *(see pp40–41)*. The city had to be repopulated by a mixture of force and encouragement. People from all over the empire moved to Istanbul, and Jews, Christians and Muslims lived together in a cosmopolitan society.

Mehmet and his successors pushed the frontiers of the empire across the Middle East and into Europe. In the early 16th century, Selim I (1512–20) conquered Egypt and assumed the title of caliph *(see p31)*, as well as establishing the Ottomans as a sea power. He is also notorious for killing all his male relatives bar one son, to ensure that there were no rivals for the succession.

Süleyman the Magnificent

Selim's one surviving son was Süleyman I, "the Magnificent" (1520–66), under whose rule the Ottoman Empire reached its maximum extent. At the time of his death the empire stretched from Algiers to the Caspian Sea and from Hungary to the Persian Gulf.

Ottoman Empire
　Maximum extent (1683)

Much of western Europe only just escaped conquest when an Ottoman army was driven back from the gates of Vienna in 1529. Süleyman's reign was a time of great artistic and architectural achievements. The architect Sinan *(see p93)* designed many mosques and other great buildings in the city, while the Ottoman arts of ceramics *(see p163)* and calligraphy *(see p97)* also flourished.

Depiction of the unsuccessful siege of Vienna by the Ottomans

1453 Mehmet the Conqueror enters Constantinople on 29 May

1458 The Ottomans conquer Athens

1461 Trebizond on the Black Sea, the last part of the Byzantine Empire, is conquered

1536 Grand Vizier İbrahim Paşa is killed on the orders of Süleyman's wife, Roxelana *(see p78)*

1561 Süleyman executes his son Beyazıt on suspicion of treason

1571 Defeat of the Ottoman navy at the Battle of Lepanto

1450　**1475**　**1500**　**1525**　**1550**

1455 Yedikule Castle *(see p117)* is built and work begins on the Grand Bazaar

1478 Topkapı Palace completed

1470 Fatih Mosque is built over the Church of the Holy Apostles

1533 Hayrettin Paşa, better known as Barbarossa, is appointed grand admiral

1556 Inauguration of Sinan's Süleymaniye Mosque *(see pp92–3)*

Süleyman I

The Sultanate of Women

Süleyman's son Selim II (1566–74), "the Sot", was not such a capable ruler, although he added Cyprus to the empire. The defeat of his navy by the Venetians at the Battle of Lepanto was a heavy blow to Ottoman ambitions to be a seafaring power. This era was also the start of the so-called "Sultanate of Women", when

The Battle of Lepanto, a defeat for the Ottoman navy

Selim's mother (the valide sultana, *see pp30–31*) and Nur Banu, his principal wife (the first *kadın*), effectively took over power and exercised it for their own ends. Corruption and intrigue became endemic, and after Selim's death Nur Banu kept her son, Murat III (1574–95), distracted by the women of the harem so that she could maintain her control over imperial affairs.

Osman II (1618–22) was the first sultan to try to reverse the decline of the empire. But when the Janissaries *(see p129)* learnt of his plans to abolish their corps, they started a revolt which eventually led to his assassination. Murat IV (1623–40) enjoyed more success in his attempts at reform and significantly reduced corruption during his stable period of rule.

The late 17th century saw many years of capable government by a succession of grand viziers from the Albanian Köprülü family. Yet their efforts were not sufficient to stem the decline in imperial fortunes, symbolized by a failed

Osman II, who failed to halt Ottoman decline

attempt to capture Vienna in 1683. The Treaty of Karlowitz in 1699 marked the start of the Ottoman withdrawal from Europe.

The Tulip Period

Ahmet III (1703–30), on his succession to the throne, left power in the hands of his capable grand vizier, İbrahim Paşa. The sultan preferred pleasure to politics. During his reign, beautiful Baroque palaces, such as Aynalı Kavak Palace *(see p129)*, fountains, mosques and yalıs *(see p141)* were built. Formal gardens were laid out and filled with tulips, Ahmet's favourite flower, which lent their name to the period of his rule. The sultan even ordered tulips to be scattered over the floor at the lavish festivals and entertainments that he staged for the Ottoman elite. He also sent an ambassador, Mehmet Çelebi, to France to investigate Western civilization and culture. On his return, Western clothes and costumes became not only acceptable for the first time, but fashionable.

1616 The Blue Mosque *(see pp80–81)* is finished after eight years of construction work by the architect Mehmet Ağa

1699 The loss of Hungary under the Treaty of Karlowitz marks the Ottomans' retreat from Europe

| 1600 | 1625 | 1650 | 1700 | 1725 |

1622 Revolt of the Janissaries. They murder Osman II in Yedikule Castle, the Prison of the Seven Towers

Domes of the Blue Mosque

1729 The first Ottoman printing press is set up in Istanbul and begins to print texts in Turkish

Ottoman Society

Beneath the sultan, Ottoman society was divided into a privileged ruling class (the *askeri*, which included the religious hierarchy, or *ulema*) and a tax-paying subject population *(reaya)*. Rank and honour, however, were not hereditary but could be gained through education or service in the army or administration. This social structure was modified during the reforms of the 19th century *(see p32)*, but Ottoman titles were only finally abolished in 1922 after the Turkish Republic was created *(see p33)*.

The grand vizier, the prime minister, was the sultan's right-hand man.

The sultan was at the apex of the social order and everyone owed al-legiance to him. He lived a life of ease and luxury, as seen in this portrait of Selim III (1789–1807). The Ottoman (Osmanlı in Turkish) sultans were always succeeded by one of their sons, but not automatically by the eldest.

Bayram Reception (c.1800)

In this painting by Konstantin Kapidagi, Selim III (1789–1807, see p32) presides over a parade of high-ranking officials during the celebration of a religious festival (see p49) at Topkapı Palace.

Ağa of the Janissaries

Minister of the Interior

Şeyhülislam (Grand Mufti)

Chief executioner

Men of high rank could be recognized by their different uniforms, above all their large and distinctive headgear, as seen in this portrait of four Ottoman officials. The turban was abolished by Mahmut II *(see p32)* in 1829 in favour of the more egalitarian fez.

The Women of the Harem

Like all other Ottoman institutions the harem was hierarchical. It was presided over by the sultan's mother, the valide sultana. Next in order of importance came the sultan's daughters. Immediately below them were the four *kadıns*, the official wives or favourites. Then came the *gözdes* (girls who had recently caught the sultan's eye), and the *ikbals* (women with whom he had already slept). Apart from the sultan's family members, all these women had entered the harem as slaves. They were kept under a watchful eye by a powerful stewardess, the *kahya kadın*.

One of the sultan's favourites *(kadıns)* as depicted in a 19th-century engraving

Black eunuchs

Sword bearer to the sultan

The Gate of Felicity *(see p56)*, in the second courtyard of Topkapı Palace, was used for such ceremonial occasions.

Chief lackey (footman)

The sultan is surrounded by his courtiers. He is the only seated figure.

Şeyhülislam (Grand Mufti)

Chief of the sultan's bodyguard

Black eunuchs

Dancing women

Valide sultana

Dwarf

The valide sultana, the most powerful woman in the harem, is the centre of attention in this festive scene. The picture was commissioned c.1689 by Madame Giradin, wife of the French ambassador.

Ottoman Titles

Ağa: leader of an organization. The most influential *ağas* were the commander of the Janissary corps, the sultan's elite troops *(see p129)*, and the Ağa of the Abode of Felicity, or chief black eunuch, who was in charge of the harem *(see pp60–61)*.

Chief black eunuch

Bey: governor of a district or province. The word is now used simply to mean "Mr".

Caliph: spiritual ruler of the Islamic world. The title was assumed by the Ottoman sultans, beginning with Selim the Grim in 1517.

Gazi: honorary title given to a victorious Islamic warrior.

Kadi: judge charged with interpreting Islamic law and Ottoman administrative codes.

Khedive: viceroy of Egypt under Ottoman rule (1867–1914). The autonomous khedives acknowledged the religious leadership of the Ottoman Empire.

Paşa: title bestowed on a senior civil servant or high-ranking army officer. According to his rank, a *paşa* was entitled to display one, two or three horsetails on his standard *(see p58)*.

Sultan: political and religious ruler of the empire.

Şeyhülislam (Grand Mufti): head of the *ulema*, a religious institution which was made up of "learned men" responsible for interpreting and enforcing Islamic law *(sharia)*.

Valide sultana: mother of the ruling sultan.

Vizier: minister of state. The four most senior ministers were called "viziers of the dome" because they attended cabinet meetings in the domed hall of the divan in Topkapı Palace *(see pp56–61)*. From the 16th century, the divan was presided over by the immensely powerful grand vizier (the prime minister).

Grand vizier

A Janissary leaps to his death in a German painting
of the Auspicious Event of 1826

The Reforming Sultans

Abdül Hamit I (1774–89) resumed the
work of reform and was succeeded by
Selim III, who instituted a wide range of
changes to the military and Ottoman society.
He was deposed by a Janissary mutiny in
1807. Mahmut II (1808–39) realized that
the Janissary corps *(see p129)* could not
be reformed, so he established a modern
army alongside them, but the Janissaries
rebelled and were massacred on 15 June
1826 in the "Auspicious Event". Soon after,
in 1829, the sultan introduced further
modernizing measures including
changes in the dress code.

Later in his reign Mahmut reorganized
central government so that a regulated

bureaucracy replaced the old system of
rule by military and religious powers. By
doing this he paved the way for his sons
Abdül Mecit (1839–61) and Abdül Aziz (1861–
76) to oversee the Tanzimat (Reordering), a
series of legislative reforms. Functionaries
were given higher salaries to deter them
from taking bribes, and the grand vizier's
post was replaced by that of prime minister.

A constitution was declared in 1876,
creating parliamentary government.
However, the Russian-Turkish War of 1877–8
led to Abdül Hamit II suspending it and ruling
alone for the next 30 years. In 1908 a bloodless
revolution by a collection of educated men –
the so-called Young Turks – finally forced the
sultan to recall parliament.

Atatürk and Westernization

Throughout the 19th- and early 20th-
centuries, the Ottoman Empire steadily
lost territory through wars with Russia and
Austria, and to emerging Balkan nation-states
such as Serbia, Greece and Bulgaria. Then, in
World War I, despite famously winning the
battle for Gallipoli in a valiant defence of the
Dardanelles *(see p172)*, the Ottoman Empire
found itself on the losing side. Istanbul was
occupied by victorious French and British

Artillery in action at Gallipoli

	1807 Much of the city is destroyed during a Janissary revolt against Mahmut II	*Dolmabahçe clocktower*	1845 First (wooden) Galata Bridge is built over the Golden Horn	1870 Schliemann begins excavation of Troy *(see p173)*	1888 Rail link with Paris leads to first run of the Orient Express *(see p68)*	
1800		**1825**	**1850**	**1875**		**190**
	1826 Mahmut II finally destroys the Janissaries in their own barracks in the "Auspicious Event"	1856 Abdül Mecit I abandons Topkapı Palace for the new Dolmabahçe Palace *(see pp130–31)*	1875 The Tünel underground railway system, the third built in the world, opens in Galata		*Orient Express poster*	

troops, and much of Western Anatolia by Greek forces. The peace treaties that followed rewarded the victors with Ottoman territory and as a result stimulated Turkish nationalists to take over power from the sultan.

A portrait of Atatürk

The history of modern Turkey is dominated by the figure of Mustafa Kemal Paşa (1881–1938), a military hero turned politician, universally known as Atatürk, or "Father of the Turks". It was at his instigation that the Turkish War of Independence was fought to regain land lost to the Allies and, in particular, Greece. At the end of this war, the present territorial limits of Turkey were established. Atatürk then started a programme of political and social change. The sultanate was abolished in 1922, and religion and state were formally separated a year later, when the country was declared a secular republic. His reforms included replacing the Arabic alphabet with a Roman one, allowing women greater social and political rights, encouraging Western dress (the fez was banned) and obliging all Turks to choose a surname.

Modern Istanbul

Another part of this process was to move the institutions of state from the old Ottoman city of Istanbul to the more centrally located Ankara, which became the capital of Turkey in 1923. Since then, Istanbul has gone through a dramatic transformation into a modern city. As

Modern tram
(see p240)

migrants from Anatolia have poured in, the population has increased, and although small communities of Jews, Arabs, Armenians and Christians remain within the city, they are now vastly outnumbered by Turks.

A booming economy has led to the building of new motorways and bridges, and the public transport network has been revolutionized with modern trams, light railways and fast catamaran sea buses (see p243). Meanwhile Istanbul has geared itself up for tourism: its ancient monuments have been restored and many new hotels and restaurants were opened in the run up to 2010, Istanbul's year as European Capital of Culture.

But, like Turkey as a whole, Istanbul is forever wrestling with a divided half-Asian, half-European identity. The influences of these contrasting cultures remain widely evident today and create the city's unique atmosphere.

The suspension bridge spanning the Bosphorus, which opened in October 1973

Turkish flag

1919–22 British and French occupy Istanbul	**1938** Atatürk dies in Dolmabahçe Palace at 9:05am on 10 November (see p131)		**1993** The Islamicist Welfare Party takes control of the Greater Istanbul Municipality	**2010** Istanbul is celebrated as European Capital of Culture
1922 Sultanate finally ends				
1925	**1950**		**1975**	**2000**
1915 Allied forces land at Gallipoli but are repulsed by Turkish troops	**1936** Haghia Sophia becomes a museum. Restoration starts	**1973** A suspension bridge is built across the Bosphorus (see p140), linking east and west Turkey	**1996** The United Nations Conference on Human Settlement (Habitat II) is held in Istanbul	**2002** Recep Tayyip Erdoğan is elected Prime Minister
	1928 Istanbul becomes the city's official name			

The Ottoman Sultans

The first Ottomans were the leaders of warlike tribes living on the borders of the Byzantine Empire. From the 13th century, however, the dynasty established itself at the head of a large empire. In their heyday, having captured Istanbul in 1453 *(see p28)*, the Ottoman sultans were admired and feared for their military strength and ruthlessness towards opponents and rival pretenders to the throne. Later sultans often led a decadent lifestyle while power was exercised by their viziers *(see p31)*.

Murat III (1574–95), whose *tuğra (see p97)* is shown above, fathers over 100 children

Selim II, "the Sot" (1566–74), prefers drinking and harem life to the affairs of state

Selim I, "the Grim" (1512–20), seen here at his coronation, assumes the title of caliph after his conquest of Egypt

Osman Gazi (1299–1326), a tribal chieftain, establishes the Ottoman dynasty

Murat I (1359–89)

Mehmet I (1413–21)

Beyazıt II (1481–1512)

1250	1300	1350	1400	1450	1500	1550

1250	1300	1350	1400	1450	1500	1550

Orhan Gazi (1326–59) is the first Ottoman to bear the title of sultan

Süleyman I, "the Magnificent" (1520–66), expands the empire and fosters a golden age of artistic achievement

Beyazıt I (1389–1402) is nicknamed "the Thunderbolt" because of the speed at which he takes strategic decisions and moves his troops from one place to another

Period of Interregnum (1402–13) while Beyazıt's sons fight each other over the succession

Murat II (1421–51), the greatest of the warrior sultans, gains notable victories against the Crusaders

Mehmet II, "the Conqueror" (1451–81), captures Constantinople in 1453. He then rebuilds the city, transforming it into the new capital of the empire

Mehmet III (1595–1603) succeeds to the throne after his mother has all but one c his 19 brothers strangle

Mustafa I (1617–18 and 1622–3), a weak and incompetent ruler, reigns for two short periods and is deposed twice

Abdül Mecit I (1839–61) presides over the reforms of the Tanzimat *(see p32)*

Mehmet VI (1918–22), the last Ottoman sultan, is forced into exile by the declaration of the Turkish Republic *(see p33)*

İbrahim, "the Mad" (1640–48), much despised, goes insane at the end of his short but disastrous reign

Mahmut II, "the Reformer" (1808–39), finally defeats the Janissaries *(see p129)*

Mehmet V (1909–18)

Süleyman II (1687–91)

Mustafa II (1695–1703)

Mahmut I (1730–54)

Mustafa III (1757–74)

Murat V (1876)

| 1650 | 1700 | 1750 | 1800 | 1850 | 1900 |

| 1650 | 1700 | 1750 | 1800 | 1850 | 1900 |

Ahmet II (1691–5)

Osman III (1754–7)

Abdül Mecit II (1922–3) is caliph only, the sultanate having been abolished in 1922 *(see p33)*

Abdül Aziz (1861–76)

Mehmet IV (1648–87)

Abdül Hamit I (1774–89)

Murat IV (1623–40)

Ahmet III (1703–30) presides over a cultural flowering known as the Tulip Period *(see p29)*

Mustafa IV 1807–8

Osman II (1618–22)

Abdül Hamit II (1876–1909) suspends parliament for 30 years and rules an autocratic police state until toppled from power by the Young Turk movement

Ahmet I (1603–17) has the Blue Mosque *(see pp80–1)* constructed in the centre of Istanbul

Selim III (1789–1807) attempts Western-style reforms but is overthrown by a revolt of the Janissaries

ISTANBUL AT A GLANCE

More than 100 places worth visiting in Istanbul are described in the *Area by Area* section of this book, which covers the sights of central Istanbul as well as those a short way out of the city centre. They range from mosques, churches, palaces and museums to bazaars, Turkish baths and parks. For a breathtaking view across Istanbul, you can climb the Galata Tower *(see p107)*, or take a ride on a ferry *(see pp242–3)* to the city's Asian shore. A selection of the sights you should not miss is given below. If you are short of time, you will probably want to concentrate on the most famous monuments, namely Topkapı Palace, Haghia Sophia and the Blue Mosque, which are all located conveniently close to each other.

Istanbul's Top Ten Sights

Topkapı Palace
See pp56–9

Dolmabahçe Palace
See pp130–31

Archaeological Museums
See pp64–7

Blue Mosque
See pp80–81

Basilica Cistern
See p78

Süleymaniye Mosque
See pp92–3

Haghia Sophia
See pp74–7

The Bosphorus Trip
See pp146–51

Grand Bazaar
See pp100–101

Church of St Saviour in Chora
See pp120–21

◄ İznik tiles in the Harem of the Topkapı Palace

Istanbul's Best: Mosques and Churches

Most visitors to Istanbul will immediately be struck by the quantity of mosques, from the imposing domed buildings dominating the skyline to the small neighbourhood mosques which would pass unnoticed were it not for their minarets. Several mosques were built as churches, but converted for Islamic worship after the Ottoman conquest *(see p28)*. Some of the most outstanding of them have since become national monuments, but no longer serve a religious function.

Eyüp Mosque
The holiest mosque in Istanbul stands beside the tomb of Eyüp Ensari, a companion of the Prophet Mohammed *(see p122)*.

Rüstem Paşa Mosque

St Saviour in Chora
The Dormition of the Virgin is one of many beautiful mosaics that fill this Byzantine church *(see pp120–21)*.

Church of the Pammakaristos
An image of Christ Pantocrator gazes down from the main dome of what was one of the most important churches in the city *(see p115)*.

Golden Horn
ABÜLEZEL PAŞA
VATAN CADDESI
ATATÜRK BULVARI
ORDU CADDE

Fatih Mosque
Rebuilt after an earthquake, this mosque was founded by Mehmet the Conqueror after his conquest of the city *(see p28)*. The inner courtyard is especially fine *(see p115)*.

Süleymaniye Mosque
Sinan, the greatest Ottoman imperial architect, built this mosque in honour of his patron, Süleyman the Magnificent *(see p28)*. He placed ablution taps in the side arches of the mosque to serve a large number of worshippers *(see pp92–3)*.

Rüstem Paşa Mosque
The fine tiles decorating this mosque date from the mid-16th century, the greatest period of İznik tile (see p163) production (see p90).

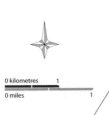

0 kilometres 1
0 miles 1

Haghia Sophia
One of the world's greatest feats of architecture, Haghia Sophia dates from AD 537. The calligraphic roundels were added in the 19th century (see pp74–7).

Atik Valide Mosque
The last major work of Sinan (see p93), this mosque was built in 1583 for the wife of Selim II. Its mihrab (niche indicating the direction of Mecca) is surrounded by İznik tiles (see p133).

İSTİKLAL CAD

NECATİ BEY CADDESİ

Bosphorus

PAŞA LİMANI CADDESİ

SEL MANIPAK CAD

ÜSKÜDAR-HAREM SAHİL YOLU

GÜNDOĞUMU CAD

ÇAVUŞDERE CAD

KENNEDY CAD

Sea of Marmara

Church of SS Sergius and Bacchus
An intricate frieze with a Greek inscription honouring the two dedicatees of this former church has survived for 1,400 years (see p84).

Blue Mosque
Istanbul's most famous landmark was built by some of the same stonemasons who later helped construct the Taj Mahal in India (see pp80–81).

Exploring Mosques

Five times a day throughout Istanbul a chant is broadcast over loudspeakers set high in the city's minarets to call the faithful to prayer. Over 99 per cent of the population is Muslim, though the Turkish state is officially secular. Most belong to the Sunni branch of Islam, but there are also a few Shiites. Both follow the teachings of the Koran, the sacred book of Islam, and the Prophet Mohammed (c.570–632), but Shiites accept, in addition, the authority of a line of 12 imams directly descended from Mohammed. Islamic mystics are known as Sufis (see p106).

Overview of the Süleymaniye Mosque complex

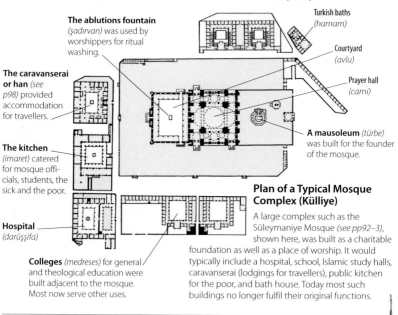

The ablutions fountain (*şadırvan*) was used by worshippers for ritual washing.

Turkish baths (*hamam*)

Courtyard (*avlu*)

The caravanserai or han (*see p98*) provided accommodation for travellers.

Prayer hall (*cami*)

A mausoleum (*türbe*) was built for the founder of the mosque.

The kitchen (*imaret*) catered for mosque officials, students, the sick and the poor.

Hospital (*darüşşifa*)

Colleges (*medreses*) for general and theological education were built adjacent to the mosque. Most now serve other uses.

Plan of a Typical Mosque Complex (Külliye)

A large complex such as the Süleymaniye Mosque (see pp92–3), shown here, was built as a charitable foundation as well as a place of worship. It would typically include a hospital, school, Islamic study halls, caravanserai (lodgings for travellers), public kitchen for the poor, and bath house. Today most such buildings no longer fulfil their original functions.

Inside a Mosque

Visitors will experience a soaring sense of space on entering the prayer hall of one of Istanbul's great mosques. Islam forbids images of living things (human or animal) inside a mosque, so there are never any statues or figurative paintings; but the geometric and abstract architectural details of the interior can be exquisite. Men and women pray separately. Women often use a screened off area or a balcony.

The müezzin mahfili is a raised platform found in large mosques. The muezzin (mosque official) stands on this when chanting responses to the prayers of the imam (head of the mosque).

The mihrab, an ornate niche in the wall, marks the direction of Mecca. The prayer hall is laid out so that most people can see it.

The minbar is a lofty pulpit to the right of the mihrab. This is used by the imam when he delivers the Friday sermon (*khutba*).

Muslim Beliefs and Practices

Muslims believe in God (Allah), and the Koran shares many prophets and stories with the Bible. However, whereas for Christians Jesus is the son of God, Muslims hold that he was just one in a line of prophets – the last being Mohammed, who brought the final revelation of God's truth to mankind. Muslims believe that Allah communicated the sacred texts of the Koran to Mohammed, via the archangel Gabriel. There are five basic duties for Muslims. The first of these is the profession of faith: "There is no God but God, and Mohammed is his Prophet". Muslims are also enjoined to pray five times a day, give alms to the poor, and fast during the month of Ramazan (see p49). Once in their lifetime, if they can afford it, they should make the pilgrimage (hajj) to Mecca (in Saudi Arabia), the site of the Kaaba, a sacred shrine built by Abraham, and also the birthplace of the Prophet.

The call to prayer used to be given by the muezzin from the balcony of the minaret. Nowadays loudspeakers broadcast the call across the city. Only imperial mosques have more than one minaret.

Prayer Times

The five daily prayer times are calculated according to the times of sunrise and sunset, and so change throughout the year. Exact times will be posted up on boards outside large mosques. Those given here are a guide.

Prayer	Summer	Winter
Sabah	5am	7am
öğle	1pm	1pm
İkindi	6pm	4pm
Akşam	8pm	6pm
Yatsı	9:30pm	8pm

Ritual ablutions must be undertaken before prayer. Worshippers wash their head, hands and feet either at the fountain in the courtyard or, more usually, at taps set in a discreet wall of the mosque.

When praying, Muslims always face the Kaaba in the holy city of Mecca, even if they are not in a mosque, where the mihrab indicates the right direction. Kneeling and lowering the head to the ground are gestures of humility and respect for Allah.

The loge (hünkar mahfili) provided the sultan with a screened-off balcony where he could pray, safe from would-be assassins.

The kürsü, seen in some mosques, is a chair or throne used by the imam while he reads extracts from the Koran.

Visiting a Mosque

Visitors are welcome at any mosque in Istanbul, but non-Muslims should try to avoid prayer times, especially the main weekly congregation and sermon on Fridays at 1pm. Take off your shoes before entering the prayer hall. Shoulders and knees should be covered. Some mosques require women to cover their hair; scarves can usually be borrowed. Do not eat, take photographs with a flash or stand close to worshippers. A contribution to a donation box or mosque official is courteous.

Board outside a mosque giving times of prayer

Istanbul's Best: Palaces and Museums

As the former capital of an empire that spanned from Algeria to Iraq and from Arabia to Hungary, Istanbul is home to a huge and diverse collection of treasures. Some, from musical instruments to priceless jewels, are housed in the beautiful former imperial palaces of the Ottoman sultans, which are worth visiting in any case for their architecture and opulent interiors. Topkapı and Dolmabahçe are the most famous palaces in Istanbul. The Archaeological Museums should also be on any itinerary of the city. This map points out these and other palaces and museums which are worth visiting for their splendid buildings or the exceptional collections they contain.

Aynalı Kavak Palace
This reclusive palace, with its airy feel and intimate proportions, shows subtler aspects of Ottoman taste. It houses a collection of Turkish musical instruments.

Archaeological Museums
Purpose-built in 1896, these superb museums have exhibits ranging from prehistory to the Byzantine era. They include this classical sculpture of the 2nd-century Roman Emperor *Hadrian*.

Museum of Calligraphy
Some of the texts in Istanbul's collection of Ottoman calligraphy *(see p97)* are by sultans, such as this panel by Ahmet III (1703–30).

Museum of Turkish and Islamic Arts
This Seljuk example is one of the many carpets *(see pp218–19)* included in this museum's display of Turkish heritage. Other collections include glassware and ceramics.

DOLAPDERE CADDE
İSTIKLAL CA
SIRASE
NECA
Golden Horn
ABDÜLEZELPAŞA CAD
MACAR KARDEŞLER CAD
VATAN CADDESİ
MİLLET CADDESİ
ATATÜRK BULVARI
ORDU CADDESİ
KENNEDY CADDESİ
KENI

Mosaic Museum
Gladiators fighting a lion are shown in one of the floors from the Great Palace *(see pp84–5)* displayed in this small museum.

Topkapı Palace

Beylerbeyi Palace
Adorning one of the
principal atriums of this
19th-century imperial
summer palace is this
elegant marble fountain. The
palace was built to entertain
visiting foreign dignitaries.

Military Museum
A highlight of this museum is
the famous Mehter Band, which
gives regular outdoor concerts
of Ottoman military music.

BARBAROS BULVARI

ÇIRAĞAN CADDESI

PAŞA LIMANI CADDESI

SELMANIPAK CADDESI

Bosphorus

ÜSKÜDAR-HAREM SAHIL YOLU

GÜNDOĞUMU CADDESI

Şale Pavilion
One of a group of pavilions built in
leafy Yıldız Park by 19th-century
sultans, the Şale Pavilion has
around 50 splendid rooms,
including the Mother-of-Pearl Hall.

Dolmabahçe Palace
This opulent 19th-century palace is home to
such marvels as 2-m (7-ft) high vases, a crystal
staircase and an alabaster bathroom.

*Sea of
Marmara*

Topkapı Palace
This huge palace was
used as the official royal
residence for 400 years.
The treasury contains a
myriad of precious
objects including the
Kasikci Diamond and this
ornate ceremonial *canteen*.

0 kilometres 1
0 miles 1

Exploring Istanbul's Collections

Each museum in Istanbul contributes a piece to the vast cultural jigsaw of this cosmopolitan city. From Ancient Greek remains and early Chinese ceramics, which arrived in the city along the great Silk Route, to 16th-century tiles commissioned for the great mosques and modern industrial machinery, each has its place in the history of Istanbul. Many of the larger museums have a wide range of exhibits and therefore feature under several of the headings below.

The Sarcophagus of the Mourning Women, Archaeological Museum

Archaeology

The archaeological fruits of the expansive Ottoman Empire are displayed in the **Archaeological Museums**, where the exhibits range from monumental 6th-century BC Babylonian friezes to exquisite classical sarcophagi and statues. Classical sculpture fills the ground floor.

Upstairs there is a gallery for the archaeology of Syria and Cyprus. Ancient oriental finds are housed in the Ancient Orient Museum, located in the same complex. The **Museum of Turkish and Islamic Arts** features specifically Muslim artifacts, including early Iraqi and Iranian ceramics as well as beautiful displays of glassware, metalwork and woodwork.

Byzantine Antiquities

Although Constantinople was the capital of the Byzantine Empire (see pp22–27) for over 1,000 years, it can be hard to get a full picture of the city in that period. The best place to start is the **Archaeological Museums**, which have displays illustrating the city's Byzantine history. Its courtyard contains the purple sarcophagi of the Byzantine emperors.

For Byzantine church mosaics, visit the **Church of St Saviour in Chora** near the city walls which has some particularly fine examples vividly depicting the lives of Christ and the Virgin Mary. The impressive **Haghia Sophia** has a few brilliant gold mosaics remaining, some dating back to the reign of Justinian (see p22). The galleries and upper walls of the **Church of the Pammakaristos** are covered with mosaics, although public access is restricted.

The **Mosaic Museum** houses mosaic floors and murals from the now-vanished Byzantine Great Palace (see pp84–5), which were discovered by archaeologists in 1938. The **Sadberk Hanım Museum** also houses several Byzantine antiquities, including icons, ceramics and jewellery.

Mosque lamp from the Archaeological Museum

Calligraphy

In the days before the printed word, Ottoman calligraphy (see p97) developed into a highly skilled artform, widely used both to ornament religious texts and legal documents and decrees. The **Museum of Calligraphy** mounts a continuous series of temporary exhibitions. Early Koranic calligraphy can be viewed in **Topkapı Palace**, the **Museum of Turkish and Islamic Arts** and the **Sakıp Sabancı Museum** (see p143).

Ceramics

Experts and amateurs come from all over the world to view the collection of Chinese ceramics and porcelain on display in the kitchens of **Topkapı Palace**. The earliest examples provided the inspiration for Turkey's indigenous ceramic production at İznik (see p163). Examples of İznik tiles can be seen on the walls of Topkapı Palace and in the city's mosques. İznik tiles and also pottery are on display in the Tiled Kiosk Museum, in the **Archaeological Museums** complex, and at the **Sadberk Hanım Museum**. A wider selection of ceramics from all over the Islamic world can be found in the **Museum of Turkish and Islamic Arts**.

Ottoman Interiors

The interiors that can be visited in Istanbul run the gamut from the classical Ottoman styling of the older parts of **Topkapı Palace** to extravagant European-inspired 19th-century decor. In the latter category, the huge **Dolmabahçe Palace** set the style. It was decorated with Bohemian glass and Hereke carpets and has an ornate central stairway

Byzantine mosaic floor in the Mosaic Museum

The opulent Süfera Salon in Dolmabahçe Palace

fashioned of crystal and brass. The **Pavilion of the Linden Tree** and the Rococo **Küçüksu Palace**, although more intimate in scale, are equally lavish in their interior style.

Textiles

The Ottomans were justifiably proud of their textile tradition, which can be admired in the huge imperial costume collection at **Topkapı Palace**, begun in 1850. The palace collection houses older materials, including kaftans dating back to the 15th century. The **Sadberk Hanım Museum** houses magnificent, mostly 19th-century pieces on the top floor and some fine examples of delicate Turkish embroidery.

On a larger scale, there are huge imperial campaign tents in the **Military Museum**, which also has a collection of miniature Janissary *(see p129)* costumes. Uniforms, nomadic tents and a renowned selection of fine carpets are on display in the **Museum of Turkish and Islamic Arts**. The collection includes rug fragments dating back to the 13th century, as well as palatial silks on a larger scale.

Kaftan from Topkapı Palace

Musical Instruments

Examples of typical Turkish instruments, such as the *saz* (lute), can be found in a museum devoted to them at **Aynalı Kavak Palace**. Those played by the Whirling Dervishes are on display at the **Mevlevi Monastery**. Instruments can also be seen, and bought, in two shops situated near the entrance to Gülhane Park *(see p63)*. Traditional Turkish military instruments can be heard being played at the **Military Museum**.

Militaria

The beautiful barges in which the Ottoman sultans were rowed around the Golden Horn and the Bosphorus are part of the **Naval Museum** collection. Naval uniforms and paintings of military scenes also feature. Weapons and armour from the 12th–20th centuries can be found in the **Military Museum**, along with a cannon, captured by the Turks during their European campaigns. There is a smaller selection of weaponry in the armoury of **Topkapı Palace**. The **Florence Nightingale Museum** (located

in the Selimiye Barracks on the Asian Side) commemorates the work of the nurse during the Crimean War. It also has some interesting military exhibits on display.

Painting

Close to Dolmabahçe Palace is Istanbul's **Museum of Fine Arts**, which offers a collection of largely late 19th- and early 20th-century Turkish paintings. Those interested in more contemporary works of art may also like to visit the changing exhibitions at the **Taksim Republic Art Gallery**.

Science and Technology

Located in a converted warehouse in the heart of Istanbul's docks is the **Rahmi M Koç Museum**. It is home to a selection of mechanical and scientific instruments dating from the early years of the Industrial Revolution, as well as an entire reconstructed bridge taken from an early 20th-century ship.

ISTANBUL THROUGH THE YEAR

Istanbul is at its best in late May and early September, when temperatures are mild and sunshine is plentiful. High season, from June to August, is the most expensive, crowded and hottest time to visit, but the summer arts and music festivals are highlights in the city's cultural calendar. Late November until March or April can be damp and dreary. However, Istanbul is still mild in autumn and winter and, with fewer tour parties around, you can enjoy the sights in peace. As well as arts and sporting events, several public holidays and religious festivals punctuate the year. It is wise to be aware of these when planning an itinerary as some sights may be closed or else crammed with locals enjoying a day out. Some of these celebrations are also fascinating spectacles in their own right.

Tulips growing in Emirgan Park, scene of the spring Tulip Festival

Spring

As the winter smog fades and sunshine increases, cafés and restaurants prepare for the first wave of alfresco dining. After a winter's diet of apples and oranges, a welcome crop of spring fruits, including fresh figs, strawberries and tart green plums, arrives in the shops. Toasted sweetcorn is sold from carts (see p208), and a spring catch of sea bream, sea bass and turbot is on the menu. Tulips, hyacinths, daffodils and pansies fill parks and gardens, and the distinctive pink buds of the Judas tree are seen along the Bosphorus. Monuments and museums are generally uncrowded in spring, and discounts are available at many hotels. In May the popular son et Lumière shows outside the Blue Mosque (see pp80–81) begin and continue until September.

Events

Easter (March or April). Pilgrimage to the Monastery of St George on Büyükada in the Princes' Islands (see p161).

International Istanbul Film Festival (late March–mid-April), selected cinemas. Screening of Turkish and foreign films and related events.

Tulip Festival (April), Emirgan Park (see p143). Displays of springtime blooms.

National Sovereignty Day (23 April). Public holiday marking the inauguration of the Turkish Republic in 1923 (see pp32–3). Children take to the streets in folk costume.

Commemoration of the Anzac Landings (25 April), Gallipoli. Britons, Australians and New Zealanders gather at the location of the Anzac landings at Gallipoli during World War I (see pp172–3).

Work and Solidarity Day

(1 May). Official public holiday when workers usually attend union-organized rallies.

Kakava Festival (early May), Edirne. A celebration of gypsy music and dance.

Youth and Sports Day (19 May). Public holiday in commemoration of the start of the War of Independence (see p33) in 1919, with sporting events and other activities held throughout the city in stadiums and on the streets.

International Istanbul Theatre Festival (May–June, every two years), various venues. European and Turkish productions.

Conquest of Istanbul (29 May), between Tophane and Karaköy and on the shores of the upper Bosphorus. Mehmet the Conqueror's taking of the city in 1453 (see p28) is re-enacted in street parades and mock battles.

Colourful evening son et Lumière show at the Blue Mosque

Average daily hours of sunshine

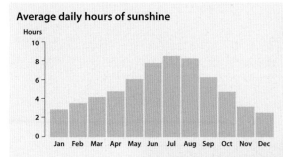

Hours

Sunshine Chart
One of Istanbul's attractions is its summer sunshine – there are about 2,500 hours each year. From May to October the city is bathed in light well into the evening, however, bursts of heavy rain are common in high summer. Winter, by contrast, is notoriously deprived of sun.

Summer

In contrast to an all-too-brief spring, the warm weather and clear skies of summer can linger on in Istanbul until November. In July and August temperatures soar and although luxury hotels have air conditioning, cheaper ones do not. Popular sights are packed with tourists throughout the high season. Picturesque locations outside Istanbul may, on the other hand, be overrun by locals. At weekends city dwellers trek out to the Belgrade Forest and Black Sea beaches (see p160) or to health clubs along the Bosphorus. Those who can afford it flee to their coastal summer homes until autumn.

For those who stay behind there is a strong summer culture. This includes a wild nightlife in hundreds of bars and night spots (see p209), and enthusiastic support for many arts festivals, which attract world-famous performers. Look out, too, for events taking place in historical buildings. You may be able to listen to classical music in Haghia Eirene (see p62) or enjoy a pop concert in the Fortress of Europe on the Bosphorus (see pp142–3). This is also the best time of year for outdoor sports such as hiking, horse-riding, water sports, golf and parachuting.

In summer, the menu focuses more on meat than fish, but vegetables and fresh fruit – such as honeydew melons,

Silk Market in Bursa, which operates all year round

cherries, mulberries, peaches and apricots – are widely available. In July and August many shops have summer sales (see p211).

Events

Silk Market (June–July), Bursa. Special market for the sale of silk cocoons (see pp166–7).
International Istanbul Music and Dance Festival (mid-June–July). Classical music, opera and dance performed in historic locations. Mozart's *Abduction from the Seraglio* is staged annually in Topkapı Palace (see pp56–61).

Scene from *Abduction from the Seraglio*, Topkapı Palace

Bursa Festival (June–July), Bursa Park. Music, folk dancing, plays, opera and shadow puppetry.
Navy Day (1 July). Parades of old and new boats along the Bosphorus.
International Istanbul Jazz Festival (July), various venues. International event with a devoted following.
International Sailing Races (July). Regatta held at the Marmara Islands (see p171).
Grease Wrestling (July), Kırkpınar, Edirne. Wrestlers smeared in olive oil grapple with each other (see p156).
Hunting Festival (3 days, late July), Edirne. Music, art and fishing displays.
Folklore and Music Festival (late July), Bursa. Ethnic dances and crafts displays.
Festival of Troy (August), Çanakkale. Re-enactment of the tale of Troy (see p173).
Victory Day (30 August). Public holiday commemorating victory over Greece in 1922.

Average monthly rainfall

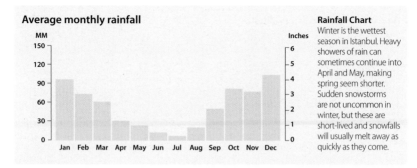

Rainfall Chart
Winter is the wettest season in Istanbul. Heavy showers of rain can sometimes continue into April and May, making spring seem shorter. Sudden snowstorms are not uncommon in winter, but these are short-lived and snowfalls will usually melt away as quickly as they come.

Autumn

Residents of Istanbul often consider their city to be at its best in autumn. As the summer heat loses its grip, chestnut sellers appear on the streets (see p208), pumpkins are sold in the markets, and fresh figs are eaten in abundance. In the surrounding countryside, cotton, wheat and sunflowers are harvested. Migratory grouper and bonito are among the tastiest types of fish which are caught at this time of year.

A popular beauty spot for its array of autumn colours is Lake Abant, 200 km (125 miles) east of Istanbul. Meanwhile, bird-watchers converge on the hills overlooking the Bosphorus to view great flocks of migratory birds heading for their warm wintering grounds in Africa (see p143).

On the cultural agenda is a world-class arts biennial and an antiques fair which blends Turkish and Western aesthetics. Several public holidays reaffirm Turkey's commitment to secularism, including Republic Day in late October, during which flags are hung from balconies. The bridges over the Bosphorus (see p140) are hung with particularly huge flags.

Street-side roasting of seasonal chestnuts

Events
Tüyap Arts Fair (September), opposite the Pera Palas Hotel (see p106). A showcase of Istanbul's artistic talent.
Yapı Kredi Festival (September), various venues. A celebration of music and dance promoting young performers.

Republic Day (29 October). Public holiday commemorating Atatürk's proclamation of the Republic in 1923 (see p33). The Turkish flag adorns buildings in the city.
Akbank Jazz Festival (October), various venues. Jazz music (see p221).
International Istanbul Fine Arts Biennial (October–November every two years, 2015, 2017). International and local avant-garde artists exhibit work in historic locations such as Haghia Eirene and the Imperial Mint (see p62), and the Basilica Cistern (see p78).
Anniversary of Death (10 November). A minute's silence is observed at 9:05am, the precise time of Atatürk's death in Dolmabahçe Palace (see pp130–31) in 1938.
Tüyap Book Fair (October), Tüyap Fair and Congress Centre. Istanbul's premier publishing event showcases prominent writers.
Efes Pilsen Blues Festival (early November), selected venues. Foreign and local blues bands play in popular music venues across the city.
Interior Design Fair (first week of November), Çırağan Palace Hotel Kempinski (see p125). Interior designers and antique dealers display up-market wares in this popular annual show.
Elit's Küsav Antiques Fair (mid-November), Military Museum (see p128). Sale of local and foreign paintings, furniture, carpets, maps, books, porcelain, textiles, silver, clocks and bronze statuary.

Crowds gathering to celebrate Republic Day on 29 October

Average monthly temperature

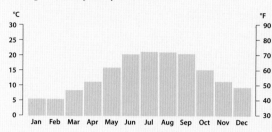

Temperature Chart
The temperature of the city rarely drops below freezing in winter, and even very cold snaps seldom last longer than three days. The heat of the long, humid summer is intensified by the lodos wind, which blows in from the Sea of Marmara. However, the northerly *poyraz* occasionally provides a cooling breeze.

Winter

There are distinct bonuses to visiting Istanbul in the winter, when even major sights are uncrowded, although the rain, fog and pollution may be off-putting. Shops in the Akmerkez, Galleria, Capitol and Carousel malls *(see p211)* hold sales, making the city a shopper's paradise for leather, woollens and fashion.

Outside Istanbul, when enough snow has fallen on the mountains, the ski season begins in Uludağ *(see p171)*, one of Turkey's most important winter sports resorts. Meanwhile baklava and cream cakes are consumed in the cosy cafés along the Bosphorus and in the old quarter of Beyoğlu *(see pp102–9)*.

View of Bebek on the Bosphorus *(see pp138–51)* in winter

founder of the famous Whirling Dervishes or the Mevlevi.
Christmas *(late December)*. Though Christmas Day is not a public holiday, major hotels organize seasonal festivities.
New Year's Day *(1 January)*. Public holiday incorporating European Christmas traditions including eating turkey, decorating trees and partying. Strings of lights adorn the main roads.
Karadam Ski Festival *(second half of February)*, Uludağ Mountain. Competitions organized by local radio stations and the Uludağ Ski Instructors' Association.

Multitude of lights to welcome in the New Year in Beyoğlu

Events
Mevlâna Festival *(17–24 December)*, Mevlevi Monastery *(see p106)*. Enthusiastic Istanbul devotees perform special dances in honour of the

Muslim Holidays

The dates of Muslim holidays vary according to the phases of the moon and therefore change from year to year. In the holy month of **Ramazan**, Muslims refrain from eating and drinking between dawn and dusk. Some restaurants are closed during the day, and tourists should be discreet when eating in public. Straight after this is the three-day **Şeker Bayramı** (Sugar Festival), when sweetmeats are prepared. Two months later the four-day **Kurban Bayramı** (Feast of the Sacrifice) commemorates the Koranic version of Abraham's sacrifice. This is the main annual public holiday in Turkey, and hotels, trains and roads are packed. Strict Muslims also observe the festivals of **Regaip Kandili, Miraç Kandili, Berat Kandili** and **Mevlid-i-Nebi**.

Festivities during Şeker Bayramı

A mesmeric view of Istanbul at sunset ▶

ISTANBUL
AREA BY AREA

SERAGLIO POINT

The hilly, wooded promontory that marks the meeting point of the Golden Horn, the Sea of Marmara and the Bosphorus occupies a natural strategic position. In Byzantine times, monasteries and public buildings stood on this site. Today it is dominated by the grandiose complex of buildings forming Topkapı Palace, the residence of the Ottoman sultans and the women of the harem for 400 years. The palace is now open to the public as a rambling museum, with lavish apartments and glittering collections of jewels and other treasures. Originally, the palace covered almost the whole of the area with its gardens and pavilions. Part of the grounds have now been turned into a public park. Adjacent to it is the Archaeological Museums, a renowned collection of finds from Turkey and the Near East.

Sights at a Glance

Museums and Palaces
1 Topkapı Palace pp56–61
2 Archaeological Museums pp64–7

Churches
4 Haghia Eirene

Historic Buildings and Monuments
3 Imperial Mint
5 Fountain of Ahmet III
9 Sublime Porte
11 Sirkeci Station

Streets and Courtyards
6 Soğukçeşme Sokağı
7 Cafer Ağa Courtyard

Parks
8 Gülhane Park

Turkish Baths
10 Cağaloğlu Baths

Restaurants pp199–202
1 Café Mese
2 Can Oba
3 Hocapaşa Pidecisi
4 Imbat
5 Karakol
6 Konyalı
7 Neyzade
8 Olive Restaurant
9 Orient Express Restaurant
10 Paşazade
11 Sarnıç
12 Şehzade Erzurum Cağ Kebabı

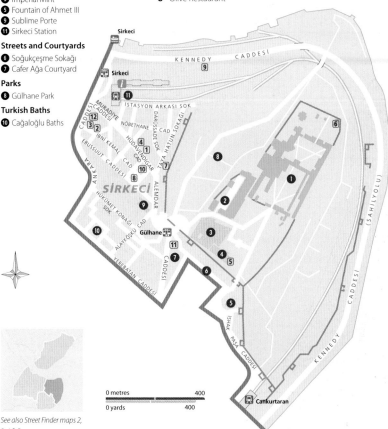

See also Street Finder maps 2, 3, 4 & 5

◀ Interior of the Harem, Topkapı Palace

For map symbols see back flap

Street-by-Street: The First Courtyard of Topkapı

The juxtaposition of Ottoman palace walls, intimately proportioned wooden houses and a soaring Byzantine church lends plenty of drama to the First Courtyard, the outer part of Topkapı Palace. This was once a service area, housing the mint, a hospital, college and a bakery. It was also the mustering point of the Janissaries (*see p129*). Nowadays, the Cafer Ağa Courtyard and Büfe, just outside the courtyard wall, offer unusual settings for refreshments. Gülhane Park, meanwhile, is one of the few shady open spaces in a city of monuments.

Gülhane Park
Once a rose garden in the outer grounds of Topkapı Palace, the wooded Gülhane Park provides welcome shade in which to escape from the heat of the city.

Ancient Orient Museum

❻ **Soğukçeşme Sokağı** Traditional, painted wooden houses line this narrow street.

❾ **Sublime Porte**
A Rococo gate stands in place of the old Sublime Porte, once the entrance to (and symbol of) the Ottoman government.

Entrance to Gülhane Park

Alay Pavilion

ALEMDAR CAD

0 metres   75
0 yards   75

Gülhane tram stop

Key

— Suggested route

SOĞUKÇEŞME S

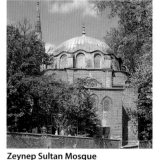

Büfes, tiny ornate kiosks, sell drinks and snacks.

Zeynep Sultan Mosque
Resembling a Byzantine church, this mosque was built in 1769 by the daughter of Ahmet III, Princess Zeynep.

❼ **Cafer Ağa Courtyard**
The cells of this former college, ranged round a tranquil courtyard café, are now occupied by jewellers, calligraphers and other artisans selling their wares.

❷ ★ Archaeological Museums

Classical statues, dazzling carved sarcophagi, Turkish ceramics and other treasures from all over the former Ottoman Empire make this complex one of the world's great collections of antiquities.

Locator Map
See Street Finder maps 2, 3, 4 & 5

Tiled Kiosk Museum
(see p67)

The Executioner's Fountain is so named because the executioner washed his hands and sword here after a public beheading.

❶ ★ Topkapı Palace

For 400 years the Ottoman sultans ruled their empire from this vast palace. Its fine art collections, opulent rooms and leafy courtyards are among the highlights of a visit to Istanbul.

Entrance to Topkapı Palace

Topkapı Palace ticket office

❸ Imperial Mint

This museum houses exhibitions on the historical background to Istanbul.

❹ Haghia Eirene

The Byzantine church of Haghia Eirene dates from the 6th century. Unusually, it has never been converted into a mosque.

Imperial Gate

❺ Fountain of Ahmet III

Built in the early 18th century, the finest of Istanbul's Rococo fountains is inscribed with poetry likening it to the fountains of paradise.

❶ Topkapı Palace

Between 1459 and 1465, shortly after his conquest of Constantinople *(see p28)*, Mehmet II built Topkapı Palace as his main residence. Rather than a single building, it was conceived as a series of pavilions contained by four enormous courtyards, a stone version of the tented encampments from which the nomadic Ottomans had emerged. Initially, the palace served as the seat of government and housed a school in which civil servants and soldiers were trained. In the 18th century, however, the government was moved to the Sublime Porte *(see p63)*. Sultan Abdül Mecit I abandoned Topkapı in 1853 in favour of Dolmabahçe Palace *(see pp130–31)*. In 1924 Topkapı was opened to the public as a museum.

★ Harem
The labyrinth of exquisite rooms where the sultan's wives and concubines lived is open to visitors *(see pp60–61)*.

KEY

① **The kitchens** contain an exhibition of ceramics, glass and silverware *(see p58)*.

② **Second courtyard**

③ **Harem ticket office**

④ **Exhibition of arms and armour** *(see p58)*

⑤ **The Gate of Felicity** is also called the Gate of the White Eunuchs.

⑥ **Throne Room**

⑦ **Exhibition of imperial costumes** *(see p58)*

⑧ **Third courtyard**

⑨ **Exhibition of miniatures and manuscripts** *(see p59)*

⑩ **Exhibition of clocks** *(see p59)*

⑪ **Pavilion of the Holy Mantle** *(see p59)*

⑫ **Circumcision Pavilion**

⑬ **The fourth courtyard** is a series of gardens dotted with pavilions.

⑭ **Konyalı Restaurant** *(see p196)*

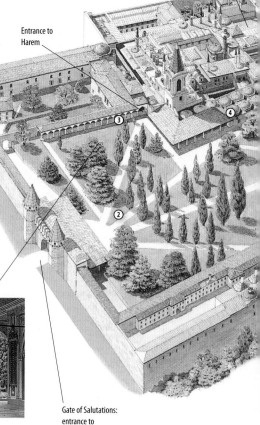

Entrance to Harem

Gate of Salutations: entrance to the palace

Divan
The viziers of the imperial council met in this chamber, sometimes watched covertly by the sultan.

İftariye Pavilion
Standing between the Baghdad and Circumcision pavilions, this canopied balcony provides views down to the Golden Horn.

VISITORS' CHECKLIST

Practical Information
Babıhümayun Cad. **Map** 3 F3.
Tel (0212) 512 04 80. **Open** 9am–4pm Wed–Mon.
Harem: **Open** 9:30am–3:30pm Wed–Mon. (book early).
w topkapisarayi.gov.tr

Transport
Sultanahmet.

Baghdad Pavilion
In 1639 Murat IV built this pavilion to celebrate his capture of Baghdad. It has exquisite blue-and-white tilework.

Library of Ahmet III
Erected in 1719, the library is an elegant marble building. This ornamental fountain is set into the wall below its main entrance.

★ Treasury
This 17th-century jewel-encrusted jug is one of the precious objects exhibited in the former treasury (*see p59*).

Exploring the Palace's Collections

During their 470-year reign, the Ottoman sultans amassed a glittering collection of treasures. After the foundation of the Turkish Republic in 1923 *(see p33)*, this was nationalized and the bulk of it put on display in Topkapı Palace. As well as diplomatic gifts and articles commissioned from the craftsmen of the palace workshops, a large number of items in the collection were brought back as booty from successful military campaigns. Many such trophies date from the massive expansion of the Ottoman Empire during the reign of Selim the Grim (1512–20), when Syria, Arabia and Egypt were conquered.

Ceramics, Glass and Silverware

The kitchens contain the palace's collection of glass, ceramics and silverware. The silverware section is currently closed for renovation.

Turkish and European pieces are overshadowed by the vast display of Chinese and, to a lesser extent, Japanese porcelain. This was brought to Turkey along the Silk Route, the overland trading link between the Far East and Europe. Topkapı's collection of Chinese porcelain is the world's second best after China itself.

The Chinese porcelain on display spans four dynasties: the Sung (10–13th centuries), followed by the Yüan (13–14th centuries), the Ming (14–17th centuries) and the Ching (17–20th centuries). Celadon, the earliest form of Chinese porcelain collected by the sultans, was made to look like jade, a stone believed by the Chinese to be lucky. The Ottomans prized it because it was said to neutralize poison in food. There are also several exquisite blue-and-white pieces, mostly of the Ming era.

Chinese aesthetics were an important influence on Ottoman craftsmen, particularly in the creation of designs for their fledgling ceramics industry at İznik *(see p163)*. Although there are no İznik pieces in the Topkapı collection, many of the tiles on the palace walls originated there. These clearly show the influence of designs used for Chinese blue-and-white porcelain, such as cloud scrolls and stylized flowers. Much of the later porcelain, particularly the Japanese Imari ware, was made specifically for the export market. The most obvious examples of this are some plates decorated with quotations from the Koran. A part of the kitchens, the old confectioners' pantry, has been preserved as it would have been when in use. On display are huge cauldrons and other utensils wielded by the palace's chefs to feed its 12,000 residents and guests.

Japanese porcelain plate

Arms and Armour

Taxes and tributes from all over the empire were once stored in this chamber, which was known as the Inner Treasury. Straight ahead as you enter is a series of horse-tail standards. Carried in processions or displayed outside tents, these proclaimed the rank of their owners. Viziers *(see p31)*, for example, merited three standards; the grand vizier, five; and the sultan's banner, nine.

The weaponry includes ornately embellished swords and several bows made by sultans themselves (Beyazıt II was a particularly masterful craftsman). The bulky iron weaponry used by European crusaders look rudimentary by comparison. Also on view are examples of 15th-century Ottoman chainmail and colourful shields. The shields have metal centres surrounded by closely woven straw painted with flowers.

Imperial Costumes

A collection of imperial costumes is displayed in the Hall of the Campaign Pages, whose task was to look after the royal wardrobe. It was a palace tradition that on the death of a sultan his clothes were carefully folded and placed in sealed bags.

As a result, it is possible to see a perfectly preserved kaftan once worn by Mehmet the Conqueror *(see p28)*. The reforms of Sultan Mahmut II included a revolution in the dress code *(see p32)*. The end of an era came as plain grey serge replaced the earlier luxurious silken textiles.

Sumptuous silk kaftan once worn by Mehmet the Conqueror

Treasury

Of all the exhibitions in the palace, the Treasury's collection is the easiest to appreciate, glittering as it does with thousands of precious and semi-precious stones. The only surprise is that there are so few women's jewels here. Whereas the treasures of the sultans and viziers were owned by the state and reverted to the palace on their deaths, those belonging to the women of the court did not.

In the first hall stands a full, diamond-encrusted suit of chainmail, designed for Mustafa III (1757–74) for ceremonial use.

Diplomatic gifts include a fine pearl statuette of a prince seated beneath a canopy, which was sent to Sultan Abdül Aziz (1861–76) from India. The greatest pieces are in the second hall. Foremost among these is the Topkapı dagger (1741). This splendid object was commissioned by the sultan from his own jewellers. It was intended as a present for the Shah of Persia, but he died before it reached him. Among other exhibits here are a selection of the bejewelled aigrettes (plumes) which added splendour to imperial turbans.

In the third hall, the 86-carat Spoonmaker's diamond is said to have been discovered in a rubbish heap in Istanbul in the 17th century, and bought from a scrap merchant for three spoons. The gold-plated Bayram throne was given to Murat III (see p34) by the Governor of Egypt in 1574 and used for state ceremonies until early this century.

It was the throne in the fourth hall, given by the Shah of Persia, which was to have been acknowledged by the equally

The Topkapı dagger

magnificent gift of the Topkapı dagger. In a cabinet near the throne is an unusual relic: a case containing bones said to be from the hand of St John the Baptist.

Miniatures and Manuscripts

It is possible to display only a tiny fraction of Topkapı's total collection of over 13,000 miniatures and manuscripts at any one time. Highlights of it include a series of depictions of warriors and fearsome creatures known as *Demons and Monsters in the Life of Nomads*, which was painted by Mohammed Siyah Qalem, possibly as early as the 12th century. It is from this Eastern tradition of miniature painting, which was also prevalent in Mogul India and Persia, that the ebullient Ottoman style of miniatures developed.

Also on show are some fine examples of calligraphy (see p97), including texts of the Koran, manuscripts in Turkish, Arabic, Persian, Latin, Hebrew and Greek, along with several firmans, or imperial decrees.

Cover of a Koran, decorated in gold filigree work

Clocks

European clocks given to, or bought by, various sultans form the majority of this collection, despite the fact that there were makers of clocks and watches in Istanbul from the 17th century.

A 17th-century watch made of gold, enamel and precious stones

The clocks range from simple, weight-driven 16th-century examples to an exquisite 18th-century English mechanism encased in mother-of-pearl and featuring a German organ which played tunes on the hour to the delight of the harem.

Interestingly, the only male European eyewitness accounts of life in the harem were written by the mechanics sent to service these instruments.

Pavilion of the Holy Mantle

Some of the holiest relics of Islam are displayed in these five domed rooms, which are a place of pilgrimage for Muslims. Most of the relics found their way to Istanbul as a result of the conquest by Selim the Grim (see p28) of Egypt and Arabia, and his assumption of the caliphate (the leadership of Islam) in 1517.

The most sacred treasure is the mantle once worn by the Prophet Mohammed. Visitors cannot actually enter the room in which it is stored; instead they look into it from an antechamber through an open doorway. Night and day, holy men continuously chant passages from the Koran over the gold chest in which the mantle is stored. A stand in front of the chest holds two of Mohammed's swords.

A glass cabinet in the anteroom contains hairs from the beard of the Prophet, a letter written by him and an impression of his footprint.

In the other rooms you can see some of the ornate locks and keys for the Kaaba (see p41) which were sent to Mecca by successive sultans.

Topkapı Palace: The Harem

The word Harem derives from the Arabic for "forbidden". A Harem was the residence of the sultan's wives, concubines and children, who were guarded by black slave eunuchs. The sultan and his sons were the only other men allowed access to the Harem, which also included the Cage, a set of rooms where the sultan's brothers were confined to avoid destabilizing succession contests. Topkapı's Harem was laid out by Sultan Murat III in the late 16th century and is a labyrinth of brilliantly tiled corridors and chambers.

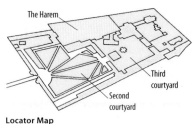

The Harem

Third courtyard

Second courtyard

Locator Map
See main illustration of the palace on pp56–7

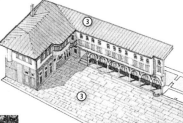

★ **Paired Pavilions**
These twin apartments, built in the 17th century for the crown prince, boast superb İznik tiles *(see p163)* and a dome lined with gilded canvas.

★ **Dining Room of Ahmet III**
A sumptuous array of fruit and flowers is painted on to the walls of this 18th-century chamber, which is also known as the Fruit Room.

Imperial Hall
The largest room in the Harem, this hall was used for entertainments. Against one wall stands a large throne, from which the sultan would view the proceedings.

Life in the Harem

The women of the Harem were slaves, gathered from the furthest corners of the Ottoman Empire and beyond. Their dream was to become a favourite of the sultan *(see p30)* and bear him a son, which on some occasions led to marriage. Competition was stiff, however, for at its height the Harem contained over 1,000 concubines, many of whom never rose beyond the service of their fellow captives. The last women eventually left in 1909.

A western view of Harem life in a 19th-century engraving

Salon of the Valide Sultana
The sultan's mother, the valide sultana *(see p31)*, was the most powerful woman in the Harem and had some of the best rooms.

Key

☐ Rooms open to the public
☐ Areas closed to the public

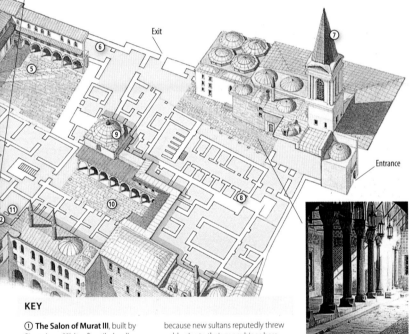

Exit

Entrance

Courtyard of the
Black Eunuchs
Marble columns line this courtyard, which still has some old-fashioned, wrought-iron lamps.

KEY

① **The Salon of Murat III**, built by Sinan *(see p93)*, has fine tiled walls, a handsome fountain and a large hearth.

② **The Library of Ahmet I** is pleasantly light and airy, with ivory-faced shutters.

③ **Apartments and courtyard of the favourites**

④ **Sultan's bathroom**

⑤ **Courtyard of the valide sultan**

⑥ **The Golden Way** is so called because new sultans reputedly threw gold coins to their concubines here.

⑦ **The Tower of Justice** offers a superb view of Topkapi's rooftops and beyond

⑧ **Barracks of the black eunuchs**

⑨ **The Harem baths** were where the concubines bathed and relaxed.

⑩ **Courtyard of the concubines**

⑪ **Valide sultan's bedchamber**

⑫ **Valide sultan's prayer room**

❷ Archaeological Museums

See pp64–7.

❸ Imperial Mint
Darphane-i Amire

First courtyard of Topkapı Palace. **Map** 3 E4 (5 F3). 🚋 Gülhane or Sultanahmet.

The Ottoman Mint opened here in 1727, but most of what can be seen today dates from the reign of Mahmut II (1808–39), when the complex was extended. In 1967, the mint moved to a new location. The buildings now house laboratories for the state restoration and conservation department, but visitors can look around the exterior of the building during office hours.

❹ Haghia Eirene
Aya İrini Kilisesi

First courtyard of Topkapı Palace. **Map** 3 E4 (5 F3). **Tel** (0212) 522 17 50. 🚋 Gülhane or Sultanahmet. **Open** by special permission and for concerts.

Though the present church dates only from the 6th century, it is at least the third building to be erected on what is thought to be the oldest site of Christian worship in Istanbul. Within a decade of the Muslim conquest of the city in 1453 *(see p28)* it

One of the four elaborately decorated sides of the Fountain of Ahmet III

had been included within the Topkapı Palace complex for use as an arsenal. Today the building, with its good acoustics, hosts concerts during the Istanbul Music Festival *(see p47)*.

Inside are three fascinating features that have not survived in any other Byzantine church in the city. The *synthronon*, the five rows of built-in seats hugging the apse, were occupied by clergymen officiating during services. Above this looms a simple black mosaic cross on a gold background, which dates from the iconoclastic period *(see p22)*, when figurative images were forbidden. At the back of the church is a cloister-like courtyard where deceased Byzantine emperors once lay in their porphyry sarcophagi. Most have been moved to the Archaeological Museums.

❺ Fountain of Ahmet III
Ahmet III Çeşmesi

Junction of İshak Paşa Cad & Babıhümayun Cad. **Map** 3 E4 (5 F4). 🚋 Gülhane or Sultanahmet.

Built in 1729, the most beautiful of Istanbul's countless fountains survived the violent deposition of Sultan Ahmet III two years later. Many of the other monuments constructed by the sultan during his reign, which has become known as the Tulip Period *(see p29)*, were destroyed. The fountain is in the delicate Turkish Rococo style, with five small domes, mihrab-shaped niches and dizzying floral reliefs.

Ottoman "fountains" do not spout jets of water, but are more like ornate public taps. They sometimes incorporated a counter, or *sebil*, from which refreshments would be served.

In this case, each of the fountain's four walls is equipped with a tap, or *çeşme*, above a carved marble basin. Over each tap is an elaborate calligraphic inscription by the 18th-century poet Seyit Vehbi Efendi. The inscription, in gold on a blue-green background, is in honour of the fountain and its founder. At each of the four corners there is a *sebil* backed by three windows covered by ornate marble grilles. Instead of the customary iced water, passers-by at this fountain would have been offered sherbets and flavoured waters in silver goblets.

The apse of Haghia Eirene, with its imposing black-on-gold cross

❻ Soğukçeşme Sokağı

Map 3 E4 (5 F3).  Gülhane.

Charming old wooden houses line this narrow, sloping cobbled lane ("the street of the cold fountain"), which squeezes between the outer walls of Topkapı Palace and the towering minarets of Haghia Sophia. Traditional houses like these were built in the city from the late 18th century onwards.

The buildings in the lane were renovated by the Turkish Touring and Automobile Club (TTOK, *see p245*) in the 1980s. Of these, nine buildings form the Ayasofya Konakları *(see p187)*, a series of attractive pastel-painted guesthouses popular with tourists. Another building has been converted by the TTOK into a library of historical writings on Istanbul, and archive of engravings and photographs of the city. A Roman cistern towards the bottom of the lane has been converted into the Sarnıç restaurant *(see p197)*.

Traditional calligraphy on sale in Cafer Ağa Courtyard

❼ Cafer Ağa Courtyard

Cafer Ağa Medresesi

Caferiye Sok. **Map** 5 E3. **Tel** (0212) 513 18 43.  Gülhane. **Open** 8:30am–8pm daily.

This peaceful courtyard at the end of an alley was built in 1559 by Sinan *(see p93)* for the chief black eunuch *(see p31)* as a *medrese* (theological college, *see p40)*. Sinan's bust presides over the café tables in the courtyard. The former students'

Ottoman Houses

The typical, smart town house of 19th-century Istanbul had a stone ground floor above which were one or two wooden storeys. The building invariably sported a *çıkma*, a section projecting out over the street. This developed from the traditional Turkish balcony, which was enclosed in the northern part of the country because of the colder climate. Wooden lattice covers, or *kafesler*, over the windows on the upper

Restored Ottoman house on Soğukçeşme Sokağı

storeys ensured that the women of the house were able to watch life on the street below without being seen themselves. Few wooden houses have survived. Those that remain usually owe their existence to tourism and many have been restored as hotels. While the law forbids their demolition, it is extremely hard to obtain insurance for them in a city that has experienced many devastating fires.

lodgings are now used to display a variety of craft goods typically including jewellery, silk prints, ceramics and calligraphy.

❽ Gülhane Park

Gülhane Parkı

Alemdar Cad. **Map** 3 E3 (5 F2).  Gülhane. **Open** daily. Museum: **Open** 9am–4:30pm Wed–Mon. Library: **Open** 10am–7pm Mon–Sat.

Gülhane Park occupies what was the lower grounds of Topkapı Palace. Today it has a neglected air but it is still a shady place to stroll and it includes a couple of interesting landmarks.

The History of Islamic Science and Technology Museum, housed in the stables, exhibits the discoveries and inventions of Islamic scientists through the history of Islam. The Alay Köşkü (Procession Kiosk) is now the **Ahmet Hamdi Tanpınar Museum and Library**, named after the one of Istanbul's most important modern writers and containing works of other famous Turkish authors as well. At the far end of the park is the Goths' Column, a well-preserved 3rd-century victory monument, surrounded by clapboard teahouses. Its name comes from the Latin inscription on it which reads: "Fortune is restored to us because of victory over the Goths".

Across Kennedy Caddesi, the main road running along the

northeast side of the park, there is a viewpoint over the busy waters where the Golden Horn meets the Bosphorus.

❾ Sublime Porte

Bab-ı Ali

Alemdar Cad. **Map** 3 E3 (5 E2).  Gülhane.

Foreign ambassadors to Ottoman Turkey were known as Ambassadors to the Sublime Porte, after this monumental gateway which once led into the offices and palace of the grand vizier. The institution of the Sublime Porte filled an important role in Ottoman society because it could often provide an effective counter-balance to the whims of sultans.

The Rococo gateway you see today was built in the 1840s. Its guarded entrance now shields the offices of Istanbul's provincial government.

Rococo decoration on the roof of the Sublime Porte

❷ Archaeological Museums
Arkeoloji Müzeleri

Although this collection of antiquities was begun only in the mid-19th century, provincial governors were soon sending in objects from the length and breadth of the Ottoman Empire. Today the complex includes three different museums – the Archaeological Museum (Arkeoloji Müzesi), the Ancient Orient Museum (Eski Şark Eserleri Müzesi) and Tiled Kiosk Museum (Çinili Köşk Müzesi). It has one of the world's richest collections of classical artifacts, and also includes treasures from the pre-classical world. The main building was erected under the directorship of Osman Hamdi Bey (1881–1910), to house his finds. This archaeologist, painter and polymath discovered the exquisite sarcophagi in the royal necropolis at Sidon in present-day Lebanon.

★ **Alexander Sarcophagus**
This fabulously carved marble tomb from the late 4th century BC is thought to have been built for King Abdalonymos of Sidon. It is called the Alexander Sarcophagus because Alexander the Great is depicted on it winning a victory over the Persians.

Key to Floorplan

- ☐ Classical Archaeology
- ☐ Children's Museum
- ☐ Thracian, Bithynian and Byzantine Collections
- ▨ Istanbul Through the Ages
- ▨ Anatolia and Troy
- ▨ Anatolia's Neighbouring Cultures
- ☐ Tiled Kiosk Museum
- ☐ Ancient Orient Museum
- ☐ Non-exhibition space

The porticoes of the museum take their design from the 4th-century BC Sarcophagus of the Mourning Women.

Sarcophagus of the Mourning Women

Outdoor café

★ **Karaman Mihrab**
This blue, richly tiled mihrab (see p40) comes from the city of Karaman in southeast Turkey, which was the capital of the Karamanid state from 1256–1483. It is the most important artistic relic of that culture.

Gallery Guide
The 20 galleries of the main building house the Archaeological Museum's important collection of classical antiquities. The four-storey wing has displays on the archaeology of Istanbul and nearby regions, and includes the Children's Museum. There are two other museums within the grounds: the Tiled Kiosk Museum, the oldest building in the complex showcasing Turkish tiles and ceramics, and the Ancient Orient Museum.

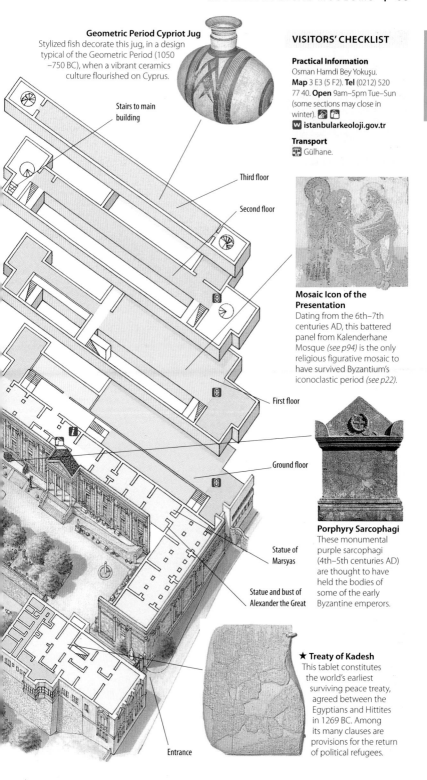

Geometric Period Cypriot Jug
Stylized fish decorate this jug, in a design typical of the Geometric Period (1050–750 BC), when a vibrant ceramics culture flourished on Cyprus.

Stairs to main building

Third floor

Second floor

First floor

Ground floor

Statue of Marsyas

Statue and bust of Alexander the Great

Entrance

Mosaic Icon of the Presentation
Dating from the 6th–7th centuries AD, this battered panel from Kalenderhane Mosque (see p94) is the only religious figurative mosaic to have survived Byzantium's iconoclastic period (see p22).

Porphyry Sarcophagi
These monumental purple sarcophagi (4th–5th centuries AD) are thought to have held the bodies of some of the early Byzantine emperors.

★ Treaty of Kadesh
This tablet constitutes the world's earliest surviving peace treaty, agreed between the Egyptians and Hittites in 1269 BC. Among its many clauses are provisions for the return of political refugees.

Exploring the Archaeological Museums

This enormous collection spans over 5,000 years, from figurines of the Mother Goddess modelled in the 3rd millennium BC to Turkish pottery thrown in the 19th century. To cover everything in one visit is impossible. Visitors with little time should not miss the breathtaking sarcophagi from the royal necropolis at Sidon. To learn more about the history of Istanbul itself you should head for the gallery exploring this theme, on the first floor of the New Building wing. Youngsters may enjoy the displays in the Children's Museum.

Classical archaeology

Monumental Bes, the ancient Egyptian god, greets visitors at the door to the main building. Hugely popular in the 1st–3rd centuries, Bes' comically grotesque appearance was an effective deterrent for evil spirits. Rooms 9 and 8 contain the highlights of the museum's entire collection: a group of sarcophagi unearthed in 1887 at Sidon (in present-day Lebanon). These are thought to have been made for a line of Phoenician kings who ruled in the 6th–4th centuries BC. Their decoration vividly shows the transition from Egyptian to Greek influence in the art of the Near East at that time.

Marble bust of Emperor Augustus

The latest and finest of them is the so-called Alexander Sarcophagus (late 4th century BC). Alexander the Great features in two decorative, high-relief friezes on the longest sides. These show a battle scene and a hunting scene. The friezes survive in almost perfect condition, showing traces of their original colouring, though the metal weapons of the soldiers and hunters have been lost.

The Sarcophagus of the Mourning Women is thought to have been made for King Straton (374–358 BC), who was known for his fondness for women. The grief-stricken females may have been members of his harem.

Rooms 14–20 contain some remarkable statues. Among them is a Roman copy of a 3rd century BC statue of Marsyas, depicting the satyr about to be flayed after daring to challenge Apollo's musical ability. A statue and bust of Alexander the Great (3rd–2nd centuries BC) show the conqueror as the perfect hero, with a meditative expression on his face. Room 18 contains realistic busts of Roman emperors.

Children's Museum

Special low cabinets are used in this part of the museum, which is designed for visiting schoolchildren. Paper and coloured crayons are to hand in a bid to stimulate future archaeologists.

Thracian, Bithynian and Byzantine Collections

This interesting gallery on the ground floor of the New Building wing displays religious and other artifacts from the ancient civilizations of Thrace and Bithynia, and from Byzantium (see pp22–27) – including a statue of Byzantine Emperor Valens. This section of the musuem also covers the architecture of the ancient world.

Bronze head of a snake from the Serpentine Column

Istanbul through the Ages

With a few well-chosen pieces and explanatory texts in Turkish and English, this gallery brilliantly chronicles Istanbul's archaeological past.

The rare Mosaic Icon of the Presentation (c.AD 600) originally adorned the Kalenderhane Mosque (see p94). One of the three snakes' heads from the Serpentine Column, which has stood headless in the Hippodrome (see p82) since the 18th century, is also displayed here. Look out too for a section of the iron chains that the Byzantines hung across both the Bosphorus and the Golden Horn to stop hostile ships (see p25).

Frieze showing the battle of Issus (333 BC), on the side panel of the Alexander Sarcophagus

Reconstruction of a mausoleum discovered at Palmyra in Syria

Anatolia and Troy

One side of this narrow, long hall chronicles the history of Anatolia (the Asiatic part of modern Turkey) from the Palaeolithic era to the Iron Age. It culminates with a room devoted to the Phrygian culture, which centred on the city of Gordion. The highlight is a recreation of an 8th-century BC royal tomb, which was housed beneath a tumulus in a juniper-wood chamber. As well as cooking utensils, the king was buried with furniture made of oak, box, yew and juniper.

The other side of the gallery traces the excavations of nine different civilizations at Troy *(see p173)*, from 3000 BC to the time of Christ. On display are a few pieces of the gold hoard known as the Schliemann treasure, after the archaeologist who first discovered it in the late 19th century. Most of the pieces were smuggled out of Turkey, however, and are now in museums around the world.

Anatolia's Neighbouring Cultures

This long gallery is also divided in two, with one side devoted to Cyprus and the other to Syria-Palestine. The Cypriot collection was assembled by the joint American and Russian consul to Cyprus, Luigi Palma di Cesnola, who systematically looted its tombs from 1865–73. Apart from some beautiful pots, the most interesting objects are the figures of plump, naked temple boys (3rd century BC). They are thought to represent boy prostitutes at temples to Aphrodite, the Greek goddess of love.

Among the Syrian exhibits are funerary reliefs, the Gezer Calendar (925 BC) – a limestone tablet bearing the oldest known Hebrew inscription – and a reconstruction of a 1st–3rd-century mausoleum from the trading oasis of Palmyra.

16th-century İznik tiled lunette in the Çinili Pavilion

Tiled Kiosk Museum

Apart from carpets, the most distinctive Turkish art form is ceramics. This is particularly seen in the sheets of tiles used to decorate the walls of mosques and pavilions such as the Çinili Pavilion in which the Tiled Kiosk Museum is located, where the entrance archway is plastered with geometric and calligraphic tiles.

In the main room there is an exquisite early 15th-century tiled mihrab from central Anatolia. Rooms 3 and 4 contain tiles and mosque lamps from the famed İznik potteries, the hub of Turkish ceramics production *(see p163)*. With the decline in quality of İznik ceramics in the late 16th century, other centres took over. One of these, Kütahya, also produced pieces of beauty and high quality (rooms 5 and 6).

Ancient Orient Museum

Although this collection contains antiquities of great rarity and beauty from the Egyptian and Hittite cultures, pride of place goes to the artifacts from the early civilizations of Mesopotamia (present-day Iraq).

The monumental glazed brick friezes from Babylon's main entrance, the Ishtar Gate, (rooms 3 and 9) date from the reign of Nebuchadnezzar II (605–562 BC), when the capital of Babylon experienced its final flowering. The elegant, 30-kg (65-lb) duck-shaped weight in Room 4 comes from a much earlier Babylonian temple (c.2000 BC).

Room 5 contains some of the earliest known examples of writing, in the form of cuneiform inscriptions on clay tablets, dating from 2700 BC. The famous Treaty of Kadesh (room 7), concluded around 1269 BC between the Egyptian and Hittite empires, was originally written on a sheet of silver. The one in this collection is a Hittite copy. The treaty includes many sophisticated clauses, including one providing for the return of a political refugee, who was "not to be charged with his crime, nor his house and wives and his children be harmed".

Glazed frieze of a bull from Ishtar Gate, Babylon

⓾ Cağaloğlu Baths
Cağaloğlu Hamamı

Prof Kazım İsmail Gürkan Cad 34, Cağaloğlu. **Map** 3 E4 (5 D3). **Tel** (0212) 522 24 24. 🚊 Sultanahmet. **Open** daily 8am–8pm.
Ⓦ cagalogluhamami.com.tr

Among the city's more sumptuous Turkish baths, the ones in Cağaloğlu were built by Sultan Mahmut I in 1741. The income from them was designated for the maintenance of Mahmut's library in Haghia Sophia (see pp74–7).

The city's smaller baths have different times at which men and women can use the same facilities. But in larger baths, such as this one, there are

Corridor leading into the Cağaloğlu Baths, built by Mahmut I

entirely separate sections. In the Cağaloğlu Baths the men's and women's sections are at right angles to one another and entered from different streets. Each consists of three parts: a *camekan*, a *soğukluk* and the main bath chamber or *hararet*, which centres on a massive octagonal massage slab.

The Cağaloğlu Baths are popular with foreign visitors because the staff are happy to explain the procedure. Even if you do not want to sweat it out, you can still take a look inside the entrance corridor and *camekan* of the men's section. Here you will find a small display of Ottoman bathing regalia, including precarious wooden clogs once worn by women on what would frequently be their only outing from the confines of the home. You can also sit and have a drink by the fountain in the peaceful *camekan*.

⓫ Sirkeci Station
Sirkeci Garı

Sirkeci İstasyon Cad, Sirkeci. **Map** 3 E3 (5 E1). **Tel** (0212) 527 00 50 or 520 65 75. 🚊 Sirkeci. **Open** daily.

This magnificent railway station was built to receive the long-anticipated Orient Express from Europe. It was officially opened in 1890, even though the luxurious train had been

Sirkeci Station, final destination of the historic Orient Express

running into Istanbul for a year by then. The design, by the German architect Jasmund, successfully incorporates features from the many different architectural traditions of Istanbul. Byzantine alternating stone and brick courses are combined with a Seljuk-style monumental recessed portal and Muslim horseshoe arches around the windows.

The station café is a good place in which to escape the bustle of the city for a while. Sirkeci serves Greece and other destinations in Europe as well as the European part of Turkey. Istanbul's other mainline railway station is Haydarpaşa (see p135), on the Asian side of the city.

The World-Famous Orient Express

The Orient Express made its first run from Paris to Istanbul in 1889, covering the 2,900-km (1,800-mile) journey in three days. Both Sirkeci Station and the Pera Palas Hotel (see p106) in Istanbul were built especially to receive its passengers. The wealthy and often distinguished passengers of "The Train of Kings, the King of Trains" did indeed include kings among the many presidents, politicians, aristocrats and actresses. King Boris III of Bulgaria even made a habit of taking over from the driver of the train when he travelled on it through his own country.

A byword for exoticism and romance, the train was associated with the orientalist view of Istanbul as a treacherous melting pot of diplomats and arms dealers. It inspired no fewer than 19 books – *Murder on the Orient Express* by Agatha Christie and *Stamboul Train* by Graham Greene foremost among them – six films and one piece of music. During the Cold War standards of luxury crashed, though a service of sorts, without even a restaurant car, continued twice weekly to Istanbul until 1977.

A 1920s poster for the Orient Express, showing a romantic view of Istanbul

Turkish Baths

No trip to Istanbul is complete without an hour or two spent in a Turkish bath *(hamam)*, which will leave your whole body feeling rejuvenated. Turkish baths differ little from the baths of ancient Rome, from which they derive, except there is no pool of cold water to plunge into at the end.

A full service will entail a period of relaxation in the steam-filled hot room, punctuated by bouts of vigorous soaping and massaging. There is no time limit, but allow at least an hour and a half. Towels and soap will be provided, but you can take toiletries with you. Three historic baths located in the old city – Çemberlitaş *(see p83)*, Hürrem Sultan Hamamı *(see p78)* and Cağaloğlu (illustrated below) – are used to catering for tourists. Most luxury hotels have their own baths *(see pp182)*.

Choosing a Service
Services, detailed in a price list at the entrance, range from a self-service option to a luxury body scrub, shampoo and massage.

The camekan (entrance hall) is
a peaceful internal courtyard near the entrance of the building. Bathers change clothes in cubicles surrounding it. The *camekan* is also the place to relax with a cup of tea after bathing.

Changing Clothes
Before changing you will be given a cloth *(peştemal)*, to wrap around you, and a pair of slippers for walking on the hot, wet floor.

Corridor from street

Basin and tap for washing

Small, star-like windows piercing the domes

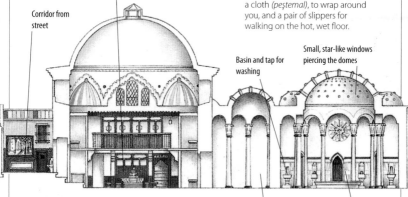

Cağaloğlu Baths

The opulent, 18th-century Turkish baths at Cağaloğlu have separate, identical sections for men and women. The men's section is shown here.

The soğukluk (intermediate room) is a temperate passage between the changing room and the *hararet*. You will be given dry towels here on your way back to the *camekan*.

In the hararet (hot room), the main room of the Turkish bath, you are permitted to sit and sweat in the steam for as long as you like.

The Exfoliating Body Scrub
In between steaming, you (or the staff at the baths) scrub your body briskly with a coarse, soapy mitt *(kese)*.

The Body Massage
A marble plinth *(göbek taşı)* occupies the centre of the hot room. This is where you will have your pummelling full-body massage.

SULTANAHMET

Istanbul's two principal monuments face each other across an area of gardens known informally as Sultanahmet Square. This part of the city gets its name from Sultan Ahmet I, who built the Blue Mosque. Opposite is Haghia Sophia, an outstanding example of early Byzantine architecture, and still one of the world's most remarkable churches. A neat oblong square next to the Blue Mosque marks the site of the Hippodrome, a chariot-racing stadium built by the Romans in around AD 200. On the other side of the Blue Mosque, Sultanahmet slopes down to the Sea of Marmara in a jumble of alleyways. Here, traditional-style Ottoman wooden houses have been built over the remains of the Great Palace of the Byzantine emperors.

Sights at a Glance

Mosques and Churches
1 Haghia Sophia pp74–7
6 Blue Mosque pp80–81
13 Sokollu Mehmet Paşa Mosque
14 Church of SS Sergius and Bacchus

Museums
5 Mosaic Museum
7 Museum of Turkish and Islamic Arts
9 Marmara University Museum of the Republic

Squares and Courtyards
3 Istanbul Crafts Centre
8 Hippodrome

Historic Buildings and Monuments
2 Basilica Cistern
4 Baths of Roxelana
10 Cistern of 1,001 Columns
11 Tomb of Sultan Mahmut II
12 Constantine's Column
15 Bucoleon Palace

Restaurants pp199–202
1 Ahırkapı Balıkçısı
2 Albura Kathisma
3 Aloran Café & Restaurant
4 Amedros
5 Balıkçı Sabahattin
6 Doy Doy
7 Doyuran Lokantası
8 Dubb
9 Faros Hotel Restaurant
10 Fes Café
11 Fuego Restaurant
12 Giritli Restaurant
13 Imren Lokantası
14 Karışma Sen Meyhane
15 Khorosani
16 Köfteci Ramiz
17 Mozaik Restaurant
18 Patara Restaurant
19 Seasons Restaurant
20 Sultanahmet Fish House
21 Tarihi Sultanahmet Köftecisi
22 The North Shield
23 Tria Elegance
24 Vonalı Celal

See also Street Finder maps 3 & 5

0 metres   250
0 yards   250

◀ The Blue Mosque in the luminescent glow of the setting sun

For map symbols see back flap

Street-by-Street: Sultanahmet Square

Two of Istanbul's most venerable monuments, the Blue Mosque and Haghia Sophia, face each other across a leafy square, informally known as Sultanahmet Square (Sultanahmet Meydanı), next to the Hippodrome of Byzantium. Also in this fascinating historic quarter are a few museums, including the Mosaic Museum, built over part of the old Byzantine Great Palace *(see pp84–5)*, and the Museum of Turkish and Islamic Arts. No less diverting than the cultural sights of this pedestrianized area are the cries of the *simit* (bagel) hawkers and carpet sellers, and the chatter of children selling postcards.

Tomb of Sultan Ahmet I
Stunning 17th-century İznik tiles *(see p163)* adorn the inside of this tomb, which is part of the outer complex of the Blue Mosque.

❻ ★ Blue Mosque
Towering above Sultanahmet Square are the six beautiful minarets of this world-famous mosque. It was built in the early 17th century for Ahmet I.

❼ Museum of Turkish and Islamic Arts
Yurts, used by Turkey's nomadic peoples, and rugs are included in this impressive collection.

Egyptian Obelisk

Sultanahmet tram stop

Firuz Ağa Mosque

Fountain of Kaiser Wilhelm II

Key

— Suggested route

Brazen Column

ATMEYDANI SOK

ATMEYDANI SOK

TAVUKHANE SOK

TORUN SOK

Serpentine Column

❽ Hippodrome
This stadium was the city's focus for more than 1,000 years before it fell into ruin. Only a few sections, such as the central line of monuments, remain.

❺ Mosaic Museum
Hunting scenes are one of the common subjects that can be seen in some of the mosaics from the Great Palace.

❷ ★ **Basilica Cistern**
This marble Medusa head is one of two classical column bases found in the Basilica Cistern. The cavernous cistern dates from the reign of Justinian *(see p22)* in the 6th century.

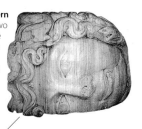

A stone pilaster next to the remains of an Ottoman water tower is all that survives of the Milion *(see p85)*, a triumphal gateway.

Locator Map
See Street Finder maps 3 & 5

❶ ★ **Haghia Sophia**
The supreme church of Byzantium is over 1,400 years old but has survived in a remarkably good state. Inside it are several glorious figurative mosaics.

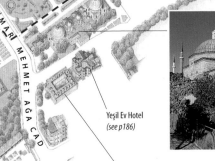

Yeşil Ev Hotel
(see p186)

❹ **Baths of Roxelana**
Sinan *(see p93)* designed these baths in the mid-16th century. In the past, the building has housed a carpet shop, but it has been restored and reopened in 2012 as public baths.

❸ **Istanbul Crafts Centre**
Visitors have a rare opportunity here to observe Turkish craftsmen practising a range of skills.

Arasta Bazaar
Eager salesmen will call you over to peruse their wares – mainly carpets and handicrafts – in this bazaar. With two long rows of shops on either side of a lane, the bazaar was once a stable yard.

0 metres   75
0 yards   75

❶ Haghia Sophia

Ayasofya

The "church of holy wisdom," Haghia Sophia is among the world's greatest architectural achievements. More than 1,400 years old, it stands as a testament to the sophistication of the 6th-century Byzantine capital. The vast edifice was built over two earlier churches and inaugurated by Emperor Justinian in 537.

Print of Haghia Sophia from the mid-19th century

In the 15th century the Ottomans converted it into a mosque: the minarets, tombs, and fountains date from this period. To help support the structure's great weight, the exterior has been buttressed on numerous occasions, which has partly obscured its original shape. Three mausoleums at the site are also open to the public.

Byzantine Frieze
Among the ruins of the monumental entrance to the earlier Haghia Sophia (dedicated in AD 415) is this frieze of sheep.

Historical Plan of Haghia Sophia

Nothing remains of the first 4th-century church on this spot, but there are traces of the second one from the 5th century, which burnt down in AD 532. Earthquakes have taken their toll on the third structure, strengthened and added to many times.

Entrance

Key

☐ 5th-century church
◼ 6th-century church
☐ Ottoman additions

★ Nave
Visitors cannot fail to be staggered by this vast space which is covered by a huge dome reaching to a height of 56 m (184 ft).

VISITORS' CHECKLIST

Practical Information
Ayasofya Sultanahmet Meydanı 1.
Map 3 E4 (5 F3). **Tel** (0212) 528 45
00. **Open** 9am–6pm Tue–Sun.
🐾 📷 ♿ ground floor only.

Transport
🚋 Sultanahmet.

★ The Mosaics
The church's splendid Byzantine mosaics include this one at the end of the south gallery. It depicts Christ flanked by Emperor Constantine IX and his wife, the Empress Zoe.

KEY

① **Outer Narthex**

② **Buttresses**

③ **Inner Narthex**

④ **Imperial Gate**

⑤ **The galleries** were originally used by women during services.

⑥ **Kürsü** *(see p41)*

⑦ **Calligraphic roundel**

⑧ **Seraphims** adorn the pendentives at the base of the dome.

⑨ **Sultan's loge**

⑩ **Brick minaret**

⑪ **Müezzin mahfili** *(see p40)*

⑫ **The Coronation Square** served for the crowning of emperors.

⑬ **Library of Sultan Mahmut I**

⑭ **The Baptistry**, part of the 6th-century church, now serves as the tomb of two sultans.

⑮ **The mausoleum of Murat III** was used for his burial in 1599. Murat had by that time sired 102 children.

⑯ **Mausoleum of Selim II**
The oldest of the three mausoleums was completed in 1577 to the plans of Sinan *(see p93)*. Its interior is entirely decorated with İznik tiles *(see p163)*.

⑰ **Mausoleum of Mehmet III**

Exit →

★ Ablutions Fountain
Built around 1740, this fountain is an exquisite example of Turkish Rococo style. Its projecting roof is painted with floral reliefs.

Exploring Haghia Sophia

Designed as an earthly mirror of the heavens, the interior of Haghia Sophia succeeds in imparting a truly celestial feel. The artistic highlights are a number of glistening figurative mosaics – remains of the decoration that once covered the upper walls but which has otherwise mostly disappeared. These remarkable works of Byzantine art date from the 9th century or later, after the iconoclastic era (see p22). Some of the patterned mosaic ceilings, however, particularly those adorning the narthex and the neighbouring Vestibule of the Warriors, are part of the cathedral's original 6th-century decoration.

Interior as it looked after restoration in the 19th century

Ground Floor

The first of the surviving Byzantine mosaics can be seen over the Imperial Gate. This is now the public entrance into the church, although previously only the emperor and his entourage were allowed to pass through it. The mosaic shows **Christ on a throne with an emperor kneeling beside him** ① and has been dated to between 886 and 912. The emperor is thought to be Leo VI, the Wise (see p23).

The most conspicuous features at ground level in the nave are those added by the Ottoman sultans after the conquest of Istanbul in 1453,

when the church was converted into a mosque.

The **mihrab** ②, the niche indicating the direction of Mecca, was installed in the apse of the church directly opposite the entrance. The **sultan's loge** ③, on the left of the mihrab as you face it, was built by the Fossati brothers. These Italian-Swiss architects undertook a major restoration of Haghia Sophia for Sultan Abdül Mecit in 1847–9.

To the right of the mihrab is the **minbar** ④, or pulpit, which was installed by Murat III (1574–95). He also erected the four **müezzin mahfilis** ⑤, marble platforms for readers of the Koran (see p40). The largest of

these is adjacent to the minbar. The patterned marble **coronation square** ⑥ next to it marks the supposed site of the Byzantine emperor's throne, or omphalos (centre of the world). Nearby, in the south aisle, is the **library of Mahmut I** ⑦, which was built in 1739 and is entered by a decorative bronze door.

Across the nave, between two columns, is the 17th-century marble **preacher's throne** ⑧, the contribution of Murat IV (1623–40). Behind it is one of several **maqsuras** ⑨. These low, fenced platforms were placed beside walls and pillars to provide places for elders to sit, listen and read the Koran.

In the northwestern and western corners of the church are two **marble urns** ⑩, thought to date from the Hellenistic or early Byzantine period. A rectangular pillar behind one of the urns, the **pillar of St Gregory the Miracle-Worker** ⑪, is believed to have healing powers. As you leave the church you pass through the Vestibule of the Warriors, so called because the emperor's bodyguards would wait here for him when he came to worship. Look behind you as you enter it at the wonderful mosaic of the **Virgin with Constantine and Justinian** ⑫ above the door. It shows Mary seated on a throne holding the infant Jesus and flanked by two of the

Floorplan of Haghia Sophia

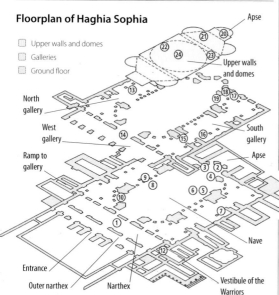

- Upper walls and domes
- Galleries
- Ground floor

Apse

Upper walls and domes

North gallery

West gallery

Ramp to gallery

South gallery

Apse

Nave

Entrance

Outer narthex

Narthex

Vestibule of the Warriors

greatest emperors of the city. Constantine, on her left, presents her with the city of Constantinople, while Justinian offers her Haghia Sophia. This was made long after either of these two emperors lived, probably in the 10th century, during the reign of Basil II *(see p23)*. Visitors exit the church by the door that was once reserved for the emperor due to its proximity to the Great Palace *(see pp84–5)*.

Figure of Christ, detail from the Deesis Mosaic in the south gallery

Galleries

A ramp leads from the ground floor to the north gallery. Here, on the eastern side of the great northwest pier, you will find the 10th-century mosaic of **Emperor Alexander holding a skull** ⑬. On the west face of the same pier is a medieval drawing of a galleon in full sail. The only point of interest in the western gallery is a green marble disk marking the location of the

Byzantine **Empress's throne** ⑭.

There is much more to see in the south gallery. You begin by passing through the so-called **Gates of Heaven and Hell** ⑮, a marble doorway of which little is known except that it predates the Ottoman conquest *(see p28)*.

Around the corner to the right after passing through this doorway is the **Deesis Mosaic** ⑯ showing the Virgin Mary and John the Baptist with Christ Pantocrator (the All-Powerful). Set into the floor opposite it is the tomb of Enrico Dandalo, the Doge of Venice responsible for the sacking of Constantinople in 1204 *(see p26)*.

In the last bay of the southern gallery there are two more mosaics. The right-hand one of these is of the **Virgin holding Christ, flanked by Emperor John II Comnenus and Empress Irene** ⑰. The other shows **Christ with Emperor Constantine IX Monomachus and Empress Zoe** ⑱. The faces of the emperor and empress have been altered.

Eight great **wooden plaques** ⑲ bearing calligraphic inscriptions hang over the nave at the level of the gallery. An addition of the Fossati brothers, they bear the names of Allah, the Prophet Mohammed, the first four caliphs and Hasan and Hussein, two of the Prophet's grandsons who are revered as martyrs.

Mosaic depicting Gabriel, on the lower wall of the apse

Upper Walls and Domes

The apse is dominated by a large and striking mosaic showing the **Virgin with the infant Jesus on her lap** ⑳. Two other mosaics in the apse show the archangels **Gabriel** ㉑ and, opposite him, Michael, but only fragments of the latter now remain. The unveiling of these mosaics on Easter Sunday 867 was a triumphal event celebrating victory over the iconoclasts *(see p23)*.

Three mosaic portraits of **saints** ㉒ adorn niches in the north tympanum and are visible from the south gallery and the nave. From left to right they depict: St Ignatius the Younger, St John Chrysostom and St Ignatius Theophorus.

In the four pendentives (the triangular, concave areas at the base of the dome) are mosaics of six-winged **seraphim** ㉓. The ones in the eastern pendentives date from 1346–55, but may be copies of much older ones. Those on the western side are 19th-century imitations that were added by the Fossati brothers.

The great **dome** ㉔ itself is decorated with Koranic inscriptions. It was once covered in golden mosaic and the tinkling sound of pieces dropping to the ground was familiar to visitors until the building's 19th-century restoration.

Mosaic of the Virgin with Emperor John II Comnenus and Empress Irene

The cavernous interior of the Byzantine Basilica Cistern

❷ Basilica Cistern

Yerebatan Sarayı

13 Yerebatan Cad, Sultanahmet.
Map 3 E4 (5 E4). **Tel** (0212) 522 12 59.
Sultanahmet. **Open** 9am–5:30pm daily (Oct–Apr 8:30am–4pm).

This vast underground water cistern, a beautiful piece of Byzantine engineering, is the most unusual tourist attraction in the city. Although there may have been an earlier, smaller cistern here, this cavernous vault was laid out under Justinian in 532, mainly to satisfy the growing demands of the Great Palace (see pp84–5) on the other side of the Hippodrome (see p82). For a century after the conquest (see p26), the Ottomans did not know of the cistern's existence. It was rediscovered after people were found to be collecting water, and even fish, by lowering buckets through holes in their basements.

Visitors tread walkways to the mixed sounds of classical music and dripping water. The cistern's roof is held up by 336 columns, each over 8 m (26ft) high. The original structure covered a total area of 9,800 sq m (105,000 sq ft) but today only about two thirds of it is visible, the rest having been bricked up in the 19th century. Water reached the cistern, which held about 100 million litres (22 million gal), from the Belgrade Forest, 20 km (12 miles) north of Istanbul, via the Valens Aqueduct (see p91).

❸ Istanbul Crafts Centre

Mehmet Efendi Medresesi

Kabasakal Cad 5, Sultanahmet.
Map 3 E4 (5 E4). **Tel** (0212) 517 67 82.
Sultanahmet. **Open** 9:30am–5:30pm daily.

If you are interested in Turkish craftwork, this for-mer Koranic college is worth a visit. You can watch skilled artisans at work: they may be binding a book, executing an elegant piece of calligraphy or painting glaze onto ceramics. Items produced here are all for sale. Others include exquisite dolls, meerschaum pipes and jewellery based on Ottoman designs.

Next door is the Yeşil Ev Hotel (see p186), a restored Ottoman building with a pleasant café in its courtyard.

❹ Baths of Roxelana

Hürrem Sultan Hamamı

Ayasofya Meydanı, Sultanahmet.
Map 3 E4 (5 E4). **Tel** (0212) 517 35 35.
Sultanahmet. **Open** 8am–10pm daily. 🆆 ayasofyahamami.com

These baths were built in 1556 for Süleyman the Magnificent (see p28) by Sinan (see p93), and are named after Roxelana, the sultan's scheming wife. They were designated for the use of the congregation of Haghia

Roxelana

Süleyman the Magnificent's power-hungry wife Roxelana (1500–58, Hürrem Sultan in Turkish), rose from being a concubine in the imperial harem to become his chief wife, or first kadın (see p30). Thought to be of Russian origin, she was also the first consort permitted to reside within the walls of Topkapı Palace (see pp56–61).

Roxelana would stop at nothing to get her own way. When Süleyman's grand vizier and friend from youth, İbrahim Paşa,

became a threat to her position, she persuaded the sultan to have him strangled. Much later, Roxelana performed her coup de grâce. In 1553 she persuaded Süleyman to have his handsome and popular heir, Mustafa, murdered by deaf mutes to clear the way for her own son Selim (see p28) to inherit the throne.

Red-and-white brick exterior of the Baths of Roxelana

Sophia (see pp74–7) when it was used as a mosque. With the women's entrance at one end of the building and the men's at the other, their absolute symmetry makes them perhaps the most handsome baths in the city. The men's section of the baths faces Haghia Sophia and has a fine colonnaded portico.

Each end of the baths starts with a *camekan*, a massive domed hall which would originally have been centred on a fountain.

Detail of a 5th-century mosaic in the Mosaic Museum

Next is a small *soğukluk*, or intermediate room, which opens into a *hararet*, or steam room. The hexagonal massage slab in each *hararet*, the *göbek taşı*, is inlaid with coloured marbles, indicating that the baths are of imperial origin.

The baths functioned as a public bathhouse for over 350 years until 1910. After their closure, they continued to be used for various purposes, including as a coal and fuel store and as a government-run carpet shop. The baths have been restored according to original specifications and fitted with authentic features. Following the renovations, the bathhouse reopened for public use in 2012.

❺ Mosaic Museum
Mozaik Müzesi

Arasta çarşısı, Sultanahmet.
Map 3 E5 (5 E5). **Tel** (0212) 518 12 05. Sultanahmet. **Open** 9am–4:30pm Tue–Sun.

Located near Arasta Bazaar, among a warren of small shops, this museum was created simply by roofing over a part of the Great Palace of the Byzantine Emperors (see pp84–5), which was discovered by archeologists in the 1930s. In its heyday the palace boasted hundreds of rooms, many of them glittering with gold mosaics.

The surviving mosaic has a surface area of 1,872 sq m (1,969 sq ft), making it one of the largest preserved mosaics in Europe. It is thought to have been created by an imperial workshop that employed the best craftsmen from across the Empire under the guidance of a master artist. In terms of imagery, the mosaic is particularly diverse, with many different landscapes depicted, including domestic and pastoral episodes, such as herdsmen with their grazing animals, as well as hunting and fighting scenes. It portrays over 150 different human and animal figures, including wild and domestic beasts. There are also scenes from mythology, with fantastical creatures featuring on the design. The mosaic is thought to have adorned the colonnade leading from the royal apartments to the imperial enclosure beside the Hippodrome, and dates from the late 5th century AD.

❻ Blue Mosque
See pp80–81.

❼ Museum of Turkish and Islamic Arts
Türk ve İslam Eserleri Müzesi

Atmeydanı Sok, Sultanahmet.
Map 3 D4 (5 D4). **Tel** (0212) 518 18 05. Sultanahmet. **Open** summer: 9am–7pm Tue–Sun; winter: 9am–5pm Tue–Sun. W tiem.gov.tr

Over 40,000 items are on display in the former palace of İbrahim Paşa (c.1493–1536), the most gifted of Süleyman's many grand viziers. Paşa married Süleyman's sister when the sultan came to the throne. The collection was begun in the 19th century and ranges from the earliest period of Islam, under the Omayyad caliphate (661–750), through to modern times.

Each room concentrates on a different chronological period or geographical area of the Islamic world, with detailed explanations in both Turkish and English. The museum is particularly renowned for its collection of rugs. These range from 13th-century Seljuk fragments to the palatial Persian silks that cover the walls from floor to ceiling in the palace's great hall.

On the ground floor, an ethnographic section focuses on the lifestyles of different Turkish peoples, particularly the nomads of central and eastern Anatolia. The exhibits include recreations of a round felt *yurt* (Turkic nomadic tent) and a traditional brown tent.

Recreated yurt interior, Museum of Turkish and Islamic Arts

🜔 Blue Mosque

Sultan Ahmet Camii

The blue mosque, which takes its name from the mainly blue İznik tilework *(see p163)* decorating its interior, is one of the most famous religious buildings in the world. Serene at any time, it is at its most magical when floodlit at night, its minarets circled by keening seagulls. Sultan Ahmet I *(see p35)* commissioned the mosque during a period of declining Ottoman fortunes, and it was built between 1609–16 by Mehmet Ağa, the imperial architect. The splendour of the plans provoked great hostility at the time, especially because a mosque with six minarets was considered a sacrilegious attempt to rival the architecture of Mecca itself.

A 19th-century engraving showing the Blue Mosque viewed from the Hippodrome *(see p82)*

KEY

① **Exit for tourists**

② **Prayer hall**

③ **The Imperial Pavilion**

④ **The loge** *(see p41)* accommodated the sultan and his entourage during mosque services.

⑤ **Mihrab**

⑥ **Minbar** The 17th-century minbar is intricately carved in white marble. It is used by the imam during prayers on Friday *(see p40)*.

⑦ **Thick piers** support the weight of the dome.

⑧ **Müezzin mahfili** *(see p40)*.

⑨ **Over 250 windows** allow light to flood into the mosque.

⑩ **The courtyard** covers the same area as the prayer hall, balancing the whole building.

⑪ **Exit to Hippodrome**

⑫ **Each minaret** has two or three balconies.

Entrance to courtyard

★ İznik Tiles
No cost was spared in the decoration of the mosque. The tiles were made at the peak of tile production in İznik *(see p163)*.

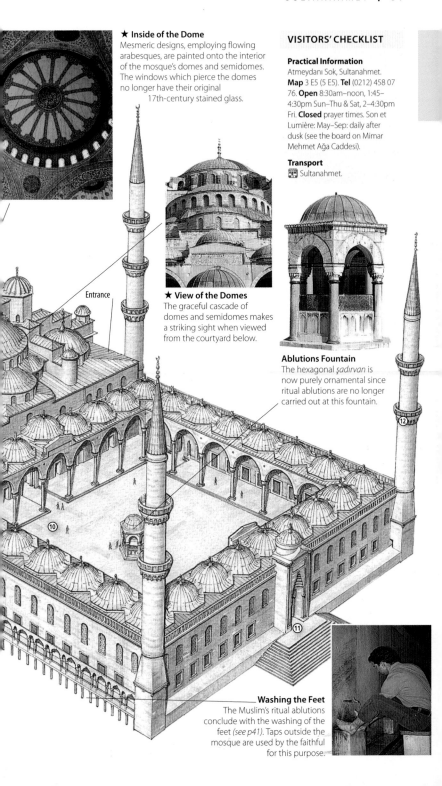

★ **Inside of the Dome**
Mesmeric designs, employing flowing arabesques, are painted onto the interior of the mosque's domes and semidomes. The windows which pierce the domes no longer have their original 17th-century stained glass.

Entrance

★ **View of the Domes**
The graceful cascade of domes and semidomes makes a striking sight when viewed from the courtyard below.

Ablutions Fountain
The hexagonal *şadırvan* is now purely ornamental since ritual ablutions are no longer carried out at this fountain.

Washing the Feet
The Muslim's ritual ablutions conclude with the washing of the feet *(see p41)*. Taps outside the mosque are used by the faithful for this purpose.

Egyptian Obelisk and the Column of Constantine Porphyrogenitus

❽ Hippodrome
At Meydanı

Sultanahmet. **Map** 3 E4 (5 D4).
🚋 Sultanahmet.

Little is left of the gigantic stadium which once stood at the heart of the Byzantine city of Constantinople (see pp24–5). It was originally laid out by Emperor Septimus Severus during his rebuilding of the city in the 3rd century AD (see p21). Emperor Constantine (see p22) enlarged the Hippodrome and connected its kathisma, or royal box, to the nearby Great Palace (see pp84–5). It is thought that the stadium held up to 100,000 people. The site is now an elongated public garden, At Meydanı, Cavalry Square. There are, however, enough remains of the Hippodrome to get a sense of its scale and importance.

The road running around the square almost directly follows the line of the chariot racing track. You can also make out some of the arches of the

Relief carved on the base of the Egyptian Obelisk

sphendone (the curved end of the Hippodrome) by walking a few steps down Nakilbent Sok. Constantine adorned the spina, the central line of the stadium, with obelisks and columns from Ancient Egypt and Greece. Conspicuous by its absence is the column which once stood on the spot where the tourist information office is now located. This was topped by four bronze horses which were pillaged during the Fourth Crusade (see p26) and taken to St Mark's in Venice. Three ancient monuments remain, however. The **Egyptian Obelisk**, which was built in 1500 BC, stood outside Luxor until Constantine had it brought to his city. This carved monument is probably only one third of its original height. Next to it is the **Serpentine Column**, believed to date from 479 BC, which was shipped here from Delphi.

Another obelisk still standing, but of unknown date, is usually referred to as the **Column of Constantine Porphyrogenitus**,

after the emperor who restored it in the 10th century AD. Its dilapidated state owes much to the young Janissaries (see p129) who routinely scaled it as a test of their bravery.

The only other structure in the Hippodrome is a domed fountain which commemorates the visit of Kaiser Wilhelm II to Istanbul in 1898.

The Hippodrome was the scene of one of the bloodiest events in Istanbul's history. In 532 a brawl between rival chariot-racing teams developed into the Nika Revolt, during which much of the city was destroyed. The end of the revolt came when an army of mercenaries, under the command of Justinian's general Belisarius, massacred an estimated 30,000 people trapped in the Hippodrome.

❾ Marmara University Museum of the Republic
Cumhuriyet Müzesi

Sultanahmet. **Map** 3 D5 (5 D5).
🚋 Sultanahmet. **Open** 10am–6pm Tue–Sun.

This fine art collection run by Marmara University is comprised of works by more than 85 artists, both from Turkey and around the world. The museum was initiated in 1973 as an etching exhibition held to celebrate 50 years of Turkey as a Republic. Today, visitors can see print paintings, calligraphy and other traditional Turkish art forms.

❿ Cistern of 1001 Columns
Binbirdirek Sarnıcı

Imran Okten Sok 4, Sultanahmet. **Map** 3 D4 (5 D4). **Tel** (0212) 518 10 01. 🚋 Çemberlitaş. **Open** 9am–6pm daily.

This cistern, dating back to the 4th century AD, is the second largest underground Byzantine cistern in Istanbul after the Basilica Cistern (see p78). Spanning an area of 64 m

Ceremonies in the Hippodrome

Beginning with the inauguration of Constantinople on 11th May 330 *(see p22)*, the Hippodrome formed the stage for the city's greatest public events for the next 1,300 years. The Byzantines' most popular pastime was watching chariot racing in the stadium. Even after the Hippodrome fell into ruins following the Ottoman conquest of Istanbul *(see p28)*, it continued to be used for great public occasions. This 16th-century illustration depicts Murat III watching the 52-day-long festivities staged for the circumcision of his son Mehmet. All the guilds of Istanbul paraded before the Sultan displaying their crafts.

Sultan Murat III

Palace of İbrahim Paşa (Museum of Turkish and Islamic Arts, *see p79*)

Column of Constantine Porphyrogenitus

Serpentine Column

Egyptian Obelisk

(210 ft) by 56 m (185 ft), the herring-bone brick roof vaults are held up by 264 marble columns – the 1,001 columns of its name is poetic exaggeration. Until not long ago, the cistern was filled with rubble and only explored by adventurous visitors, but it has been transformed into an atmospheric shopping complex specializing in jewellery, carpets and tiles and other merchandise inspired by Ottoman culture.

⓫ Tomb of Sultan Mahmut II

Mahmut II Türbesi

Divanyolu Cad, Çemberlitaş.
Map 3 D4 (4 C3). ⬛ Çemberlitaş.
Open 9:30am–4:30pm daily.

This large octagonal mausoleum is in the Empire style (modelled on Roman architecture), made popular by Napoleon. It was built in 1838, the year before Sultan Mahmut II's death and is shared by sultans Mahmut II, Abdül Aziz and Abdül Hamit II *(see pp34–5)*. Within, Corinthian pilasters divide up walls which groan with symbols of victory and prosperity. The huge tomb dominates a cemetery that has beautiful headstones, a fountain and a good café.

⓬ Constantine's Column

Çemberlitaş

Yeniçeriler Cad, Çemberlitaş.
Map 3 D4 (4 C3). ⬛ Çemberlitaş.
Çemberlitaş Baths: Vezirhani Cad 8.
Tel (0212) 511 25 35. **Open** 6am–midnight daily.

A survivor of both storm and fire, this 35-m (115-ft) high column was constructed in AD 330 as part of the celebrations to inaugurate the new Byzantine capital *(see p22)*. It once dominated the magnificent Forum of Constantine *(see p25)*. Made of porphyry brought from Heliopolis in Egypt, it was originally surmounted by a Corinthian capital bear- ing a statue of Emperor Constantine dressed as Apollo. This was brought down in a storm in 1106. Although what is left is relatively unimpressive, it has been carefully preserved. In the year 416 the 10 stone drums making up the column were reinforced with metal rings. These were renewed in 1701 by Sultan Mustafa II, and consequently the column is known as Çemberlitaş (the Hooped Column) in Turkish. In English it is sometimes referred

Constantine's Column

to as the Burnt Column because it was damaged by several fires, especially one in 1779 which decimated the Grand Bazaar *(see pp100–1)*.

A variety of fantastical holy relics were supposedly entombed in the base of the column, which has since been encased in stone to strengthen it. These included the axe which Noah used to build the ark, Mary Magdalen's flask of anointing oil, and remains of the loaves of bread with which Christ fed the multitude.

Next to Constantine's Column, on the corner of Divanyolu Caddesi, stand the Çemberlitaş Baths. This splendid *hamam* complex *(see p69)* was commissioned by Nur Banu, wife of Sultan Selim II, and built in 1584 to a plan by the great Sinan *(see p93)*. Although the original women's section no longer survives, the baths still have separate facilities for men and women. The staff are used to foreign visitors, so this is a good place for your first experience of a Turkish bath.

⓭ Sokollu Mehmet Paşa Mosque

Sokollu Mehmet Paşa Camii

Şehit Çeşmesi Sok, Sultanahmet. **Map** 3 D5 (4 C5). Çemberlitaş or Sultanahmet. **Open** daily.

Built by the architect Sinan *(see p93)* in 1571–2, this mosque was commissioned by Sokollu Mehmet Paşa, grand vizier to Selim II *(see p34)*. The simplicity of Sinan's design solution for the mosque's sloping site has been widely admired. A steep entrance stairway leads up to the mosque courtyard from the street, passing beneath the teaching hall of its *medrese* *(see p40)*, which still functions as a college. Only the tiled lunettes above the windows in the portico give a hint of the jewelled mosque interior to come.

Inside, the far wall around the carved mihrab is entirely covered in İznik tiles *(see p163)* of a sumptuous green-blue hue. This tile panel, designed specifically for the space, is complemented by six stained-glass windows. The "hat" of the *minbar* is covered with the same tiles. Most of the mosque's other walls are of plain stone, but they are enlivened by a few more tile panels. Set into the wall over the entrance there is a small piece of greenish stone which is supposedly from the Kaaba, the holy stone at the centre of Mecca.

Interior of the 16th-century Sokollu Mehmet Paşa Mosque

The Byzantine Church of SS Sergius and Bacchus, now a mosque

⓮ SS Sergius and Bacchus' Church

Küçük Ayasofya Camii

Küçük Ayasofya Cad. **Map** 3 D5 (4 C5). Çemberlitaş or Sultanahmet. **Open** daily.

Commonly referred to as "Little Haghia Sophia", this church was built in 527, a few years before its namesake *(see pp74–7)*. It too was founded by Emperor Justinian *(see p22)*, together with his empress, Theodora, at the beginning of his long reign. Ingenious and highly decorative, the church gives a somewhat higgledy-piggledy impression both inside and out and is one of the most charming of all the city's architectural treasures.

Inside, an irregular octagon of columns on two floors supports a broad central dome composed of 16 vaults. The mosaic

Reconstruction of the Great Palace

In Byzantine times, present-day Sultanahmet was the site of the Great Palace, which, in its heyday, had no equal in Europe and dazzled medieval visitors with its opulence. This great complex of buildings – including royal apartments, state rooms, churches, courtyards and gardens – extended over a sloping, terraced site from the Hippodrome to the imperial harbour on the shore of the Sea of Marmara. The palace was built in stages, be-ginning under Constantine in the 4th century. It was enlarged by Justinian following the fire caused by the Nika Revolt in 532 *(see p82)*. Later emperors, especially the 9th-century Basil I *(see p23)*, extended it further. After several hundred years of occupation, it was finally abandoned in the second half of the 13th century in favour of Blachernae Palace *(see p119)*.

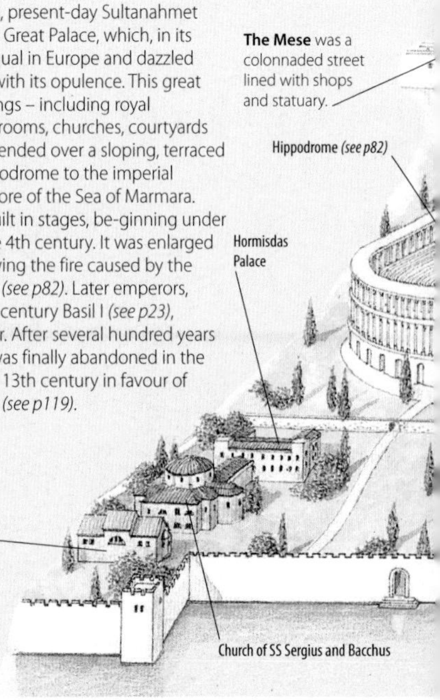
The Mese was a colonnaded street lined with shops and statuary.
Hippodrome *(see p82)*
Hormisdas Palace
Church of SS Peter and Paul
Church of SS Sergius and Bacchus

decoration which once adorned some of the walls has long since crumbled away. However, the green and red marble columns, the delicate tracery of the capitals and the carved frieze running above the columns are original features of the church.

The inscription on this frieze, in boldly carved Greek script, mentions the founders of the church and St Sergius, but not St Bacchus. The two saints were Roman centurions who converted to Christianity and were martyred. Justinian credited them with saving his life when, as a young man, he was implicated in a plot to kill his uncle, Justin I. The saints supposedly appeared to Justin in a dream and told him to release his nephew.

The Church of SS Sergius and Bacchus was built between two important edifices to which it was connected, the Palace of Hormisdas and the Church of SS Peter and Paul, but has outlived them both. After the conquest of Istanbul in 1453 *(see p28)* it was converted into a mosque.

⓯ Bucoleon Palace
Bukoleon Sarayı

Kennedy Cad, Sultanahmet. **Map** 3 E5. 🚊 Sultanahmet.

Finding the site of what remains of the Great Palace of the Byzantine emperors requires precision. It is not advisable to visit the ruins alone as they are usually inhabited by tramps.

Take the path under the railway from the Church of SS Sergius and Bacchus, turn left and walk beside Kennedy Caddesi, the main road along the shore of the Sea of Marmara for about 400 m (450 yards). This will bring you to a stretch of the ancient sea walls, constructed to protect the city from a naval assault. Within these walls you will find a creeper-clad section of stonework pierced by three vast windows framed in marble. This is all that

now survives of the Bucoleon Palace, a maritime residence that formed part of the sprawling Great Palace. The waters of a small private harbour lapped right up to the palace and a private flight of steps led down in to the water, allowing the emperor to board imperial caïques. The ruined tower just east of the palace was a lighthouse, called the Pharos, in Byzantine times.

Fragment of the Bucoleon Palace wall that remains intact

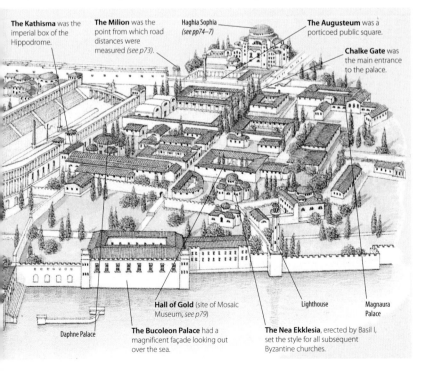

The Kathisma was the imperial box of the Hippodrome.

The Milion was the point from which road distances were measured *(see p73)*.

Haghia Sophia *(see pp74–7)*

The Augusteum was a porticoed public square.

Chalke Gate was the main entrance to the palace.

Hall of Gold (site of Mosaic Museum, *see p79*)

Lighthouse

Magnaura Palace

Daphne Palace

The Bucoleon Palace had a magnificent façade looking out over the sea.

The Nea Ekklesia, erected by Basil I, set the style for all subsequent Byzantine churches.

THE BAZAAR QUARTER

Trade has always been important in a city straddling the continents of Asia and Europe. Nowhere is this more evident than in the warren of streets lying between the Grand Bazaar and Galata Bridge. Everywhere, goods tumble out of shops onto the pavement. Look through any of the archways in between shops and you will discover hidden courtyards or hans *(see p98)* containing feverishly industrious workshops. With its

seemingly limitless range of goods, the labyrinthine Grand Bazaar is at the centre of all this commercial activity. The Spice Bazaar is equally colourful but smaller and more manageable.

Up on the hill, next to the university, is Süleymaniye Mosque, a glorious expression of 16th-century Ottoman culture. It is just one of numerous beautiful mosques in this area.

Sights at a Glance

Mosques and Churches

1 New Mosque
3 Rüstem Paşa Mosque
5 Süleymaniye Mosque *pp92–3*
6 Church of St Theodore
9 Prince's Mosque
10 Kalenderhane Mosque
11 Tulip Mosque
12 Bodrum Mosque
20 Atik Ali Paşa Mosque
21 Nuruosmaniye Mosque
22 Mahmut Paşa Mosque

Bazaars, Hans and Shops

2 Spice Bazaar

8 Vefa Bozacısı
16 Book Bazaar
17 Valide Hanı
18 Grand Bazaar *pp100–101*

Museums and Monuments

7 Valens Aqueduct
13 Forum of Theodosius
14 Museum of Calligraphy

Squares and Courtyards

15 Beyazıt Square
19 Çorlulu Ali Paşa Courtyard

Waterways

4 Golden Horn

☐ **Restaurants** *pp199–202*
1 Aslan Restaurant
2 Aynen Dürüm
3 Bizim Mutfak
4 Borsa
5 Can Restaurant
6 Çiğ Köfteci Ali Usta
7 Daruzziyafe
8 Gaziantep Burç Ocakbaşı
9 Hamdi
10 Havuzlu
11 Kahve Dünyası
12 Kardeşler Pilav Evi
13 Kral Kokoreç
14 Makarna Sarayı
15 Nar Lokanta
16 Nuruosmaniye Köftecisi
17 Ocakbası Dürüm Ve Kebap Salonu
18 Şark Kahvesi
19 Seref Buryan

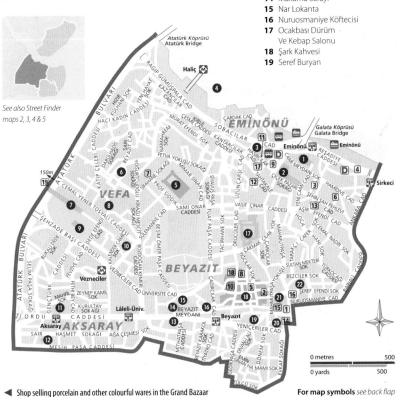

See also Street Finder maps 2, 3, 4 & 5

◀ Shop selling porcelain and other colourful wares in the Grand Bazaar

For map symbols *see back flap*

Street-by-Street: Around the Spice Bazaar

The narrow streets around the Spice Bazaar encapsulate the spirit of old Istanbul. From here buses, taxis and trams head off across the Galata Bridge and into the interior of the city. The blast of ships' horns signals the departure of ferries from Eminönü to Asian Istanbul. It is the quarter's shops and markets, though, that are the focus of attention for the eager shoppers who crowd the Spice Bazaar and the streets around it, sometimes breaking for a leisurely tea beneath the trees in its courtyard. Across the way, and entirely aloof from the bustle, rise the domes of the New Mosque. On one of the commercial alleyways which radiate out from the mosque, an inconspicuous doorway leads up stairs to the terrace of the serene, tile-covered Rüstem Paşa Mosque.

❸ ★ Rüstem Paşa Mosque
The interior of this secluded mosque is a brilliant pattern-book made of İznik tiles (see p163) of the finest quality.

0 metres   75

0 yards   75

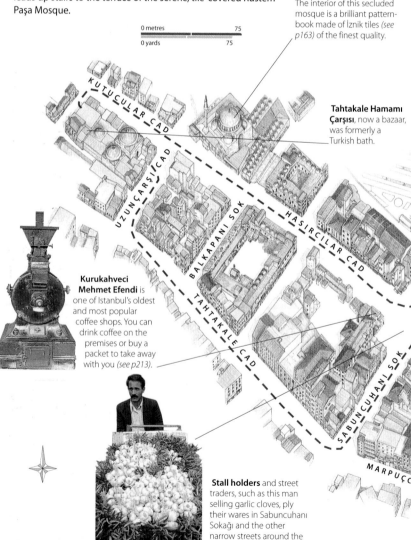

Tahtakale Hamamı Çarşısı, now a bazaar, was formerly a Turkish bath.

Kurukahveci Mehmet Efendi is one of Istanbul's oldest and most popular coffee shops. You can drink coffee on the premises or buy a packet to take away with you (see p213).

Stall holders and street traders, such as this man selling garlic cloves, ply their wares in Sabuncuhanı Sokağı and the other narrow streets around the Spice Bazaar.

Eminönü is the port from which ferries depart to many destinations (see p242) and for trips along the Bosphorus (see pp146–51). It bustles with activity as traders compete to sell drinks and snacks.

Locator Map
See Street Finder map 2, 3, 4, & 5

The royal pavilion, a suite of beautifully tiled private rooms, is linked by a passage to the sultan's loge inside the New Mosque.

Galata Bridge

Eminönü sea bus boarding point

Eminönü bus terminal

RESADIYE CAD

Eminönü tram stop

CAMIS CAD

CAMI MEYDANI SOK

YENI CAMI CAD

EK PAZARI SOK

Tea Gardens

Mausoleum of Turhan Hatice Valide Sultan, mother of Mehmet IV

Pet market and garden centre

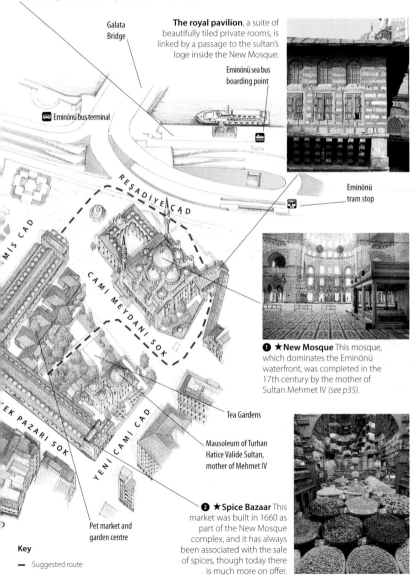

❶ ★**New Mosque** This mosque, which dominates the Eminönü waterfront, was completed in the 17th century by the mother of Sultan Mehmet IV (see p35).

❷ ★**Spice Bazaar** This market was built in 1660 as part of the New Mosque complex, and it has always been associated with the sale of spices, though today there is much more on offer.

Key

— Suggested route

❶ New Mosque
Yeni Cami

Yeni Cami Meydanı, Eminönü.
Map 3 D2. 🚇 Eminönü. **Open** daily.

Situated at the southern end of Galata Bridge, the New Mosque is one of the most prominent mosques in the city. It dates from the time when a few women from the harem became powerful enough to dictate the policies of the Ottoman sultans *(see p29)*. The mosque was started in 1597 by Safiye, mother of Mehmet III, but building was suspended on the sultan's death as his mother then lost her position. It was not completed until 1663, after Turhan Hadice, mother of Mehmet IV, took up the project.

Though the mosque was built after the classical period of Ottoman architecture, it shares many traits with earlier imperial foundations, including a monumental courtyard. The mosque once had a hospital, school and public baths.

The turquoise, blue and white floral tiles decorating the interior are from İznik *(see p163)* and date from the mid-17th century, though by this time the quality of the tiles produced there was already in decline. More striking are the tiled lunettes and bold Koranic frieze decorating the porch between the courtyard and the prayer hall.

At the far left-hand corner of the upper gallery is the sultan's loge *(see p41)*, which is linked to his personal suite of rooms *(see p89)*.

A selection of nuts and seeds for sale in the Spice Bazaar

❷ Spice Bazaar
Mısır Çarşısı

Cami Meydanı Sok. **Map** 3 D2 (4 C1).
🚇 Eminönü. **Open** 8am–7pm Mon–Sat.

This cavernous, L-shaped market was built in the early 17th century as an extension of the New Mosque complex. Its revenues once helped maintain the mosque's philanthropic institutions.

In Turkish the market is named the Mısır Çarşısı – the Egyptian Bazaar – because it was built with money paid as duty on Egyptian imports. In English it is usually known as the Spice Bazaar. From medieval times spices were a vital and expensive part of cooking and they became the market's main produce. The bazaar came to specialize in spices from the orient, taking advantage of Istanbul's site on the trade route between the East (where most spices were grown) and Europe.

Stalls in the bazaar stock spices, herbs and other foods such as honey, nuts, sweetmeats and *pastirma* (cured beef). Today's expensive Eastern commodity, caviar, is also available, the best variety being

Iranian. Nowadays an eclectic range of other items can be found in the Spice Bazaar, including everything from household goods, toys and clothes to exotic aphrodisiacs. The square between the two arms of the bazaar is full of commercial activity, with cafés, and stalls selling plants and pets.

Floral İznik tiles adorning the interior of Rüstem Paşa Mosque

❸ Rüstem Paşa Mosque
Rüstem Paşa Camii

Hasırcılar Cad, Eminönü. **Map** 3 D2.
🚇 Eminönü. **Open** daily.

Raised above the busy shops and warehouses around the Spice Bazaar, this mosque was built in 1561 by the great architect Sinan *(see p93)* for Rüstem Paşa, son-in-law of and grand vizier to Süleyman I *(see p28)*. Rents from the businesses in the bazaar were intended to pay for the upkeep of the mosque.

The staggering wealth of its decoration says something about the amount of money that the corrupt Rüstem managed to salt away during his career. Most of the interior is covered in İznik tiles of the very highest quality.

The New Mosque, a prominent feature on the Eminönü waterfront

The four piers are adorned with tiles of one design but the rest of the prayer hall is a riot of different patterns, from abstract to floral. Some of the finest tiles can be found on the galleries. All in all, there is no other mosque in the city adorned with such a magnificent blanket of tiles.

The mosque is also notable for its numerous windows: it was built with as many as the structure would allow.

❹ Golden Horn
Haliç

Map 3 D2. 🚇 Eminönü. 🚌 55T, 99A.

Often described as the world's greatest natural harbour, the Golden Horn is a flooded river valley which flows southwest into the Bosphorus. The estuary attracted settlers to its shores in the 7th century BC and later enabled Constantinople to become a rich and powerful port. According to legend, the Byzantines threw so many valuables into it during the Ottoman conquest (see p28), that the waters glistened with gold. Today, however, belying its name, the Golden Horn has become polluted by the numerous nearby factories.

For hundreds of years the city's trade was conducted by ships that off-loaded their goods into warehouses lining the Golden Horn. Nowadays, though, the great container ships coming to Istanbul use ports on the Sea of

Marmara. Spanning the mouth of the Horn is the Galata Bridge, which joins Eminönü to Galata. The bridge, built in 1994, opens in the middle to allow access for tall ships. It is a good place from which to appreciate the complex geography of the city and admire the minaret-filled skyline.

The functional Haliç Bridge replaced the raffish charm of a pontoon bridge. The second is the Haliç Metro Bridge, a cable-stayed bridge that will be connected with the Taksim-Yenikapı metro by 2015. It is located between the Galata Bridge and the Unkapanı Bridge. That is the third bridge, Unkapanı (also known as Atatürk), south of these, and the fourth, the Galata Bridge, is further up the Horn near the end of the city walls.

❺ Süleymaniye Mosque
See pp92–3.

❻ Church of St Theodore
Vefa Kilise Camii

Vefa Cad, Cami Sok, Vefa. **Map** 2 B2. 🚌 28, 61B, 87.

Apart from its delightfully dishevelled ancient exterior, very little else remains of the former Byzantine Church of St Theodore. The elaborate church was built in the 12th–14th centuries, the last great era of Byzantine

construction. It was converted into a mosque following the Ottoman conquest of the city in 1453 (see p28).

One feature that is still evident in the south dome in its outer porch is a 14th-century mosaic of the Virgin Mary surrounded by the Prophets. The fluted minaret makes a sympathetic addition.

The 4th-century Valens Aqueduct crossing Atatürk Bulvarı

❼ Valens Aqueduct
Bozdoğan Kemeri

Atatürk Bulvarı, Saraçhane. **Map** 2 A3. 🚇 Laleli. 🚌 28, 61B, 87. Ⓜ Vezneciler.

Emperor Valens built this mighty aqueduct, supported by two imposing rows of arches, in the late 4th century AD. Part of the elaborate water system feeding the palaces and fountains of the Byzantine capital, it brought water from the Belgrade Forest (see p160) and mountains over 200 km (125 miles) away to a vast cistern which stood in the vicinity of what is now Beyazıt Square (see p96).

The aqueduct supplied the city's water until the late 19th century, when it was made obsolete by a modern water distribution network. The original open channels, however, had by this stage already been replaced first by clay pipes and then by iron ones.

The structure was repaired many times during its history, latterly by sultans Mustafa II (1695–1703) and Ahmet III (see p29). It was originally 1,000 m (3,300 ft) long, of which 625 m (2,050 ft) remain.

Fisherman on the modern Galata Bridge spanning the Golden Horn

❺ Süleymaniye Mosque
Süleymaniye Camii

Istanbul's most important mosque is both a tribute to its architect, the great Sinan, and a fitting memorial to its founder, Süleyman the Magnificent *(see p28)*. It was built above the Golden Horn in the grounds of the old palace, Eski Saray *(see p96)*, between 1550–57. Like the city's other imperial mosques, the Süleymaniye Mosque was not only a place of worship, but also a charitable foundation, or *külliye (see p40)*. The mosque is surrounded by its former hospital, soup kitchen, schools, caravanserai and bath house. This complex provided a welfare system which fed over 1,000 of the city's poor – Muslims, Christians and Jews alike – every day.

Courtyard
The ancient columns that surround the courtyard are said to have come originally from the kathisma, the Byzantine royal box in the Hippodrome *(see p82)*.

KEY

① **Café in a sunken garden**

② **Muvakkithane Gateway**
The main courtyard entrance (now closed) contained the rooms of the mosque astronomer, who determined prayer times.

③ **İmaret Gate**

④ **The caravanserai** provided lodging and food for travellers and their animals

⑤ **Tomb of Sinan**

⑥ **Minaret**

⑦ **The Tomb of Roxelana** contains Süleyman's beloved wife *(see p78)*.

⑧ **Graveyard**

⑨ **These marble benches** were used to support coffins before burial.

⑩ **Addicts Alley"** is so called because the cafés here once sold opium and hashish as well as coffee and tea.

⑪ **The medreses** *(see p40)* to the south of the mosque house a library containing 110,000 manuscripts

⑫ **Former hospital and asylum**

İmaret
The kitchen – now a restaurant, Dârüzziyafe *(see p199)* – fed the city's poor as well as the mosque staff and their families. The size of the millstone in its courtyard gives an idea of the amount of grain needed to feed everyone.

★ Mosque Interior
A sense of soaring space and calm strikes you as you enter the mosque. The effect is enhanced by the fact that the height of the dome from the floor is exactly double its diameter.

VISITORS' CHECKLIST

Practical Information
Prof Siddik Sami Onar Caddesi, Vefa. **Map** 2 C3 (4 A1). **Tel** (0212) 522 02 98. **Open** daily. **Closed** at prayer times.

Transport
🚇 Beyazıt or Eminönü, then 10 mins walk.

Entrance

⑦

⑧

⑨

⑩

⑪

★ Tomb of Süleyman
Ceramic stars said to be set with emeralds sparkle above the coffins of Süleyman, his daughter Mihrimah and two of his successors, Süleyman II and Ahmet II.

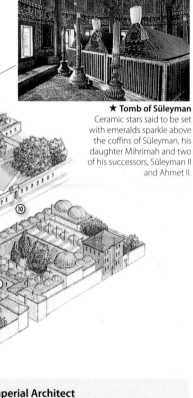

Sinan, the Imperial Architect

Like many of his eminent contemporaries, Mimar Sinan (c.1490–1588) was brought from Anatolia to Istanbul in the devşirme, the annual roundup of talented Christian youths, and educated at one of the elite palace schools. He became a military engineer but won the eye of Süleyman I, who made him chief imperial architect in 1538. With the far-sighted patronage of the sultan, Sinan – the closest Turkey gets to a Renaissance architect – created masterpieces which demonstrated his master's status as the most magnificent of monarchs. Sinan died aged 98, having built 131 mosques and 200 other buildings.

Bust of the great architect Sinan

❶ Vefa Bozacısı

Katip Çelebi Cad 104/1, Vefa.
Map 2 B2. **Tel** (0212) 519 49 22.
🚌 61B, 90. 🚇 Vezneciler.
Open 8am–midnight daily.

With its wood-and-tile interior and glittering glass-mosaic columns, this unusual shop and bar has changed little since the 1930s. It was founded in 1876 to sell *boza*, a popular winter drink made from bulgur (cracked wheat, *see p195*). In summer a slightly fermented grape juice known as *şıra* is sold. The shop's main trade throughout the whole year, however, is in wine vinegar.

Inside the shop you will see a glass from which Kemal Atatürk *(see p33)* drank *boza* in 1937, enshrined beneath a glass dome.

Bottles of *boza*, a wheat-based drink, in the Vefa Bozacısı

❷ Prince's Mosque

Şehzade Camii

Şehzade Başı Cad 70, Saraçhane.
Map 2 B3. 🚇 Laleli. 🚇 Vezneciler.
Open daily. Tombs: **Open** 9am–5pm Tue–Sun.

This mosque complex was erected by Süleyman the Magnificent *(see p28)* in memory of his eldest son by Roxelana *(see p78)*, Şehzade (Prince) Mehmet, who died of smallpox at the age of 21. The building was Sinan's *(see p93)* first major imperial commission and was completed in 1548. The architect used a delightful decorative style in designing this mosque before abandoning it in favour of the classical austerity of his later work. The mosque is approached through

Dome of the Prince's Mosque, Sinan's first imperial mosque

an elegant porticoed inner courtyard, while the other institutions making up the mosque complex, including a *medrese (see p40)*, are enclosed within an outer courtyard.

The interior of the mosque is unusual and was something of an experiment in that it is symmetrical, having a semi-dome on each of its four sides.

The three tombs located to the rear of the mosque, belonging to Şehzade Mehmet himself and grand vi-ziers İbrahim Paşa and Rüstem Paşa *(see p90)*, are the finest in the city. Each has beautiful İznik tiles *(see p163)* and lustrous original stained glass. That of Şehzade Mehmet also boasts the finest painted dome in Istanbul.

On Fridays you will notice a crowd of women flocking to another tomb within the complex, that of Helvacı Baba, as they have done for over 400 years. Helvacı Baba is said to

miraculously cure crippled children, solve fertility problems and find husbands or accommodation for those who beseech him.

❿ Kalenderhane Mosque

Kalenderhane Camii

16 Mart Şehitleri Cad, Saraçhane.
Map 2 B3. 🚇 Üniversite. 🚇 Vezneciler. **Open** prayer times only.

Sitting in the lee of the Valens Aqueduct *(see p91)*, on the site where a Roman bath once stood, is this Byzantine church with a chequered history. It was built and re-built several times between the 6th and 12th centuries, before finally being converted into a mosque shortly after the conquest in 1453 *(see p28)*. The mosque is named after the Kalender brotherhood of dervishes which used the church as its headquarters for some years after the conquest.

The building has the cruciform layout characteristic of Byzantine churches of the period. Some of the decora-tion remaining from its last incarnation, as the Church of Theotokos Kyriotissa (her Ladyship Mary, Mother of God), also survives in the prayer hall with its marble panelling and in the fragments of fresco in the narthex (entrance hall). A series of frescoes depicting the life of St Francis of Assisi were re-moved in the 1970s and are no longer on public view.

A shaft of light illuminating the interior of Kalenderhane Mosque

The Baroque Tulip Mosque, housing a marketplace in its basement

⓫ Tulip Mosque
Lâleli Camii

Ordu Cad, Lâleli. **Map** 2 B4. 🚇 Lâleli.
🚌 Vezneciler. **Open** prayer times
only.

Built from 1760–64, this mosque
complex is the best example
in the city of the Baroque style,
of which its architect, Mehmet
Tahir Ağa, was the greatest
exponent. Inside the mosque,
a variety of gaudy, coloured
marble covers all of its surfaces.

More fascinating is the area
underneath the main body
of the mosque. This is a great
hall supported on eight piers,
with a fountain in the middle.
The hall is now used as a
subterranean marketplace,
packed with Eastern Europeans
and Central Asians haggling
over items of clothing.

The nearby Büyük Taş Hanı (see
p98), or Big Stone Han, is likely to
have been part of the mosque's
original complex but now houses
a number of leather shops and a
restaurant. To get to it turn left
outside the mosque into Fethi
Bey Caddesi and then take the
second left into Çukur Çeşme

Sokağı. The main courtyard of
the han is at the end of a long
passage situated off this lane.

⓬ Bodrum Mosque
Bodrum Camii

Sait Efendi Sok, Laleli. **Map** 2 A4.
🚇 Laleli. **Open** prayer times only.

Narrow courses of brick
forming the outside walls, and a
window-pierced dome, betray
the early origins of this mosque
as a Byzantine church. It was
built in the early 10th century
by co-Emperor Romanus I
Lacapenus (919–44) as part of
the Monastery of Myrelaion and
adjoined a small palace. The
palace was later converted into
a nunnery where the emperor's
widow, Theophano, lived out
her final years. She was eventually buried in a sanctuary
chapel beneath the church,
which is closed to the public.

In the late 15th century the
church was converted into a
mosque by Mesih Paşa, a
descendant of the Palaeologus
family, the last dynasty to rule
Byzantium. The building was

gutted by fire several times
and nothing remains of its
internal decoration. Today it is
still a working mosque and is
accessed via a stairway which
leads up to a raised piazza filled
with coat stalls.

⓭ Forum of Theodosius
Theodosius Forumu

Ordu Cad, Beyazıt. **Map** 2 C4 (4 A3).
🚇 Üniversite or Beyazıt.

Constantinople (see pp24–5)
was built around several large
public squares or forums. The
largest of them stood on the
site of present-day Beyazıt
Square. It was originally known
as the Forum Tauri (the Forum
of the Bull) because of the huge
bronze bull in the middle of it
in which sacrificial animals,
and sometimes even criminals,
were roasted.

After Theodosius the
Great enlarged it in the late 4th
century, the forum took his
name. Relics of the triumphal
arch and other structures can
be found on either side of the
tram tracks along Ordu Caddesi.
The huge columns, with a motif
reminiscent of a peacock's tail,
are particularly striking. Once
the forum had become derelict,
these columns were reused all
over the city. Some can be seen
in the Basilica Cistern (see p78).
Other fragments from the forum
were built into Beyazıt Hamamı,
a Turkish bath (see p69) further
west down Ordu Caddesi, now
a bazaar.

Peacock feather design on a column from
the Forum of Theodosius

⓮ Museum of Calligraphy
Türk Vakıf Hat Sanatları Müzesi

Beyazıt Meydanı, Beyazıt. **Map** 2 C4 (4 A3). **Tel** (0212) 527 58 51. Üniversite. **Open** 9am–4pm Tue–Sat. with assistance.

The pretty courtyard in which this museum has been installed was once a *medrese (see p40)* of Beyazıt Mosque, situated on the other side of the square.

Its changing displays are taken from the massive archive belonging to the Turkish Calligraphy Foundation. As well as some beautiful manuscripts, including some dating back to the 13th century, there are examples of calligraphy on stone and glass. There is also an exhibition of tools used in calligraphy. One of the cells in the *medrese* now contains a waxwork tableau of a master calligrapher with his pupils.

The museum is likely to reopen in 2015 after renovation.

Beyazıt Tower, within the wooded grounds of Istanbul University

⓯ Beyazıt Square
Beyazıt Meydanı

Ordu Cad, Beyazıt. **Map** 2 C4 (4 A3). Beyazıt.

Always filled with crowds of people and huge flocks of pigeons, Beyazıt Square is the most vibrant space in the old part of the city. Throughout the week the square is the venue for a flea market, where everything from carpets *(see pp218–19)* and

The fortress-like entrance to Istanbul University, Beyazıt Square

Central Asian silks to general bric-a-brac can be purchased. When you have tired of rummaging, there are several cafés.

On the northern side of the square is the Moorish-style gateway leading into Istanbul University. The university's main building dates from the 19th century and once served as the Ministry of War. Within the wooded grounds rises Beyazıt Tower. This marble fire-watching station was built in 1828 on the site of Eski Saray, the palace first inhabited by Mehmet the Conqueror *(see p28)* after Byzantium fell to the Ottomans. Two original timber towers were destroyed by fire. The tower is now illuminated, indicating weather conditions through the use of different lights.

On the square's eastern side is Beyazıt Mosque, which was commissioned by Beyazıt II and completed in 1506. It is the oldest surviving imperial mosque in the city. Behind the impressive outer portal is a harmonious courtyard with an elegant domed fountain at its centre. Around the courtyard are columns made of granite and green and red Egyptian porphyry, and a pavement of multi-coloured marble. The layout of the mosque's interior, with its central dome and surrounding semidomes, is heavily inspired by the design of Haghia Sophia *(see pp74–7)*.

⓰ Book Bazaar
Sahaflar Çarşısı

Sahaflar Çarşısı Sok, Beyazıt. **Map** 2 C4 (4 A3). Üniversite. **Open** 8am–8pm daily.

This charming booksellers' courtyard, on the site of the Byzantine book and paper market, can be entered either from Beyazıt Square or from inside the Grand Bazaar *(see pp100–1)*. Racks are laden with all sorts of books, from tourist guides to academic tomes.

During the early Ottoman period *(see pp27–9)*, printed books were seen as a corrupting European influence and were banned in Turkey. As a result the bazaar only sold manuscripts. Then on 31 January 1729 İbrahim Müteferrika (1674–1745) produced the first printed book in the Turkish language, an Arabic dictionary. His bust stands in the centre of the market today. Note that book prices are fixed and cannot be haggled over.

Customers browsing in the Book Bazaar

The Art of Ottoman Calligraphy

Calligraphy is one of the noblest of Islamic arts. Its skills were handed down from master to apprentice, with the aim of the pupil being to replicate perfectly the hand of his master. In Ottoman Turkey, calligraphy was used to ornament firmans (imperial decrees) as well as poetry and copies of the Koran. However, many examples are also to be found on buildings, carved in wood and applied to architectural ceramics. The art of the calligrapher in all cases was to go as far as possible in beautifying the writing without altering the sense of the text. It was particularly important that the text of the Koran should be accurately transcribed. With the text of a firman, made to impress as much as to be read, the calligrapher could afford to add more flourishes.

The great calligraphers of the Ottoman period were Şeyh Hamdullah (1436–1520), whose work is seen in this Koran, Hafız Osman (1642–98) and Ahmet Karahisari (d.1556). Their pupils also achieved great renown.

Floral decorations

Ornamental loops

The sultan's tuğra was his personal monogram, used in place of his signature. It would either be drawn by a calligrapher or engraved on a wooden block and then stamped on documents. The tuğra incorporated the sultan's name and title, his patronymic and wishes for his success or victory – all highly stylized. This is the tuğra of Selim II (1566–74).

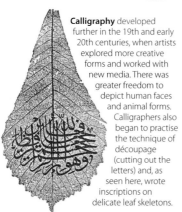

Calligraphy developed further in the 19th and early 20th centuries, when artists explored more creative forms and worked with new media. There was greater freedom to depict human faces and animal forms. Calligraphers also began to practise the technique of découpage (cutting out the letters) and, as seen here, wrote inscriptions on delicate leaf skeletons.

The later sultans were taught calligraphy as part of their education and became skilled artists. This panel, from the 19th century, is by Mahmut II (1808–39).

Breathing techniques were probably practised by some calligraphers in order to achieve the steadiness of hand required for their craft.

Burnisher

Knife for cutting pen nib

The calligrapher's tools and materials included a burnisher, usually made of agate, which was used to prepare the paper. A knife was used to slit the reed nib of the pen before writing.

⓱ Valide Han
Valide Han

Junction of Tarakçılar Sok and Çakmakçılar Yokuşu, Beyazıt. **Map** 2 C3 (4 B2). 🚇 Beyazıt, then 10 mins walk. **Open** 9:30am–5pm Mon–Sat.

If the Grand Bazaar *(see pp100–101)* seems large, it is sobering to realize that it is only the covered part of an huge area of seething commercial activity which reaches all the way to the Golden Horn *(see p91)*. As in the Grand Bazaar, most manufacturing and trade takes place in hans, courtyards hidden away from the street behind shaded gateways.

The largest han in Istanbul is Valide Han. It was built in 1651 by Kösem, the mother of Sultan Murat IV. You enter it from çakmakçılar Yokuşu through a massive portal. After passing through an irregularly shaped forecourt, you come out into a large courtyard centring on a Shiite mosque. This was built when the han became the centre of Persian trade in the city. Today, the han throbs to the rhythm of hundreds of weaving looms.

A short walk further down çakmakçılar Yokuşu is Büyük Yeni Han, hidden behind another impressive doorway. This Baroque han, built in 1764,

Carpet shops in Çorlulu Ali Paşa Courtyard

has three arcaded levels. The entrance is on the top level, where distinctive bird cages are among the wares.

In the labyrinth of narrow streets around these hans, artisans are grouped according to their wares: on Bakırcılar Caddesi, for instance, you will find metal workers, while the craftsmen of Uzunçarşı Caddesi make wooden items.

⓲ Grand Bazaar
See pp100–101.

Hans of Istanbul
The innumerable hans that dot the centre of Istanbul originally provided temporary accommodation for travellers, their pack animals and their wares. The typical han was built as part of a mosque complex *(see pp40–41)*. It consists of two- or three-storey buildings around a courtyard. This is entered via a large gateway which can be secured by a heavy wooden door at night. When vans and lorries replaced horses and mules, the city's hans lost their original function and most of them were converted into warrens of small factories and workshops. These working

Café in Büyük Taş Han, near the Tulip Mosque *(see p95)*

hans are frequently in bad repair, but in them you can still sense the entrepreneurial, oriental atmosphere of bygone Istanbul.

⓳ Çorlulu Ali Paşa Courtyard
Çorlulu Ali Paşa Külliyesi

Yeniçeriler Cad, Beyazıt. **Map** 4 B3. 🚇 Beyazıt. **Open** daily.

Like many others in the city, the *medrese (see p40)* of this mosque complex outside the Grand Bazaar has become the setting for a tranquil outdoor café. It was built for çorlulu Ali Paşa, son-in-law of Mustafa II, who served as grand vizier under Ahmet III *(see p29)*. Ahmet later exiled him to the island of Lésvos and had him executed there in 1711. Some years later his family smuggled his head back to Istanbul and interred it in the tomb built for him. The complex is entered from Yeniçeriler Caddesi by two alleyways. Several carpet shops now inhabit the *medrese* and rugs are hung and spread all around, waiting for prospective buyers. The carpet shops share the *medrese* with a *kahve*, a traditional café *(see p208)*, which is popular with locals and students from the nearby university. It advertises itself irresistibly as the "Traditional Mystic Water Pipe and Erenler Tea Garden". Here you can sit and drink tea, and perhaps smoke a nargile (bubble pipe), while deciding which carpet to buy *(see pp218–19)*.

Situated across Bıleycılar Sokak, an alleyway off Çorlulu Ali Paşa Courtyard, is the Koca Sinan Paşa tomb complex, the courtyard of which is another tea garden. The charming *medrese*, mausoleum and *sebil* (a fountain where water was handed out to passers-by) were built in 1593 by Davut Ağa, who succeeded Sinan *(see p93)* as chief architect of the empire. The tomb of Koca Sinan Paşa, grand vizier under Murat III and Mehmet III, is a striking 16-sided structure.

Just off the other side of Yeniçeriler Caddesi is Gedik Paşa Hamamı, thought to be the oldest working Turkish baths *(see p69)* in the city. It was built around 1475 for Gedik Ahmet Paşa, grand vizier under Mehmet the Conqueror *(see p28)*.

The dome and minaret of the mosque of Atik Ali Paşa

⑳ Atik Ali Paşa Mosque

Atik Ali Paşa Camii

Yeniçeriler Cad, Beyazıt. **Map** 3 D4 (4 C3). 🚇 Çemberlitaş. 🚌 61B. **Open** daily. 📷

Secreted behind walls in the area south of the Grand Bazaar, this is one of the oldest mosques in the city. It was built in 1496 during the reign of Beyazıt II, the successor of Mehmet the Conqueror, by his eunuch grand vizier, Atik Ali Paşa. The mosque stands in a small garden. It is a simple rectangular structure entered through a deep stone porch.

In an unusual touch, its mihrab is contained in a kind of apse. The other buildings which formed part of the mosque complex – its kitchen (*imaret*), *medrese* and Sufi monastery (*tekke*) – have all but disappeared during the widening of the busy Yeniçeriler Caddesi.

㉑ Nuruosmaniye Mosque

Nuruosmaniye Camii

Vezirhanı Cad, Beyazıt. **Map** 3 D4 (4 C3). 🚇 Çemberlitaş. 🚌 61B. **Open** daily. 📷

Nuruosmaniye caddesi, a street lined with carpet and antique shops, leads to the gateway of the mosque from which it gets its name. Mahmut I began the mosque in 1748, and it was finished by his brother, Osman III in 1755. It was the first in the city to exhibit the exaggerated traits of the Baroque, as seen in its massive cornices. Its most striking features, however, are the enormous unconcealed arches supporting the dome, each pierced by a mass of windows. Light floods into the plain square prayer hall, allowing you to see the finely carved wooden calligraphic frieze which runs around the walls above the gallery.

On the other side of the mosque complex is the Nuruosmaniye Gate. This leads into Kalpakçılar Caddesi, the Grand Bazaar's street of jewellery shops *(see p214)*.

The tomb of Mahmut Paşa, behind the mosque named after him

㉒ Mahmut Paşa Mosque

Mahmut Paşa Camii

Vezirhanı Cad, Beyazıt. **Map** 3 D3 (4 C3). 🚇 Çemberlitaş. 🚌 61B. **Open** daily. 📷

Built in 1462, just nine years after Istanbul's conquest by the Ottomans, this was the first large mosque to be erected within the city walls. Unfortunately, it has been over-restored and much of its original charm lost.

The mosque was funded by Mahmut Paşa, a Byzantine aristocrat who converted to Islam and became grand vizier under Mehmet the Conqueror. In 1474 his disastrous military leadership incurred the sultan's fury, and he was executed. His tomb, behind the mosque, is unique in Istanbul for its Moorish style of decoration, with small tiles in blue, black, turquoise and green set in swirling geometric patterns.

Rows of windows illuminating the prayer hall of Nuruosmaniye Mosque

⑱ Grand Bazaar

Kapalı Çarşı

Nothing can prepare you for the Grand Bazaar. This labyrinth of streets covered by painted vaults is lined with thousands of booth-like shops, whose wares spill out to tempt you and whose shopkeepers are relentless in their quest for a sale. The bazaar was established by Mehmet II shortly after his conquest of the city in 1453 *(see p28)*. It can be entered by several gateways, two of the most useful being Çarşıkapı Gate (from Beyazıt tram stop) and Nuruosmaniye Gate (from Nuruosmaniye Mosque). It is easy to get lost in the bazaar in spite of the signposting. Most of the bazaar's goods were once manufactured and traded behind the scenes in a large area made up of secluded courtyards called hans *(see p98)*.

Key

— Suggested route

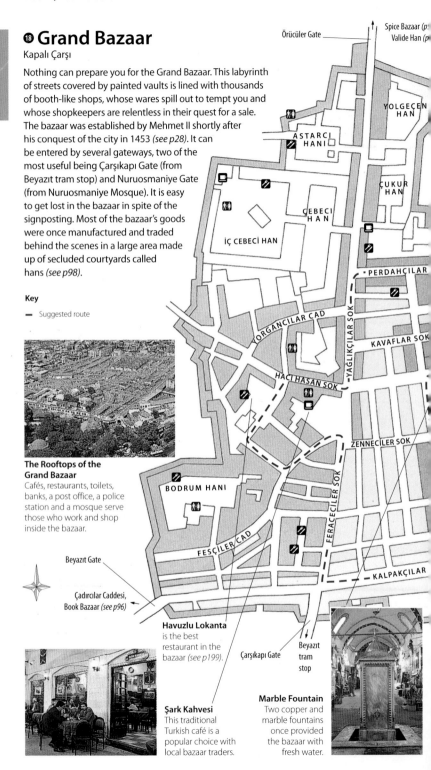

Örücüler Gate

Spice Bazaar (p
Valide Han (p

YOLGEÇEN HAN

ASTARCI HANI

ÇUKUR HAN

CEBECİ HAN

İÇ CEBECİ HAN

PERDAHÇILAR

YORGANCILAR CAD

YAĞLIKÇILAR SOK

KAVAFLAR SOK

HACI HASAN SOK

ZENNECİLER SOK

BODRUM HANI

FERACECİLER SOK

FESÇİLER CAD

KALPAKÇILAR

The Rooftops of the Grand Bazaar
Cafés, restaurants, toilets, banks, a post office, a police station and a mosque serve those who work and shop inside the bazaar.

Beyazıt Gate

Çadırcılar Caddesi, Book Bazaar *(see p96)*

Havuzlu Lokanta
is the best restaurant in the bazaar *(see p199)*.

Çarşıkapı Gate

Beyazıt tram stop

Şark Kahvesi
This traditional Turkish café is a popular choice with local bazaar traders.

Marble Fountain
Two copper and marble fountains once provided the bazaar with fresh water.

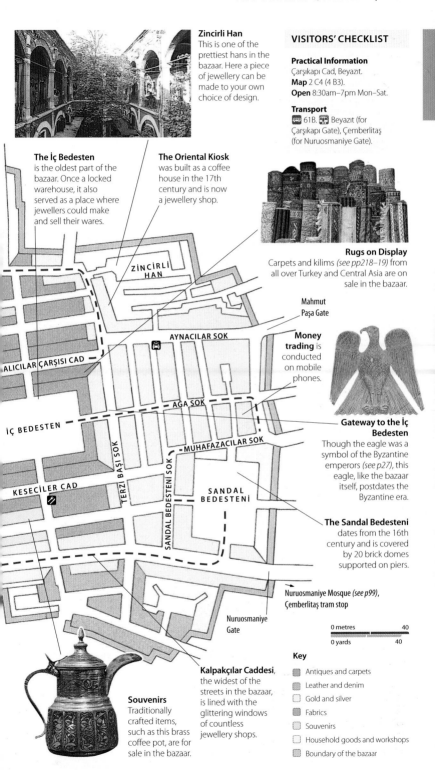

Zincirli Han
This is one of the prettiest hans in the bazaar. Here a piece of jewellery can be made to your own choice of design.

The İç Bedesten
is the oldest part of the bazaar. Once a locked warehouse, it also served as a place where jewellers could make and sell their wares.

The Oriental Kiosk
was built as a coffee house in the 17th century and is now a jewellery shop.

Rugs on Display
Carpets and kilims (see pp218–19) from all over Turkey and Central Asia are on sale in the bazaar.

Money trading is conducted on mobile phones.

Gateway to the İç Bedesten
Though the eagle was a symbol of the Byzantine emperors (see p27), this eagle, like the bazaar itself, postdates the Byzantine era.

The Sandal Bedesteni
dates from the 16th century and is covered by 20 brick domes supported on piers.

Nuruosmaniye Mosque (see p99), Çemberlitaş tram stop

Mahmut Paşa Gate

ZİNCİRLİ HAN

AYNACILAR SOK

ALICILAR ÇARŞISI CAD

AĞA SOK

İÇ BEDESTEN

MUHAFAZACILAR SOK

TERZİ BAŞI SOK

SANDAL BEDESTENİ SOK

KESECİLER CAD

SANDAL BEDESTENİ

Nuruosmaniye Gate

Kalpakçılar Caddesi,
the widest of the streets in the bazaar, is lined with the glittering windows of countless jewellery shops.

Souvenirs
Traditionally crafted items, such as this brass coffee pot, are for sale in the bazaar.

| 0 metres | 40 |
| 0 yards | 40 |

Key

- Antiques and carpets
- Leather and denim
- Gold and silver
- Fabrics
- Souvenirs
- Household goods and workshops
- Boundary of the bazaar

BEYOĞLU

For centuries Beyoğlu, a steep hill north of the Golden Horn, was home to the city's foreign residents. First to arrive here were the Genoese. As a reward for their help in the reconquest of the city from the Latins in 1261 *(see p26)*, they were given the Galata area, which is now dominated by the Galata Tower. During the Ottoman period, Jews from Spain, Arabs, Greeks and Armenians settled in communities here. From the 16th century the great European powers established embassies in the area to further their own interests within the lucrative territories of the Ottoman Empire. The district has not changed much in character over the centuries and is still a thriving commercial quarter today.

Sights at a Glance

Historic Buildings and Monuments
❶ Pera Palas Hotel
❸ Mevlevi Lodge
❹ Galata Tower
⓫ Tophane Fountain

Mosques and Churches
❺ Church of SS Peter and Paul
❻ Arab Mosque
❼ Azap Kapı Mosque
❾ Yeraltı Mosque
❿ Kılıç Ali Paşa Mosque
⓬ Nusretiye Mosque

Museums
❷ Pera Museum
❽ Ottoman Bank Museum
⓭ Istanbul Museum of Modern Art

Quarters
⓮ Çukurcuma
⓯ Taksim

☐ Selected Restaurants *pp199–202*
1 5 Kat
2 Ada Café & Bookstore
3 Ara Kafe
4 Bambi Café
5 By Corbaci Soup Bar
6 Cezayir
7 Çok Çok Thai
8 Date
9 Datli Maya
10 Hacıbaba
11 İsmail Kebab
12 Kahve6
13 Karaköy Lokantası
14 Kitchenette
15 Klemuri
16 La Mouette
17 Litera Café
18 Münferit
19 Ninja
20 White Mill Café

See also Street Finder maps 3, 6 & 7

0 metres 500
0 yards 500

◀ Galata Tower, one of the city's most distinctive sights

For map symbols *see back flap*

Street-by-Street: İstiklâl Caddesi

The pedestrianized İstiklal Caddesi is Beyoğlu's main street. Once known as the Grande Rue de Pera, it is lined by late 19th-century apartment blocks and European embassy buildings whose grandiose gates and façades belie their use as mere consulates since Ankara became the Turkish capital in 1923 *(see p33)*. Hidden from view stand the churches which used to serve the foreign communities of Pera (as this area was formerly called), some still buzzing with worshippers, others just quiet echoes of a bygone era. The once seedy backstreets of Beyoğlu, off İstiklâl Caddesi, are now filled with trendy jazz bars, shops selling handcrafted jewellery, furniture and the like. Crowds are also drawn by the area's cinemas and numerous stylish restaurants. Be aware that the street numbers on İstiklal Caddesi are in the process of being changed.

❶ ★ **Pera Palas Hotel** This hotel is an atmospheric period piece. Many famous guests, including Agatha Christie, Ernest Hemingway and Alfred Hitchcock have stayed here since it opened in 1892.

St Mary Draperis is a Franciscan church dating from 1789. This small statue of the Virgin stands above the entrance from the street. The vaulted interior of the church is colourfully decorated. An icon of the Virgin, said to perform miracles, hangs over the altar.

Tünel underground funicular to Karaköy

Tünel Square

❸ ★ **Mevlevi Lodge** A peaceful garden surrounds this small museum of the Mevlevi Sufi sect *(see p106)*. On the last Sunday of every month visitors can see dervishes perform their famous swirling dance.

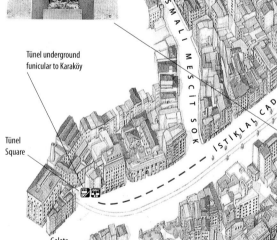

Galata Tower

Swedish Consulate

Russian Consulate

Galatasaray Fish Market
(Balık Pazarı) mainly sells fresh fish, but inside you will also discover numerous delicatessens offering everything from meats and cheeses through to delicious sweetmeats and pickles.

Locator Map
See Street Finder map 3, 6 & 7

British Consulate

HAMALBAŞI CAD

Armenian church

ET CAD

İSTİKLAL CAD

YENİ ÇARŞI CAD

Taksim →

Galatasaray High School

Çiçek Pasajı was originally a flower market. Its stalls have now been replaced by bars and restaurants, which are particularly lively in the evenings.

Dutch Consulate

❷ Pera Museum
Oriental paintings, Anatolian weights and measures and Kütahya tiles and ceramics are part of the collection.

Key

— Suggested route

0 metres   75
0 yards   75

The Church of the Panaghia serves the now much reduced Greek Orthodox population of Beyoğlu. Dedicated to the Virgin Mary, it contains this beautiful classical iconostasis.

For map symbols *see back flap*

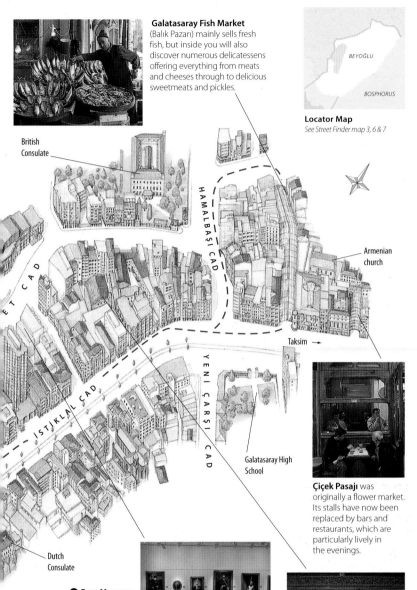

The elegant Grand Orient bar in the Pera Palas Hotel

❶ Pera Palas Hotel
Pera Palas Oteli

Meşrutiyet Cad 98–100, Tepebaşı.
Map 7 D5. **Tel** (0212) 251 45 60.
🚇 Tünel. ♿ by arrangement. 📷 by appointment only. 🌐 **perapalas.com**

The Pera Palas (see p188) has attained a legendary status. Relying on the hazy mystique of yesteryear, it has changed little since it opened in 1892, mainly to cater for travellers on the Orient Express (see p68). It still evokes images of uniformed porters and exotic onward destinations such as Baghdad. The Grand Orient bar serves cocktails beneath its original chandeliers, while the patisserie attracts customers with its irresistible cakes and genteel ambience.

Former guests who have contributed to the hotel's reputation include Mata Hari, Greta Garbo, Jackie Onassis, Sarah Bernhardt, Josephine Baker and Atatürk (see p33), whose favourite room is now a museum. A room used by the writer Agatha Christie can be visited on request.

Sufism and the Whirling Dervishes

Sufism is the mystical branch of Islam (see pp40–41). The name comes from *suf*, the Arabic for wool, for Sufis were originally associated with poverty and self-denial, and often wore rough woollen clothes next to the skin. Sufis aspire to a personal experience of the divine. This takes the form of meditative rituals, involving recitation, dance and music, to bring the practitioner into direct, ecstatic communion with Allah. There are several sects of Sufis, the most famous of which are the Mevlevi, better known as the Whirling Dervishes on account of their ritual spinning dance.

Painting of the Whirling Dervishes (1837) at the Mevlevi Lodge

❷ Pera Museum
Pera Müzesi

Meşrutiyet Cad 141, Tepebaşı.
Map 7 D4. **Tel** (0212) 334 99 00.
Tünel. 🚌 From Taksim Square down Tarlabaşı. **Open** 10am–7pm Tue–Sat, noon–6pm Sun. **Closed** 1 Jan, first day of Religious Holidays. ♿ 📷 (disabled visitors enter free). 📱 🌐 **peramuzesi.org.tr**

The Pera Museum was opened in June 2005 by the Suna and İnan Kıraç Foundation, with the aim of providing a cultural centre. It is housed in a historic building, formerly the Hotel Bristol. Notable collections include Ottoman weights and measures, over 400 examples of 18th-century Kütahya tiles and ceramics, and the Suna and İnan Kıraç Foundation's exhibition of Orientalist art. This collection brings together works by European artists inspired by the Ottoman world from the 17th century to the early 19th century. It also covers the last two centuries of the Ottoman Empire and provides an insight into upper class lives, customs and dress. The Pera also provides spaces for modern art exhibitions.

❸ Mevlevi Lodge
Mevlevi Tekkesi

Galip Dede Cad 15, Beyoğlu. **Map** 7 D5. **Tel** (0212) 245 41 41. 🚇 Tünel. **Open** 9am–4pm Wed–Mon. 📷

Although Sufism was banned by Atatürk in 1924, this monastery has survived as the Divan Edebiyatı Müzesi, a museum of *divan* literature (classical Ottoman poetry). The monastery belonged to the most famous sect of Sufis, who were known as the Whirling Dervishes. The original dervishes were disciples of the mystical poet and great Sufi master "Mevlana" (Our Leader) Celaleddin Rumi, who died in Konya, in central

The peaceful courtyard of the Mevlevi Lodge

Anatolia in 1273. Tucked away off a street named after one of the great poets of the sect, Galip Dede, the museum centres on an 18th-century lodge, within which is a beautiful octagonal wooden dance floor. Here, for the benefit of visitors, the *sema* (ritual dance) is performed by a group of latter-day Sufi devotees on the last Sunday of every month. At 3pm a dozen or so dancers unfurl their great circular skirts to whirl round the room in an extraordinary state of ecstatic meditation, accompanied by haunting music.

Around the dance floor are glass cases containing a small exhibition of artifacts belonging to the sect, including hats, clothing, manuscripts, photographs and musical instruments. Outside, in the calm, terraced garden, stand the ornate tombstones of ordinary sect members and prominent sheikhs (leaders).

❹ Galata Tower
Galata Kulesi

Büyük Hendek Sok, Beyoğlu. **Map** 3 D1. **Tel** (0212) 293 81 80. Tünel. **Open** 9am–7pm daily. Restaurant & show. **Open** 8pm–midnight daily. galatatower.net

The most recognizable feature on the Golden Horn, the Galata Tower is 60-m (196-ft) high and topped by a conical tower. Its origins date from the 6th century

Doorway into the main courtyard of the Church of SS Peter and Paul

when it was used to monitor shipping. After the conquest of Istanbul in 1453, the Ottomans turned it into a prison and naval depot. In the 18th century, aviation pioneer, Hezarfen Ahmet Çelebi, attached wings to his arms and "flew" from the tower to Üsküdar. The building was subsequently used as a fire watchtower.

The tower has been renovated and on the ninth floor there is a restaurant with nightly shows of folk music and belly dancing. The unmissable view from the top encompasses the city's skyline and beyond as far as Princes' Islands *(see p161)*.

❺ Church of SS Peter and Paul
Sen Piyer Kilisesi

Galata Kulesi Sok 44, Karaköy. **Map** 3 D1. **Tel** (0212) 249 23 85. Tünel. **Open** 7am–5pm Mon–Sat & 10:30am–noon Sun.

When their original church was requisitioned as a mosque (to become the nearby Arab Mosque) in the early 16th century, the Dominican brothers of Galata moved to this site, just below the Galata Tower. The present building, dating from 1841, was built by the Fossati brothers, architects of Italian-Swiss origin who also worked on the restoration of Haghia Sophia *(see pp74–7)*. The church's rear wall is built into a section of Galata's old Genoese ramparts.

According to Ottoman regulations, the main façade of the building could not be directly on a road, so the church is reached through a courtyard, the entrance to which is via a tiny door on the street. Ring the bell to gain admittance.

The church is built in the style of a basilica, with four side altars. The cupola over the choir is sky blue, studded with gold stars. Mass is said here in Italian every morning.

❻ Arab Mosque
Arap Camii

Kalyon Sok 1, Galata. **Map** 3 D1. Tünel. **Open** prayer times only.

The Arabs after whom this mosque was named were Moorish refugees from Spain. Many settled in Galata after their expulsion from Andalusia following the fall of Granada in 1492. The church of SS Paul and Dominic, built in the first half of the 14th century by Dominican monks, was given to the settlers for use as a mosque. It is an unusual building for Istanbul: a vast, strikingly rectangular Gothic church with a tall square belfry which now acts as a minaret. The building has been restored several times, but of all the converted churches in the city it makes the least convincing mosque.

The distinctive Galata Tower, as seen from across the Golden Horn

Azap Kapı Mosque, built by the great architect Sinan

⑦ Azap Kapı Mosque
Azap Kapı Camii

Tersane Cad, Azapkapı. **Map** 2 C1. 🚇 Tünel. 🚌 46H, 61B. **Open** prayer times only.

Delightful though they are, this little mosque complex and fountain are somewhat overshadowed by the stream of traffic thundering over the adjacent Atatürk Bridge. The trees surrounding the mosque, however, help to screen it from the noise. It was built in 1577–8 by Sinan (see p93) for Grand Vizier Sokollu Mehmet Paşa and is considered to be one of Sinan's more attractive mosques. Unusually, the entrance is up a flight of internal steps.

⑧ Ottoman Bank Museum
Osmanlı Bankası Müzesi

Bankalar Cad 35–37, Karaköy. **Map** 3 D1. **Tel** (0212) 334 22 70. 🚇 Tünel. 🚌 25E, 56. **Open** 10am–6pm daily. 🚻 📷 ♿ 🅦 obmuseum.com

The Ottoman Bank Museum has the most interesting collection of state archives in Turkey. Exhibits include Ottoman banknotes, promissory notes from officials at the imperial palace and photos of the Empire's ornately crafted branches. Outstanding are the 6,000 photographs of the bank's employees – a unique social registry.

⑨ Yeraltı Mosque
Yeraltı Camii

Karantina Sok, Karaköy. **Map** 3 E1. 🚇 Tünel. **Open** daily.

This mosque, literally "the underground mosque", contains the shrines of two Muslim saints, Abu Sufyan and Amiri Wahibi, who died during the first Arab siege of the city in the 7th century (see p23). It was the discovery of their bodies in the cellar of an ancient Byzantine fortification in 1640 that led to the creation of first a shrine on the site and later, in 1757, a mosque.

The tombs of the saints are behind grilles at the end of a low, dark prayer hall, the roof of which is supported by a forest of pillars.

⑩ Kılıç Ali Paşa Mosque
Kılıç Ali Paşa Camii

Necatibey Cad, Tophane. **Map** 7 E5. 🚌 25E, 56. 🚋 Tophane. **Open** daily.

This mosque was built in 1580 by Sinan, who was by then in his 90s. The church of Haghia Sophia (see pp74–7) provided the architect with his inspiration. İznik tiles adorn the mihrab and there is a delightful deep porch before the main door. Above the entrance portal is an inscription giving the date when the mosque was established.

Kılıç Ali Paşa, who commissioned the mosque, had a colourful life. Born in Italy, he was captured by Muslim pirates and later converted to Islam in the service of Süleyman the Magnificent (1520–66). He served as a naval commander under three sultans and after retiring asked Murat III (see p29) where to

Detail of a carved panel on Tophane Fountain

build his mosque. The sultan is said to have replied "in the admiral's domain, the sea". Taking him at his word, Kılıç Ali Paşa re-claimed part of the Bosphorus for his complex.

⑪ Tophane Fountain
Tophane Çeşmesi

Tophane İskele Cad, Tophane. **Map** 7 E5. 🚌 25E, 56. 🚋 Tophane.

Beside Kılıç Ali Paşa Mosque stands a beautiful but abandoned Baroque fountain, built in 1732 by Mahmut I. With its elegant roof and dome, it resembles the fountain of Ahmet III (see p62). Each of the four walls is entirely covered in low-relief floral carving, which would once have been gaily painted.

The name, meaning "cannon foundry fountain", comes from the brick and stone foundry building on the hill nearby. Established in 1453 by Mehmet the Conqueror (see p28) and rebuilt several times, the foundry no longer produces weapons but is still owned by the military.

⑫ Nusretiye Mosque
Nusretiye Camii

Meclis-i Mebusan Cad, Tophane. **Map** 7 E5. 🚌 25E, 56. **Open** daily.

The baroque "Mosque of Victory" was built in the 1820s by Kirkor Balyan (see p130), who went on to found a dynasty of architects. This ornate building seems more like a large palace pavilion than a mosque, with its decorative out-buildings and marble terrace.

Commissioned by Mahmut II to commemorate his abolition of the Janissary corps in 1826 (see p32), it faces the Selimiye Barracks (see p134), across the Bosphorus, which housed the

Koranic inscription in İznik tiles at the Kılıç Ali Paşa Mosque

The window-filled dome and arches of Nusretiye Mosque

New Army that replaced the Janissaries. The Empire-style swags and embellishments celebrate the sultan's victory. The marble panel of calligraphy around the interior of the mosque is particularly fine, as is the pair of *sebils* (kiosks for serving drinks) outside.

⓭ Istanbul Museum of Modern Art
İstanbul Modern Sanat Müzesi

Meclis-i Mebusan Cad, Liman İşletmeleri Sahası, Antrepo 4, Karaköy. **Map** 7 F5. **Tel** (0212) 334 73 00. Tophane. 56. **Open** 10am–6pm Tue–Sun.
w istanbulmodern.org

The Istanbul Modern, a new building perched on the Golden Horn, opened in 2005 as the most upbeat and thoroughly contemporary museum in Turkey. It houses both permanent collections and temporary exhibitions, providing a show-case for many of the eccentric and talented personalities who have shaped modern art in Turkey from the early 20th century to the present day. Many of the works are from the private collection of the Eczacıbaşı family, who founded the museum. Exhibits include abstract art, landscapes and watercolours as well as a sculpture garden and a stunning display of black and white photography.

⓮ Çukurcuma

Map 7 E4. Taksim. Museum of Innocence: Çukurcuma Cad, Dalgıç Çıkmazı, Beyoğlu. **Open** 10am–6pm Tue–Sun.

This charming old quarter of Beyoğlu, radiating from a neighbourhood mosque on Çukurcuma Caddesi, has become an important centre for Istanbul's furnishings and antiques trades. The old warehouses and houses in this district have been converted into shops and show-rooms, where modern uphol-stery materials are piled up in carved marble basins and antique cabinets. It is worth browsing here to discover hidden treasures, ranging from valuable paintings and prints and 19th-century Ottoman embroidery to 1950s biscuit boxes.

Suzani textiles *(see p212)* on sale in Çukurcuma

The district is also home to Nobel prize winner Orhan Pamuk's Masumiyet Müzesi **(Museum of Innocence)**. Set in a 19th-century house, the museum celebrates Pamuk's novel of the same name. The exhibits relate to the items used and owned by the characters in the novel.

⓯ Taksim

Map 7 E3. Taksim. Taksim. Taksim Republic Art Gallery: İstiklâl Cad No. 2, Taksim. **Tel** (0212) 245 78 32. **Open** daily.

Centring on the vast Taksim Square (Taksim Meydanı), the Taksim area is the hub of activity in modern Beyoğlu. Taksim means "water distribution centre"; from the early 1700s, it was from this site that water from the Belgrade Forest *(see p160)* was distributed throughout the city. The original stone reservoir, built in 1732 by Mahmut I, still stands at the top of İstiklâl Caddesi. In the southwest of the square is the 1928 Monument of Independence, by the Italian artist Canonica. It shows Atatürk *(see pp32–3)* and the other founding fathers of the modern Turkish Republic.

Further up near the entrance to İstiklâl Caddesi is Taksim Cumhuriyet Sanat Galerisi **(Taksim Republic Art Gallery)**. As well as temporary exhibitions, the gallery has a permanent display of Istanbul landscapes by some of Turkey's most important 20th-century painters.

Flower sellers in Taksim Square

GREATER ISTANBUL

Away from the city centre there are many sights which repay the journey to visit them. Greater Istanbul has been divided into five areas shown on the map below; each also has its own map to help you get around. Closest to the centre are the mosques and churches of Fatih, Fener and Balat: most conspicuously the gigantic Fatih Mosque. Across the Golden Horn (see p91) from Balat are two sights worth seeing: Aynalı Kavak Palace and a fascinating industrial museum. The Theodosian Walls, stretching from the Golden Horn to the Sea of Marmara, are one of the city's most impressive monuments. Along these walls stand several ancient palaces and churches: particularly interesting is the Church of St Saviour in Chora, with its stunning Byzantine mosaics. Beyond the walls, up the Golden Horn, is

Eyüp, a focus of pilgrimage to Muslims, where you can visit a number of fine mausoleums and walk up the hill to the historic café associated with the French writer Pierre Loti. Following the Bosphorus northwards past Beyoğlu (see pp102–9) brings you to the Dolmabahçe Palace, one of the top sights of Istanbul. This opulent fantasy created in the 19th century by Sultan Abdül Mecit I requires a lengthy visit. Beyond it is peaceful Yıldız Park containing yet more beautiful palaces and pavilions. Not all visitors to Istanbul make it to the Asian side, but if you have half a day to spare it is only a short ferry trip from Eminönü (see pp242–3). Its attractions include some splendid mosques, a handsome railway station and a small museum dedicated to British nurse, Florence Nightingale.

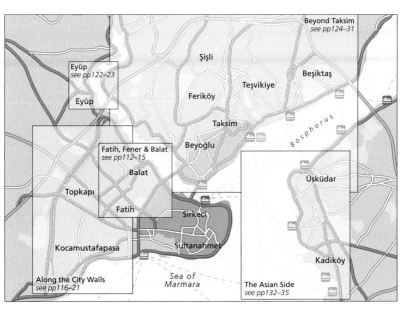

Beyond Taksim
see pp124–31

Şişli

Eyüp
see pp122–23

Eyüp

Beşiktaş

Teşvikiye

Feriköy

Taksim

Bosphorus

Beyoğlu

Fatih, Fener & Balat
see pp112–15

Balat

Üsküdar

Topkapı

Fatih

Sirkeci

Kocamustafapasa

Sultanahmet

Kadıköy

Along the City Walls
see pp116–21

Sea of
Marmara

The Asian Side
see pp132–35

Key

- ▨ Central Istanbul
- ▢ Greater Istanbul
- ▬ Main road
- ▭ Motorway
- ═ Other road
- ▬ City Walls
- --- Ferry route

0 kilometres   1

0 miles   1

◀ Modest interiors of the Church of St Saviour in Chora

For map symbols see back flap

Fatih, Fener and Balat

A visit to these neighbourhoods is a reminder that for centuries after the Muslim conquest *(see p28)*, Jews and Christians made up around 40 per cent of Istanbul's population. Balat was home to Greek-speaking Jews from the Byzantine era onwards; Sephardic Jews from Spain joined them in the 15th century. Fener became a Greek enclave in the early 16th century and many wealthy residents rose to positions of prominence in the Ottoman Empire. Hilltop Fatih is linked to the city's radical Islamic tradition and you will see far more devout Muslims here than anywhere else in Istanbul. All three areas are residential, their maze of streets the preserve of washing lines and children playing.

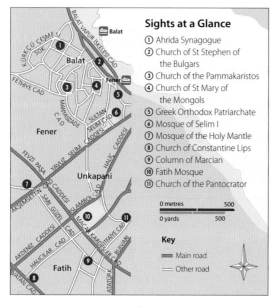

Sights at a Glance

① Ahrida Synagogue
② Church of St Stephen of the Bulgars
③ Church of the Pammakaristos
④ Church of St Mary of the Mongols
⑤ Greek Orthodox Patriarchate
⑥ Mosque of Selim I
⑦ Mosque of the Holy Mantle
⑧ Church of Constantine Lips
⑨ Column of Marcian
⑩ Fatih Mosque
⑪ Church of the Pantocrator

```
0 metres      500
0 yards       500
```

Key

▬▬ Main road
— Other road

❶ Ahrida Synagogue

Ahrida Sinagogu

Gevgili Sok, Balat. **Map** 1 C1. 🚌 55T, 99A. **Open** by appointment. 🚫

The name of Istanbul's oldest and most beautiful synagogue is a corruption of Ohrid, a town in Macedonia from which its early congregation came. It was founded before the Muslim conquest of the city in 1453 and, with a capacity for up to 500 worshippers, has been in constant use ever since. However, tourists can only visit by prior arrangement with a guided tour company *(see p228)*. The synagogue's painted walls and ceilings, dating from the late 17th century, have been restored to their Baroque glory. Pride of place, however, goes to the central Holy Ark, covered in rich tapestries, which contains rare holy scrolls.

During an explosion of fervour that swept the city's Jewish population in the 17th century, the religious leader Shabbetai Zevi (1629–76), a self-proclaimed messiah, started preaching at this synagogue. He was banished from the city and later converted to Islam. However, a significant number of Jews held that Zevi's conversion was a subterfuge and his followers, the Sabbatians, exist to this day.

❷ Church of St Stephen of the Bulgars

Bulgar Kilisesi

Mürsel Paşa Cad 85, Balat. **Map** 1 C1. 🚌 55T, 99A. 🚢 Balat. **Closed** for renovation.

Astonishingly, this entire church was cast in iron, even the internal columns and galleries. It was created in Vienna in 1871, shipped all the way to the Golden Horn *(see p91)* and assembled on its shore. The church was needed for the Bulgarian community who had broken away from the authority of the Greek Orthodox Patriarchate just up the hill. Today, it is still used by this community, who keep the marble tombs of the first Bulgarian patriarchs permanently decorated with flowers. The church stands in a pretty little park that is dotted with trees and flowering shrubs and which runs down to the edge of the Golden Horn.

The Church of St Stephen of the Bulgars, wholly made of iron

❸ Church of the Pammakaristos

Fethiye Camii

Fethiye Cad, Draman. **Map** 1 C2. 🚌 90, 90B. **Open** prayer times only. 🚫

This Byzantine church is one of the hidden secrets of Istanbul. It is rarely visited despite the important role it has played in the history of the city and its breathtaking series of mosaics. For over 100 years after the

Byzantine façade of the Church of the Pammakaristos

Ottoman conquest it housed the Greek Orthodox Patriarchate, but was converted into a mosque in the late 16th century by Murat III *(see p34)*. He named it the Mosque of Victory to commemorate his conquests of Georgia and Azerbaijan.

The charming exterior is obviously Byzantine, with its alternating stone and brick courses and finely carved marble details. The main body of the building is the working mosque, while the extraordinary mosaics are in a side chapel. This now operates as a museum and officially you need to get permission in advance from Haghia Sophia *(see pp74–7)* to see it. However, the caretaker, if around, may simply let you in.

Dating from the 14th century, the great Byzantine renaissance *(see p27)*, the mosaics show holy figures isolated in a sea of gold, a reflection of the heavens. From the centre of the main dome, Christ Pantocrator ("the All-Powerful"), surrounded by the Old Testament prophets, stares solemnly down. In the apse another figure of Christ, seated on a jewel-encrusted throne, gives his benediction. On either side are portraits of the Virgin Mary and John the Baptist beseeching Christ. They are overlooked by the four archangels, while the side apses are filled with other saintly figures.

❹ Church of St Mary of the Mongols
Kanlı Kilise

Tevkii Cafer Mektebi Sok, Fener. **Map** 1 C2. **Tel** (0212) 521 71 39. 55T, 99A. **Open** by appointment.

Consecrated in the late 13th century, the Church of St Mary of the Mongols is the only Greek Orthodox church in Istanbul to have remained continuously in the hands of the Greek community since the Byzantine era. Its immunity from conversion into a mosque was decreed in an order signed by Mehmet the Conqueror *(see p28)*. A copy of this is kept by the church to this day.

The church gets its name from the woman who founded it, Maria Palaeologina, an illegitimate Byzantine princess who was married off to a Mongol khan, Abagu, and lived piously with him in Persia for 15 years. On her husband's assassination, she returned to Constantinople, built this church and lived out her days in it as a nun.

A beautiful Byzantine mosaic which depicts Theotokos Pammakaristos ("the All-Joyous Mother of God") is the church's greatest treasure.

❺ Greek Orthodox Patriarchate
Ortodoks Patrikhanesi

Sadrazam Ali Paşa Cad 35, Fener. **Tel** (0212) 525 54 16. 55T, 99A. **Open** 9am–5pm daily.

This walled complex has been the seat of the patriarch of the Greek Orthodox Church since the early 17th century. Though nominally head of the whole church, the patriarch is now shepherd to a diminishing flock in and around Istanbul.

As you walk up the steps to enter the Patriarchate through a side door you will see that the main door has been welded shut. This was done in memory of Patriarch Gregory V, who was hanged here for treason in 1821 after encouraging the Greeks to overthrow Ottoman rule at the start of the Greek War of Independence (1821–32). Antagonism between the Turkish and Greek communities worsened with the Greek occupation of parts of Turkey in the 1920s *(see p33)*. There were anti-Greek riots in 1955, and in the mid-1960s many Greek residents were expelled. Today the clergy here is protected by a metal detector at the entrance.

The Patriarchate centres on the basilica-style Church of St George, which dates back to 1720. Yet the church contains much older relics and furniture. The patriarch's throne, the high structure to the right of the nave, is thought to be Byzantine, while the pulpit on the left is adorned with fine Middle Eastern wooden inlay and Orthodox icons.

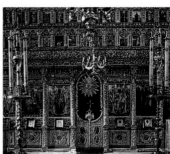

Church of St George in the Greek Orthodox Patriarchate

İznik tile panel capping a window in the Mosque of Selim I

❻ Mosque of Selim I

Yavuz Sultan Selim Camii

Yavuz Selim Cad, Fener. **Map** 1 C2. 55T, 90, 90B, 99A. **Open** daily.

This much-admired mosque is also known locally as Yavuz Sultan Mosque: Yavuz, "the Grim", being the nickname the infamous Selim acquired (see p28). It is idyllic in an off-beat way, which seems at odds with the barbaric reputation of the sultan.

The mosque, built between 1519 and 1522, sits alone on a hill beside a sunken parking lot, once the Byzantine Cistern of Aspar. Sadly it is rarely visited and has an air of neglect, yet the mosque's courtyard gives an insight into concept of paradise in Islam. At the centre of this lovely garden is an octagonal, domed fountain, surrounded by trees filled with chirruping birds.

The windows set into the porticoes in the courtyard are capped by early İznik tiles (see p163). These were made by the cuerda seca technique, in which each colour is separated during the firing process, thus affording the patterns greater definition.

Similar tiles lend decorative effect to the prayer hall, with its fine mosque furniture (see pp40–41) and woodwork.

❼ Mosque of the Holy Mantle

Hırka-i Şerif Camii

Keçeciler Cad, Karagümrük. **Map** 1 B3. 28, 87, 90, 91. **Open** daily.

Built in the Empire Style in 1850, this mosque was designed to house a cloak (hırka) in the imperial collection which once belonged to and was worn by the Prophet Moham-med. This resides in a sanctuary directly behind the mihrab. The mosque's minarets are in the form of Classical columns, and its balconies styled like Corinthian capitals. The interior of the octagonal prayer hall, meanwhile, has a plethora of decorative marble. Abdül Mecit I, the mosque's patron, was jointly responsible for the design of its calligraphic frieze.

Knocker, Mosque of the Holy Mantle

❽ Church of Constantine Lips

Fenari İsa Camii

Vatan Cad, Fatih. **Map** 1 B4. 90B. **Open** daily.

This 10th-century monastic church, dedicated to the Immaculate Mother of God, was founded by Constantine Lips Dungarios, a commander of the Byzantine fleet. Following the Byzantine reconquest

Byzantine brickwork exterior of the Church of Constantine Lips

of the city in 1261 (see p26), Empress Theodora, wife of Michael VIII Palaeologus (see pp26–7), added a second church. She also commissioned a funerary chapel, where she and her sons were buried.

This unusual history has given the structure its present rambling appearance. In an idiosyncratic touch, there are also four tiny chapels perched on the roof around the main dome. Another highlight is the building's eastern exterior wall. This is decorated with a tour de force of brick friezes, typical hallmarks of Byzantine churches of this period. When the church was con-verted into a mosque in 1496, it adopted the name Fenari İsa, or the Lamp of Jesus. This was in honour of İsa (Turkish for Jesus), the leader of a Sufi brotherhood (see p106) who worshipped here at that time. Inside the mosque, which is still in use today, are well-restored capitals and decorated cornices.

❾ Column of Marcian

Kız Taşı

w Cad, Saraçhane. **Map** 1 C4 (2 A3). 28, 87, 90, 91.

Standing in a little square, this 5th-century Byzantine column was once surmounted by a statue of the Emperor Marcian (AD 450–57). On its base you can still see a pair of Nikes, Greek winged goddesses of victory, holding an inscribed medallion.

Interestingly, the column's Turkish name translates as the Maiden's Column, suggesting that it was mistaken for the famous Column of Venus. According to legend, this column was said to sway at the passing of an impure maid. It originally stood nearby and is thought to have been employed as one of the largest columns in the Süleymaniye Mosque (see pp92–3).

Chandelier hanging in the light and airy interior of Fatih Mosque

⓾ Fatih Mosque

Fatih Camii

Macar Kardeşler Cad, Fatih. **Map** 1 C3.
28, 87, 90, 91. **Open** daily.

A spacious outer courtyard surrounds this vast Baroque mosque, which is the third major structure on this site. The first was the Church of the Holy Apostles *(see p25)*, the burial place of most of the Byzantine emperors. When Mehmet the Conqueror *(see p28)* came to construct a mosque here, the church's crumbling remains provided a symbolic location. But the first Fatih Mosque collapsed in an earthquake in 1766, and most of what you see today was the work of Mehmet Tahir Ağa, the chief imperial architect under Mustafa III. Many of the buildings he constructed around the prayer hall, including eight Koranic colleges *(medreses)* and a hospice, still stand.

The only parts of Mehmet the Conqueror's mosque to have survived are the three porticoes of the courtyard, the ablutions fountain, the main gate into the prayer hall and, inside, the mihrab. Two exquisite forms of 15th-century decoration can be seen over the windows in the porticoes: İznik tiles made using the *cuerda seca* technique and lunettes adorned with calligraphic marble inlay.

Inside the prayer hall, stencilled patterns decorate the domes, while the lower level of the walls is revetted with yet more tiles – although these are inferior to those used in the porticoes.

The tomb of Mehmet the Conqueror stands behind the prayer hall, near that of his consort Gülbahar. His sarcophagus and turban are both appropriately large. It is a place of enormous gravity, always busy with supplicants.

If you pay a visit to the mosque on a Wednesday, you will also see the weekly market *(see p214)* which turns the streets around it into a circus of commerce. From tables piled high with fruit and vegetables to lorries loaded with unspun wool, this is a real spectacle, even if you don't buy anything.

⓫ Church of the Pantocrator

Zeyrek Camii

İbadethane Sok, Küçükpazar.
Map 2 B2. 28, 61B, 87.
Open prayer times daily.

Empress Irene, the wife of John II Comnenus *(see p21)*, founded the Church of the Pantocrator ("Christ the Almighty") during the 12th century. This hulk of Byzantine masonry was once the centrepiece of one of the city's most important religious foundations, the Monastery of the Pantocrator. As well as a monastery and church, the complex included a hospice for the elderly, an asylum and a hospital. In this respect it prefigured the social welfare system provided by the great imperial mosque complexes that the Ottomans later built in the city *(see p40)*.

The church, now a mosque, boasts a magnificent figurative marble floor. It is composed of three interlinked chapels. The one with the highest dome was built by Empress Irene. Emperor John II added another as a mortuary chapel when Irene died in 1124, and he later filled the area between with a third apsed chapel. The rest of the Comnenus dynasty and many of the Palaeologus imperial family were interred within these chapels.

Shortly after the Muslim conquest in 1453 *(see p28)*, the building was converted into a mosque. A caretaker may let you in outside prayer times in the afternoons.

Church of the Pantocrator, built by Empress Irene in the 12th century

Along the City Walls

Istanbul's land walls are one of the most impressive remains of the city's Byzantine past. Pierced by monumental gates and strengthened by towers, they encompass the city centre in a great arc, stretching all the way from Yedikule, on the Sea of Marmara, to Ayvansaray, on the Golden Horn (see p91). The suburbs that lie adjacent to the walls, particularly Edirnekapı and Topkapı, are mainly working-class, residential districts, interspersed with areas of wasteland which are unsafe to explore alone. Dotted around these suburbs, however, are important remnants of the city's past, particularly the Byzantine period. The outstanding sight here is the Church of St Saviour in Chora (see pp120–21), with its beautifully preserved mosaics and frescoes.

Silivrikapı, one of the gateways through the Theodosian Walls

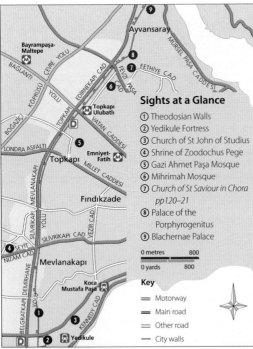

Sights at a Glance

1. Theodosian Walls
2. Yedikule Fortress
3. Church of St John of Studius
4. Shrine of Zoodochus Pege
5. Gazi Ahmet Paşa Mosque
6. Mihrimah Mosque
7. *Church of St Saviour in Chora pp120–21*
8. Palace of the Porphyrogenitus
9. Blachernae Palace

0 metres 800
0 yards 800

Key

= Motorway
= Main road
= Other road
— City walls

Theodosius II (408–50). In 447 an earthquake destroyed 54 of the towers but these were immediately rebuilt, under threat of the advancing Attila the Hun. Subsequently the walls resisted sieges by Arabs, Bulgarians, Russians and Turks. Even the determined armies of the Fourth Crusade (see p26) only managed to storm the ramparts along the Golden Horn, while the land walls stood firm.

Mehmet the Conqueror finally breached the walls in May 1453 (see p28). Successive Ottoman sultans then kept the walls in good repair until the end of the 17th century.

Large stretches of the walls, particularly around Belgratkapı (Belgrade Gate) have been rebuilt. Byzantine scholars have criticized the restoration for insensitive use of modern building materials, but the new sections do give you an idea of how the walls used to look.

Many, although not all, of the gateways are still in good repair. Mehmet the Conqueror directed his heaviest cannon at the St Romanus and Charsius gates. Under the Ottomans, the former became known as Topkapı, the Gate of the Cannon (not to be confused

❶ Theodosian Walls

Teodos II Surları

From Yedikule to Ayvansaray.
Map 1 A1. 🚃 Topkapı, Ulubatlı.

With its 11 fortified gates and 192 towers, this great chain of double walls sealed Constantinople's landward side against invasion for more than a thousand years. Extending for a distance of 6.5 km (4 miles) from the Sea of Marmara to the Golden Horn, the walls are

built in layers of red tile alternating with limestone blocks. Different sections can be reached by metro, tram, train or bus; but to see their whole length you will need to take a taxi or dolmuş (see p238) along the main road that runs outside them.

The walls were built between AD 412–22, during the reign of

Carving of the Byzantine eagle over Yedikule Gate

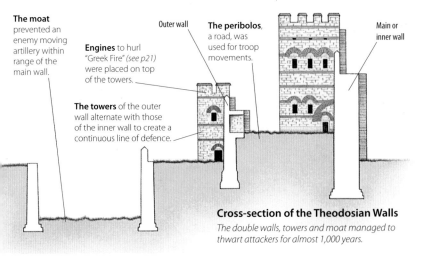

The moat prevented an enemy moving artillery within range of the main wall.

Outer wall

Engines to hurl "Greek Fire" (see p21) were placed on top of the towers.

The peribolos, a road, was used for troop movements.

Main or inner wall

The towers of the outer wall alternate with those of the inner wall to create a continuous line of defence.

Cross-section of the Theodosian Walls

The double walls, towers and moat managed to thwart attackers for almost 1,000 years.

---

with Topkapı Palace, *see pp56–61*). Unfortunately, a section of walls close to this gate was demolished in the 1950s to make way for a road, Millet Caddesi. The Charsius Gate (now called Edirnekapı), Silivrikapı, Yeni Mevlanakapı and other original gates still give access to the city. The Yedikule Gate (which stands beside the fortress of the same name) has an imperial Byzantine eagle (*see p27*) carved above its main archway.

❷ Yedikule Fortress
Yedikule Müzesi

Kule Meydanı 4, Yedikule.
Tel (0212) 585 89 33. 🚌 31, 80, 93T.
Open 9am–5pm daily.

Yedikule, the "Fortress of the Seven Towers", is built on to the southern section of the Theodosian Walls. Its seven towers are connected by thick walls to make a five-sided fortification. One of the sides, with four towers spaced along it, is formed by a stretch of the land walls themselves.

The fortress as it is today incorporates both Byzantine and Ottoman features. The two stout, square marble towers built into the land walls once flanked the Golden Gate (now blocked up), the triumphal entrance into medieval Byzantium (*see p24*) built by Theodosius II. Imperial processions would enter the city

through this gate to mark the investiture of a new emperor or in celebration of a successful military campaign. When it was first built, the gate was covered in gold plate and the façade decorated with sculptures, including a statue of a winged Victory, four bronze elephants and an image of Emperor Theodosius himself.

In the 15th century, Mehmet the Conqueror added the three tall, round towers that are not part of the land walls, and the connecting curtain walls, to complete the fortress.

After viewing the castle from the outside, you can enter through a doorway in the northeastern wall. The tower immediately to your left as you enter is known as the *yazılı kule*, "the tower with inscriptions".

This was used as a prison for foreign envoys and others who fell foul of the sultan. These hapless individuals carved their names, dates and other details on the walls and some of these inscriptions are still visible.

Executions were carried out in Yedikule Castle, in the northern of the two towers flanking the Golden Gate. Among those executed here was the 17-year-old Osman II (*see p35*). In 1622 he was dragged to Yedikule by his own Janissaries (*see p129*), after four years of misrule, which included, it is alleged, using his own pages as targets for archery practice.

The walkway around the ramparts is accessible via a steep flight of stone steps. It offers good views of the land walls and nearby suburbs, and also of the cemeteries.

Aerial view of Yedikule Fortress with the Sea of Marmara behind

❸ Church of St John of Studius

İmrahor Camii

İmam Aşir Sok, Yedikule. 🚌 80, 80B, 80T. 🚆 Yedikule.

Istanbul's oldest surviving church, St John of Studius, is now a mere shell consisting only of its outer walls. However, you can still get an idea of the original beauty of what was once part of an important Byzantine institution.

The church was completed in AD 463 by Studius, a Roman patrician who served as consul during the reign of Emperor Marcian (450–57). Originally connected to the most powerful monastery in the Byzantine Empire, in the late 8th century it was a spiritual and intellectual centre under the rule of Abbot Theodore, who was buried in the church's garden. The abbot is venerated today in the Greek Orthodox Church as St Theodore.

Until its removal by the soldiers of the Fourth Crusade (see p26), the most sacred relic housed in the church was the head of St John the Baptist. The emperor would visit the church each year for the Beheading of the Baptist feast on 29 August.

In the 15th century the church housed a university and was converted into a mosque. The building was abandoned in 1894 when it was severely damaged by an earthquake.

The church is a perfect basilica, with a single apse at the east end, preceded by a narthex and a courtyard. It has a magnificent entrance portal, with carved Corinthian capitals and a sculpted architrave and cornice. Inside, it is empty, apart from a colonnade of six columns of verdigris.

The Shrine of Zoodochus Pege, founded on a sacred spring

❹ Shrine of Zoodochus Pege

Balıklı Kilise

Seyit Nizam Cad 3, Silivrikapı. **Tel** (0212) 582 30 81. 🚆 Seyitnizam. 🚌 93T. **Open** 8am–4pm daily.

The Fountain of Zoodochus Pege ("Life-Giving Spring") is built over Istanbul's most famous sacred spring, which is believed to have miraculous powers. The fish swimming in it are supposed to have arrived though a miracle which occurred shortly before the fall of Constantinople (see p28). They are said to have leapt into the spring from a monk's frying pan on hearing him declare that a Turkish invasion of Constantinople was as likely as fish coming back to life.

The spring was probably the site of an ancient sanctuary of Artemis. Later, with the arrival of Christianity, a church was built around it, which was dedicated to the Virgin Mary. The spring was popular throughout the Byzantine era, especially on Ascension Day, when the emperor would visit it. The church was destroyed and rebuilt many times over the years by various Byzantine emperors, but the present one dates from 1833. The inner

courtyard is filled with tombs of bishops and patriarchs of the Greek Orthodox Church.

❺ Gazi Ahmet Paşa Mosque

Gazi Ahmet Paşa Camii

Undeğirmeni Sok, Fatma Sultan. 🚇 Ulubatlı. 🚆 Topkapı. 🚌 93T. **Open** Prayer times only.

One of the most worthwhile detours along the city walls is the Gazi Ahmet Paşa Mosque, also known as Kara Ahmet Paşa. This lovely building, with its peaceful leafy courtyard and graceful proportions, is one of Sinan's (see p93) lesser known achievements. He built it in 1554 for Kara Ahmet Paşa, a grand vizier of Süleyman the Magnificent (see p28).

The courtyard is surrounded by the cells of a *medrese* and a *dershane*, or main classroom. Attractive apple-green and yellow İznik tiles (see p163) grace the porch, while blue-and-white ones are found on the east wall of the prayer hall. These tiles date from the mid-16th century. Of the three galleries, the wooden ceiling under the west one

Tilework over *medrese* doorway at Kara Ahmet Paşa Mosque

is elaborately painted in red, blue, gold and black.

Outside the city walls, nearby, is tiny Takkeci İbrahim Ağa Mosque, which dates from 1592. Wooden-domed, it has some particularly fine İznik tile panels.

❻ Mihrimah Mosque

Mihrimah Camii

Sulukule Cad, Edirnekapı. **Map** 1 A2. 🚌 28, 87, 91. **Open** daily.

An imposing monument located just inside the city walls, the Mihrimah Mosque complex was built by Sinan between 1562 and 1565. Mihrimah, the daughter of Süleyman the Magnificent (see p28), was then the recently

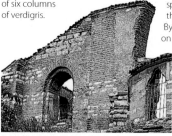

Ruins of the Church of St John of Studius

widowed wife of Rüstem Paşa, a grand vizier who gave his name to the tiled mosque near the Spice Bazaar *(see pp90–91)*.

This mosque rests on a platform, occupying the highest point in the city. Its profile is visible from far away on the Bosphorus and also when approaching Istanbul from Edirne *(see pp156–9)*.

The building is square in shape, with four strong turrets at its corners, and is surmounted by a 37-m (121-ft) high dome. The single minaret is tall and slender, so much so that it has twice been destroyed by earthquakes. On the second occasion, in 1894, the minaret crashed through the roof of the mosque. The 20th-century stencilling on the inside of the prayer hall was added following this accident.

The interior is illuminated by numerous windows, some of which have stained glass. The supporting arches of the sultan's loge *(see p41)* have been skilfully painted to resemble green-and-white marble. The carved marble *minbar* is also impressive.

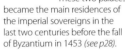

Stained-glass window in the Mihrimah Mosque

❼ Church of St Saviour in Chora

See pp120–21.

❽ Palace of the Porphyrogenitus

Tekfur Sarayı

Şişehane Cad, Edirnekapı. **Map** 1 B1. **Tel** (0212) 522 175. 🚌 87, 90, 126. **Open** daily.

Only glimpses of the former grandeur of the Palace of the Porphyrogenitus (Sovereign) during its years as an imperial residence are discernible from the sketchy remains. Its one extant hall, now open to the

elements, does, however, have an attractive three-storey façade in typically Byzantine style. This is decorated in red brick and white marble, with arched doorways at ground level and two rows of windows overlooking a courtyard.

The palace, also known as Tekfur Palace Museum, dates from the late Byzantine era and is the only surviving palace from this period. Its exact age is debatable since the technique of alternating stone with three courses of brick is typical of the 10th century, whereas its geometrical designs were common in the 14th century. It was most likely constructed as an annexe of nearby Blachernae Palace. These two palaces became the main residences of the imperial sovereigns in the last two centuries before the fall of Byzantium in 1453 *(see p28)*.

During the reign of Ahmet III (1703–30, *see p29*) the last remaining İznik potters *(see p163)* moved to the palace. However, by this time their skills were in decline and the tiles made here never acquired the

excellence of those created at the height of production in İznik. Cezri Kasım Paşa Mosque in Eyüp *(see p123)* has some fine examples of these tiles.

❾ Blachernae Palace

Anemas Zindanları

İvaz Ağa Cad, Ayvansaray. 🚌 55T, 99A.

As the city walls approach the Golden Horn you come to the scant remains of Blachernae Palace. These consist of a tower in the city wall, known as the Prison of Anemas, a terrace to the east (the present site of the İvaz Efendi Mosque), and another tower to the south of the terrace, known as the Tower of Isaac Angelus.

The origins of the palace date as far back as AD 500, when it was an occasional residence for imperial visitors to the shrine of Blachernae. It was the great Comnenus emperors *(see p23)* who rebuilt the structure in the 12th century, transforming it into a magnificent palace.

The remains of the marble decoration and wall frescoes in the Anemas tower indicate that this was probably an imperial residence. Although you can walk around the site, you will be unable to gain access into the towers unless the caretaker is there.

Brick and marble façade in the Palace of the Porphyrogenitus

❼ Church of St Saviour in Chora

Kariye Müzesi

Some of the very finest Byzantine mosaics and frescoes can be found in the Church of St Saviour in Chora. Little is known of the early history of the church, although its name "in Chora", which means "in the country", suggests that the church originally stood in a rural setting. The present church dates from the 11th century. Between 1315–21 it was remodelled and the mosaics and frescoes added by Theodore Metochites, a theologian, philosopher and one of the elite Byzantine officials of his day.

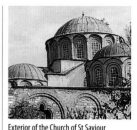

Exterior of the Church of St Saviour in Chora

The Genealogy of Christ

Theodore Metochites, who restored St Saviour, wrote that his mission was to relate how "the Lord himself became a mortal on our behalf". He takes the *Genealogy of Christ* as his starting point: the mosaics in the two domes of the inner narthex portray 66 of Christ's forebears.

The crown of the southern dome is occupied by a figure of Christ. In the dome's flutes are two rows of his ancestors: Adam to Jacob ranged above the 12 sons of Jacob. In the northern dome, there is a central image of the Virgin and Child with the kings of the House of David in the upper row and lesser ancestors of Christ in the lower row.

The Life of the Virgin

All but one of the 20 mosaics in the inner narthex depicting the *Life of the Virgin* are well preserved. This cycle is based mainly on the apocryphal Gospel of St James, written in the 2nd century, which gives an account of the Virgin's life. This was popular in the Middle Ages and was a rich source of material for ecclesiastical artists.

Among the events shown are the first seven steps of the Virgin, the Virgin entrusted to Joseph and the Virgin receiving bread from an angel.

The Infancy of Christ

Scenes from the *Infancy of Christ*, based largely on the New Testament, occupy the semicircular panels of the outer narthex. They begin on the north wall of the outer

Mosaic showing Christ and his ancestors, in the southern dome of the inner narthex

Guide to the Mosaics and Frescoes

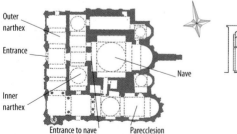

- Outer narthex
- Entrance
- Inner narthex
- Nave
- Entrance to nave
- Parecclesion

Key

- ▨ The Genealogy of Christ
- ▨ The Life of the Virgin
- ▨ The Infancy of Christ
- ▨ Christ's Ministry
- ▨ Other Mosaics
- ▨ The Frescoes

Outer narthex looking east

Outer narthex looking west

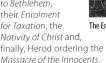

narrthex with a scene of Joseph being visited by an angel in a dream. Subsequent panels include Mary and Joseph's *Journey to Bethlehem*, their *Enrolment for Taxation*, the *Nativity of Christ* and, finally, Herod ordering the *Massacre of the Innocents*.

The Enrolment for Taxation

Christ's Ministry

While many of the mosaics in this series are badly damaged, some beautiful panels remain. The cycle occupies the vaults of the seven bays of the outer narthex and some of the south bay of the inner narthex. The most striking mosaic is the portrayal of Christ's tempta-tion in the wilderness, in the second bay of the outer narthex.

Theodore Metochites presents St Saviour in Chora to Christ

Other Mosaics

There are three panels in the nave of the church, one of which, above the main door from the inner narthex, illustrates the *Dormition of the Virgin*. This mosaic, protected by a marble frame, is the best preserved in the church. The Virgin is depicted laid out on a bier, watched over by the Apostles, with Christ seated behind. Other devotional panels in the two narthexes include one, on the east wall of the south bay of the inner narthex, of the *Deësis*, depicting Christ with the Virgin Mary and unusually, without St John. Another, in the inner narthex over the door into the nave, is of Theodore Metochites himself, shown wearing a large turban, and humbly presenting the restored church as an offering to Christ.

The Frescoes

The frescoes in the parecclesion are thought to have been painted just after the mosaics were completed, probably in around 1320. The most engaging of the frescoes –

VISITORS' CHECKLIST

Practical Information
Kariye Camii Sok, Edirnekapı.
Map 1 B1. **Tel** (0212) 631 92 41.
Open 9am–4pm Thu–Tue.

Transport
28, 86 or 90, then
5 minutes' walk

which reflect the purpose of the parecclesion as a place of burial – is the *Anastasis*, in the semidome above the apse. In it, the central figure of Christ, the vanquisher of death, is shown dragging Adam and Eve out of their tombs. Under Christ's feet are the gates of hell, while Satan lies before him. The fresco in the vault overhead depicts *The Last Judgment*, with the souls of the saved on the right and those of the damned to the left.

Figure of Christ from the *Anastasis* fresco in the parecclesion

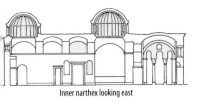

Inner narthex looking east

Parecclesion and outer narthex looking south

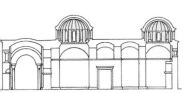

Inner narthex looking west

Parecclesion and outer narthex looking north

Eyüp

As the burial place of Eyüp Ensari, the standard bearer of the Prophet Mohammed, the village of Eyüp is a place of pilgrimage for Muslims from all over the world. Its sacrosanct status has kept it a peaceful place of contemplation, far removed from the squalid effects of industrialization elsewhere on the Golden Horn *(see p91)*. The wealthy elite established mosques and street fountains in the village but, above all, they chose Eyüp as a place of burial. Their grand mausoleums line the streets surrounding Eyüp Sultan Mosque, while the cypress groves in the hills above the village are filled with the gravestones of ordinary people.

Gateway to the Baroque Complex of Valide Sultan Mihrişah

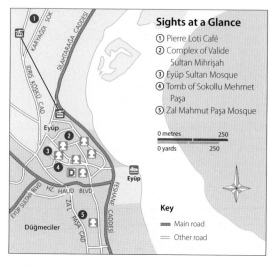

Sights at a Glance

① Pierre Loti Café
② Complex of Valide Sultan Mihrişah
③ Eyüp Sultan Mosque
④ Tomb of Sokollu Mehmet Paşa
⑤ Zal Mahmut Paşa Mosque

0 metres 250
0 yards 250

Key

▬▬ Main road
═══ Other road

❷ Complex of Valide Sultan Mihrişah

Mihrişah Valide Sultan Külliyesi

Seyit Reşat Cad. 🚌 39, 55T, 99A. **Open** 9am–6pm Tue–Sun.

Most of the northern side of the street leading from Eyüp Mosque's northern gate is occupied by the largest Baroque *külliye (see p40)* in Istanbul, although unusually it is not centred on a mosque. Built for Mihrişah, mother of Selim III *(see p35)*, the *külliye* was completed in 1791.

The complex includes the ornate marble tomb of Mihrişah and a soup kitchen, which is still in use today. There is also a beautiful grilled fountain *(sebil)*, from which an attendant once served water and refreshing drinks of sweet sherbet to passers-by.

❶ Pierre Loti Café

Piyer Loti Kahvehanesi

Gümüşsuyu Karyağdı Sok 5, Eyüp. **Tel** (0212) 581 26 96.
🚌 39, 55T, 99A. **Open** 8:30am–midnight daily.

This famous café stands at the top of the hill in Eyüp Cemetery, about 20 minutes' walk or short funicular ride up Karyağdı Sokağı from Eyüp Mosque, from where it commands sweeping views down over the Golden Horn. It is named after the French novelist and Turkophile Pierre Loti, who frequented a café in Eyüp – claimed to be this one – during his stay here in 1876. Loti, a French naval officer, fell in love with a married Turkish woman and wrote an autobiographical novel,

Aziyade, about their affair. The café is prettily decked out with 19th-century furniture and the waiters wear period clothing.

The path up to the café passes by a picturesque array of tombstones, most of which date from the Ottoman era. Just before the café on the right, a few tall, uninscribed tombstones mark the graves of executioners.

Period interior of the Pierre Loti Café *(see p208)*

❸ Eyüp Sultan Mosque

Eyüp Sultan Camii

Cami-i Kebir Sok. **Tel** (0212) 564 73 68.
🚌 39, 55T, 99A. **Open** daily.

Mehmet the Conqueror built the original mosque on this site in 1458, five years after his conquest of Istanbul *(see p28)*, in honour of Eyüp Ensari. That building fell into ruins, probably as a result of an earthquake, and the present mosque was completed in 1800, by Selim III *(see p35)*.

The mosque's delightful inner courtyard is a garden in which two huge plane trees grow on a platform. This platform was the setting for the Girding of the Sword of Osman, part of a sultan's inauguration from the days of Mehmet the Conqueror.

The mosque itself is predominantly covered in gleaming white marble.

Opposite the mosque is the tomb of Eyüp Ensari himself, believed to have been killed during the first Arab siege of Constantinople in the 7th century *(see p23).* The tomb dates from the same period as the mosque and most of its decoration is in the Ottoman Baroque style. Both the outer wall of the tomb facing the mosque, and most of its interior, have an impressive covering of tiles, some of them from İznik *(see p162).*

Zal Mahmut Paşa Mosque, as viewed from its tomb garden

Visitors at the tomb of Eyüp Ensari, Mohammed's standard bearer

❹ Tomb of Sokollu Mehmet Paşa
Sokollu Mehmet Paşa Türbesi

Cami-i Kebir Sok. 🚌 39, 55T, 99A. **Open** 9:30am–4:30pm Tue–Sun.

Grand vizier *(see p31)* Sokollu Mehmet Paşa commissioned his tomb around 1574, five years before he was assassinated by a madman in Topkapı Palace *(see pp56–61).* Of Balkan royal blood, he started his career as falconer royal and steadily climbed the social order until he became grand vizier to Süleyman the Magnificent *(see p28)* in 1565. He held this position through the reign of Selim II *(see p29)* and into that of Murat III. The architect Sinan *(see p93)* built this elegantly proportioned

octagonal tomb. It is notable for its stained glass, some of which is original.

A roofed colonnade connects the tomb to what was formerly a Koranic school.

❺ Zal Mahmut Paşa Mosque
Zal Mahmut Paşa Camii

Zal Paşa Cad. 🚌 39, 55T, 99A. **Open** daily.

Heading south from the centre of Eyüp, it is a short walk to Zal Mahmut Paşa Mosque. The complex was built by Sinan for the man who assassinated Mustafa, the first-born heir of Süleyman the Magnificent.

Probably erected some time in the 1560s, the mosque is notable for the lovely floral tiles around its mihrab, and for its carved marble *minbar* and *müezzin mahfili (see p40).* Proceeding down some stone steps to the north of the mosque you will come to a garden. In it stands the large tomb of Zal Mahmut Paşa and his wife, said to have both died on the same day.

On the same street, Cezri Kasım Paşa Mosque (1515) is a small mosque with a pretty portal and a tiled mihrab. Most of the tiles were produced at the Palace of the Porphyrogenitus *(see p119)* in the first half of the 18th century.

Ottoman Gravestones

The Ottoman graveyard was a garden of the dead, where the living happily strolled without morbid inhibitions. The gravestones within it were often lavishly symbolic: from their decoration you can tell the sex, occupation, rank and even the number of children of the deceased. As the turban was banned in 1829 *(see p32),* only the fez appears on men's gravestones erected after that date.

Women's *graves have a flower for each child.*

A turban's *size reflected a gentleman's status.*

This hat *indicates the grave of a member of a Sufi order.*

A fez *was worn by a paşa, or public servant (see p30).*

Beyond Taksim

The area to the north of Taksim Square *(see p109)* became fashionable in the 19th century, when sultans built palaces along the Bosphorus and in the wooded hills above it. The extravagant Dolmabahçe Palace, built by Abdül Mecit I *(see p32)*, started the trend. High-ranking court officials soon followed, and the area achieved a glamour that it retains to this day. Two other sights worth seeing are on the northern shore of the Golden Horn. Aynalı Kavak Palace is the last surviving trace of a grand palace built by Ahmet III *(see p29)*, while the Rahmi Koç Museum, in nearby Hasköy, is an interesting industrial museum. Hasköy became a royal park in the 15th century and later supported fruit orchards, before dockyards brought industrialization to the area in the 19th century.

Ortaköy's fashionable waterfront square and ferry landing

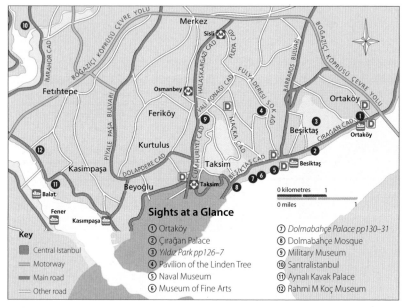

Sights at a Glance

① Ortaköy
② Çırağan Palace
③ Yıldız Park *pp126–7*
④ Pavilion of the Linden Tree
⑤ Naval Museum
⑥ Museum of Fine Arts
⑦ *Dolmabahçe Palace pp130–31*
⑧ Dolmabahçe Mosque
⑨ Military Museum
⑩ Santralistanbul
⑪ Aynalı Kavak Palace
⑫ Rahmi M Koç Museum

Key

■ Central Istanbul
═ Motorway
━ Main road
─ Other road

Cobbled Ortaköy side street lined with cafés and shops

❶ Ortaköy

Map 9 F3. 🚌 25E, 40.

Crouched at the foot of Bosphorus Bridge *(see p140)*, the suburb of Ortaköy has retained a village feel. Life centres on İskele Meydanı, the quayside square, which used to be busy with fishermen unloading the day's catch. Nowadays, though, Ortaköy is better known for its lively Sunday market *(see p215)*, which crowds out the square and surrounding streets, and its shops selling the wares of local artisans. It is also the location for a thriving bar and café scene, which in the summer especially is the hub of Istanbul's nightlife *(see p221)*.

Mecidiye Mosque (or Ortaköy Camii), the suburb's most impressive landmark, is on the waterfront. Built in 1855 by Nikoğos Balyan, who was responsible for Dolmabahçe Palace *(see pp130–31)*, it has grace and originality, with window-filled tympanum arches and corner turrets.

Ortaköy also has a Greek Orthodox church, Haghios Phocas, and a synagogue, Etz Ahayim. The origins of both date from the Byzantine era.

❷ Çırağan Palace

Çırağan Sarayı

Dolmabahçe Cad, Beşiktaş. **Map** 9 D3.
Tel (0212) 236 90 00. 🚌 25E, 40.
w ciragan-palace.com

Sultan Abdül Mecit I started work on Çırağan Palace in 1864, but it was not completed until 1871, during the reign of Abdül Aziz (see p32). It replaced an earlier wooden palace where torch-lit processions were held during the Tulip Period (see p29).

The palace was designed by Nikogos Balyan. At the sultan's request he added Arabic touches from sketches of Moorish buildings such as the Alhambra at Granada in Spain. Externally this is reflected in the honeycomb capitals over its windows. The sultan entered Çırağan Palace directly from the Bosphorus, through the ornate ceremonial gates along its shoreline.

Çırağan Palace had a sad, short history as an imperial residence. Abdül Aziz died here in 1876, supposedly committing suicide – although his friends believed he had been murdered. His successor, Murat V (see p35), was imprisoned in the palace for a year after a brief reign of only three months. He died in the Malta Pavilion (see p127) 27 years later, still a prisoner. The palace was eventually destroyed by fire in 1910. It remained a burnt out shell for many years,

Baroque-style staircase at the Pavilion of the Linden Tree

before being restored in 1990 as the Çırağan Palace Kempinski (see p188).

❸ Yıldız Park

See pp126–7.

❹ Pavilion of the Linden Tree

Ihlamur Kasrı

Dolmabahçe Cad, Beşiktaş. **Map** 8 B2.
Tel (0212) 236 90 00. 🚌 26 (from Eminönü). **Open** 9am–5pm Tue–Wed & Fri–Sun. 🚫 📷.

This one-time residence of sultans, dating from the early 19th century, stands in beautiful, leafy gardens which are planted with magnolias and camellias, and decorated with ornamental fountains. Today, the gardens are a somewhat incongruous reminder of the city's Ottoman past, situated in the midst of the modern suburbs of Teşvikiye and Ihlamur.

As the pavilion's name suggests, the area was once a grove of lime (linden) trees, and the gardens are all that remain of what was previously a vast wooded park. This park was a favourite retreat and hunting ground of the Ottoman sultans. In the early 19th century, Abdül

Mecit I (see p32) often came here and stayed in the original pavilion on this site. That building was so unassuming that the French poet Alphonse de Lamartine (1790–1869) expressed great surprise that a sultan should have entertained him in a humble cottage, with a gardener working in plain view through the windows.

In 1857 Abdül Mecit chose Nikogos Balyan, who had by then finished Dolmabahçe Palace with his father, to design another residence here. Two separate pavilions were built, the grander of which is the Ceremonial Pavilion, or Mabeyn Köşkü, used by the sultan and his guests. The Entourage Pavilion, or Maiyet Köşkü, a short distance away, was reserved for the sultan's retinue, including the women of the harem. Both buildings are open to visitors – the Entourage Pavilion is currently a café and bookshop.

The pavilions are constructed mainly of sandstone and marble. Their façades are in the Baroque style, with double stairways, many decorative embellishments and hardly a single straight line to be seen. The ornate interiors of the buildings reflect 19th-century Ottoman taste, incorporating a mixture of European styles. With their mirrors, lavish furnishings and gilded details, they are similar to but less ostentatious than those of Dolmabahçe Palace.

Çırağan Palace, notable for the Moorish-style embellishments above its windows

⑤ Yıldız Park

Yıldız Parkı

Yıldız Park was originally laid out as the garden of the first Çırağan Palace *(see p125)*. It later formed the grounds of Yıldız Palace, an assortment of buildings from different eras now enclosed behind a wall and entered separately from Ihlamur-Yıldız Caddesi. Further pavilions dot Yıldız Park, which, with its many ancient trees and exotic shrubs, is a favourite spot for family picnics. The whole park is situated on a steep hill and, as it is a fairly long climb, you may prefer to take a taxi up to the Şale Pavilion and walk back down past the other sights.

Bridge over the lake in the grounds of Yıldız Palace

Yıldız Palace

The palace is a collection of pavilions and villas built in the 19th and 20th centuries. Many of them are the work of the eccentric Sultan Abdül Hamit II (1876–1909, *see p35*), who made it his principal residence as he feared a seaborne attack on Dolmabahçe Palace *(see pp130–31)*.

The main building in the entrance courtyard is the **State Apartments** (Büyük Mabeyn), dating from the reign of Sultan Selim III (1789–1807, *see p35*), but not presently open to the public. Around the corner, the **City Museum** (Şehir Müzesi) has a display of Yıldız porcelain. The Italianate building opposite it is the former armoury, or Silahhane. Next door to the City Museum is the **Yıldız Palace Museum**, housed in what was once the Marangozhane, Abdül Hamit's carpentry workshop. This has a changing collection of art and objects from the palace.

A monumental arch leads from the first courtyard to the harem section of the palace. On the left beside the arch is a pretty greenhouse, the

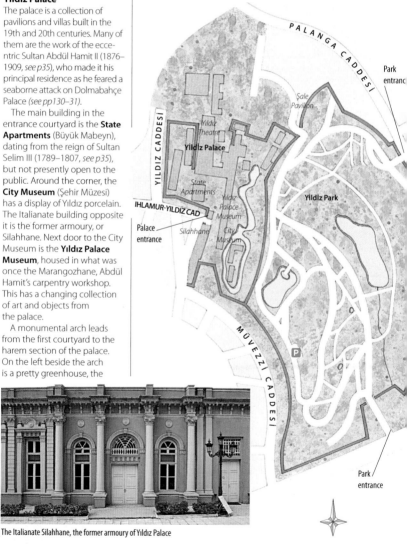

The Italianate Silahhane, the former armoury of Yıldız Palace

Limonluk Serası (Lemon House).

Further on, **Yıldız Palace Theatre** is now a museum. It was completed in 1889 by Abdül Hamit, who encouraged all forms of Western art. The decor of the theatre's restored interior is mainly blue and gold. The stars on the domed ceiling are a reference to the name of the palace: *yıldız* means "star" in Turkish.

Abdül Hamit sat alone in a box over the entrance. Since no one was allowed to sit with his back to the sultan, the stalls were not used. Backstage, the former dressing rooms are given over to displays on the theatre, including costumes and playbills.

The lake in the palace grounds is shaped like Abdül Hamit's *tuğra (see p97)*. A menagerie was kept on the islands in the lake where 30 keepers tended tigers, lions, giraffes and zebras.

Salon in the lavish Şale Pavilion

Park entrance

PALANGA CADDESİ

AĞAN CADDESİ

0 metres 250
0 yards 250

Key

🔲 Buildings of palace

— Park wall/Palace wall

VISITORS' CHECKLIST

Practical Information
Çırağan Cad, Beşiktaş. **Map** 9 D2.
Yıldız Palace: **Tel** (0212) 258 30 80.
Open 9:30am–4pm Wed–Sun.
🏛 Şale Pavilion: **Tel** (0212) 259
45 70. **Open** 9:30am–4:30pm.
Closed Mon & Thu. 🏛 Malta &
Çadır Pavilions: **Tel** (0212) 258 94
53. **Open** 9am–9pm daily. (Malta
Pavilion until 10:30pm). Imperial
Porcelain Factory: **Tel** (0212) 260
23 70. **Open** 9am–noon,
1–4:30pm Mon–Fri.

Transport
🚌 25E, 40, 56.

Şale Pavilion

The single most impressive building in the park, the Şale Pavilion (Şale Köşkü) was among those erected by Abdül Hamit II. Although its façade appears as a whole, it was in fact built in three stages.

The first, left-hand section of the buildling was designed to resemble a Swiss chalet. It probably dates from the 1870s. Winston Churchill, Charles de Gaulle and Nicolae Ceauşescu have all stayed in its rooms.

The second section was added in 1889, to accommodate Kaiser Wilhelm II on the first ever state visit of a foreign monarch to the Ottoman capital. The 14-room suite includes a dining room known as the Mother-of-Pearl Salon (Sedefli Salon) after the delicate inlay that covers almost all of its surfaces.

The third section was also built for a visit by Kaiser Wilhelm II, this time in 1898. Its reception chamber is the grandest room in the whole pavilion. The vast silk Hereke carpet *(see p218)* covering its floor was painstakingly hand-knotted by 60 weavers.

Malta and Çadır Pavilions

These two lovely pavilions were built in the reign of Abdül Aziz (1861–76, *see p32*). Both formerly served as prisons but are now open as cafés. Malta Pavilion, also a restaurant, has a superb view and on Sunday is a haunt for locals wanting to relax and read the newspapers.

Mithat Paşa, reformist and architect of the constitution, was among those imprisoned in Çadır Pavilion, for instigating the murder of Abdül Aziz. Meanwhile, Murat V and his mother were locked away in Malta Pavilion for 27 years after a brief incarceration in Çırağan Palace *(see p125)*.

Façade of Çadır Pavilion, which has now been refurbished as a café

Imperial Porcelain Factory

In 1895 this factory opened to feed the demand of the upper classes for European-style ceramics to decorate their homes. The unusual building was designed to look like a stylized European medieval castle, complete with turrets and portcullis windows.

The original sugar bowls, vases and plates produced here depict idealized scenes of the Bosphorus and other local beauty spots; they can be seen in museums and palaces all over Istanbul. The factory is normally not open to visitors but the mass-produced china of today is on sale in its shop.

❺ Naval Museum
Deniz Müzesi

Hayrettin Paşa İskelesi Sok, Beşiktaş.
Map 8 B4. **Tel** (0212) 261 00 40.
🚌 25E, 28, 40, 56. **Open** 9am–noon,
1:30–5:30pm Wed–Sun. 🐾 🖼

This museum is located next
to the ferry landing in Beşiktaş.
One building, the Caïques
Gallery, is devoted to huge
imperial rowing boats, or
caïques (some of them manned
by replica oarsmen), dating
from the 17th century. The
largest of these, at 40 m (130 ft),
was used by Mehmet IV and
powered by 144 oarsmen. The
rowing boats used by Atatürk
(see p32) look tiny in comparison:
it is remarkable
to think that he
entertained
heads of
state in
them. The
exhibits in the
neighbouring
main museum
include oil
paintings of
various military
scenes, ship
figureheads, naval uniforms,
and objects from, and
paintings of, Atatürk's yacht,
the Savarona.

**Rowing boat
used by Atatürk**

❻ Museum of Fine Arts
Resim ve Heykel Müzesi

Hayrettin Paşa İskelesi Sok, Beşiktaş.
Map 8 B4. **Tel** (0212) 261 42 98.
🚌 25E, 28, 40, 56. **Open** noon–4pm
Wed–Sun.

This building adjacent to
Dolmabahçe Palace (see pp130–
31) houses a fine collection of
19th- and 20th-century paintings
and sculpture. In the 1800s, the
westernization of the Ottoman
Empire (see pp32–3) led
artists such as Osman Hamdi
Bey (1842–1910, see p64) to
experiment with Western-style
painting. While their styles rely
heavily on European art forms,
the subject matter of their work
gives a glimpse into the oriental
history of the city. Look out
for Woman with Mimosas,
Portrait of a Young Girl and

**Woman with Mimosas by Osman Hamdi
Bey, Museum of Fine Arts**

Man with a Yellow Robe, all
by Osman Hamdi Bey, Sultan
Ahmet Mosque by Ahmet Ziya
Akbulut (1869–1938), and
Âşık, a statue of a poet by İsa
Behzat (1867–1944).

❼ Dolmabahçe Palace
See pp130–31.

❽ Dolmabahçe Mosque
Dolmabahçe Camii

Meclis-i Mebusan Cad, Kabataş.
Map 8 A5. 🚋 Kabataş. 🚌 25E, 40.
Open daily.

Completed at the same time
as Dolmabahçe Palace, in 1853,
the mosque standing beside it
was also built by the wealthy
Balyan family. Its slim minarets
were constructed in the form of
Corinthian columns, while great
arching windows lighten the

interior. Inside, the decoration
includes fake marbling
and trompe l'oeil.

❾ Military Museum
Harbiye Askeri Müzesi

Vali Konağı Cad, Harbiye. **Map** 7 F1.
Tel (0212) 233 27 20. 🚌 46H.
🚇 Osmanbey. **Open** 9am–5pm
Wed–Sun. Mehter Band performances:
3–4pm Wed–Sun. 🐾 🖼

This impressive museum traces
the history of Turkey's conflicts
from the conquest of Constantinople in 1453 (see p28) through
to modern warfare. The building
used to be the military academy
where Atatürk studied from 1899
to 1905. His classroom has been
preserved as it was then.

The museum is also the
main venue for performances
by the Mehter Band, which was
first formed in the 14th-century
during the reign of Osman I (see
p27). From then until the 19th
century, the band's members
were Janissaries, who would
accompany the sultan into
battle and perform songs about
Ottoman hero-ancestors and
battle victories.

Some of the most striking
weapons on display on the
ground floor are the curved
daggers (cembiyes) carried by
foot soldiers in the 15th century.
These are decorated with plant,
flower and geometric motifs
in relief and silver filigree. Other
exhibits include 17th-century
copper head armour for horses
and Ottoman shields made
from cane and willow covered
in silk thread.

Dolmabahçe Mosque, a landmark on the Bosphorus shoreline

Cembiyes – Ottoman curved daggers – on display in the Military Museum

A moving portrayal of trench warfare, commissioned in 1995, is included in the section concerned with the ANZAC landings of 1915 at Chunuk Bair on the Gallipoli peninsula *(see p32)*.

Upstairs, the most spectacular of all the exhibits are the tents used by sultans on their campaigns. They are made of silk and wool with embroidered decoration.

⓾ Santralistanbul

Kazim Karabekir Cad 1, Eyüp. **Tel** (0212) 311 78 78. 🚌 47; also free shuttle every 30 minutes from Kabataş ferry port. **Open** 10am–6pm (till 8pm only on weekends).

Inaugurated in July 2007 and housed in the first power station built in the city during the Ottoman Period, santralistanbul is an innovative art park that includes, among other things, a centre for contemporary arts, a museum of energy, and living quarters for guest artists, architects and designers.

⓫ Aynalı Kavak Palace
Aynalı Kavak Kasrı

Kasımpaşa Cad, Hasköy. **Map** 6 A3. **Tel** (0212) 250 40 94. 🚌 47, 54. **Open** 9:30am–4pm. **Closed** Mon & Thu. 🐾

Aynali Kavak Palace is the last vestige of a large Ottoman palace complex on the once lovely Golden Horn *(see p91)*. Originally it stood in extensive gardens covering an area of 7,000 sq m (75,300 sq ft). Inscriptions dated 1791 can be found all over the palace, but it is thought to have been built earlier by Ahmet III during the Tulip Period *(see p29)*, because of traces around the building of an older style of architecture.

The palace is built on a hill and as a result has two storeys on the southwest side and a single storey to the northeast. It retains some beautiful Ottoman features. These include the upper windows on the southwest façade, which are decorated with stained glass set in curvilinear stucco tracery. Particularly

striking is the composition room, which Sultan Selim III (1789–1807) is thought to have used for writing music.

The audience chamber is adorned with an inscription in gold on blue which describes the activities of Selim III while he stayed at the palace.

There is also a superb exhibition of archaic Turkish musical instruments permanently on show, in honour of Selim III, who contributed a great deal to Turkish classical music.

In summer, popular concerts of classical Turkish music are held here.

Audience chamber of Aynalı Kavak Palace on the Golden Horn

⓬ Rahmi M Koç Museum
Rahmi M Koç Müzesi

Hasköy Cad 27, Eyüp. **Tel** (0212) 369 66 00. 🚌 47. **Open** 10am–5pm Tue–Fri, 10am–7pm Sat, Sun. 🐾

Situated in Hasköy, this old 19th-century factory, which once produced anchors and chains, now houses an eclectic collection named after its industrialist founder, Rahmi M Koç. The building itself, with its four small domes, vaulted passageways and original wooden fittings is one of the museum's highlights.

The theme of the industrial age loosely connects exhibitions on aviation, transport, steam engines and scientific instruments. Exhibits range from mechanical toys and scale models of machinery to an entire recreated ship's bridge. Two fine restaurants are located on the premises.

Janissaries

The Janissary (New Army) corps was formed in the 14th century to serve as the sultan's elite fighting force. Its ranks were filled by *devşirme,* the levy of Christian youths brought to Istanbul to serve the sultan. A highly professional and strong army, it was instrumental in the early expansion of the Ottoman Empire and, as well as a fighting force, it acted as the sultan's personal guard. However, discipline eventually began to weaken, and by 1800 the Janissaries had become a destabilizing element in society. They mutinied and overthrew many sultans until their final demise under Mahmut II in 1826 *(see p32)*.

Janissaries depicted in a 16th-century miniature

❼ Dolmabahçe Palace
Dolmabahçe Sarayı

Sultan Abdül Mecit *(see p35)* built Dolmabahçe Palace in 1856. As its designers he employed Karabet Balyan and his son Nikogos, members of the great family of Armenian architects who lined the Bosphorus *(see pp138–51)* with many of their creations in the 19th century. The extravagant opulence of the Dolmabahçe belies the fact that it was built when the Ottoman Empire was in decline. The sultan financed his great palace with loans from foreign banks. The palace can only be visited on a guided tour, of which two are on offer. The best tour takes you through the Selamlık (or Mabeyn-i Hümayun), the part of the palace that was reserved for men and which contains the state rooms and the enormous Ceremonial Hall. The other tour goes through the Harem, the living quarters of the sultan and his entourage. If you only want to go on one tour, visit the Selamlık.

★ Crystal Staircase
The apparent fragility of this glass staircase stunned observers when it was built. In the shape of a double horseshoe, it is made from Baccarat crystal and brass, and has a polished mahogany rail.

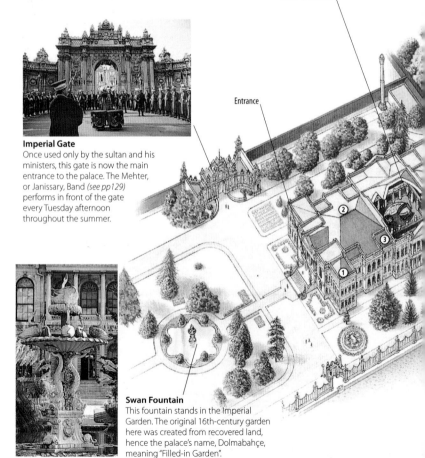

Imperial Gate
Once used only by the sultan and his ministers, this gate is now the main entrance to the palace. The Mehter, or Janissary, Band *(see pp129)* performs in front of the gate every Tuesday afternoon throughout the summer.

Entrance

Swan Fountain
This fountain stands in the Imperial Garden. The original 16th-century garden here was created from recovered land, hence the palace's name, Dolmabahçe, meaning "Filled-in Garden".

★ **Ceremonial Hall**
This magnificent domed hall was designed to hold 2,500 people. Its chandelier, reputedly the heaviest in the world, was bought in England.

VISITORS' CHECKLIST

Practical Information
Dolmabahçe Cad, Beşiktaş.
Map 8 B4. **Tel** (0212) 236 90 00.
Open 9am–4pm (last adm) Tue, Wed & Fri–Sun (Oct–Feb: last adm 3pm). **Closed** the first day of religious festivals.

Transport
🚌 25E, 40.

Blue Salon
On religious feast days the sultan's mother would receive his wives and favourites in the Harem's principal room.

KEY

① **The Red Room** was used by the sultan to receive ambassadors.

② **The Süfera Salon**, where ambassadors waited for an audience with the sultan, is one of the most luxurious rooms in the palace.

③ **Selamlık**

④ **The Zülveçheyn, or Panorama Room**

⑤ **Main shore gate**

⑥ **Reception room of the sultan's mother**

⑦ **Sultan Abdül Aziz's bedroom** had to accommodate a huge bed built especially for the 150-kg (23-stone) amateur wrestler.

⑧ **Atatürk's Bedroom** is part of the palace tour. Atatürk (*see pp32–3*) died in this room at 9:05am on 10 November 1938. All the clocks in the palace, such as this one near the crystal staircase, are stopped at this time.

⑨ **The Rose-coloured salon** was the assembly room of the Harem.

⑩ **Harem**

★ **Main Bathroom**
The walls of this bathroom are revetted in finest Egyptian alabaster, while the taps are solid silver. The brass-framed bathroom windows afford stunning views across the Bosphorus.

The Asian Side

The Asian side of Istanbul comprises the two major suburbs of Üsküdar and Kadıköy, which date from the 7th century BC (see p21). Üsküdar (once known as Scutari after the 12th-century Scutarion Palace which was located opposite Leander's Tower) was the starting point of Byzantine trade routes through Asia. It retained its importance in the Ottoman period and today is renowned for its many classical mosques.

A number of residential districts radiate from Üsküdar and Kadıköy. Moda is a pleasant leafy suburb famous for its ice cream, while there is a lighthouse and an attractive park at Fenerbahçe. From there it is a short walk up to bustling Bağdat Caddesi, one of Istanbul's best-known shopping streets.

The distinctive Leander's Tower, on its own small island

❷ Şemsi Paşa Mosque

Şemsi Paşa Camii

Sahil Yolu, Üsküdar. **Map** 10 A2. 🚊 Üsküdar. 🚢 Üsküdar. **Open** daily.

This is one of the smallest mosques to be commissioned by a grand vizier (see p31). Its miniature dimensions combined with its picturesque waterfront location make it one of the most attractive mosques in the city.

Şemsi Ahmet Paşa succeeded Sokollu Mehmet Paşa (see p84) as grand vizier, and may have been involved in his murder. Sinan (see p93) built this mosque for him in 1580.

The garden, which overlooks the Bosphorus, is surrounded on two sides by the medrese (see p40), with the mosque on the third side and the sea wall on the fourth. The mosque itself is unusual in that the tomb of Şemsi Ahmet is joined to the main building, divided from the interior by a grille.

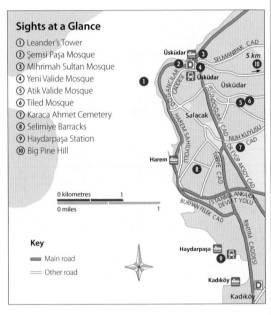

Sights at a Glance

① Leander's Tower
② Şemsi Paşa Mosque
③ Mihrimah Sultan Mosque
④ Yeni Valide Mosque
⑤ Atik Valide Mosque
⑥ Tiled Mosque
⑦ Karaca Ahmet Cemetery
⑧ Selimiye Barracks
⑨ Haydarpaşa Station
⑩ Big Pine Hill

Key

━━ Main road
═══ Other road

❶ Leander's Tower

Kız Kulesi

Üsküdar. **Map** 10 A3. **Tel** (0216) 342 47 47. 🚢 Üsküdar.
Ⓦ **kizkulesi.com.tr**

Located offshore from Üsküdar, the tiny, white Leander's Tower is a well-known Bosphorus landmark. The islet on which this 18th-century tower stands was the site of a 12th-century Byzantine fortress built by Manuel I Comnenus.

The tower has served as a quarantine centre during a cholera outbreak, a lighthouse, a customs control point and a maritime toll gate. It is now a restaurant and nightclub.

The tower is known in Turkish as the "Maiden's Tower" after a legendary princess, said to have been confined here after a prophet foretold that she would die from a snakebite. The snake duly appeared from a basket of figs and struck the fatal blow. The English name of the tower derives from the Greek myth of Leander, who swam the Hellespont (the modern-day Dardanelles, see p172) to see his lover Hero.

Şemsi Paşa Mosque, built by Sinan for Grand Vizier Şemsi Ahmet Paşa

❸ Mihrimah Sultan Mosque

Mihrimah Sultan Camii

Hakimiyeti Milliye Cad, Üsküdar.
Map 10 B2. 🚇 Üsküdar. 🚌 Üsküdar.
Open daily.

One of Üsküdar's most prominent landmarks, the Mihrimah Sultan Mosque (also known as İskele Mosque), is named after the daughter of Süleyman, the Magnificent and wife of Grand Vizier Rüstem Paşa *(see p90)*. A massive structure on a raised platform, it was built by Sinan between 1547 and 1548.

Without space to build a courtyard, Sinan constructed a large protruding roof which extends to cover the *şadırvan* (ablutions fountain) in front of the mosque. The porch and interior are rather gloomy as a result. This raised portico is an excellent place from which to look down on the main square below, in which stands the Baroque Fountain of Ahmet III, built in 1726.

Fountain set into the platform below the Mihrimah Sultan Mosque

❹ Yeni Valide Mosque

Yeni Valide Camii

Hakimiyeti Milliye Cad, Üsküdar.
Map 10 B2. 🚇 Üsküdar. 🚌 Üsküdar.
Open daily.

Across the main square from Mihrimah Sultan Mosque, the Yeni Valide Mosque, or New Mosque of the Sultan's Mother, was built by Ahmet III between

The *mektep* (Koranic school) over the gate of Yeni Valide Mosque

1708 and 1710 to honour his mother, Gülnuş Emetullah. The complex is entered through a large gateway, with the *mektep* (Koranic school) built above it. This leads into a spacious courtyard. The buildings in the complex date from an important turning point in Ottoman architecture. The mosque is in the classical style, yet there are Baroque embellishments on the tomb of the Valide Sultan, the neighbouring *sebil* (kiosk from which drinks were served) and the *şadırvan*.

❺ Atik Valide Mosque

Atik Valide Camii

Çinili Camii Sok, Üsküdar. **Map** 10 C3.
🚌 12C (from Üsküdar). **Open** prayer times only.

The Atik Valide Mosque, set on the hill above Üsküdar, was among Istanbul's most extensive mosque complexes. Translated as the Old Mosque of the Sultan's Mother, the mosque was built for Nur Banu, the Venetian-born wife of Selim II ("the Sot") and the mother of Murat III. She was the first of the sultans' mothers to rule the Ottoman Empire from the harem *(see p29)*.

Dome in the entrance to Atik Valide Mosque

Sinan completed the mosque, which was his last major work, in 1583. It has a wide shallow dome which rests on five semidomes, with a flat arch over the entrance portal.

The interior is surrounded on three sides by galleries, the undersides of which retain the rich black, red and gold stencilling typical of the period. The *mihrab* apse is almost completely covered with panels of fine İznik tiles *(see p163)*, while the mihrab itself and the *minbar* are both made of beautifully carved marble. Side aisles were added to the north and south in the 17th century, while the grilles and architectural *trompe l'oeil* paintings on the royal loge in the western gallery date from the 18th century.

Outside, a door in the north wall of the courtyard leads down a flight of stairs to the *medrese*, where the *dershane* (classroom) projects out over the street below, supported by an arch. Of the other buildings in the complex, the *şifahane* (hospital) is the only one which has been restored and is open to the public. Located just to the east of the mosque, it consists of 40 cells around a courtyard and was in use well into the 20th century.

Women attending an Islamic class in the Tiled Mosque

❻ Tiled Mosque
Çinili Camii

Çinili Camii Sok, Üsküdar. **Map** 10 C3. 🚌 Üsküdar, then 20 mins walk. **Open** prayer times only.

This pretty little mosque is best known for the fine tiles from which it takes its name. It dates from 1640 and is noticeably smaller than other royal foundations of the 17th century. This is partly because by the middle of the century much of Istanbul's prime land had already been built on, and the size of the plot did not allow for a larger building. There was also a trend away from endowing yet more enormous mosque complexes in the city.

The mosque was founded by Mahpeyker Kösem Sultan. As the wife of Sultan Ahmet I (see p35), and mother of sultans Murat IV and İbrahim the Mad, she wielded great influence. Indeed, she was one of the last of the powerful harem women (see p29).

In the courtyard is a massive, roofed ablutions fountain. The adjacent medrese (see p40), however, is tiny. The façade and interior of the mosque are covered with İznik tiles (see p163) in turquoise, white, grey and a range of blues. There are none of the red and green pigments associated with the heyday of İznik tile production, but the designs are still exquisite. Even the conical cap of the marble minbar is tiled, and the carving on the minbar itself is picked out in green, red and gold paint.

The mosque's Turkish bath is on Çinili Hamam Sokağı. It has been renovated and is used by local residents.

❼ Karacaahmet Cemetery
Karacaahmet Mezarlığı

Nuh Kuyusu Cad, Selimiye. **Map** 10 C4. 🚌 12. **Open** daily. Tomb: **Open** daily.

Sprawling over a large area, this cemetery is a pleasant place in which to stroll among old cypress trees and look at ancient tombstones. The earliest dated stone is from 1521, although the cemetery itself, one of the largest in Turkey, is thought to date from 1338.

The carvings on each tombstone tell a story (see p123). A man's tomb is indicated by a fez or a turban. The style of the turban denotes the status of the deceased. Women's stones are adorned with carved flowers, hats and shawls.

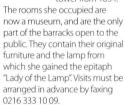
Crimean War memorial in the British War Cemetery

Standing on the corner of Gündoğumu Caddesi and Nuh Kuyusu Caddesi is the tomb of Karaca Ahmet himself. This warrior died fighting in the Turkish conquest of the Byzantine towns of Chrysopolis and Chalcedon (Üsküdar and Kadıköy) in the mid-14th century. The tomb and monument to his favourite horse date from the 19th century.

❽ Selimiye Barracks
Selimiye Kışlası

Çeşme-i Kebir Cad, Selimiye. **Map** 10 B5. **Tel** (0216) 343 73 10. 🚉 Harem. 🚌 12. **Open** 9am–5pm Sat.

The Selimiye Barracks were originally built by Selim III in 1799 to house his New Army, with which he hoped to replace the Janissaries (see p129). He failed in his attempt, and was deposed and killed in a Janissary insurrection in 1807–8 (see p32). The barracks burnt down shortly afterwards. The present building, which dominates the skyline of the Asian shore, was started by Mahmut II in 1828, after he had finally disbanded the Janissary corps. Abdül Mecit I added three more wings between 1842 and 1853. The barracks were used as a military hospital during the Crimean War (1853–6). They became famously associated with Florence Nightingale, who lived and worked in the northeast tower from 1854. The rooms she occupied are now a museum, and are the only part of the barracks open to the public. They contain their original furniture and the lamp from which she gained the epitaph "Lady of the Lamp". Visits must be arranged in advance by faxing 0216 333 10 09.

Two other sites near the barracks – the Selimiye Mosque

Visitor praying at the tomb of the warrior Karaca Ahmet

Haydarpaşa Station, terminus for trains arriving from Anatolia

and the British War Cemetery – are both worth seeing. Built in 1804, the mosque is in a peaceful, if somewhat neglected, garden courtyard. The interior is filled with light from tiers of windows set in high arches. It is simply decorated with a classically painted dome and grey marble *minbar*. The royal pavilion in the northwest corner of the compound is flanked by graceful arches.

The British War Cemetery is a short walk south, on Burhan Felek Caddesi. It contains the graves of men who died in the Crimean War, in World War I at Gallipoli *(see p172)* and in World War II in the Middle East. There is no sign outside and opening hours vary, but the caretaker will usually be there to let you in.

❾ Haydarpaşa Station

Haydarpaşa Garı

Haydarpaşa İstasyon Cad, Haydarpaşa. **Tel** (0216) 336 04 75 or 336 20 63. ⛴ Haydarpaşa or Kadıköy. **Open** daily.

The waterfront location and grandeur of Haydarpaşa Station, together with the neighbouring tiled jetty, make it an impressive point of arrival or departure in Istanbul. The first Anatolian railway line, which was built in 1873, ran from here to İznik *(see p162)*. The extension of this railway was a major part of Abdül Hamit II's drive to modernize the Ottoman Empire. Lacking

sufficient funds to continue the project, he applied for help to his German ally, Kaiser Wilhelm II. The Deutsche Bank agreed to invest in the construction and operation of the railway. In 1898 German engineers were contracted to build the new railway lines running across Anatolia and beyond into the far reaches of the Ottoman Empire. At the same time a number of stations were built. Haydarpaşa, the grandest of these, was completed in 1908. Trains run from Haydarpaşa into the rest of Asia. It is currently closed for renovation *(see p237)*.

Florence Nightingale

A 19th-century painting of Florence Nightingale in Selimiye Barracks

The British nurse Florence Nightingale (1820–1910) was a tireless campaigner for hospital, military and social reform. During the Crimean War, in which Britain and France fought on the Ottoman side against the Russian Empire, she organized a party of 38 British nurses. They took charge of medical services at the Selimiye Barracks in Scutari (Üsküdar) in 1854. By the time she returned to Britain in 1856, at the end of the war, the mortality rate in the barracks had decreased from 20 to 2 percent, and the fundamental principles of modern nursing had been established. On her return home, Florence Nightingale opened a training school for nurses.

❿ Big Pine Hill

Büyük Çamlıca

Çamlıca. 🚌 11F, KÇ1; then 30 mins walk. Park: **Open** 9am– 11pm daily.

On a clear day the view from the top of this hill takes in the Princes' Islands, the Sea of Marmara, the Golden Horn and Beyoğlu, and the Bosphorus as far as the Black Sea. It is even possible to see snow-capped Mount Uludağ near Bursa *(see p171)* to the south. Big Pine Hill, 4 km (2.5 miles) east of Üsküdar, is the highest point in Istanbul, at 261 m (856 ft) above sea level. Even the forest of radio and TV masts further down the slopes of the hill does not obscure the view.

The park at the summit, which was created by the Turkish Touring and Automobile Club *(see p183)* in 1980, is laid out with gardens, marble kiosks and two 18th-century-style cafés.

Neighbouring Küçük Çamlıca (Little Pine Hill), located to the south, is rather less cultivated and consequently attracts fewer tourists to its little tea garden. It is another lovely place for a stroll, again with beautiful views.

Picturesque view of the Bosphorus, one of the world's busiest waterways ▶

BEYOND ISTANBUL

THE BOSPHORUS

If the noise and bustle of the city get too much, nothing can beat a trip up the Bosphorus *(see pp146–51)*, the straits separating Europe and Asia, which join the Black Sea and the Sea of Marmara. The easiest way to travel is by boat. An alternative is to explore the sights along the shores at your own pace. For much of their length the shores are lined with handsome buildings: wooden waterside villas known as yalıs, graceful mosques and opulent 19th-century palaces. The grander residences along the Bosphorus have

waterfront entrances. These date from the days when wooden caïques, boats powered by a strong team of oarsmen, were a popular form of transport along the straits among the city's wealthier inhabitants. Interspersed between the monumental architecture are former fishing villages, where you will find some of Istanbul's finest clubs and restaurants. The Bosphorus is especially popular in summer, when the cool breezes off the water provide welcome relief from the heat of the city.

Sights at a Glance

Museums and Palaces
- 2 Beylerbeyi Palace
- 4 Küçüksu Palace
- 5 Aşiyan Museum
- 9 Sakıp Sabancı Museum
- 10 Maslak Pavilion
- 11 Khedive's Palace
- 13 Sadberk Hanım Museum

Towns and Villages
- 3 Bebek
- 7 Kanlıca
- 12 Beykoz
- 14 Rumeli Kavağı

Historic Buildings
- 1 Bosphorus Bridge
- 6 Fortress of Europe

Parks
- 8 Emirgan Park

Key
- ▨ Central Istanbul
- ▨ Greater Istanbul
- ▭ Motorway
- ▬ Main road

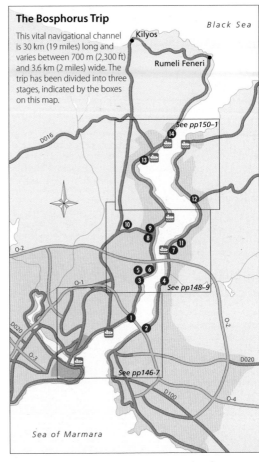

The Bosphorus Trip

This vital navigational channel is 30 km (19 miles) long and varies between 700 m (2,300 ft) and 3.6 km (2 miles) wide. The trip has been divided into three stages, indicated by the boxes on this map.

Black Sea

Kilyos

Rumeli Feneri

See pp150–1

See pp148–9

See pp146–7

Sea of Marmara

0 kilometres   5
0 miles   5

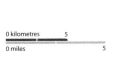

◀ The imposing Bosphorus Bridge, also known as the Atatürk Bridge

For map symbols *see back flap*

The Bosphorus suspension bridge between Ortaköy and Beylerbeyi

❶ Bosphorus Bridge

Boğaziçi Köprüsü

Ortaköy and Beylerbeyi. **Map** 9 F2. 🚌 40, 200, 202 (double deckers from Taksim).

Spanning the Bosphorus between the districts of Ortaköy and Beylerbeyi, this was the first bridge to be built across the straits that divide Istanbul. Construction began in February 1970 and finished on 29 October 1973, the 50th anniversary of the inauguration of the Turkish Republic (see p33). It is the world's ninth longest suspension bridge, at a length of 1,074 m (3,524 ft), and it reaches 64 m (210 ft) above water level.

❷ Beylerbeyi Palace

Beylerbeyi Sarayı

Beylerbeyi Cad, Asian side. **Tel** (0216) 321 93 20. 🚌 15 (from Üsküdar). 🚢 from Üsküdar. **Open** 9:30am–5pm Tue, Wed & Fri–Sun (Oct–Apr until 4pm). 🐾 🎟

Designed in the Baroque style by Sarkis Balyan, Beylerbeyi Palace seems fairly restrained compared to the excesses of the earlier Dolmabahçe (see pp130–31) or Küçüksu (see p142) palaces. It was built for Sultan Abdül Aziz (see p32) in 1861 as a summer residence and a place to entertain visiting heads of state. Empress Eugénie of France visited Beylerbeyi on her way to the opening of the Suez Canal in 1869 and had her face slapped by the sultan's

mother for daring to enter the palace on the arm of Abdül Aziz. Other regal visitors to the palace included the Duke and Duchess of Windsor.

The palace looks its most attractive from the Bosphorus, from where its two bathing pavilions – one for the harem and the other for the selamlık (the men's quarters) – can best be seen.

The most attractive room is the reception hall, which has a pool and fountain. Running water was popular in Ottoman houses for its pleasant sound and cooling effect in the heat.

Egyptian straw matting is used on the floor as a form of insulation. The pretty crystal chandeliers are mostly Bohemian and the carpets (see pp218–19)

Landing at the top of the stairs in Beylerbeyi Palace

are from Hereke. Despite her initial reception, Empress Eugénie of France was so delighted by the elegance of the palace that she had a copy of the window in the guest room made for her bedroom in Tuileries Palace, in Paris.

❸ Bebek

European side. 🚌 25E, 40.

Bebek is one of the most fashionable villages along the Bosphorus. It is famous for its marzipan (badem ezmesi, see p213), and for the cafés which line its waterfront. It was once a favourite location for summer residences and palaces of Ottoman aristocrats, and at the end of the 19th century, caïques (see p128) of merrymakers would set off on moonlit cruises from the bay, accompanied by a boat of musicians. The women in the party would trail pieces of velvet or satin edged with silver fishes in the

Detail of the gate of the Egyptian Consulate, Bebek

water behind them while the musicians played to the revellers.

One of the hosts of these parties was the mother of the last Khedive of Egypt (see p31), Abbas Hilmi II. Built in the late 19th century, the only remaining monumental architecture in Bebek is the Egyptian Consulate, which, like the Khedive's Palace (see p144), was commissioned by Abbas Hilmi II. The steep, mansard roof of this yalı is reminiscent of 19th-century northern French architecture. There are lighter Art Nouveau touches including the railings draped in wrought-iron vines and a rising sun between the two turrets, symbolizing the beginning of the new century.

The khedive used the yalı as a summer palace until he was deposed by the British in 1914. From then on to the present day it has been used as the Egyptian Consulate.

Yalıs on the Bosphorus

Old yalı at Kandilli, Asian side

At the end of the 17th century, *paşas*, grand viziers and other distinguished citizens of Ottoman Istanbul began to build themselves elegant villas – yalıs – along the shores of the Bosphorus. These served as summer residences, and the styles employed reflected their owners' prestige. Since then, the yalıs that have been built have become larger and more elaborate, adopting Baroque, Art Nouveau and modern styles of architecture. Most of them still conform to a traditional plan, making maximum use of the waterfront and, inside, having a large sitting room surrounded by bedrooms.

Köprülü Amcazade Hüseyin Paşa Yalı *(see p149)*, near Anadolu Hisarı, was built in 1699 and is the oldest building on the shores of the Bosphorus. Early yalıs, like this one, were built at the water's edge, but in later years they were constructed a little way inland.

A *cumba*, or bay window, projects over the water.

Traditional wooden yalıs were normally painted rust red, a colour known as "Ottoman rose".

Later yalıs, built from the 18th century, were painted in pastel shades.

A bracket supports the projecting upstairs rooms.

Fethi Ahmet Paşa Yalı *(see p147)*, or Mocan Yalı, at Kuzguncuk, was built in the late 18th century. Among visitors were the composer Franz Liszt and the architect Le Corbusier. Famous as the "Pink Yalı", after its boldly decorated exterior, the house is almost invisible from the land.

Baroque influence is clearly visible in the ornately carved balcony.

Ethem Pertev Yalı *(see p149)*, at Kanlıca, is a prime example of the so-called "cosmopolitan period" of yalı building, between 1867 and 1908. It has a boat house below and combines intricate wood carving, a later development, with the more traditional features of a yalı...

Boat house under the yalı

The Egyptian Consulate *(see p148)* at Bebek clearly shows the influence of Art Nouveau, with its wrought iron railings worked into a leaf design. It was commissioned by the Khedive of Egypt *(see p140)* in around 1900.

French-style mansard roof

Ornamental details were inspired by Austrian Art Nouveau designs.

A narrow quay often separates 19th-century yalıs from the shore.

❹ Küçüksu Palace
Küçüksu Kasrı

Küçüksu Sahili–Anadoluhisarı Beykoz, Asian side. **Tel** (0216) 332 02 37. 🚌 15 (from Üsküdar) or 101 (from Beşiktaş). **Open** 9:30am–5pm Tue, Wed, Fri–Sun (Oct–Apr until 4pm).

Marble-fronted Küçüksu Palace has one of the prettiest façades on the shores of the Bosphorus. Particularly attractive is the curving double staircase which leads up to its main waterside entrance.

Sultan Abdül Mecit I *(see p32)* employed court architect Nikogos Balyan *(see p130)* to build this palace to accommodate his entourage on their visits to the Sweet Waters of Asia. This was the romantic name European visitors gave to the Küçüksu and Göksu rivers. For centuries the Ottoman nobility liked to indulge in picnics in the meadows between the streams.

On the completion of Küçüksu Palace in 1856, the sultan complained that it was too plain and demanded more ornamentation, including his monogram engraved on the façade. Later, in the reign of Abdül Aziz *(see p32)*, the façade was further embellished, with the result that it is hard to follow the lines of the original architecture.

The room arrangement is typically Ottoman, with a large central salon opening on to four corner rooms on each floor. The interior decor was carried out by Séchan, the decorator of the Paris Opera, soon after the palace was finished. The carpets are fine examples from Hereke *(see pp218–19)* and the chandeliers Bohemian crystal.

Küçüksu Palace, an ornate Bosphorus residence built in 1856

On the shore near Küçüksu Palace is the picturesque, turreted Fountain of the Valide Sultan Mihrişah. Dating from 1796, it is in the Baroque style.

Kıbrıslı Yalı, just south of the palace, was built in 1760. At over 60 m (200 ft), its brilliant white façade is the longest of any yalı *(see p141)* along the Bosphorus. A little further south again is Kırmızı Yalı, the Red Yalı, which is so called for its distinctive crimson colour and was built for one of Sultan Mahmut II's gardens in the 1830s.

❺ Aşiyan Museum
Aşiyan Müzesi

Aşiyan Yolu, Bebek, European side. **Tel** (0212) 263 69 86. 🚌 25E, 40. **Open** 9am–4pm Tue–Sat.

Aşiyan, or bird's nest, is the former home of Tevfik Fikret (1867–1915), a teacher, utopian visionary and one of Turkey's leading poets. The wooden mansion, built by Fikret himself in 1906, is an attractive example of Turkish vernacular architecture. The views from its upper-storey balcony are stunning.

On show are the poet's possessions and *Sis* (Fog), a painting by Caliph Abdül Mecit (1922–24), inspired by Fikret's poem of that name.

❻ Fortress of Europe
Rumeli Hisarı

Yahya Kemal Cad, European side. **Tel** (0212) 263 53 05. 🚌 25E, 40. **Open** 9:30am–4:30pm Thu–Tue. 🎫

This fortress was built by Mehmet the Conqueror in 1452 as his first step in the conquest of Constantinople *(see p28)*. Situated at the narrowest point of the Bosphorus, the fortress controlled a major Byzantine supply route. Across the straits is Anadolu Hisarı, or the Fortress of Asia, which was built in the 14th century by Beyazıt I.

The Fortress of Europe's layout was planned by Mehmet himself. While his grand vizier *(see p31)* and two other viziers were each responsible for the building of one of the three great towers, the sultan took charge of the walls. In the spirit of competition which evolved, the fortress was completed in four months.

The Fortress of Europe, built by Mehmet the Conqueror to enable him to capture Constantinople

The new fortress was soon nicknamed Boğazkesen – meaning "Throat-cutter" or "Strait-cutter". It was garrisoned by a force of Janissaries (see p129). These troops trained their cannons on the straits to prevent the passage of foreign ships. After they had sunk a Venetian vessel, this approach to Constantinople was cut off. Following the conquest of the city, the fortress lost its importance as a military base and was used as a prison, particularly for out-of-favour foreign envoys and prisoners-of-war.

The structure was restored in 1953. Open-air theatre performances are now staged here during the Istanbul Music and Dance Festival (see p47).

Café serving the yoghurt for which Kanlıca is famous

❼ Kanlıca

Asian side. 🚌 15, 101.

A delicious, creamy type of yoghurt is Kanlıca's best known asset. The İskender Paşa Mosque, overlooking the village square, is a minor work by Sinan (see p93), built for Sultan Süleyman's vizier İskender Paşa in 1559–60. There have been changes to the original building: the wooden dome has been replaced by a flat roof, and the porch was added later.

There are a number of yalıs in and around Kanlıca, including the Köprülü Amcazade Hüseyin Paşa Yalı (see p141), the oldest surviving Bosphorus yalı, just south of the village. This was built in 1698 by Mustafa II's grand vizier Hüseyin Paşa, the fourth grand vizier from the Köprülü family. The Treaty of Karlowitz, in which the Ottomans

acknowledged the loss of territory to Austria, Venice, Poland and Russia, was signed here in 1699 (see p29). All that remains of the yalı, which is not open to visitors, is a T-shaped salon, its dome only saved by wooden props.

❽ Emirgan Park ✓
Emirgan Parkı

Emirgan Sahil Yolu, European side.
Tel (0212) 277 57 82. 🚌 25E, 40.
Open 7am–10:30pm daily.
🚫 for vehicles.

Emirgan Park is the location of some famous tulip gardens, which are at their finest for the annual Tulip Festival in April (see p46). Tulips originally grew wild on the Asian steppes and were first propagated in large quantities in Holland. They were later reintroduced to Turkey by Mehmet IV (1648–87). The reign of his son Ahmet III is known as the Tulip Period (see p29) because of his fascination with the flowers.

In the late 19th century Sultan Abdül Aziz gave the park to the Egyptian Khedive (see p31), İsmail Paşa, and its three pavilions date from that era. They are known by their colours. The Sarı Köşk (Yellow Pavilion), built in the style of a Swiss chalet, suffered fire damage in 1954 and was re-built in concrete with a façade resembling the original. The Beyaz Köşk (White Pavilion) is a Neo-Classical style mansion, while the Pembe Köşk (Pink

Pretty tulips at Pembe Köşk in Emirgan Park

Pavilion) is in the style of a traditional Ottoman house. All three are now cafés.

❾ Sakıp Sabancı Museum
Sakıp Sabancı Müzesi

İstinye Cad 22, Emirgan 34467.
Tel (0212) 229 55 18. 🚌 40, 41 from Taksim Sq; any bus to İstinye or Sarıyer.
Open 10am–5pm Tue, Thu, Fri; 10am–7pm Wed & Sat; noon–5pm Sun. **Closed** 1 Jan, 1st day of religious hols. 🚫 🚫 ♿ 🖥 📷
W muze.sabanciuniv.edu

With a superb view over the Bosphorus, the Sakıp Sabancı Museum is also known as the Horse Mansion (Atlı Köşk). Exhibitions comprise over 400 years of Ottoman calligraphy and other Koranic and secular art treasures. The collection of paintings is exquisite, with works by Ottoman court painters and European artists enthralled with Turkey.

Birds of the Bosphorus

In September and October, thousands of white storks and birds of prey fly over the Bosphorus on their way from their breeding grounds in eastern Europe to wintering regions in Africa. Large birds usually prefer to cross narrow straits like the Bosphorus rather than fly over an expanse of open water such as the Mediterranean. Among birds of prey on this route you can see the lesser spotted eagle and the honey buzzard. The birds also cross the straits in spring on their way to Europe but, before the breeding season, they are fewer in number.

The white stork, which migrates over the straits

Hot-house plants in the conservatory at Maslak Pavilions

⑩ Maslak Pavilions

Maslak Kasırları

Büyükdere Cad, Maslak. **Tel** (0212) 276 10 22. 🚌 40S (from Taksim). **Open** 9:30am–5pm Tue, Wed & Fri–Sun (Nov–Feb until 4pm).

This small group of buildings was a royal hunting lodge and country residence, much prized for its glorious views. The pavilions were built in the early and mid-19th century, when the focus of Istanbul court life moved away from Topkapı Palace (see pp56–61), in the centre of the city, to the sultans' lavish estates along the shore of the Bosphorus. The buildings are thought to date mainly from the reign of Abdül Aziz (1861–76). He gave Maslak to his nephew Abdül Hamit in the hope that he would then stop sailing at Tarabya (see p150), which his uncle regarded as unsafe.

The four main buildings are less ornate than other 19th-century pavilions in Istanbul. This is possibly due to the austere character of Abdül Hamit. He personally crafted the balustrades of the beautiful central staircase in the Kasr-ı Hümayun (the Pavilion of the Sultan) during his stay here. His initials in Western script – AH – can also be seen in the headpieces over the mirrors. The pavilion's lounge retains an Oriental feel, with a low sofa and a central coal-burning brazier.

Jason and the Symplegades

The upper Bosphorus features in the Greek myth of Jason's search for the Golden Fleece. The Argonauts, Jason's crew, helped a local king, Phineus, by ridding him of the harpies (female demons) sent by Zeus to torment him. In return, the king advised them on how to tackle the Symplegades, two rocks at the mouth of the Bosphorus which were reputed to clash together, making passage impossible. His advice was to send a dove in advance of the ship; if it went through safely, so would the ship. This the Argonauts duly did, and the rocks clipped the dove's tail feathers. The Argo then went through with only some damage to its stern.

Jason and the Argonauts making their way through the Symplegades

Behind the small but elegant Mabeyn-i Hümayun (the Private Apartments) is a large conservatory full of camellias, ferns and banana plants. Nearby, at the edge of the forest stands a tiny octagonal folly with an ornate balcony called the Çadır Köşkü, or Tent Pavilion, which now serves as a bookshop. The Paşalar Dairesi (the Apartments of the Paşa) are located at the other side of the complex.

⑪ Khedive's Palace

Hidiv Kasrı

Hidiv Kasrı Yolu 32, Çubuklu. **Tel** (0216) 413 96 64. 🚌 15, 15A, 15P (from Üsküdar) or 221 (from Taksim), then 5 mins' walk from Kanlıca. **Open** 9am–11pm daily (May–Oct: to 10:30pm). 🖥 🌐 hidivkasri.com

Built in 1907 by the last khedive (hereditary viceroy of Egypt, see p31), Abbas Hilmi II, this summer palace is one of the city's most striking buildings of its era. Its tower is an imposing landmark for those travelling up the Bosphorus.

The Italian architect Delfo Seminati based the design of the palace on an Italianate villa, throwing in Art Nouveau and Ottoman elements. Most impressive of all is the round entrance hall. This is entered through Art Nouveau glass doors and features a stained-glass skylight above a central fountain surrounded by eight pairs of elegant columns.

Renovated by the Turkish Touring Club (TTOK, see p245), the palace is now a luxury restaurant.

⑫ Beykoz

Asian shore. 🚌 15 (from Üsküdar) or 221 (from Taksim).

Beykoz is famous for its walnuts (beykoz means "prince's walnut") and for the glass produced here in the 1800s. The distinctive, mainly opaque, Beykoz glass (see p213), with its rich colours and graceful designs, can be seen in museums all over Turkey. Nowadays, the village's

Fountain in the village square at Beykoz

main attraction is its fish restaurants, which serve excellent turbot.

A fine fountain stands in the central square. Built on the orders of Sultan Mahmut I *(see p35)*, it is called the İshak Ağa Çeşmesi, after the customs inspector who commissioned it in 1746. It has a large domed and colonnaded loggia, and 10 conduits spouting a constant stream of water.

Industrialization, mainly bottling and leather factories, has taken its toll, and only a few buildings hint at the village's former splendour. An attractive 19th-century waterside mansion, Halil Ethem Yalı, interestingly combines Neo-Classical and Neo-Baroque styles. It stands on İbrahim Kelle Caddesi, south of the ferry landing.

⓭ Sadberk Hanım Museum
Sadberk Hanım Müzesi

Piyasa Cad 27–29, Büyükdere.
Tel (0212) 242 38 13. 🚌 25E.
Open 10am–6pm Thu–Tue. 🎫 📷
🌐 **sadberkhanimmuzesi.org.tr**

Occupying two archetypal wooden Bosphorus yalis *(see p141)*, the Sadberk Hanım Museum was the first private museum to open in Turkey, in 1981. The larger of these yalıs,

the Azaryan Yalı, is the former summer house of the wealthy Koç family. A four-storey mansion, it was built in 1911 and, like many buildings of the time, was inspired by European architecture. The distinctive criss-crossed wooden slats on its façade distinguish it from the neighbouring buildings. It contains some fine ethnographic artifacts collected by Sadberk Hanım, wife of the industrialist Vehbi Koç, to whom the museum is dedicated. She found many of them in the Grand Bazaar *(see pp100–101)* and in Istanbul's other markets. A number of exhibits are laid out in tableaux depicting 19th-century Ottoman society. These include a henna party, at which the groom's female relatives would apply henna to the hands of his bride; and a circumcision bed, with a young boy dressed in traditional costume. Also worth seeking out in this section is a display of infinitely delicate *oya*, Turkish embroideries. These remarkably life-like pieces imitate garlands of flowers, such as carnations, roses, hyacinths and lilies and were used to fringe scarves and petticoats. Some of the examples on show were made in palace harems in the 18th century.

Attic vase, Sadberk Hanım Museum

The neighbouring building is called the Sevgi Gönül Wing. Also dating from the early 20th century, it was bought to house the archaeological collection of Hüseyin Kocabaş, a friend of the Koç family. Displays are ordered chronologically, ranging from the late Neolithic period (5400 BC) to the Ottoman era.

Exhibits are changed from time to time, but typically include Assyrian cuneiform tablets dating from the second millennium BC, Phrygian metalwork and Greek pottery from the late Geometric Period (750–680 BC). Among other items are Byzantine reliquary and pendent crosses, and a selection of Roman gold jewellery.

⓮ Rumeli Kavağı

European shore. 🚌 25A (from Beşiktaş). 🚢 Rumeli Kavağı.

This pretty village has a broad selection of restaurants specializing in fish and fried mussels. They are clustered around the harbour from where there are views of the wild, rocky shores on the approach to the Black Sea. On the hill above Rumeli Kavağı are the scant remains of a castle, İmros Kalesi, built by Manuel I Comnenus *(see p23)* in the 12th century to guard its customs point.

Further up the Bosphorus, the shore road leads from Rumeli Kavağı to Altın Kum beach. This small strip of sand backed by restaurants is popular with local people.

The fishing village of Rumeli Kavağı, on the upper Bosphorus

The Bosphorus Trip

One of the great pleasures of a visit to Istanbul is a cruise up the Bosphorus. You can go on a pre-arranged guided tour or take one of the small boats that tout for passengers at Eminönü. But there is no better way to travel than on the official trip run by Istanbul Sea Bus Company (İDO, *see pp242–3*), which is described on the following pages. The İDO Bosphorus Cruise makes a round-trip to the upper Bosphorus two or three times daily, stopping at six piers along the way. You can return to Eminönü on the same boat or make your way back by bus, dolmuş or taxi. A 2-hour cruise also departs daily from Eminönü and Üsküdar.

Locator Map

Naval Museum *(see p128)*

Dolmabahçe Palace
This opulent 19th-century palace *(see pp130–31)* has a series of ornate gates along the waterfront. These were used by the sultan to enter the palace from his imperial barge.

Barbaros Hayrettin Paşa

İnönü Stadium

Kabataş

Museum of Fine Arts *(see p128)*

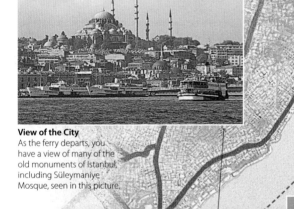

View of the City
As the ferry departs, you have a view of many of the old monuments of Istanbul, including Süleymaniye Mosque, seen in this picture.

Dolmabahçe Mosque was completed in 185 a year before the palace *(see p128)*.

Galata Bridge

Karaköy

Eminönü

Leander's Tower
One the landmarks of the city, this white tower stands prominently in mid-channel, a short way off the Asian shore *(see p132)*.

Eminönü Port
The official Bosphorus ferry departs from Istanbul's busiest ferry terminal.

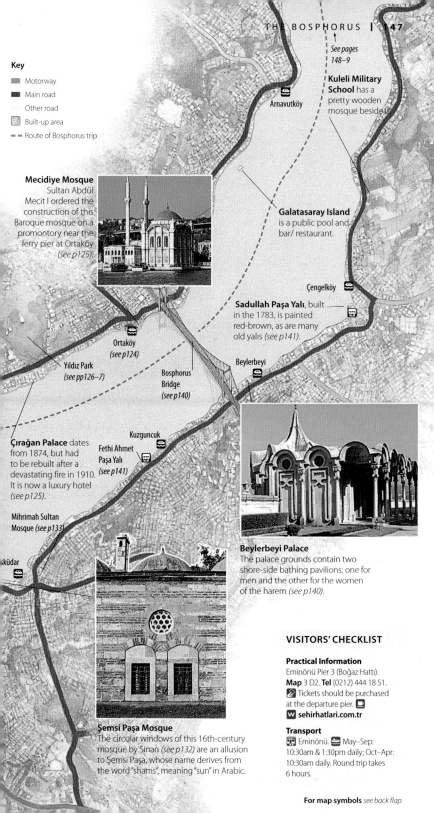

See pages
148–9

Kuleli Military School has a pretty wooden mosque beside it

Arnavutköy

Key

▬ Motorway

▬ Main road

　 Other road

▦ Built-up area

▬ ▬ Route of Bosphorus trip

Mecidiye Mosque
Sultan Abdül Mecit I ordered the construction of this Baroque mosque on a promontory near the ferry pier at Ortaköy *(see p125)*

Galatasaray Island is a public pool and bar/ restaurant.

Çengelköy

Sadullah Paşa Yalı, built in the 1783, is painted red-brown, as are many old yalıs *(see p141)*.

Ortaköy
(see p124)

Beylerbeyi

Yıldız Park
(see pp126–7)

Bosphorus Bridge
(see p140)

Çırağan Palace dates from 1874, but had to be rebuilt after a devastating fire in 1910. It is now a luxury hotel *(see p125)*.

Kuzguncuk

Fethi Ahmet Paşa Yalı
(see p141)

Mihrimah Sultan Mosque *(see p133)*

sküdar

Beylerbeyi Palace
The palace grounds contain two shore-side bathing pavilions: one for men and the other for the women of the harem *(see p140)*.

VISITORS' CHECKLIST

Practical Information
Eminönü Pier 3 (Boğaz Hattı).
Map 3 D2. **Tel** (0212) 444 18 51.
⚠ Tickets should be purchased at the departure pier. ☐
Ⓦ sehirhatlari.com.tr

Transport
🚇 Eminönü. ⛴ May–Sep: 10:30am & 1:30pm daily; Oct–Apr: 10:30am daily. Round trip takes 6 hours.

Şemsi Paşa Mosque
The circular windows of this 16th-century mosque by Sinan *(see p132)* are an allusion to Şemsi Paşa, whose name derives from the word "shams", meaning "sun" in Arabic.

For map symbols *see back flap*

The Middle Bosphorus

North of Arnavutköy, the outskirts of Istanbul give way to attractive towns and villages, such as Bebek with its bars and cafés. The Bosphorus flows fast and deep as the channel reaches its narrowest point – 700 m (2,300 ft) across – on the approach to the Fatih Sultan Mehmet bridge. It was at this point that the Persian emperor Darius and his army crossed the Bosphorus on a pontoon bridge in 512 BC, on their way to fight the Greeks. Two famous old fortresses face each other across the water near here. Several elegant yalıs are also found in this part of the strait, particularly in the region known to Europeans as the Sweet Waters of Asia.

Locator Map

İstinye Bay
This huge natural bay, the largest inlet on the Bosphorus, has been used as a dock for centuries. There is a fish market along the quay every morning.

Emirgan Park
Situated above the pretty village of Emirgan, this park is famous for its tulips in spring (see p46). The grounds contain pleasant cafés and pavilions (see p143).

The Bosphorus University, one of the most prestigious in Turkey, enjoys spectacular views. Almost all teaching here is in English.

Fortress of Europe
Situated at the narrowest point on the Bosphorus, this fortress (see p142) was built by Mehmet II in 1452, as a prelude to his invasion of Constantinople (see p28).

Bebek (see p140)

Egyptian Consulate (see p140)

Kandil

Arnavutköy

See pages 146–7

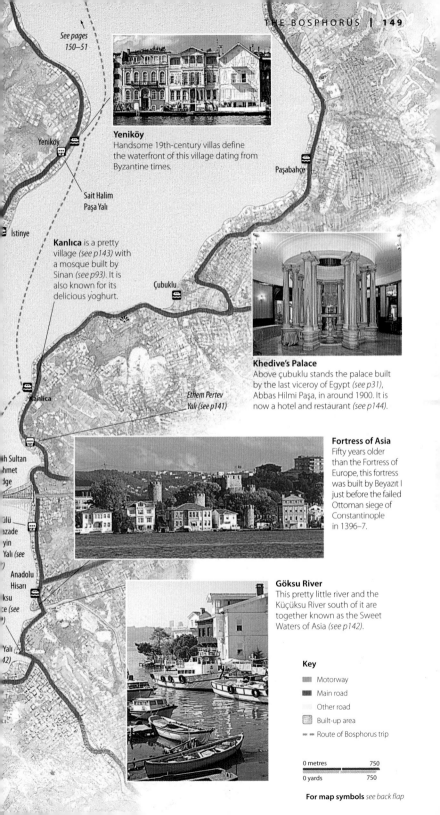

See pages 150–51

Yeniköy
Handsome 19th-century villas define the waterfront of this village dating from Byzantine times.

Paşabahçe

Sait Halim Paşa Yalı

İstinye

Kanlıca is a pretty village *(see p143)* with a mosque built by Sinan *(see p93)*. It is also known for its delicious yoghurt.

Çubuklu

Kanlıca

Khedive's Palace
Above çubuklu stands the palace built by the last viceroy of Egypt *(see p31)*, Abbas Hilmi Paşa, in around 1900. It is now a hotel and restaurant *(see p144)*.

Ethem Pertev Yalı (see p141)

h Sultan
hmet
dge

ilü
azade
yin
Yalı (see
')

Anadolu
Hisarı

ksu
:e (see
)

Yalı (
42)

Fortress of Asia
Fifty years older than the Fortress of Europe, this fortress was built by Beyazıt I just before the failed Ottoman siege of Constantinople in 1396–7.

Göksu River
This pretty little river and the Küçüksu River south of it are together known as the Sweet Waters of Asia *(see p142)*.

Key
- Motorway
- Main road
- Other road
- Built-up area
- ▪ ▪ Route of Bosphorus trip

| 0 metres | 750 |
| 0 yards | 750 |

For map symbols *see back flap*

The Upper Bosphorus

In the 19th century ambassadors to Turkey built their summer retreats between Tarabya and Büyükdere, on the European side of the Bosphorus. As the hills fall more steeply towards the shore along the upper reaches of the straits, the built-up area peters out. There is time to explore and take lunch at Anadolu Kavaği on the Asian side before the boat returns to Eminönü. You can also catch a bus or dolmuş back to the city. The Bosphorus itself continues for 8 km (5 miles) or so to meet the Black Sea, but the land on both sides of this stretch is now under military control.

Locator Map

Sadberk Hanım Museum
This museum, housed in two wooden yalıs, has a variety of interesting exhibits. These include antiquities from Greece and Rome, and Ottoman craftwork *(see p145)*.

Büyükdere

Sarıyer

Tarabya Bay
The small village set within a lovely bay first attracted wealthy Greeks in the 18th century. The bay still thrives as an exclusive resort with up-market fish restaurants.

Huber Köşk
a 19th-cent... yalı owned... the governme...

Fishing on the Bosphorus

A multitude of fishing vessels ply the waters of the Bosphorus, ranging from large trawlers returning from the Black Sea to tiny rowing boats from which a line is cast into the water. On a trip up the Bosphorus you often see seine nets spread out in circles, suspended from floats on the surface. The main types of fish caught are mackerel, mullet, *hamsi* (similar to anchovy, *see p196*) and sardine. Much of the fish caught is sold at Istanbul's principal fish market in Kumkapı.

Fishing boats at Sarıyer, the main fishing port on the Bosphorus

Rumeli Kavağı
This village is the most northerly ferry stop on the European side *(see p145)*. From here the Bosphorus widens out to meet the Black Sea.

Rumeli Kavağı

Anadolu Kavağı

Anadolu Kavağı
A short climb from this village – the last stop on the trip – brings you to a ruined 14th-century Byzantine fortress, the Genoese Castle, from which there are great views over the straits.

Beykoz
Beykoz is the largest fishing village along the Asian shore. Close to its village square, which has this fountain dating from 1746, are several fish restaurants which are very popular in summer *(see p144)*.

Beykoz

Halil
Ethem Yalı
(see p145)

See pages 148–9

Key

■ Main road
Other road
▨ Built-up area
– – Route of Bosphorus trip

| 0 metres | 750 |
| 0 yards | 750 |

For map symbols *see back flap*

EXCURSIONS FROM ISTANBUL

Standing at a natural crossroads, Istanbul makes a good base for excursions into the neighbouring areas of Thrace and Anatolia – European and Asian Turkey respectively. Whether you want to see great Islamic architecture, immerse yourself in a busy bazaar, relax on an island or catch a glimpse of Turkey's rich birdlife, you will find a choice of destinations within easy reach of the city.

On public holidays and weekends nearby resorts become crowded with Istanbul residents taking a break from the noisy city. For longer breaks, they head for the Mediterranean or Aegean, so summer is a good time to explore the Marmara and western Black Sea regions while they are quiet.

The country around Istanbul varies immensely from lush forests to open plains and, beyond them, impressive mountains. The Belgrade Forest is one of the closest green areas to the city if you want a short break. The Princes' Islands, where the pine forests and monasteries can be toured by a pleasant ride in a horse-and-carriage, are also just a short boat trip away from the city. Further away, through rolling fields of bright yellow sunflowers, is Edirne, the former Ottoman capital. The town stands on a site first settled in the 7th century BC. It is visited today for its fine mosques, especially the Selimiye.

South of the Sea of Marmara is the pretty spa town of Bursa, originally a Greek city which was founded in 183 BC. The first Ottoman capital, it has some fine architecture.

Near the mouth of the straits of the Dardanelles (which link the Sea of Marmara to the Aegean) lie the ruins of the legendary city of Troy, dating from as early as 3600 BC. North of the Dardanelles are cemeteries commemorating the battles which were fought over the Gallipoli peninsula during World War I.

Boats in Burgaz Harbour on the Princes' Islands, a short ferry ride from Istanbul

◄ Yeşil Türbe, also known as the Green Tomb, Bursa

Exploring Beyond Istanbul

Within a radius of 250 km (150 miles) of Istanbul there are many destinations worth visiting. To the northwest is Edirne, an attractive riverside town and the location of several fine mosques. South of Istanbul is Bursa, which lies at the foot of Uludağ, a mountain famed for its skiing. Closer to Istanbul are the Black Sea resorts of Şile, Polonezköy and Kilyos, and the Princes' Islands, which are easily reached by ferry. The war cemeteries of the Dardanelles and the site of ancient Troy require a longer trip.

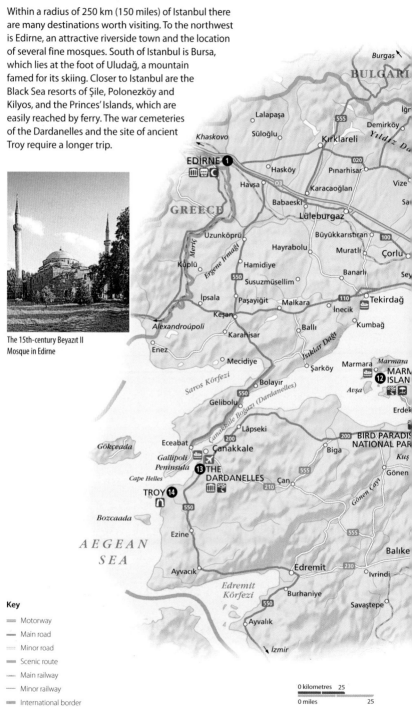

The 15th-century Beyazıt II Mosque in Edirne

Key

- Motorway
- Main road
- Minor road
- Scenic route
- Main railway
- Minor railway
- International border

For map symbols see back flap

0 kilometres 25
0 miles 25

Sights at a Glance

View over the picturesque city of Bursa

Getting Around

The road network around Istanbul is steadily improving, and modern, cheap and efficient coaches *(see p244)* will get you to most places. Ferries and sea buses *(see p244)* cross the Sea of Marmara to ports on its southern shore and reach both the Princes' and Marmara Islands.

One of the main ski runs in Uludağ National Park

❶ Edirne

Standing on the river Tunca near the border with Greece, Edirne is a provincial university town which is home to one of Turkey's star attractions, the Selimiye Mosque *(see pp158–9)*. As this huge monument attests, Edirne was historically of great importance. It dates back to AD 125, when the Roman Emperor Hadrian joined two small towns to form Hadrianopolis, or Adrianople. For nearly a century, from when Murat I *(see p27)* took the city in 1361 until Constantinople was conquered in 1453 *(see p28)*, Edirne was the Ottoman capital. The town has one other claim to fame – the annual grease wrestling championships in June.

Entrance arch, Mosque of the Three Balconies

predecessors in Bursa *(see pp164–71)*, the mosque has an open courtyard, setting a precedent for the great imperial mosques of Istanbul. The plan of its interior was also innovative. With minimal obstructions, the mihrab and *minbar* can both be seen from almost every corner of the prayer hall. Like the minarets, the dome, too, was the largest of its time.

Entrance to Beyazıt II Mosque viewed from its inner courtyard

☐ Beyazıt II Mosque

Beyazıt II KülliyesiYeniimaret Mah Beyazit Cad. **Open** daily. Health Museum: **Tel** (0284) 212 09 22. **Open** 9:30am–5:30pm daily.

Beyazıt II Mosque stands in a peaceful location on the northern bank of the Tunca River, 1.5 km (1 mile) from the town centre. It was built in 1484–8, soon after Beyazıt II *(see p34)* succeeded Mehmet the Conqueror *(see p28)* as sultan.

The mosque and its courtyards are open to the public. Of the surrounding buildings in the complex, the old hospital, which incorporated an asylum, has been converted into the Health Museum. Disturbed patients were treated in the asylum – a model of its time – with water, colour and flower therapies. The Turkish writer Evliya Çelebi (1611–84) reported that singers and instrumentalists would play soothing music here three times a week. Overuse of hashish was

one of the commonest afflictions. The colonnaded inner mosque courtyard, unlike most later examples, covers three times the area of the mosque itself. Inside, the weight of the impressive dome is supported on sweeping pendentives.

☐ Mosque of the Three Balconies

Üç Şerefeli Camii Hükümet Cad. **Open** daily.

Until the fall of Constantinople, this was the grandest building in the early Ottoman state. It was finished in 1447 and takes its name from the three balconies adorning its southeast minaret, at the time the tallest in existence. In an unusual touch, the other three minarets of the mosque are each of a different design and height. Unlike its

☐ Old Mosque

Eski Cami Talat Paşa Asfaltı. **Open** daily.

The oldest of Edirne's major mosques, this is a smaller version of the Great Mosque in Bursa *(see p166)*. The eldest son of Beyazıt I *(see p34)*, Süleyman, began the mosque in 1403, but it was his youngest son, Mehmet I, who completed it in 1414.

A perfect square, the mosque is divided by four massive piers into nine domed sections. On either side of the prayer hall entrance there are massive Arabic inscriptions proclaiming "Allah" and "Mohammed".

Grease Wrestling

The Kırkpınar Grease Wrestling Championships take place at the end of June, in Sarayiçi Er Meydanı, a field near Edirne. Established in 1346, the event is famed throughout Turkey. Before competing,

Grease wrestlers parading before they fight

the wrestlers dress in knee-length leather shorts *(kispet)* and grease themselves from head to foot in diluted olive oil. The master of ceremonies, the *cazgır*, then invites the competitors to take part in a high-stepping, arm-flinging parade across the field, accompanied by music played on a deep-toned drum *(davul)* and a single-reed oboe *(zurna)*. Wrestling bouts can last up to 2 hours and involve long periods of frozen, silent concentration interspersed by attempts to throw down the opponent.

▥ Rüstem Paşa Caravanserai

Rüstem Paşa Kervansarayı
İki Kapılı Han Cad 57.
Tel (0284) 212 61 19.

Sinan (see p93) designed this
caravanserai for Süleyman's
most powerful grand vizier,
Rüstem Paşa (see p90), in
1560–61. It was constructed
in two distinct parts. The larger
courtyard, or han (see p98),
which is now the Rüstem Paşa
Kervansaray Hotel (see p193),
was built for the merchants of
Edirne, while the smaller courtyard, now a student hostel, was
an inn for other travellers.

A short walk away, on the
other side of Saraçlar Caddesi,
is the Semiz Ali Paşa Bazaar,
where Edirne's merchants still
sell their wares. This is another
work of Sinan, dating from 1589.
It consists of a long, narrow
street of vaulted shops.

▥ Museum of Turkish and Islamic Arts

Türk ve İslam Eserleri Müzesi
Kadir Paşa Mektep Sok.
Tel (0284) 225 16 25.
Open 9am–noon, 1:30–5pm
Tue–Sun. ▨

Edirne's small collection of
Turkish and Islamic works of
art is attractively located in

the medrese of the Selimiye
Mosque (see pp158–9).
The museum's first room is
devoted to the local sport of
grease wrestling. It includes
enlarged reproductions of
miniatures depicting 600 years
of the sport. These show the
wrestling stars resplendent
in their leather shorts, their
skin glistening with olive oil.

Other objects on display
include the original doors of
the Beyazıt II Mosque. There
are also military exhibits. Among
them are some beautiful 18th-
century Ottoman shields, with
woven silk exteriors, and
paintings of military subjects.

The tranquil 15th-century Muradiye Mosque

VISITORS' CHECKLIST

Practical Information
210 km (130 miles) NW of Istanbul.
▨ 150,000. **D** Rüstem Paşa
Kervan Saray Hotel. **ℹ** Hürriyet
Meydanı 17, (0284) 213 92 08.
▨ Mon–Thu, Sat. ▨ Grease
Wrestling (late Jun); Liberation
Day (25 Nov). **W** kirkpinar.org

Transport
▨ Ayşekadin, (0284) 235 26 73.
▨ Talat Paşa Cad, (0284) 225 19 79.

▣ Muradiye Mosque

Muradiye Camii
Küçükpazar Cad.
Open prayer times only.

This mosque was
built as a zaviye (dervish
hospice) in 1421 by
Murat II (see p34),
who dreamt that the
great dervish leader
Celaleddin Rumi (see
p106) asked him to build
one in Edirne. Only later
was it converted into a
mosque. Its interior is
notable for its massive
inscriptions, similar to
those in the Old Mosque,
and for some fine early
15th-century İznik tiles
(see p163).

Edirne City Centre

① Beyazıt II Mosque
② Mosque of the Three Balconies
③ Old Mosque
④ Rüstem Paşa Caravanserai
⑤ Selimiye Mosque see pp158–9
⑥ Museum of Turkish and Islamic Arts
⑦ Muradiye Mosque

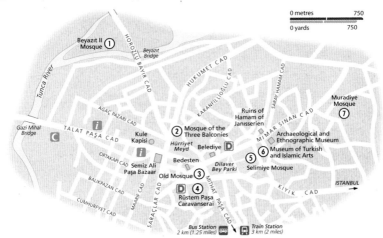

Edirne: Selimiye Mosque

Selimiye Camii

The Selimiye is the greatest of all the Ottoman mosque complexes, the apogee of an art form and the culmination of a lifetime's ambition for its architect, Sinan *(see p93)*. Built on a slight hill, the mosque is a prominent landmark. Its complex includes a *medrese (see p40)*, now housing the Museum of Turkish and Islamic Arts *(see p157)*, a school and the Kavaflar Arasta, a covered bazaar.

Selim II *(see p29)* commissioned the mosque. It was begun in 1569 and completed in 1575, a year after his death. The dome was Sinan's proudest achievement. In his memoirs, he wrote: "With the help of Allah and the favour of Sultan Selim Khan, I have succeeded in building a cupola six cubits wider and four cubits deeper than that of Haghia Sophia". In fact, the dome is of a diameter comparable to and slightly shallower than that of the building *(see pp74–7)* Sinan had so longed to surpass.

★ **Minarets**
The mosque's four slender minarets tower to a height of 84 m (275 ft). Each one has three balconies. The two northern minarets contain three intertwining staircases, each one leading to a different balcony.

KEY

① **The columns** supporting the arches of the courtyard are made of old marble, plundered from Byzantine architecture.

② **The müezzin mahfili** *(see p40)* still retains original, intricate 16th-century paintwork on its underside. Beneath it is a small fountain.

③ **Mihrab**, cut from Marmara marble

④ **Entrance from Kavaflar Arasta**

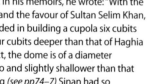

Ablutions Fountain
Intricate, pierced carving decorates the top of the 16-sided open *şadırvan* (ablutions fountain), which stands in the centre of the courtyard. The absence of a canopy helps to retain the uncluttered aspect of the courtyard.

Courtyard Portals
Alternating red and honey-coloured slabs of stone were used to build the striking arches above the courtyard portals. This echoes the decoration of the magnificent arches running around the mosque courtyard itself.

★ Dome
The dome masterfully dominates the entire interior of the mosque. Not even the florid paintwork – the original 16th-century decoration underwent restoration in the 19th century – detracts from its effect.

★ Minbar
Many experts claim that the Selimiye's *minbar*, with its conical tiled cap, is the finest in Turkey. Its lace-like side panels are exquisitely carved.

Main entrance

VISITORS' CHECKLIST

Practical Information
Mimar Sinan Cad, Edirne.
Tel (0284) 213 97 35.
Open daily. **Closed** prayer times.

The Interior
The mosque is the supreme achievement of Islamic architecture. Its octagonal plan allows for a reduction in the size of the buttresses supporting the dome. This permitted extra windows to be incorporated, making the mosque exceptionally light inside.

Sultan's Loge
The imperial loge is supported on green marble columns. They are connected by pointed arches, whose surrounds are adorned with floral İznik tiles *(see p163)*. Unusually, its ornately decorated mihrab contains a shuttered window, which opened on to countryside when the mosque was first built.

❷ Kilyos

27 km (17 miles) N of Istanbul.
🚌 1,665. **D** from Sarıyer.

Kilyos, on the shore of the
Black Sea, is the closest seaside
resort to Istanbul and very
popular. It has a long, sandy
beach and temptingly clear
water, but visitors should not
swim here in the absence of
a lifeguard because there are
dangerous currents be-neath
the calm surface.

A 14th-century Genoese
castle perches on a cliff top
overlooking the town but it
is not open to visitors. The
three ruined towers on the
left of the main approach road
into the village were formerly
water control towers. They
were part of the system that
once brought water here
from the Belgrade Forest.

❸ Belgrade Forest

Belgrad Ormanı

20 km (12 miles) N of Istanbul. 🚌 42,
40S from Taksim to Çayırbaşı, then 42
to Bahçeköy. Park: **Tel** (0212) 226 13
14. **Open** May–Sep: 6am–9pm daily;
Oct–Apr: 7am–7:30pm. 🏊 ♿

One of the most popular
escapes from the city, the
Belgrade Forest is the only
sizeable piece of woodland
in the immediate vicinity of
Istanbul. The forest is made
up of pines, oaks, beeches,
chestnuts and poplars, beneath
which a profusion of wild
flowers grow in spring. Within
it is a huge woodland park, best
visited during the week, since
it attracts hordes of picnickers
at weekends. The main entrance
to the park is near
the village of
Bahçeköy and the
popular Neşetsuyu
picnic area is a half-
hour stroll from
this gate.

The park's other
attractions are the
relics of the dams,
reservoirs and
aqueducts used for
over 1,000 years to
transport spring
water in to Istanbul.

Büyük Bent, a Byzantine dam and reservoir in the Belgrade Forest

The oldest structure, Büyük
Bent (Great Reservoir), dates
back to the early Byzantine era.
It is a pleasant half-hour walk
from Neşetsuyu picnic area.
Meanwhile, the Sultan Mahmut
Dam, outside the park's gate,
is a fine curve of marble which
dates from 1839.

Eğri Kemer (Crooked Aqueduct)
and Uzun Kemer (Long
Aqueduct) are on the D010
road between Levent and
Kısırmandıra and are best reached
by taxi. Both have impressive
rows of arches. The former
probably dates from the 12th
century, while Sinan *(see p93)*
built the latter for Süleyman
the Magnificent *(see p28)*.

❹ Şile

72 km (45 miles) NE of Istanbul.
🚌 25,372. 🚌 from Üsküdar.

The quintessential Black Sea
holiday village of Şile has a
number of fine, sandy beaches
and a black-and-white striped

Şile, a holiday resort and centre for cotton production

cliff-top lighthouse. In antiquity,
the village, then known as
Kalpe, was a port used by ships
sailing east from the Bosphorus.

Şile's lighthouse, the largest in
Turkey, was built by the French
for Sultan Abdül Mecit *(see p32)*
in 1858–9; it can be visited
after dusk. Apart from tourism,
the main industry is now the
production of a coarse cotton
which is made into clothing
and sold in shops along
Üsküdar Caddesi.

❺ Polonezköy

25 km (16 miles) NE of Istanbul.
🚌 500. 🚌 221 from Taksim to
Beykoz, then dolmuş.

Polonezköy was originally called
Adampol, after the Polish Prince
Adam Czartoryski who bought
prime arable land here in 1842
for Polish emigrants settling in
Turkey. Soon after, in 1853, the
Poles formed a band of Cossack
soldiers to fight for Abdül Mecit
I *(see p32)* in the Crimea. After
this he granted them the land
as a tax-free haven.

Polonezköy's rustic charm
is now big business, and a
number of health spas and
villas have sprung up. A couple
of restaurants *(see p207)* still
serve the pork for which the
town was once famous.

The surrounding beech forest,
which offers pleasant walks, has
now been protected from further
development. As part of this scheme, the locals have even waived
their rights to collect firewood.

❻ Princes' Islands

Adalar

12 km (7 miles) SE of Istanbul.
🚉 16,171. 🚢 8–10 crossings daily
from Kabatas to Büyükada. 🛈 (0216)
382 70 71.

The pine-forested Princes'
Islands are a welcome break
from the bustle of the city,
just a short ferry ride southeast
from Istanbul. When leaving
the European side, most ferries
call at the four largest of
the nine islands: Kınalıada,
Burgazada, Heybeliada and
finally Büyükada.

Easily visited on a
day trip, the islands take
their name from a royal
palace built by Justin II
on Büyükada, then
known as Prinkipo
(Island of the Prince)
in 569. During the
Byzantine era the islands
became infamous as a
place of exile. Members
of the royal family and
public figures were
often banished to the
monasteries here.

**Door to the
Monastery of
St George**

In the latter half of the
19th century, with the launch
of a steamboat service from
Istanbul, several wealthy
expatriates settled on the
islands, including Leon Trotsky.
From 1929–33 he lived at 55
Çankaya Caddesi, one of the
finest mansions on Büyükada.

Büyükada, the largest island,
attracts the most visitors with its
sandy beaches and *fin-de-siècle*
elegance. Its 19th-century

atmosphere is enhanced by
the omnipresence of horse-
drawn phaetons. These quaint
carriages are the only form of
public transport on Büyükada
(and Heybeliada) since
motorized transport is banned.
At the top of Büyükada's wooded
southern hill, in a clearing, stands
the Monastery of St George. It
is a 20th-century structure, built
on Byzantine foundations.

To the left of the ferry pier on
Heybeliada, the second largest
island, is the imposing former
Naval High School (Deniz Harp
Okulu), built in 1942. The
island's northern hill is
the stunning location
of the Greek Orthodox
School of Theology
(built in 1841). The school
is now closed but its
library, famous among
Orthodox scholars, is still
open. The island also
has a pleasant beach on
its south coast at Çam
Limanı Köyü.

The smaller
islands of Kınalıada
and Burgazada are less
developed and are peaceful
places to stop off for a meal.

❼ Termal

38 km (24 miles) SE of Istanbul.
🚉 5,018. 🚢 from Kabataş to Yalova.
🛈 Termal-Yalova, (0226) 675 74 00.

This small spa buried deep
in a wooded valley has been
patronized by ruling elites since
the Roman era. Termal is 12 km

Ornamental fountain at Atatürk's former
house at Termal

(7 miles) from the port of Yalova.
Its popularity was revived by
Sultan Abdül Hamit II *(see p35)* in
the early 20th century, when he
refurbished the **Yalova Termal
Baths**, now part of the Ministry
of Health complex of five baths
and four hotels. Facilities include
Turkish baths *(see p69)*, a sauna
and a swimming pool.

Atatürk enjoyed taking the
waters here. The small chalet-
style house he built at the
bottom of the valley, now the
Atatürk Museum, preserves
some of his possessions.

🛁 Yalova Termal Baths
Termal. **Tel** (0226) 675 74 00.
Open 8am–10pm daily.

🏛 Atatürk Museum
Atatürk Köşkü, Termal. **Tel** (0226) 675
70 28. **Open** May–Oct: 9am–5pm Tue,
Wed, Fri–Sun; Nov–Apr: 9:30am–4pm.

The harbour of Burgazada, one of the relaxed and picturesque Princes' Islands near Istanbul

❽ İznik

87 km (54 miles) SE of Istanbul. 🚗 20,100. 🚌 Yeni Mahalle, Yakup Sok, (0224) 757 25 83. 🛈 Belediye Hizmet Binası, Kılıçaslan Cad 97, (0224) 757 10 10. 🛒 Wed. 🎪 İznik Fair (5–10 Oct); Liberation Day (28 Nov).

Grand domed portico fronting the Archaeological Museum

A charming lakeside town, İznik gives little clue now of its former glory as, at one point, the capital of the Byzantine Empire. Its most important legacy dates, however, from the 16th century, when its kilns produced the finest ceramics ever to be made in the Ottoman world.

The town first reached prominence in AD 325, when it was known as Nicaea. In that year Constantine (see p22) chose it as the location of the first Ecumenical Council of the Christian Church. At this meeting, the Nicene Creed, a statement of doctrine on the nature of Christ in relation to God, was formulated.

The Seljuks (see p23) took Nicaea in 1081 and renamed it İznik. It was wrested back from them in 1097 by the First Crusade on behalf of Emperor Alexius I Comnenus. After the capture of Constantinople in 1204 (see p28), the city was capital of the 'Empire of Nicaea', a remaining fragment of the Byzantine Empire, for half a century. In 1331, Orhan Gazi (see p34)

captured İznik and incorporated it into the Ottoman Empire. İznik still retains its original layout. Surrounded by the **city walls**, its two main streets are in the form of a cross, with minor streets running out from them on a grid plan. The walls still more or less delineate the town's boundaries. They were built by the Greek Lysimachus, then ruler of the town, in 300 BC, but they were frequently repaired by both the Byzantines and later the Ottomans. They cover a total of 3 km (2 miles) in circumference and are punctuated by huge gateways. The main one of these, Istanbul Gate (İstanbul Kapısı), is at the city's northern limit. It is decorated with a carved relief of fighting horsemen and is flanked by Byzantine towers.

One of the town's oldest surviving monuments, the ruined **Haghia Sophia Mosque**, stands at the intersection of

Istanbul Gate from within the city walls

the main streets, Atatürk Caddesi and Kılıçaslan Caddesi. The current building was erected after an earthquake in 1065. The remains of a fine mosaic floor, and also of a Deësis, a fresco that depicts Christ, the Virgin and John the Baptist, are protected from damage behind glass screens.

Just off the eastern end of Kılıçaslan Caddesi, the 14th-century **Green Mosque** (Yeşil Cami) is named after the tiles covering its minaret. Unfortunately, the originals have been replaced by modern copies of an inferior quality.

Opposite the mosque, the Kitchen of Lady Nilüfer (Nilüfer Hatun İmareti), one of İznik's loveliest buildings, now houses the town's **Archaeological Museum**. This imaret was set up in 1388 by Nilüfer Hatun, wife of Orhan Gazi, and also served as a hospice for wandering dervishes. Entered through a spacious five-domed portico, the central domed area is flanked by two further domed rooms. The museum has displays of Roman antiquities and glass as well as some examples of Seljuk and Ottoman tiles.

🅲 **Haghia Sophia Mosque**
Müze Cad. **Tel** (0224) 757 12 06.
Open daily (after prayer).

🅲 **Green Mosque**
Müze Sok. **Open** daily (after prayer).

🏛 **Archaeological Museum**
Müze Sok. **Tel** (0224) 757 10 27.
Open by appointment. ♿

Green Mosque, İznik, named after the green tiles adorning its minaret

İznik Ceramics

Towards the end of the 15th century, the town of İznik began to produce large quantities of ceramic bowls, jars and, later, tiles for the many palaces and mosques of Istanbul. Drawing on local deposits of fine clay and inspired by imported Chinese ceramics, the work of the craftsmen of İznik soon excelled both technically and aesthetically. İznik pottery is made from hard, white "fritware", which is akin to porcelain. This style of pottery was invented in Egypt in around the 12th century. It is covered by a bright, white slip (a creamy mixture of clay and water) and a transparent glaze. Early İznik pottery is brilliant blue and white. Later, other colours, especially a vivid red, were added. The potteries of İznik reached their height in the late 16th and early 17th centuries but shortly after fell into decline.

Chinese porcelain, which was imported into Turkey from the 14th century and of which there is a large collection in Topkapı Palace (*see pp56–61*), often inspired the designs used for İznik pottery. During the 16th century, İznik potters produced imitations of pieces of Chinese porcelain such as this copy of a Ming dish.

Rock and wave border pattern

Cobalt blue and white was the striking combination of colours used in early İznik pottery (produced between c.1470–1520). The designs used were a mixture of Chinese and Arabesque, as seen on this tiled panel on the wall of the Circumcision Chamber in Topkapı Palace. Floral patterns and animal motifs were both popular at this time.

Damascus ware was the name erroneously given to ceramics produced at İznik during the first half of the 16th century. They had fantastic floral designs in the new colours of turquoise, sage green and manganese. When such tiles were discovered at Damascus, the similar İznik pots were wrongly assumed to have been made there.

Armenian bole, an iron-rich red colour, began to be used in around 1550, as seen in this 16th-century tankard. New, realistic tulip and other floral designs were also introduced, and İznik ware enjoyed its heyday, which lasted until around 1630.

Miniature depicting potters

Wall tiles were not made in any quantity until the reign of Süleyman the Magnificent (1520–66). Süleyman used İznik tiles to refurbish the Dome of the Rock in Jerusalem. Some of the best examples are seen in Istanbul's mosques, notably in the Süleymaniye (*see pp92–3*), Rüstem Paşa Mosque (*pp90–91*) and, here, in this example from the Blue Mosque (*pp80–81*).

❾ Bursa

Bursa extends in a swathe along the northern foothills of Mount Uludağ *(see p171)*. A settlement known as Prusa was reputedly established here in the 3rd century BC by Prusias I of Bithynia. However, it was the Romans who first spotted the potential of Bursa's mineral springs: today there are an estimated 3,000 baths in the city. In 1326 Bursa became the first capital of the Ottoman Empire, following its capture by Orhan Gazi *(see p27)*.

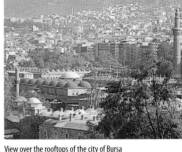

View over the rooftops of the city of Bursa

Today Bursa is a provincial capital whose status as one of Turkey's foremost centres of commerce and industry is evident in its broad boulevards and busy shops and bazaars. Apart from the central market area *(see pp166–7)*, the most frequented sightseeing area is Yeşil, on the eastern side of the Gök River, where the Green Mosque and Green Tomb are the main attractions.

🄲 Yıldırım Beyazıt Mosque

Yıldırım Beyazıt Camii Yıldırım Cad.
Open daily.

This mosque is named after Beyazıt I *(see p34)*, whose nickname was "Yıldırım", meaning "thunderbolt". This referred to the speed with which he reacted to his enemies. Built in 1389, just after Beyazıt became sultan, the mosque at first doubled as a lodge for Sufi dervishes *(see p106)*. It has a lovely portico with five domed bays.

Inside, the interior court (a covered "courtyard" in Bursa mosques, which prefigures the open courtyards preferred by later Ottoman architects) and prayer hall are divided by an impressive arch. This rises from two mihrab-like niches. The walls of the prayer hall itself are adorned with several bold and attractive pieces of calligraphic design *(see p97)*.

🄱 Green Tomb

Yeşil Türbe Yeşil Cad. **Open** daily.
🄰 donation.

The tomb of Mehmet I *(see p32)*, which stands elevated above the mosque among tall cypress trees, is one of the city's most prominent landmarks. It was built between 1414 and 1421. The tomb is much closer to the Seljuk *(see p23)* style of architecture than Classical Ottoman. Its exterior is covered in green tiles, although these are mainly 19th-century replacements for the original faïence. However, a few older tiles survive around the entrance portal.

The interior, entered through a pair of superbly carved wooden doors, is simply dazzling. The space is small and the ornamentation, covering a relatively large surface area, is breathtaking in its depth of colour and detail. The mihrab has especially intricate tile panels, including a representation of a mosque lamp hanging from a gold chain between two candles.

The sultan's magnificent sarcophagus is covered in exquisite tiles and adorned by a long Koranic inscription. Nearby sarcophagi contain the remains of his sons, daughters and nursemaid.

🄲 Green Mosque

Yeşil Cami Yeşil Cad. **Open** daily.
Bursa's most famous monument was commissioned by Mehmet I in 1412, but it remained unfinished at his death in 1421 and still lacks a portico. Nevertheless, it is the finest Ottoman mosque built before the conquest of Constantinople *(see p28)*.

The main portal is tall and elegant, with an intricately carved canopy. It opens into the entrance hall. Beyond this is an interior court, with a carved fountain at its centre. A flight of three steps leads up from here into the prayer hall. On either side of the steps are niches where worshippers once left their shoes *(see p41)*. Above the entrance to the court is the sultan's loge, resplendent in richly patterned tiles created using the *cuerda seca* technique. They are in beautiful greens, blues and yellows, with threads of gold which were added after firing. The tiling of the prayer hall was carried out by Ali İbn İlyas Ali, who learnt his art in Samarkand. It was the first

The Green Tomb and Green Mosque, Bursa's most distinctive monuments

time that tiles were used extensively in an Ottoman mosque and set a precedent for the later widespread use of İznik tiles *(see p163)*. The tiles covering the walls of the prayer hall, which is well lit by floor-level windows, are simple, green and hexagonal. Against this plain backdrop, the effect of the mihrab is especially glorious. Predominantly turquoise, deep blue and white, with touches of gold, the mihrab's tiles depict flowers, leaves, arabesques and geometric patterns. The mosque's exterior was also once clad in tiles, but they have since disappeared.

🏛 Museum of Turkish and Islamic Arts

Türk ve İslam Eserleri Müzesi Yeşil Cad. **Tel** (0224) 327 76 79. **Open** 10am–5pm Tue–Sun. 🖼

This museum is housed in a fine Ottoman building, the former *medrese (see p40)* of the Green Mosque. A colonnade surrounds its courtyard on three sides and the cells leading off from it, formerly used by the students, are now exhibition galleries. At the far end of the

VISITORS' CHECKLIST

Practical Information
90 km (60 miles) S of Istanbul. 🚆 1,995,000. 🚌 Atatürk Cad; Osman Gazi Cad. 🛈 Ulucami Parkı, Orhangazi Altgeçidi, No. 1 (0224) 220 18 48. 🎪 Textiles Fair (mid-Apr); Bursa Festival (12 Jun–12 Jul).

Transport
✈ 20 km (12 miles) NW. 🚌 Kıbrıs Şehitler Cad, (0224) 261 54 00.

courtyard is the large, domed hall which was originally the main classroom.

Exhibits dating from the 12th–20th centuries include Seljuk and Ottoman ceramics, elaborately decorated Korans and costumes ranging from linen dervish robes to ornate wedding gowns. A display on Turkish baths *(see p69)* features embroidered towels and exotic high-heeled silver bath clogs. There is also a recreated setting of a traditional circumcision room, complete with a four-poster bed.

Façade of the Museum of Turkish and Islamic Arts

Bursa City Centre

① Yıldırım Beyazıt Mosque
② Green Tomb
③ Green Mosque
④ Museum of Turkish and Islamic Arts
⑤ Tophane Citadel
⑥ Osman Gazi Tomb
⑦ Alaeddin Mosque
⑧ Muradiye Mosque
⑨ Hüsnü Züber House
⑩ Archaeological Museum

Key

Street-by-Street area
See pp166–7

Bursa: The Market Area

Bursa's central market area is a warren of streets and ancient Ottoman courtyards (hans). The area is still central to Bursa's commercial activity and is a good place to experience the life of the city. Here too you can buy the local fabrics for which the town is famous, particularly handmade lace, towelling and silk. The silkworm was introduced to the Byzantine Empire in the 6th century and there is still a brisk trade in silk cocoons carried out in Koza Han all year round. Among the many other items on sale today are the lovely hand-painted, camel-skin Karagöz puppets *(see p170)*.

★ **Covered Bazaar**
The great bazaar, built by Mehmet I in the 15th century, consists of a long hall with domed bays, adjoining by a high, vaulted hall. The Bedesten is home to jewellers' shops.

★ **The Great Mosque**
A three-tiered ablutions fountain stands beneath the central dome of this monumental mosque, which was erected in 1396–9.

Şengül
Hamamı
Turkish
baths

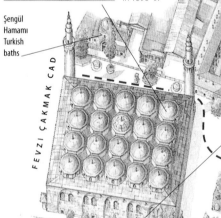

FEVZI ÇAKMAK CAD

KOZA PARKI

ATATÜRK CAD

Bey Han (also called Emir Han) was built as part of the Orhan Gazi Mosque complex, to provide revenue for the mosque's upkeep.

Cafés

The Bey Hamamı
(1339) is the oldest Turkish baths building in the world. It now houses workshops.

Koza Park
The gardens in front of Koza Han, with their fountains, benches and shaded café tables, are a popular meeting place for locals and visitors throughout the day.

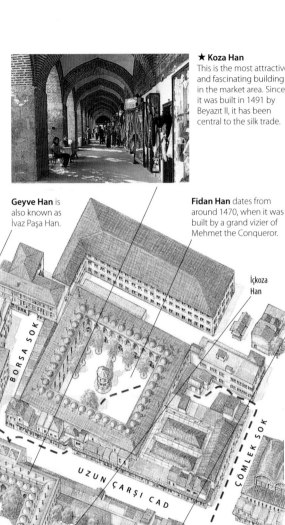

★ Koza Han
This is the most attractive and fascinating building in the market area. Since it was built in 1491 by Beyazıt II, it has been central to the silk trade.

Flower Market
The numerous bunches of flowers for sale in the streets around the town hall make a picturesque sight in the midst of Bursa's bustling market area.

Geyve Han is also known as İvaz Paşa Han.

Fidan Han dates from around 1470, when it was built by a grand vizier of Mehmet the Conqueror.

İçkoza Han

BORSA SOK

UZUN ÇARŞI CAD

ÇÖMLEK SOK

0 metres   40
0 yards   40

The Belediye, Bursa's town hall, is a Swiss chalet-style, half-timbered building that forms a surprising landmark in the centre of the town.

BELEDIYE CAD

Orhan Gazi Mosque
Built in 1339, just 13 years after the Ottoman conquest of Bursa, this mosque is the oldest of the city's imperial mosques.

Key
— Suggested route

Bursa: Tophane and Muradiye

Tophane, the most ancient part of Bursa, is distinguished by its clocktower which stands on top of a hill. This area was formerly the site of the citadel and is bounded by what remains of the original Byzantine walls. It is also known as Hisar, which means "fortress" in Turkish. If you continue westwards for 2 km (1mile), crossing the Cilimboz River, you come to the historic district of Muradiye. The 15th-century Muradiye Mosque, from which this suburb takes its name, is one of the most impressive royal mosque and tomb complexes in the city.

before his father died. Orhan brought his father's body to be buried in the baptistry of a converted church and he himself was later buried in the nave. The tombs that can be seen today date from 1868. They were rebuilt after the destruction of the church and the original tombs in an earthquake in 1855. Fragments of the church's mosaic floor survive inside the tomb of Orhan Gazi.

Exploring Tophane

Tophane's northern limit is marked by the best preserved section of the citadel walls, built on to an outcrop of rock. At the top is a pleasant park filled with cafés, which also contains the imposing clocktower and the tombs of the founders of the Ottoman dynasty. From here you can look down on the lower part of Tophane, where archetypal Ottoman houses still line many of the twisting streets. Pınarbaşı Kapısı, at Tophane's southern point, is the gate through which Orhan Gazi entered Bursa in 1326 (see p27).

🏰 Tophane Citadel

Hisar
Osman Gazi Cad. **Open** daily. 🚻
The citadel walls can be viewed from a set of steps which lead uphill from the intersection of Cemal Nadir Caddesi and Atatürk Caddesi. These steps end at the tea gardens above. The citadel fell into Turkish hands when Orhan Gazi's troops broke through its walls. Later, he built a wooden palace inside the citadel and had the old Byzantine ramparts refortified. The walls had until this era delimited the entire

circumference of the ancient city. However, Orhan began to encourage Bursa's expansion and developed the present-day commercial heart of the city further to the east.

South of Hastalaryurdu Caddesi is an area notable for its old Ottoman houses (see p63). Most of these have over-hanging upper storeys. They consist of a timber frame filled in with adobe and plastered over, then painted in bright colours. Kaleiçi Sokağı, which can be reached down Karadut Sokağı from Hastalaryurdu Caddesi, is one of the best streets of such houses.

🏛 Tombs of Osman and Orhan Gazi

Osman & Orhan Gazi Türbeleri. Ulu Cami Cad. **Open** daily. 🎁 donation.
Osman Gazi began the process of Ottoman expansion in the 13th century (see p27) and attempted to capture Bursa. But it was his son, Orhan, who took the city just

Tomb of Osman Gazi, the first great Ottoman leader

🅒 Alaeddin Mosque

Alaeddin Camii
Alaeddin Mahallesi.
Open prayer times only. 🖂
Further exploration in the Tophane area reveals the Alaeddin Mosque, the oldest in Bursa, built within 10 years of the city's conquest. It is in the form of a simple domed square, fronted by a portico of four Byzantine columns with capitals. The mosque was commissioned by Alaeddin Bey, brother of and vizier (see p41) to Orhan Gazi.

Exploring Muradiye

Muradiye is a leafy, largely residential district. Close to the Muradiye Mosque are the Hüsnü Züber House and the Ottoman House, two fine examples of traditional Turkish homes. To the north is a park, among the attractions of which are a boating lake and the Archaeological Museum.

🅒 Muradiye Mosque

Muradiye Külliyesi Murat II Cad.
Open daily. 🎁 donation.
This mosque complex was built by Murat II, father of Mehmet the Conqueror (see p28), in the early 15th century. The mosque itself is preceded by a graceful domed portico. Its wooden door is finely carved and the interior decorated with early İznik tiles (see p163). The medrese, beside the mosque, now serves as a dispensary.

Popular café in the park above the ancient citadel walls in Tophane

Octagonal tomb of Mustafa in the grounds of Muradiye Mosque

It is a perfectly square building, with cells surrounding a central garden courtyard. Its *dershane*, or main classroom, is richly tiled and adorned with an ornate brickwork façade.

The mosque garden, with its cypresses, well-tended flower beds and fountains, is one of Bursa's most tranquil retreats. Murat II was the last Ottoman sultan to be buried in Bursa and his mausoleum, standing in the garden beside the mosque and *medrese*, was completed in 1437. His earth-filled sarcophagus lies beneath an opening in the roof. The eaves above the tomb's 16th-century porch still retain their original painted decoration. There are 11 other tombs in the garden, several of which were built for murdered princes. One such is the tomb of Mustafa, a son of Süleyman the

Magnificent, who was disposed of to clear the way for his younger brother, Selim II, "the Sot" (see p78). According to an inscription, Selim had the octagonal mausoleum built for his brother. The interior is decorated with some particularly beautiful İznik tile panels depicting carnations, tulips and hyacinths. The tiles date from the best İznik period, the late 16th century.

🞀 Hüsnü Züber House

Hüsnü Züber Evi, Yaşayan Müze Uzunyol Sok 3, Muradiye. **Tel** (0224) 221 35 42. **Open** 10am–midday, 1–5pm Tue–Sun. 🞂 🞀 Ottoman House: **Tel** (0224) 285 48 13. **Open** 10am–5pm Tue–Sun.

Among the numerous well-preserved houses in the Muradiye district is the Hüsnü Züber House. This 150-year-old mansion has been opened as a museum by its present owner, the artist Hüsnü Züber. It was originally a guest house for visiting dignitaries, later becoming the Russian Consulate and, most recently, a private residence. The house is an interesting example of vernacular architecture. The upper storey projects over the street in the traditional manner of Ottoman houses (see p65). Overlooking the interior courtyard, which has rooms arranged around it

on three sides, there is a loggia. Originally this would have been open, but it is now glazed. Meanwhile, inside the house, the decorative wooden ceilings (some with hand-painted borders) are particularly attractive.

Hüsnü Züber's private collection of interesting carved wooden objects is now displayed here. These include spoons, musical instruments and even farming utensils. They are all decorated with Anatolian motifs by a unique technique of engraving by burning known as pyrogravure.

The 18th-century **Ottoman House** (Osmanlı Evi) stands on the square in front of the Muradiye Mosque. The upper storey of this fine house is adorned with elaborately patterned brickwork. Shutters and grilles hide the windows.

Hüsnü Züber House, dating from the mid-19th century

🞀 Archaeological Museum

Arkeoloji Müzesi
Kültür Parkı. **Tel** (0224) 234 49 18. **Open** 10am–5pm Tue–Sun. 🞂

Finds dating from the third millennium BC up to the Ottoman conquest of Bursa are collected in this museum. In the first hall there are clasps, vessels and an inscription from the Phrygian period. Other exhibits include Roman and Hellenistic jewellery and ceramics, a number of Roman statues of Cybele, goddess of nature, and a Roman bronze of the god Apollo with strange, lifelike eyes. There are also displays of Byzantine religious objects and coins.

Muradiye Mosque, constructed by Murat II

Bursa: Çekirge

With a name which translates literally as "Realm of the Crickets", Çekirge still earns Bursa the tag of yeşil, or "green", by which it is known in Turkey. This leafy western spa suburb of the city has attracted visitors to its mineral springs since Roman times. In the 6th century the Emperor Justinian (see p22) built a bathhouse here and his wife Theodora later arrived with a retinue of 4,000. Çekirge is also the location of most of the city's finest hotels and the area's hillside setting affords some spectacular views.

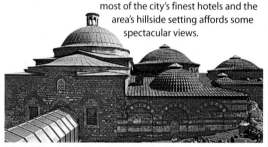
Çekirge's Old Spa, dating back to the 14th-century reign of Murat I

❶ New Spa

Yeni Kaplıca
Mudanya Yolu 6. **Tel** (0224) 236 69 68.
Open daily 5am–midnight.

Despite their name, the New Spa baths have a substantial pedigree. They were rebuilt in 1552 by Rüstem Paşa, grand vizier (see p31) to Süleyman the Magnificent (see p28). The sultan is said to have ordered their rebuilding in gratitude after his recovery from gout when bathing in the Byzantine baths that stood on this site.

The central pool is surrounded with bays adorned with beautiful but damaged İznik tiles (see p163). They are not open to women. Within the same complex, however, there are two other baths: the modern Kaynarca baths which is for women and the Karamustafa baths for couples.

🏨 Çelik Palas Hotel

Çelik Palas Otel Çekirge Cad 79.
Tel (0224) 233 38 00.

This five-star hotel stands on one of Bursa's main thoroughfares. Built in 1933, it is the city's oldest, most prestigious spa hotel. Atatürk (see pp32–3) frequented its baths. Open to both sexes, their centrepiece is an attractive circular pool in a domed marble room.

❷ Old Spa

Eski Kaplıca Hotel Kervansaray,
Çekirge Meydanı, Kervansaray.
Tel (0224) 233 93 00.
Open 8am–10:30pm daily.

The Old Spa baths were established by Murat I in the late 14th century and renovated in 1512, during the reign of Beyazıt II. Remnants of an earlier building, said to date from the reign of Emperor Justinian (see p22), are also visible. These include some Byzantine columns and capitals in the hararet (steam room) of the men's section (see p69). You enter the baths through the Kervansaray Termal Hotel. Spring water, said to cure skin diseases and rheumatism, bubbles into the central pool of both the men's and women's sections at 45 °C (113 °F). The women's baths are not as old or grand, but are still the most attractive women-only ones in Bursa.

❸ Murat I Hüdavendigar Mosque

Murat I Hüdavendigar Camii
I. Murat Cad, Çekirge. **Open** daily.

Bursa's most unusual mosque was built for Murat I, self-styled Hüdavendigar, meaning "Creator of the Universe", in 1385. It is unlike any other mosque in the Ottoman world: its prayer hall is on the ground floor, with the medrese built around a second storey.

The façade looks more like that of a palace than a mosque, with a five-arched portico surmounted by a colonnade. This colonnade in turn has five sets of double-arched windows divided by Byzantine columns. Inside, the domed court and prayer hall rise through both storeys. The upper storey colonnade leads to the cells of the medrese.

On this level, passageways lead around both sides of the mosque to a mysterious room, located over the mihrab, whose original purpose is unknown.

Karagöz Shadow Puppets

Suspended above Çekirge Caddesi is an imposing monument to the town's two famous scapegoats, Karagöz and Hacıvat. According to legend, these local clowns were executed in the 14th century for distracting their fellow workers while building the Orhan Gazi Mosque (see p167). It is said that Sultan Orhan (see p34) created a shadow play about them in remorse.

In fact, shadow puppet theatre arrived in Turkey later and is thought to have originated in Southeast Asia. Selim I is reported to have brought it back to Istanbul after his Egyptian campaign in 1517. The camel-skin puppets are 35–40 cm (14–16 in) high, brightly dyed and oiled to aid translucency. They are still made today and can be purchased in an antique shop in the Bedesten run by Şinasi Çelikkol, who also occasionally puts on shows.

Cadı, a witch in the Karagöz puppet shows

Uludağ National Park, a popular ski resort in winter

❿ Uludağ National Park
Uludağ Milli Parkı

100 km (60 miles) S of Istanbul.
Tel (0224) 283 21 97. 🚠 Teleferik to
Sarıalan, then dolmuş. **Open** daily.
🚗 only for vehicles.

One of a number of Turkish
mountains to claim the title
of Mount Olympus, Uludağ
was believed by the Bithynians
(of northwest Asia Minor) to be
the home of the gods. In the
Byzantine era, it was home to
several monastic orders. After
the Ottoman conquest of Bursa,
Muslim dervishes *(see p106)*
moved into their abandoned
monasteries. Nowadays, however, no traces of Uludağ's former
religious communities remain.

A visit to Uludağ National Park
is especially enjoyable in spring
or summer, when its alpine
heights are relatively cool and it
becomes a popular picnic area.
The park includes 109.26 sq km
(258.6 sq miles) of woodland.
As you ascend, the deciduous
beech, oak and hazel gradually
give way to juniper and aspen,
and finally to dwarf junipers. In
spring, hyacinths and crocuses
blanket the wooded slopes.

In winter, Uludağ is
transformed into Turkey's
most fashionable ski resort.
The industry centres on the
Oteller region, which has
good alpine-style hotels.

Osman Gazi *(see p27)* is
supposed to have founded
seven villages for his seven
sons and their brides in the
Bursa region. **Cumalıkızık**,

on the lower slopes of Uludağ,
is the most perfectly preserved
of the five surviving villages and
is now registered as a national
monument. Among its houses
are many 13th century semi-
timbered buildings. The village
can be reached by minibus
from Bursa.

⓫ Bird Paradise National Park
Kuşcenneti Milli Parkı

115 km (70 miles) SW of Istanbul.
Tel (0266) 735 54 22. 🅳 from
Bandırma. **Open** 8am–8pm daily. ♿

An estimated 255 species of
birds visit Bird Paradise National
Park at the edge of Kuş Gölü, the
lake formerly known as Manyas
Gölü. Located on the great
migratory paths between Europe
and Asia, the park is a happy
combination of plant cover,
reed beds and includes a lake,
which supports at least 20
species of fish.

At the entrance to the park,
there is a small museum with
displays about various birds.

Spoonbill wading in the lake at
Bird Paradise National Park

Binoculars are provided at the
desk and visitors make their way
to an observation tower.

Two main groups of birds visit
the lake: those that come here
to breed (March–July), and those
which pass by during migration,
either heading south (November)
or north (April–May). Among
the numerous different birds
that breed around the lake are
the endangered Dalmatian
pelican, the great crested grebe,
cormorants, herons, bitterns and
spoonbills. The migratory birds,
which can be seen in spring
and autumn, include storks,
cranes, pelicans and birds of
prey such as sparrowhawks
and spotted eagles.

Sandy beach on Avşa, the most popular of
the Marmara Islands

⓬ Marmara Islands
Marmara Adaları

120 km (75 miles) SW of Istanbul.
🚢 from Yenikapı. 🛈 Neyire Sıtkı Cad
31/3, Erdek, (0266) 835 11 69.

This beautiful archipelago
in the Sea of Marmara is a
popular destination with Turkish
holiday-makers, particularly
with residents of Istanbul.

The loveliest of the islands is
Avşa, whose sandy beaches and
regular summer ferry service
make it popular with Turks and,
increasingly, foreign tourists.
The ferry arrives at Türkeli on
the west coast. Transport to the
most popular beach, at Mavi
Koy, is by a tractor-pulled train.

Marmara, the largest
island, has one beach, north
of Marmara village at Çınarlı.
It is famous for producing the
prized Proconnesian marble.

⑬ The Dardanelles
Çanakkale Boğazı

200 km (125 miles) SW of Istanbul.
🚢 Çanakkale–Eceabat car ferry.
🚌 Çanakkale. ℹ️ Çanakkale İskele
Meydanı 27, (0286) 217 11 87.

Named after Dardanus, an ancient king of Çanakkale, the Dardanelles are the straits that link the Aegean Sea to the Sea of Marmara, and which separate European Turkey from Asia. Some 40 km (25 miles) long and narrowing to little more than a kilometre (half a mile) wide, they are steeped in legend and have been of strategic importance for thousands of years. In modern times they are probably best known as the setting for a disastrous Allied campaign during World War I.

The classical name for this channel of water was the Hellespont. According to legend, the Greek goddess Helle fell into the straits from the back of a golden winged ram. In another tale, the lovelorn Leander swam nightly across the Hellespont to meet his lover, Hero, until one night he drowned. The English Romantic poet Byron swam across the straits in 1810, in emulation of Leander, and remarked on the hazardous nature of the currents.

Çanakkale, the old town at the mouth of the Dardanelles, has two museums. The **Military and Naval Museum** is a short walk from the ferry docks. Its collection includes a pocket

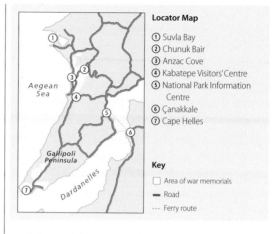

Locator Map

① Suvla Bay
② Chunuk Bair
③ Anzac Cove
④ Kabatepe Visitors' Centre
⑤ National Park Information Centre
⑥ Çanakkale
⑦ Cape Helles

Aegean Sea

Gallipoli Peninsula

Dardanelles

Key

☐ Area of war memorials
▬ Road
--- Ferry route

watch that saved the life of Atatürk (see pp32–3) when he was hit by shrapnel. The **Archaeological Museum**, south of the town centre, has exhibits from ancient Troy.

To the west is the beautiful **Gallipoli** (Gelibolu) **Peninsula**. Part of this land is a national park, with an information centre near Eceabat. The peninsula, which is now quite tranquil, was the scene of horrific battles that took place in 1915. The objectives of the Allied forces' invasion of Gallipoli were to capture Istanbul, force Turkey into submission and open a strategic supply route to Russia. The campaign began on 25 April 1915 with the landings of British and French troops at **Cape Helles**, and the Anzacs (Australian and New Zealand forces) at what they thought was the beach at Kabatepe. But currents had swept the Anzac force about 1.5 km (1 mile) to the north, to a place now known as **Anzac Cove**, near Arı Burnu. Here the soldiers were faced with unknown and tough terrain, including a cliff.

The Turks managed to retain the high ground of **Chunuk Bair**. The battle here lasted three days, during which 28,000 men were

Mehmetcik Memorial near Anzac Cove

killed. When the Allied forces failed to make headway, more British troops landed at **Suvla Bay** on 6 August. This new offensive might have been successful, but Allied intelligence continually underestimated the Turks and the difficult ground. The terrible slaughter of deadlocked trench warfare continued until the Allies were finally evacuated on 19 December. More than 500,000 Allied and Turkish troops lost their lives and the whole peninsula is scattered with battlefield sites and war memorials. The best place to begin a tour of the war memorials and cemeteries is at the **Kabatepe Visitors' Centre**, which houses a small collection of memorabilia including weapons, uniforms and soldiers' poignant letters home. North of here, near Anzac Cove, are several cemeteries and monuments. Chunuk Bair, now a peaceful pine grove above the beaches, has a memorial to the New Zealanders who died and some reconstructed Turkish trenches. The British Memorial is at Cape Helles, on the peninsula's tip. Further east along the coast stand both the French Memorial and the vast Çanakkale Şehitleri

The Çanakkale Şehitleri Memorial, honouring the Turkish dead

Memorial to the Turks who died defending Gallipoli.

🏛 Military Museum

Çimenlik Kalesi, Çanakkale. **Tel** (0286) 213 17 30. **Open** 9am–noon, 1:30–5:30pm Tue, Wed & Fri–Sun. 🖼

🏛 Archaeological Museum

Atatürk Cad, Çanakkale. **Tel** (0286) 217 67 40. **Open** 8:30am–5:30pm. **Closed** Mon. 🖼

ℹ National Park Information Centre

Near Eceabat. **Tel** (0286) 814 11 28. **Open** 9am–6pm Mon–Fri. Park: **Open** daily. 🖼

ℹ Kabatepe Visitors' Centre

Near Kabatepe. **Tel** (0286) 814 12 97. **Open** 9am–6pm daily. 🖼

⑭ Troy

Truva

350 km (220 miles) SW of Istanbul. 🚌 from Çanakkale. ℹ Çanakkale İskele Meydanı 27, (0286) 217 11 87. **Open** 8am–7pm daily (Nov–Apr: until 5pm). 🖼

In Homer's epic poem, the *Iliad*, the city of Troy is besieged by the Greeks for ten years. For centuries Troy was assumed by many to be as mythical as Achilles, Hector and the other heroes in the tale. But a handful of 19th-century archaeologists were convinced that Homer had based his story on the

Model of the legendary wooden horse at Troy

events that happened to a real city and that traces of it could be found by searching near the Dardanelles. In 1865 British Consul Frank Calvert began investigating some ruins in Hisarlık. This interested the German archaeologist Heinrich Schliemann who soon found evidence of an ancient city resembling the layout of Homer's Troy. Over the last hundred years most historians have come to accept that this city must at least have inspired

Homer, and was possibly even called Troy and besieged at the time specified in the story.

The settlement mound in fact has nine distinct levels (labelled Troy I–IX) representing 3,000 years of habitation. Sadly, the remains are sparse, and it takes some imagination to evoke an image of a city. Many structures were made of mud bricks and obviously levelled before new settlements were built on top.

The city Homer refers to is probably Troy VI (1800–1250 BC), while the Greek and Roman levels, when the city was known as Ilion, are Troy VIII (700–300 BC) and Troy IX (300 BC–AD 1) respectively.

What has survived includes a defence wall, palaces and houses from various periods, two sanctuaries (probably 8th century BC) and a Roman theatre. The grandest dwelling is the Pillar House, near the southern gate. Some believe this is the Palace of King Priam mentioned in the *Iliad*.

More conspicuous is a re-creation of the wooden horse, inside which a small group of the Greeks supposedly hid. There is also a visitors' centre with a video and a scale model of the site.

Schliemann's Search for Ancient Troy

Heinrich Schliemann used a fortune amassed in business to realize his life-long dream of discovering ancient Troy. He began

Schliemann's wife wearing some of the excavated treasure

excavating some likely sites in the 1860s and started on the ruins at Hisarlık in 1870. An amateur, Schliemann drove a great trench through the mound, destroying some walls in his haste. He soon claimed to have found Troy, though he knew not all his findings pointed to this. His greatest find – a hoard of gold and silver jewellery that he smuggled to Germany, calling it "Priam's Treasure" *(see p67)* – pre-dates Homer's Troy by 1,000 years. Some of the treasure disappeared after World War II only to reappear spectacularly in Moscow in August 1994.

THREE GUIDED WALKS

With its frenetic atmosphere, traditional cafés at almost every corner and historic sights from centuries of different rulers, Istanbul is a wonderful city for walkers.

On the following five pages are routes for three walks that take you through three different areas of Istanbul. They will take you past many of the most interesting sights. The areas covered range from the old Greek and Jewish neighbourhoods of Balat and Fener, where historic synagogues can still be seen amid traditional tripe shops, to the wonderful aromas of coffee, spices and fresh fish permeating the air in the Galata region of the city. For a little more elegance, a stroll along İstiklâl Caddesi will confirm why this area of Istanbul has the reputation for celebrating its European side, rather than Asian, while the Istanbul Modern Art Museum (see p109) is the finest venue in the city for contemporary art. All the walks are intended to be done at a leisurely pace, and there are plenty of suggestions for refreshment stops along each route. In addition to these walks, each of the four areas of Istanbul described in the Area-by-Area section of this book has a walk on its Street-by-Street map.

CHOOSING A WALK

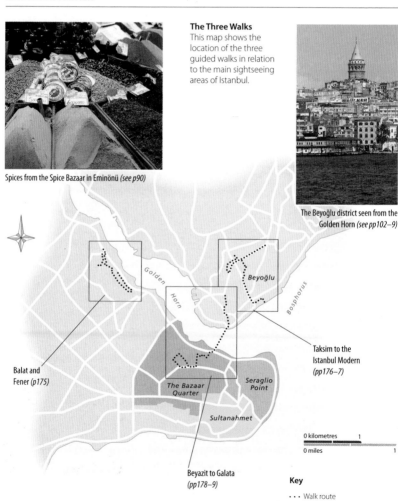

Spices from the Spice Bazaar in Eminönü (see p90)

The Three Walks
This map shows the location of the three guided walks in relation to the main sightseeing areas of Istanbul.

The Beyoğlu district seen from the Golden Horn (see pp102–9)

Balat and Fener (p175)

Beyazit to Galata (pp178–9)

Taksim to the Istanbul Modern (pp176–7)

Beyoğlu

Seraglio Point

The Bazaar Quarter

Sultanahmet

Golden Horn

Bosphorus

0 kilometres 1
0 miles 1

Key
• • • Walk route

A 45-Minute Walk in Balat and Fener

The Balat and Fener neighbourhoods epitomize the cultural diversity and tolerance that was the hallmark of the Ottomans. Fener was predominantly a Greek area, while Balat was Jewish, and this walk guides you around the ancient churches, synagogues, Turkish baths and mosques in the atmospheric back streets. They may have seen better days, but a rejuvenation scheme is putting life back into this picturesque locality.

Tips for Walkers

Starting point: Ahrida Synagogue.
Length: 1.5 km (1 mile).
Getting there: From Eminönü bus terminus, take No 99 or any bus displaying Eyüp or Ayvansaray. Ask the driver to let you off at Balat. There are also ferry points at Fener and Balat.
Stopping-off points: Hotel Daphnis ⑬ is a good spot to stop for a meal.

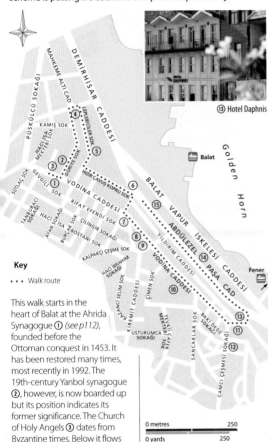

⑬ Hotel Daphnis

Key

• • • Walk route

This walk starts in the heart of Balat at the Ahrida Synagogue ① (see p112), founded before the Ottoman conquest in 1453. It has been restored many times, most recently in 1992. The 19th-century Yanbol synagogue ②, however, is now boarded up but its position indicates its former significance. The Church of Holy Angels ③ dates from Byzantine times. Below it flows a sacred spring and every 14 September supplicants of all religions gather here to pray for cures from their ailments.

Walk to Leblebiciler Sokak and nearby is Afilli Cezve ④, a small café popular for its Turkish coffee. Further along is Agora ⑤, one of Istanbul's nicest taverns (*meyhane*). Turn left on Hızır Çavuş Köprü Sokak and continue down this road until you reach Köfteci Arnavut ⑥. This traditional meatball restaurant has been serving its loyal customers since 1947.

0 metres 250
0 yards 250

Turn right and then left on to Vodina Caddesi and on your right is Tahtalı Minare Hamam ⑦, one of the oldest Turkish baths in the city, dating from the 1500s. Note the boiler room chimney on the roof. A short distance further on your right is Tahtalı Minare Mosque ⑧, built by Fatih Sultan Mehmet II in 1458. Next door is the Tomb of Hazreti Hüseyin Sadık ⑨, who was buried as a *gazi* (warrior of the faith) in the 1450s. Continue down the road and you will be able to see the cross of Aya Yorgi Metokhi Church ⑩ (no public access) above its high wall.

At the end of the road turn left and on the right is the Greek Orthodox Patriarchate ⑪ (see p113), seat of the Greek church since 1601. Look at the red-brick building on the ramparts above. This is the Fener Greek Boys High School ⑫, established in Byzantine times. On the left is the Hotel Daphnis ⑬. Turn left onto Abdülezel Paşa Caddesi and the stone building on your right is the Women's Library ⑭, the city's sole female-only information centre. Further up is the Church of St Stephen of the Bulgars ⑮ (see p112). From here the Fener ferry point will take you back to the city centre.

The narrow, winding back streets of the Balat district

For map symbols *see back flap*

A 90-Minute Walk from Taksim Square to the Istanbul Modern Art Museum

It was in the Pera district that Constantinople's cosmopolitan population lived and worked in the 19th century, where the embassies and palatial residences mirrored the lifestyle of Topkapı Palace, on the opposite side of the Golden Horn. Once known as the "Paris of the East", life centred on the main street of Pera, today's İstiklâl Caddesi. Even today the Avrupa Pasajı and Balık Pazar markets seem wistfully unchanged, especially when contrasted with the remarkable Pera Museum and the sophisticated Istanbul Modern Art Museum.

④ A Çiçek Pasajı restaurant

⑥ Avrupa Pasajı bazaar

Along İstiklâl Caddesi

Begin the walk in Taksim Square ① at the Independence Monument, completed by Pietro Canonica in 1928, that depicts Atatürk with his political contemporaries. Before following the vintage tram line down İstiklâl Caddesi, have a look at the octagonal stone tower, known as the Maksem ②, on the corner of Taksim Caddesi. Dating from 1832, it was once used as a reservoir – you can still see carved bird houses and remains of a fountain. It now houses an art gallery. On your right is the French Cultural Centre, while on the left, further down at No. 83 is a traditional sweet shop, Hacı Bekir, dating from 1777. Saray Muhallebicisi ③ is perfect for a coffee and one of the renowned pastries.

Market shopping

Pass Yeşilçam Sokak, the home of Turkish cinema, and at Şarabi Wine House, turn into the former flower market, Çiçek

Pasajı ④, built by Italian architect Michel Capello in 1856, and now filled with restaurants. At Stop Restaurant, veer left then right on Sahne Sokak, which forms the backbone of the Fish Market, or Balık Pazar ⑤.

Return along Sahne Sokak and stroll down the arcaded Hall of Mirrors, or Avrupa Pasajı ⑥ on the right. The Neo-Renaissance interior, with marble floors and classical statues, was once lit by gas lamps and mirrors amplified the light.

Turn right and then left onto Meşrutiyet Caddesi and follow the road around to the left with the British Consulate General ⑦ on your right. Follow this street down, past TRT (Turkish Radio and Television) and the celebrated but now faded Grand Hotel de Londres

until you reach the exquisite Pera Museum ⑧ (once the Bristol Hotel), where the philanthropic Suna and İnan Kiraç Foundation exhibits its art collection and Turkish tiles.

⑯ Dome of the Kılıç Ali Paşa Mosque

Historic buildings

Walk through the Odakule Arkade and turn left on to İstiklâl Caddesi. Opposite the Galatasary High School is the Old Beyoğlu Post Office ⑨. A campaign to keep it open was unsuccessful and the Baroque marble building was closed in 1998. Originally a wealthy merchant's residence, it still has an ornamental fountain in the penthouse.

Take the second right onto Tornacıbaşı Sokak, which

⑳ Istanbul Modern Art Museum

takes you past the Greek Orthodox school, Zografyon ⑩ on the left. In front of you is Galatasaray Hamamı ⑪, Turkish baths built in 1481 and in use ever since.

Take the steep cobbled street that descends beside the Turkish baths, Çapanoğlu Sokak, which becomes a staircase at the bottom. Turn right onto Harbiye Sokak and you will reach French Street, or Fransız Sokağı ⑫ on the left, where an elegant French ambience meets classy Beyoğlu. Enjoy lunch or a glass of wine at one of the French-style cafés.

Refreshed, continue along French Street and at the end turn right onto Boğazkesen Caddesi and continue

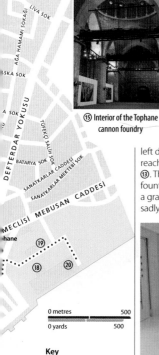

⑮ Interior of the Tophane cannon foundry

left down the hill until you reach Tomtom Kaptan Mosque ⑬. The pretty 17th-century fountain here, which was once a grand landmark, is now sadly neglected.

Tips for Walkers

Starting point: Taksim Square.
Length: 2.5 km (1.5 miles).
Getting there: From Sultanahmet, take the tramway to Karaköy, from where you can ride the Tünel funicular train to Tünel Square at the southern end of İstiklâl Caddesi in Beyoğlu. Travel up İstiklâl Caddesi by nostalgic tram to Taksim Square.
Stopping-off points: The fish market on Sahne Sokak has lots of cheerful eateries. Cezayir Street is ideal for an elegant drink.

Shopping and museums

Çukurcuma Caddesi (see p109) and Tomtom Kaptan Sokak intersect here and both have curio shops such as Tüterler ⑭ at No. 186. At the bottom of this street on the corner of Defterdar Yokuşu is the Tophane ⑮, once an Ottoman cannon foundry.

Cross Necatibey Caddesi over the tramline to the 16th-century Kılıç Ali Paşa Mosque ⑯ (see p108), one of the last masterpieces of architect Mimar Sinan. Opposite is the Tophane Fountain ⑰ (see p108) built in 1732, which now bestows locally bottled drinking water. From here you can also see the Baroque Clock Tower ⑱.

Continue left along Salı Pazarı ⑲ with its shops, restaurants and narghile (pipe) smokers. A sign directs you to the Istanbul Modern Art Museum ⑳ (see p109), with its collection of contemporary Turkish art.

To get back to the city centre, catch the west-bound tram which takes you directly back to Sultanahmet over the Galata Bridge.

```
0 metres          500
0 yards           500
```

Key

• • • Walk route

⑧ Pera Museum

A 90-Minute Walk from Beyazit to Galata

Istanbul is a seductive mix of ancient and modern, religious and secular, and this walk will give you a flavour of both. Starting at Beyazit Tower in the city's historic quarter, the route takes you through narrow shopping streets brimming with energy, over the Galata Bridge with its stunning views of the Bosphorus, to the Beyoğlu district and trendy Tünel area, where the shops, bars and cafés lend Istanbul its chic reputation.

Magnificent façade of Süleymaniye Mosque

Mimar Sinan architecture

Start at Prof Sıddık Sami Onar Caddesi, from where you can see the striking Beyazit Tower ①, also visible from much of the surrounding area. It was built in 1828 as a fire watch and stands in the grounds of Istanbul University ②, which once served as the Ministry of War and whose huge, ornamental gates are a worthy

photographic subject in themselves. Bear right on the same street past the stunning Süleymaniye Mosque ③ (see pp92–3). This breathtaking structure was completed in 1557 by the architect Mimar Sinan (see p93). Keep going until you reach Şifahane Sokak. Turn right into the street and, if you are feeling peckish or thirsty, you can make a pit stop at historic Dârüzziyafe restaurant ④, with its 16th-century detailing, housed in the former soup kitchens of the Süleymaniye Mosque (see p199).

Turn right on to Mimar Sinan Caddesi and at the bottom of the street, on the corner in front of you, is the tomb of the architect Mimar Sinan ⑤ – a poignant tribute to the great man even if its design is a little humble compared to his own creations.

Coffee and spices

Turn left onto Ismetiye Caddesi and then left again on to Uzunçarsı Caddesi. Walk to the end of the street until you reach bustling Tahtakale Caddesi, where you can jostle with the locals who come here to shop for bargains on everything from electronic goods to clothing. On the right is the Tahtakale Hamamı Çarşısı ⑥, a 16th century Turkish bathhouse that has been renovated and turned into a shopping centre. There is also a lovely café under the domed roof where you can stop to refuel.

Turn down any of the side streets to the left and you will come to Hasircilar Caddesi ⑦, famed for its spice shops, coffee stalls and delis. Walk towards the end of the street, turn left

on to Tahmis Caddesi and you will reach Kurukahreci Mehmet Efendi ⑧, a traditional coffee shop, opened in 1871, famous for its range of blends.

Galata Bridge

Walk to Galata Bridge ⑨ for fantastic views of the city. You can either stroll across the top and watch the many amateur fishermen suspending their

---

Tips for Walkers

Starting point: Beyazit Tower.
Length: 1 km (0.5 miles).
Getting there: Get off at Beyazit on the tramway that runs from Zeytinburnu near the airport to Eminönü, or take either the T4 or 61B bus, both of which run from Taksim to Sultanahmet.
Stopping off points: You are never far from a café or bar in Istanbul, but the obvious halfway stopping off point is at one of the numerous cafés or bars on Galata Bridge. The Tünel district also has plenty of elegant taverns (meyhanes) and restaurants if you want to end your walk with a leisurely lunch or dinner and ponder over a glass of wine.

Tünel (İstiklal Caddesi)

Key

••• Walk route

0 metres 250
0 yards 250

Fishermen hoping for a catch on Galata Bridge

Judaism to Islam

Walk up Harraççi Ali Sokak until you reach the Jewish Museum ⑪ on Karaköy Meydani. This 17th-century museum, once a synagogue, now contains a fascinating collection of old photographs, documents and religious objects relating to the city's Jewish population.

From here, walk up Camekan Sokak to the Gothic-looking Beyoğlu Hospital ⑫, built in 1904 as a British naval hospital. Continue until you come to the Galata Tower ⑬ *(see p107)* in Galata Square, the focal point of the district. The 360° viewing deck at the top of the tower gives the perfect vantage point from which to see almost the entire city laid out before you.

Now turn right and left on to Yüsek Kaldirim Caddesi ⑭, a steep cobblestone street lined with music shops selling just about every conceivable musical instrument you can think of, both traditional and

hi-tech. Tucked away off to the right on Galip Dede Caddesi is the Mevlevi Monastery ⑮ *(see p106)*, once home to the Whirling Dervishes.

Chic Tünel

At the top of the street, at Tünel Square, you have the option to catch the underground funicular ⑯ back down to Karaköy. The one-stop subway was opened in 1876 and is the third-oldest underground system in the world after London and New York. However do not miss the opportunity to experience this fashionable neighbourhood. Just opposite the funicular is Tünel Geçidi, an open-air passage lined with Ottoman buildings, most of which have now been turned into apartments with shops and cafés at ground level. For a refreshing iced coffee in sumptuous Viennese-style surroundings, pop into the KV restaurant ⑰, before making your way to ARtrium ⑱ to pick up some high-class antiques.

To get back to the city centre, from Tünel square you can take a 10-minute tram ride back to the Sultanahmet district. Alternatively you can head to the ferry port of Kasımpaşa and take a ferry to the Haliç Hatti stop across the water.

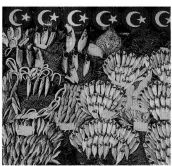

⑧ Coffee machine, Kurukahveci Mehmet Efendi

rods into the water below in hope of a catch, or go down the steps and walk along the lower deck, where there are a number of cafés, bars and restaurants. After a leisurely moment spent taking in the breathtaking views of the Bosphorus below, continue to the bustling and aromatic Karaköy fish market ⑩, where you can buy some of the freshest, cheapest fish Istanbul has to offer.

Fresh fish at the Karaköy fish market

TRAVELLERS' NEEDS

WHERE TO STAY

Whether you feel like staying in an Ottoman palace, taking a room in a restored mansion or a traditional wooden house, or even spending a night in a converted prison, you will find the hotel of your choice in Istanbul. As tourism continues to boom, the city's hotels and guesthouses now cater to every kind of taste and budget. Accommodation in Istanbul tends to be clustered around the main sightseeing areas. Sultanahmet has many of the city's historic hotels, guesthouses and boutique hotels. Beyoğlu, across the Golden Horn, is a good place to look for three- and four-star hotels, including the grand old hotels of the 19th century. Design hotels are also proliferating in all areas.

The hotels listed on pages 186–9 have been chosen from the best the city can offer across all price ranges. Each hotel is given a brief description and details are provided about the facilities available. For a broad range, check the website www.istanbulhotels.com. *Cornucopia*, a glossy magazine about Turkey, offers a hand-picked selection available for booking at www.cornucopiahotels.com. Information on other types of accommodation can be found on page 185.

Choosing a Hotel

Many hotels in Istanbul are rated by the Ministry of Culture and Tourism according to a star system. They range from comfortable, but basic one-star hotels to five-star luxury hotels. Other types of accommodation licensed by the Ministry are the converted buildings known as Special Licence hotels. A further category is the accommodation licensed by the Greater Istanbul Municipality. These hotels offer perfectly reasonable facilities, but with less stringent standards.

Accommodation is available in most central areas of the city. The Sultanahmet district is conveniently situated within walking distance of most of the city's major sights. Many of the Special Licence hotels in this area are tucked away on formerly residential side streets. There are guesthouses along Divanyolu Caddesi, the main road, and along the slopes leading down

Lounge of the Ceylan Intercontinental Hotel *(see p189)* in Taksim

to the Sea of Marmara. Along with these, there are also middle-range hotels in central Sultanahmet.

Beyoğlu, the old European centre of Istanbul, is within easy reach of the best sights in the city. This area has innumerable impressive hotels that are comfortable and dependable, international chain hotels and some stylish recent additions.

The Asian side of Istanbul is mainly residential, but has some hotels, though they are generally used more by Turks than foreigners and tourists.

Luxury Hotels

There has been rapid growth in the number of luxury hotels in the city, and most international chains are now represented in Istanbul. Almost all five-star hotels here boast spectacular views of Marmara or Bosphorus, and between them they have some of the best international restaurants in the city. All the major hotels have swimming pools and health clubs. Many of them also have Turkish baths. Conference facilities are provided, and many hotels have extensive entertainment facilities. Most of them can also arrange tours of Istanbul and nearby places through local companies. They also provide facilities for disabled visitors, arrange special activities for children *(see p184)* and have wireless Internet in all their rooms.

Special Licence Hotels

A number of the city's old buildings have been renovated

The luxurious Four Seasons Hotel *(see p187)*, formerly a prison

◀ Tourists dining along Galata Bridge at night

and transformed into historic hotels. However, due to the nature of the buildings in which they are housed, some of these hotels cannot provide facilities such as lifts. They belong to a separate category, the Special Licence hotels, and are under independent private management.

These hotels constitute some of Istanbul's most interesting and attractive hotels. They are often located in the residential streets of historic areas, and range from small, modestly priced traditional wooden houses to luxury Ottoman mansions and townhouses. Special Licence hotels, whether large or small, are generally of a high standard. The authentic period decor of many of them gives even the larger ones a warm atmosphere. The listings on the following pages provide plenty of examples, especially of boutique Special Licence hotels in Sultanahmet. Increasingly, many of the city's boutique-style hotels are opting not to apply for official ratings or stars. This does not, however, imply any lack of standards or amenities. In fact,

Lovely view from the rooftop terrace of the historic Adahan Istanbul *(see p188)*

Latticed window of a Special Licence hotel

these establishments are contributing to the continually rising standards of accommodation in the city. All have their own websites on which you can take a virtual tour, compare prices and facilities, and make a booking.

Cheaper Hotels

Istanbul has plenty of cheap, comfortable accommodation, which meets the standards of the Turkish Ministry of Culture and Tourism. However, if you are choosing one of the cheaper hotels, do not base your decision on the façade or lobby, which may look brand new.

One-star hotels provide the most basic facilities, but often have rooms with a private shower and toilet. Two- and three-star hotels have more comfortable rooms and usually a café or bar. Many three-star hotels offer rooms with a TV and mini-bar.

Guesthouses vary in terms of facilities. Most provide bedlinen and towels, and the better ones will have rooms with ensuite bathrooms. All should have communal cooking facilities. While cheaper hotels usually have central heating, they are unlikely to have air conditioning, but an electric fan

may be provided. Some small hotels may not provide hot water 24 hours a day.

What to Expect

All hotels listed in this book are comfortable and welcoming. Front desk staff usually speak English, and will be able to offer information on sights and travel.

At some budget and mid-range hotels you may need to specify if you want a double bed rather than two singles when booking or checking in.

Most hotels with three or more storeys will have a lift. However, there may not be a lift in a Special Licence hotel because of the problems of installing one in an older building. Facilities for wheelchair users are increasingly found in hotels these days.

Noise can be a problem even in some smart hotels, so in busy areas choose a room that does not face a main street. If you are not satisfied with your room, you can always ask for another.

Breakfast is included in the price of the room and typically consists of a generous open buffet, including cold meats, fruits, cereals and yoghurt. Many larger hotels have restaurants that serve à la carte meals. Upmarket hotels have at least one dining room serving evening meals, but some of the smaller, cheaper hotels do not. It is a good idea to check while booking and confirm by email or fax before you visit.

Pretty façade of Yeşil Ev *(see p186)*, a Special Licence hotel

Reception desk at the Hilton Istanbul *(see p189)*

Prices and Discounts

Hotel prices are quoted in US dollars, Euros and Turkish Lira (TL). Prices are per room, not per person. All prices usually include breakfast and tax. Apart from top-class hotels, which have standard prices that do not change through the year, tariffs differ according to the season.

The busy season, when hotel prices tend to be at their highest, is from April to the end of October. During the brief Christmas and New Year period, the higher summer tariffs are applied. There are few single rooms, but all hotels offer a single room rate of slightly more than half the price of a double room.

Lounge area of the Empress Zoe *(see p186)*

It is always worth attempting to bargain with hotels, but do not expect to get a discount. For longer stays of a week or more, you may be able to get a reduction. Some hotels also offer discounts for Internet bookings, cash payments, or out-of-season stays. However, do not expect a room with any kind of a view if you have got it at a discount.

While you will always be able to find a room of a reasonable standard, it is advisable to book in advance for the best hotels or those of your choice during the busy season. You can book any hotel listed in this guide directly, by telephone, fax and e-mail. Nearly all hotels also have their own website registration forms and are included in the major booking websites. You may be asked to give your credit card details, which will guarantee your reservation. If you cannot find a place in any of the hotels that fall in your preferred price range, try one of the established travel companies based in Istanbul, such as **Gazella Travel Designer**, **Meptur**, Plan Tours *(see p239)* or **VIP Tourism**. If you arrive without a reservation, the tourist information offices *(see p229)* in the airport, Sirkeci Station, Sultanahmet Square or Karaköy International Maritime Terminal will help you find a hotel, but they will not make a reservation for you.

Checking Out and Paying

Guests are expected to check out by midday, but hotels will usually keep luggage for collection later. All hotels accept the major credit cards, as well as Turkish lira and other currencies. VAT is always included in the room price. It is usual to leave a few dollars, or its equivalent, in the room for the cleaner, and to give a tip to the receptionist to be divided among the staff. Phone calls and mini-bar drinks can add to the size of your bill.

Children

Children up to six years of age are often not charged for rooms, and pay 50 per cent until 12 years old. It is possible to negotiate a discount for older children who share a room with their parents. Most hotels also have cots.

Some hotels arrange special entertainment for children. The Swissôtel *(see p189)* offers a weekend package.

Hostels

For those on a tight budget, Istanbul has a number of inexpensive hostels, mostly in the Sultanahmet area. A popular hostel in Istanbul is the **Sultan Hostel**. This hostel is right in the heart of the Sultanahmet district, close to Haghia Sophia, Topkapı Palace and the Grand Bazaar. The Sultan is a member of the International Youth Hostel Federation (IYHF) and offers a discount for members. There is also a travel agent who can help with travel arrangements and a currency exchange. On the same street, the **Orient Hostel** is a youth hostel with excellent facilities, including a rooftop café, a bar and a safe. The tour operator Gençtur is also affiliated to the IYHF and can provide information on other hostels.

Double room in the Kariye *(see p187)*

Classy interiors at the excellent design hostel, #Bunk *(see p188)*

Camping

Camping and caravanning in Turkey have steadily gained popularity in recent years. There is an ever-increasing variety of excellent camping sites with self-catering facilities open in the summer season, which lasts from May until October. **Londra Kamping** is open through the year. It has facilities for washing and cooking, a fast-food restaurant, bar, pool table and football pitch. As well as providing facilities for camping, it also has two-room bungalows for rent. On the Black Sea coast, but to the east of the Bosphorus, is another equally attractive and popular camp site, the **Kumbaba Moteli**, situated 2 km (1.2 miles) outside the Şile resort *(see p160)*. This site is open between May and September, and offers hot showers and cooking facilities.

For further details, contact the **Turkish Camping and Caravanning Association**, which is helpful and informative. The association also has a website with comprehensive listings of sites throughout the country.

Self-catering

Istanbul has a growing number of apartment hotels providing fully furnished apartments for those who prefer more homely surroundings. We have included a number of stand-out apartments, which are handy for tourists in the listings. The **Akmerkez Residence**, which is mostly used by businessmen, is in the upmarket Akmerkez shopping mall in Etiler *(see p211)*. Its luxuriously decorated flats have air conditioning and all the domestic appliances.

The **Entes Apart Hotel** has compact modern apartments. Global real estate franchises, such as **Century 21** and **Remax**, can assist in finding long- or short-term rental accommodation.

View over Dolmabahçe Mosque from the Swissôtel *(see p189)*

Recommended Hotels

The accommodation options featured in this guide have been selected from across a wide price range for their excellent facilities, good location and value. These include stylish, modern hotels as well as hotels steeped in history. Visitors can also consider staying in one of the well-furnished apartment hotels. For a more intimate experience, there are several acclaimed guesthouses and boutique options, along with hostels for those on a budget. The DK Choice hotels are extra special. The places highlighted as DK Choice are the very best of the pack chosen for being outstanding in some way. They may stand in beautiful surroundings, be a historically important building, or may just be incredibly charming.

DIRECTORY

Travel Agents

Gazella Travel Designer
Ulus Mah Öztopuz
Cad 16, Beşiktaş.
Tel (0212) 233 15 98.
Ⓦ gazella.com

Meptur
Büyükdere Cad 26, Mecidiyeköy.
Tel (0212) 275 02 50.
Ⓦ meptur.com.tr

VIP Tourism
Cumhuriyet Cad 167a, Harbiye.
Tel (0212) 368 48 00.
Ⓦ viptourism.com.tr

Youth Hostels

Orient Hostel
Akbıyık Cad 9, Sultanahmet.
Map 3 E5 (5 E5). **Tel** (0212) 517
94 93. Ⓦ orienthostel.com

Sultan Hostel
Akbıyık Cad 17, Sultanahmet.
Map 3 E5 (5 E5). **Tel** (0212) 516
92 60. Ⓦ sultanhostel.com

Camping

Kumbaba Moteli
Şile. **Tel** (0216) 711 50 38.
Fax (0216) 711 48 51.

Londra Kamping
Londra Asfaltı, Bakırköy.
Tel (0212) 560 42 00.
Fax (0212) 559 34 38.

**Turkish Camping and
Caravanning Association**
Bestekar sok, No. 62/12
Kavaklıdere, Ankara.
Tel (0312) 466 19 97.
Ⓦ kampkaravan.org.tr

Self-catering

Akmerkez Residence
Akmerkez Shopping & Business
Centre, Etiler.
Tel (0212) 282 01 20.
Ⓦ akmerkez.com.tr

Century 21
Topçular Kışla Cad 5, Rami-Eyüp.
Tel (0212) 493 26 00.
Ⓦ century21.com.tr

Entes Apart Hotel
İpek Sok 19, Taksim.
Map 7 E4.
Tel (0212) 293 22 08.
Ⓦ entesapart.com

Remax
Tel (0212) 232 48 20.
Ⓦ remax.com.tr

Where to Stay

Apartments

Seraglio Point

Romantic Mansion Istanbul $$
*Nöbethane Cad, Tayahatun
Sok 28, Sirkeci*
Tel (0212) 638 96 35   **Map** 5 E1
W romanticmansion.com
Three lovely flats in a self-sufficient
pink and white building. Views of
Gulhane Park from the terrace.

Beyoğlu

Galata Flats $$
Tünel Meydani 84, 34430
Tel (0212) 244 26 76   **Map** 7 D5
W galataflats.com
Ideal for longer stays, with homely
comforts and plenty of space. All
the flats are serviced daily.

Galateia Residence $$
Sahkulu Bostan Sok 9–11 Tunel, 34425
Tel (0212) 245 30 32   **Map** 7 D5
W galateiaresidence.com
A range of large, well-designed
apartments with superb transport
links. Extensive concierge service.

DK Choice

Baylo Suites $$$
Galata Kulesi Sok 24, 34420
Tel (0212) 245 98 60   **Map** 3 D1
W baylosuites.com
Four self-contained apartments
in a historic Galata building,
lovingly restored by a mother-
daughter team – Istanbul's first
historic restoration project to
meet American ecological
standards. Many original features
have been preserved, and a
gallery downstairs sells historic
prints, postcards and maps.

Simple and classy bedroom interiors
at Baylo Suites, Beyoğlu

Boutique Hotels

Seraglio Point

DK Choice

The Kybele Hotel $
*Yerebatan Cad 35,
Sultanahmet, 34410*
Tel (0212) 511 77 66   **Map** 5 E3
W kybelehotel.com
Four thousand coloured glass
lamps decorate this wooden
Sultanahmet townhouse, while
antique gramophones vie for
attention with heavy fabrics and
equally rich wallpaper. Yet, the
Kybele never feels overdone,
only welcoming and relaxed.

Sirkeci Konak $$
Taya Hatun Sok 5, 34120, Sirkeci
Tel (0212) 528 43 44   **Map** 5 E2
W sirkecikonak.com
Traditionally designed with spacious
rooms, a pool, sauna and *hamam*.

Sultanahmet

Aruna $
*Cankurtaran Mah, Ahirkapi
Sok 74, 34122*
Tel (0212) 458 54 88   **Map** 5 F5
W arunahotel.com
Homely, with private Jacuzzi or
hamam-style bathrooms in suites.

Dersaadet $
*Küçük Ayasofya Cad, Kapıağası
Sok 5, 34400*
Tel (0212) 458 07 60   **Map** 5 D5
W dersaadethotel.com
A striking, red, wooden building
close to the Blue Mosque. Antique
decor; friendly, professional staff.

Hippodrome Hotel $
Mimar Mehmet Ağa Cad 38, 34400
Tel (0212) 517 68 89   **Map** 5 F5
W hippodromehotel.com
Small, but with a variety of rooms,
including an apartment that can
accommodate up to six adults.

Hotel Empress Zoe $
Akbiyik Cad 10, 34122
Tel (0212) 518 43 60   **Map** 5 F4
W emzoe.com
Ancient masonry and a 15th-
century *hamam* create a rustic feel.

Hotel Nena $
Klodfarer Cad 8–10, 34122
Tel (0212) 516 52 64   **Map** 5 D4
W istanbulhotelnena.com
Stylish and charming hotel
with a leafy courtyard café and
terrace restaurant.

Hotel Nomade $
Ticarethane Sok 15, 34410
Tel (0212) 513 81 72   **Map** 5 D3
W hotelnomade.com
Beautifully detailed and
well-appointed rooms.

Hotel Turkoman $
*Asmalı Çeşme Sok 2, Adliye
Yanı, 34490*
Tel (0212) 516 29 56   **Map** 5 D4
W turkomanhotel.com
Down-to-earth, with 18 simple
and comfortable rooms, helpful
staff and incredible views.

Hotel Valide Sultan Konağı $
Ishakpasa Cad Kutlugün Sok 1, 34122
Tel (0212) 517 65 58   **Map** 5 F4
W hotelvalidesultan.com
Family-run, with an emphasis on
service. Quaint, antique furnishings,
but all modern conveniences.

Aren Suites $$
Küçükayasofya Cad, Gelinlik Sok 13
Tel (0212) 517 31 26   **Map** 5 D5
W arensuites.com
Many rooms look out over the
Sea of Marmara. Helpful staff.

Hotel Ibrahim Pasha $$
Terzihane Sok 7, 34122
Tel (0212) 518 03 94   **Map** 5 D4
W ibrahimpasha.com
Located just off the Hippodrome,
away from traffic. Elegant rooms
where old meets new.

Seven Dreams $$
Seyit Hasan Sok 14
Tel (0212) 518 72 67   **Map** 5 F4
W sevendreamshotel.com
Traditional and vine-clad on the
outside, hip and modern inside.

Yeşil Ev $$
Kabasakal Cad 5, 34122
Tel (0212) 517 67 85   **Map** 5 E4
W yesilev.com.tr
This hotel ushered in a
new era of boutique tourism
in Sultanahmet. It still remains
one of the best options here.

Bazaar Quarter

New House Hotel $
*Emin Sinan Mah, Evkaf Sok 6,
Cemberlitas, 34400*
Tel (0212) 638 81 76   **Map** 5 E5
W hotelnewhouse.com

Set between Grand Bazaar and Sultanahmet. Ottoman- and modern-style rooms.

Beyoğlu

Lush Hotel $
Sıraselviler Cad 12, 34433
Tel (0212) 243 95 95 **Map** 7 E4
🅦 lushhotel.com
Award winning boutique hotel close to the city's nightlife – 14 apartments also available.

Sub Hotel $
Necatibey Cad 91, Karaköy, 34435
Tel (0212) 243 00 05 **Map** 3 E1
🅦 subistanbul.com
Ultra stylish design. Ideally placed for art galleries and café culture.

The House Hotel Galatasaray $
Firuzağa Mah, Bostanbaşı Cad 19, 34425
Tel (0212) 252 04 22 **Map** 7 E4
🅦 thehousehotel.com
Homeliest of the House Hotels in a stylishly restored townhouse.

Georges Hotel Galata $$$
Serdar-ı Ekrem Cad 24, 34425
Tel (0212) 244 24 23 **Map** 7 D5
🅦 georges.com
First-class luxury and great views in a grand old townhouse.

Witt Istanbul Suites $$$
Defterdar Yokuşu 26, Cihangir, 34433
Tel (0212) 293 15 00 **Map** 7 E5
🅦 wittistanbul.com
Huge rooms with kitchenettes and neat design touches.

Greater Istanbul

Kariye Hotel $
Kariye Camii Sok 6, Edirnekapi
Tel (0212) 534 84 14 **Map** 1 B1
🅦 kariyeotel.com
Next door to the Church of St Saviour in Chora. Good value.

Khalkedon Hotel $
Moda Cad, Tellaizade Sok 2, Kadikoy
Tel (0216) 700 13 40
🅦 khalkedonhotelistanbul.com
It's a bargain, on the Asian side of Istanbul. Clean, comfortable and close to the ferries to Europe.

The House Hotel Nişantaşı $$$
Abdi İpekçi Cad 34, Nişantaşı, 34367
Tel (0212) 224 59 99 **Map** 7 F1
🅦 thehousehotel.com
The House chain's most fashionable address; set above the Prada store.

Bosphorus

The House Hotel Bosphorus $$$
Salhane Sok 1, Ortaköy, 34347
Tel (0212) 327 77 87 **Map** 8 A3
🅦 thehousehotel.com

Picturesque setting of The House Hotel Bosphorus

Celebrity favourite; by a scenic waterside square, close to the city's exclusive night spots.

Beyond Istanbul

Assos Nazlihan Hotel $
İskele Mevkii Behramkale Ayvacık
Tel (0286) 721 73 85/86
🅦 www.assosnazlihan.com
A converted warehouse by the harbour in a historic village.

Acqua Verde $$
Kurfallı Yakuplu Cad 34980, Şile
Tel (0216) 721 71 43
🅦 acquaverde.com.tr
Set on the reed-lined banks of a river where it meets the Black Sea.

Hotel Maşukiye $$
Soğuksu Mah, Sarmasik Sok, 41295, Kartepe Maşukiye/Kocaeli
Tel (0262) 354 38 99
🅦 hotelmasukiye.com
Close to an unspoilt lake, under 15 km (9 miles) from a ski resort.

Otel Kaikias $
Kale Arkası Mevkii, Bozcaada/ Çanakkale
Tel (0286) 697 02 50
🅦 kaikias.com
Close to the beach, on an island famous for its wines.

Villa Pine Garden Ağva $$$
Yeni Köy 19, Şile-Ağva
Tel (0216) 725 76 56
🅦 villapinegarden.com
Luxurious retreat on the Black Sea coast, with colour-themed rooms.

Historic Hotels

Seraglio Point

Ottoman Hotel Imperial $
Caferiye Sok 6/1, 34400, Sultanahmet
Tel (0212) 513 61 51 **Map** 5 E3
🅦 ottomanhotelimperial.com
A converted Ottoman hospital that offers sheer opulence. Traditional Ottoman-style rooms.

Ayasofya Konakları $$
Soğuk Çeşme Sok, Sultanahmet, 34400
Tel (0212) 513 36 00 **Map** 5 F3
🅦 ayasofyakonaklari.com
19th-century wooden Ottoman mansions along a leafy cobbled street. Pretty courtyard café.

Sultanahmet

Deluxe Golden Horn Hotel $$
Binbirdirek Meydanı Sok 1, 34400
Tel (0212) 518 17 17 **Map** 5 D4
🅦 goldenhornhotel.com
One of the few hotels to maintain an atmosphere of the Orient Express era. Pleasingly traditional.

Four Seasons Sultanahmet $$$
Tevkifhane Sok 1, 34110
Tel (0212) 402 30 00 **Map** 5 F4
🅦 fourseasons.com
Originally an Ottoman prison, now offers ample pampering, plus a herb-scented garden.

Bazaar Quarter

Legacy Ottoman $
Hamidiye Cad 16, Eminönü, 34112
Tel (0212) 527 67 67 **Map** 5 D1
🅦 legacyottomanhotel.com
Impressive early 20th-century complex that dominates the bustling market. Simple rooms.

Beyoğlu

Büyük Londra Oteil (Grand Hotel de Londres) $
Meşrutiyet Cad 53, 34430, Tepebaşı
Tel (0212) 245 06 70 **Map** 7 D4
🅦 londrahotel.net
Well-maintained, with a terrace bar and an eccentric array of knick-knacks in public areas.

Palazzo Donizetti $
Asmalimescit Sok 55, 34400
Tel (0212) 249 51 51 **Map** 7 D4
🅦 palazzodonizetti.com
A grand old building reminiscent of a European château, with a continental approach to luxury.

For more information on types of hotels *see page 185*

Impressive entrance to the Pera Palace Hotel Jumeirah, Beyoğlu

Adahan Istanbul $$
General Yazgan Sokağı 14, 34430
Tel (0212) 243 85 81   **Map** 7 D5
W adahanistanbul.com
Sensitively restored historic apartment building. Large rooms, high ceilings and simple design.

Pera Palace Hotel Jumeirah $$$
Meşrutiyet Cad 52, 34430, Tepebaşı
Tel (0212) 377 40 00   **Map** 7 D5
W jumeirah.com
Quintessential Istanbul hotel with suites named after famous guests.

Greater Istanbul

Splendid Palas Hotel $$
23 Nisan Cad 53, Büyükada
Tel (0216) 382 69 50
W splendidhotel.net
The most venerable hotel on the Princes' Islands. Undeniable charm, and a historic heritage.

Bosphorus

Çırağan Palace Kempinski $$$
Çırağan Cad 32, Beşiktaş
Tel (0212) 326 46 46   **Map** 9 E3
W kempinski.com
The only Istanbul hotel to occupy a royal Ottoman palace. Waterside terrace with heated infinity pool.

DK Choice

Sumahan on the Water $$$
Kuleli Cad 43, 34684
Tel (0216) 422 80 00
W sumahan.com
A multi-award winning converted distillery. Every room has a sea view, and some open onto a lawn terrace. The hotel offers a boat shuttle service, in case guests ever feel like leaving the spa and excellent restaurant.

Beyond Istanbul

Raşitler Bağ Evi, Safranbolu $
Değirmenbaşı Sok 65, Safranbolu
Tel (0370) 725 13 45
W rasitlerbagevi.com
One of the Ottoman mansions that make Safronbolu a World Heritage Site. Nearly 300 years old.

Uğurlu Mansions, Kastamonu $
Şeyh Şaban-ı Veli Cad 51, 37100, Kastamonu
Tel (0366) 212 82 02/04
W ugurlukonagi.com
Two 19th-century Ottoman mansions in a Black Sea town. The breakfasts alone are worth the drive.

Hostels and Guesthouses
Sultanahmet

Akdeniz Hotel Guest House $
Haci Tahsin Bey Sok 7, 34410
Tel (0212) 520 20 99
W istanbulakdenizhotel.com
Modest guesthouse with clean, comfortable rooms, and a *hamam* nearby. Ask for a discount.

Hotel Sultanahmet $
Divanyolu Cad 20
Tel (0212) 527 02 39   **Map** 5 D5
W hotelsultanahmet.com
Great location and views; simple rooms make it easy on the pocket.

Sultan Hostel $
Akbıyık Cad 17, 34122
Tel (0212) 516 92 60   **Map** 5 F4
W sultanhostel.com
Ideal for backpackers. Both private and dorm rooms. Safe, close to main sights, and a pub downstairs.

Bazaar Quarter

Beyazit Hostel $
Gedik Paşa Cad, Hattat Sok 19, Beyazıt
Tel (0212) 517 11 31   **Map** 4 B4
W beyazithostel.com
Basic, clean, comfortable and safe accomodation near the Grand Bazaar.

Beyoğlu

DK Choice

#Bunk $
Balik Sok 7, 34435
Tel (0212) 244 88 08   **Map** 7 D4
W bunkhostels.com
A great and original idea – low price accommodation with a cool design philosophy, makes #Bunk the perfect base for a social city break. The group hopes to expand to more properties soon.

Chill Out Hostel and Café $
Balyoz Sok 3
Tel (0212) 249 47 84   **Map** 6 D5
W chillouthostelistanbul.com
Private rooms and dorms popular with those who want to enjoy the nightlife. Friendly staff.

Beyond Istanbul

Geçim Pansiyon $
Avşaadası, 10940, Avşaadası
Tel (0535) 926 10 20
W gecimpansiyon.net
On an island in the Sea of Marmara reached by ferry from Istanbul and Tekirdağ.

Hoşköy Başkır Pansiyon $
Hoşköy – Şarköy/Tekirdağ
Tel (0282) 538 61 08
W hoskoypansiyon.com
Good place for a night break when driving or hiking. Set in a sleepy village. Vineyards nearby.

Rustepaşa Kervansaray $
İki Kapılıhan Cad 57, Edirne, 22100
Tel (0284) 212 61 19
W edirnekervansarayhotel.com
Converted 16th-century caravanserai. Small, but comfortable rooms.

Modern Hotels
Seraglio Point

Arden City Hotel $
Kazım Ismail Gürkan Cad 2, Sultanahmet
Tel (0212) 528 93 93   **Map** 5 E3
W hotelarden.com
Recently renovated, with some rooms overlooking the Sea of Marmara. Quick service, good value for money.

Elegant room interior at #Bunk, a design hostel in Beyoğlu

Gulhane Park Hotel $
Nöbethane Cad 1, 34112, Sirkeci
Tel (0212) 519 68 68   **Map** 5 E1
w gulhaneparkhotel.com.tr
Overlooking the Topkapı Palace gardens with fairly-priced rooms, a gym and *hamam*.

**Hagia Sophia Hotel
Istanbul Old City** $$$
Yerebatan Cad 13, 34110, Sultanahmet
Tel (0212) 444 93 32   **Map** 5 E3
w hsoldcity.com
Smart and modern option in the heart of the Old City, with an English-style pub. Good for business clients and sightseers.

Sultanahmet

Antea Palace Hotel & Spa $
Cinci Meydanı Sok 16, 34122
Tel (0212) 458 36 36   **Map** 4 C5
w hotelanteapalace.com
A Best Western hotel. Not the most beautiful rooms, but the spa and fitness facilities make up for it.

Armada $
Ahırkapı Sok 24, 34122
Tel (0212) 455 44 55   **Map** 5 F5
w armadahotel.com.tr
Popular with tour groups serious about seeing the sights. The terrace restaurant has one of the best views in the city.

Blue House/Mavi Ev $$
Dalbasti Sok 14
Tel (0212) 638 90 10   **Map** 5 E5
w bluehouse.com.tr
Family run with first-class service. Tasteful rooms, three restaurants and all the necessary amenities.

Pierre Loti Hotel $$
Piyer Loti Cad 1, 34400
Tel (0212) 518 57 00   **Map** 4 C4
w pierrelotihotel.com
Everything needed for a comfortable and hassle-free stay, including spa and *hamam* treatments.

Sura Hotel $$
Ticarethane Sok 45
Tel (0212) 513 66 66   **Map** 5 D3
w surahotels.com
This hotel has many striking features: rooms are colour-coded by floor and suites come with rain showers or free-standing baths.

Bazaar Quarter

Antik Cisterna $
Sekbanbaşı Sok 10, Beyazıt, 34130
Tel (0212) 638 58 58   **Map** 4 A3
w antikhotel.com
Four-star hotel with a 1,500-year-old cistern in the basement now used as an entertainment venue. Floors themed by historical events.

Sophisticated and luxurious lobby of The Edition in Levent, Greater Istanbul

Bulvar Palace Hotel $
Atatürk Bulvarı 36 Sarachane
Tel (0212) 528 58 81   **Map** 2 A3
w hotelbulvarpalas.com
Ideal for large groups who want to explore the city by coach. Independent travellers may also find the roadside location convenient.

Grand Beyazid Hotel $
Mithatpaşa Cad, Abuhayat Sok 5 34490, Beyazıt
Tel (0212) 638 46 41   **Map** 4 A4
w hotelbeyazid.com
Just outside the main tourist area, and of a similar standard to more expensive hotels.

Beyoğlu

Ceylan Intercontinental $$$
Asker Ocağı Cad 1, Taksim, 34435
Tel (0212) 368 44 44   **Map** 7 F3
w istanbul.intercontinental.com.tr
High-quality hospitality from this world renowned group of hotels. Centrally located in a modern building.

Taksim $$$
Taksim Meydani
Tel (0212) 334 83 00   **Map** 7 E4
w taksim.themarmarahotels.com
Landmark hotel, which towers over much of the city. Even the relatively low gym and pool areas offer superb bird's eye views.

Martı $$$
Abdülhak Hamit Cad 25/B, Taksim, 34435
Tel (0212) 987 40 00   **Map** 7 E3
w martiistanbulhotel.com
Elegant five-star hotel, one of the latest projects by interior designer, Zeynep Fadillioglu. Top floor spa and gym have wonderful views.

Greater Istanbul

W Hotel $$
Suleyman Seba Cad 22, Akaretler Beşiktaş, 34357
Tel (0212) 381 21 21   **Map** 8 B4
w wistanbul.com.tr
Set amidst shops and galleries, aims for a young, cool crowd.

Hilton Istanbul $$$
Cumhuriyet Cad, Harbiye, 34367
Tel (0212) 315 60 00   **Map** 7 F2
w placeshilton.com
Surrounded by a park; the brand's first foray beyond the USA has built up quite a reputation.

Swissôtel The Bosphorus $$$
Bayildim Cad 2, 34330, Beşiktaş
Tel (0212) 326 11 00   **Map** 8 A4
w swissotel.com.tr
Huge windows give jaw-dropping vistas across the Bosphorus. One of Istanbul's top five luxury hotels.

DK Choice

The Edition $$$
Büyükdere Cad 136, 34330
Tel (0212) 317 77 00
w editionhotels.com
The Edition is in the heart of Istanbul's business district, but once inside, enter a private world of luxury. Should visitors want to venture outside, there is a convenient Metro connection to the sightseeing and shopping areas. The popular bar and restaurant is managed by Cipriani's.

Beyond Istanbul

Almira, Bursa $
Ulubatli Hasan Bulvari 5, 16200, Bursa
Tel (0224) 250 20 20
w almira.com.tr
A good hotel with a music venue, restaurants, bars, shopping and swimming pools on site.

Anzac $
Saat Kulesi Meydani 8, 17100 Canakkale
Tel (0286) 217 77 77
w anzachotel.com
Good base to explore the beaches and vineyards of the Dardanelles. The Gallipoli campaign is commemorated here on April 25.

**Hotel Çelik Palace
Thermal Spa** $$
Çekirge Cad 79, 16000, Bursa
Tel (0224) 233 38 00
w celikpalasotel.com
The star attraction is the biggest thermal pool in the city. Best to relax after skiing on Uludağ or exploring Bursa's Ottoman sights.

For more information on types of hotels *see page 185*

WHERE TO EAT AND DRINK

Istanbul's restaurants range from the informal lokanta and kebab house, which are found on almost every street corner, to the gourmet restaurants (restoran) of large hotels. There are a variety of international restaurants in the city that offer fare from France to Japan at middle to high prices. Pages 190–93 illustrate the most typical Turkish dishes, and the phrase book on pages 279–80 will help you tackle the menu. On page 193, you will find a guide to drinks

available. The restaurants listed on pages 196–207 have been chosen from the best that Istanbul has to offer across all price ranges, from casual eateries to award-winning restaurants. They have been recommended for their quality of food, service and value for money. A detailed description is provided with examples of signature dishes. Light meals and snacks sold by street vendors and served in cafés and bars are described on pages 208–9.

Where to Look

Istanbul's smartest and most expensive restaurants are con-centrated in the European parts of the city: along the Bosphorus in Ortaköy; in and around Taksim; in the chic shopping districts of Nişantaşı, Maçka, Bebek and Teşvikiye; and in the modern residential suburbs of Levent and Etiler, west of the Bosphorus. The best gourmet restaurants for both Western and Turkish food are often in five-star hotels.

Beyoğlu district has the liveliest restaurants, cafés and fast-food eateries, particularly around İstiklal Caddesi (see pp104–5), which cater to a young crowd. Sultanahmet, and the neigh-bouring districts of Sirkeci, Eminönü and Beyazıt, are full of inexpensive restaurants serving the local population. There are also some stylish restaurants with modern decor in these areas. Further afield, in areas such as Fatih, Fener, Balat and Eyüp, there are plenty of cheap restaurants, cafés and bakeries.

Types of Restaurant

The most common type of restaurant is the traditional lokanta – an ordinary restaurant offering a variety of dishes, often listed by the entrance. Home-made dishes comprise hot meat and vegetable dishes displayed in steel containers. Other options may be sulu yemek (a stew) and et (grilled meat and kebabs).

Equally ubiquitous is the Turkish kebab house (kebapçı or ocakbaşı). Along with grilled meats, most kebab houses serve lahmacun, a very thin dough base with minced meat, onions and tomato sauce on top (see p192). Cheaper restaurants also serve pide, a flattened bread base, served with toppings like eggs, cheese or lamb. There are also a few specialist pide restaurants.

If you have had too much to drink you may welcome tripe soup (işkembe), a Turkish cure for hangovers, before going to bed. İşkembe restaurants stay open until early morning. The atmosphere is always informal

The Pierre Loti Coffee House in Eyüp (see p202)

and lively in Istanbul's innumerable fish restaurants (balık lokantası). The best ones are located on the shores of the Bosphorus (see pp204–6) and in Kumkapı, on the Sea of Marmara, which is like one large open-air restaurant in summer. A typical fish restaurant will offer a large variety of mezes (see p194) before you order your main course from the day's catch. Skipjack tuna (palamut), fresh sardines (sardalya) and sea bass (levrek) are the most popular fish. Also popular are Black Sea hamsi (a kind of anchovy), istavrit (bluefin) and mezgit (whiting). As fish become scarcer and more expensive, farmed fish has become more widely accepted, particularly alabalık (trout) and çipura (a type of bream). Fish is served fried or grilled and often accom-panied by a large salad and a bottle of rakı (see p195). Most fish restaurants in busy areas will not accept reservations, but if you cannot find a table at one

Beautiful hanging garden at Nar Lokanta (see p199), Bazaar Quarter

Diners at the Konyalı Restaurant *(see p196)* in Topkapı Palace

restaurant, you will probably find one at another nearby. International culinary experiences are encouraging local chefs to be more adventurous and innovative; the best are crafting superb, original food in a beautiful ambience. Wealthier Turks frequent the foreign restaurants found in a number of neighbourhoods, while global icons such as Starbucks and Gloria Jean's are becoming part of everyday life.

A *meyhane* is a tavern, serving alcohol and a variety of *mezes*. These are more casual and attract a younger crowd. The accent is mostly on drinking; there is usually *fasil* music and musicians who play atmospheric tunes on a zither or drum.

Opening Hours

Turks eat lunch between 12:30 and 2pm, and dinner around 8pm. Ordinary restaurants and kebab houses are open from

about 11am to 11pm, while fish restaurants serve all day and stay open later. International restaurants have strict opening hours, usually from noon to 3:30pm and 7:30pm to midnight. *Meyhanes* will be open from 7pm until well after midnight. Most restaurants are open daily, but some are closed only on Sunday. During Ramazan *(see p49)*, when Muslims fast from sunrise to sunset, many restaurants are closed. Some only shut during daylight hours and then serve special Ramazan meals, while others, especially in religious areas such as Fatih and Eyüp, close for the whole month. In sightseeing areas, however, there is always one open somewhere.

What to Expect

Since July 2009, smoking has been banned in all indoor establishments, although illegal lighting up is not unheard of.

Cheaper restaurants and kebab houses often do not serve alcohol. Others cannot because they are near a mosque or religious site. When alcohol is served, it can be expensive.

Accessibility for wheelchairs is somewhat hit or miss. Restaurants are often multi-level with family rooms on the upper

floors, and ground-floor restaurants often have a step leading up to the entrance. Lifts are not common outside of large hotels and offices. Many restaurants offer options for vegetarians.

In local Turkish restaurants in conservative parts of the city and outside Istanbul, women should look for the *aile salonu* sign. This denotes an area set aside for women and children; single women will be unwelcome in the main restaurant.

Turks are proud of their hospitality and service. Upmarket restaurants offer good service, but the same standards may not always apply in cheaper places.

Service and Paying

The major credit cards are widely accepted, except in the cheaper restaurants, kebab houses, local *bufés* (snack kiosks) and some *lokantas*. Restaurants usually display the credit card sign if they accept this form of payment. Value-added tax (*KDV* in Turkish) is always included. Some places add 10 per cent for service

A selection of pastries

while others leave it to the discretion of the customer.

Recommended Restaurants

All the restaurants on the pages that follow have been carefully selected to offer a cross-section of the best options from across the city – from the smartest and most upmarket establishments to the best budget food eateries. Restaurants and cafés in Istanbul offer a wide range of cuisines, including Ottoman, fusion, and international dishes, but you should not miss the traditional Turkish restaurants (*lokanta, meyhane*) either. The DK Choice restaurants are extra special. These are the truly exceptional establishments – those that boast superb cuisine, presentation, service and location, or just offer something unique that simply has to be experienced.

Delicious fried and grilled mackerel sold on the Eminönü quayside *(see p208)*

The Flavours of Istanbul

The wide range of climatic zones across Turkey make it one of the few countries that can grow all its own food. Tea is cultivated in the mountains by the Black Sea and bananas in the sultry south. The Anatolian plain in between is criss-crossed by wheat fields and rich grasslands on which cattle graze, providing top quality meat and dairy produce. Fruit and vegetables flourish everywhere and fish abound in the salty seas that lap the nation's shores. Freshness is the hallmark of this varied cuisine, drawn from the many cultures that were subject to nearly five centuries of Ottoman rule.

Nar (pomegranates)

A stall in the Spice Bazaar, one of Istanbul's oldest markets

The Anatolian Steppe

The steppe stretching from Central Asia to Anatolia is one of the oldest inhabited regions of the world. Dishes from this vast area are as varied as the different ethnic groups that live here, but are mainly traditional and simple. To fit in with a mainly nomadic way of life, food generally needed to be quick and easy to prepare. Turkey's most famous culinary staples, yogurt, flat bread and the kebab, originate in this region.

The common use of fruits, such as pomegranates, figs and apricots, in Turkish savoury dishes stems from Persian influences, filtering down with the tribes that came from the north of the steppe. From the Middle East, further south, nomads introduced the occasional fiery blash of chilli. Its use was once an essential aid to preserving meat in the searing desert heat.

Ottoman Cuisine

It was in the vast, steamy kitchens of the Topkapı Palace that a repertoire of mouthwatering dishes to rival the celebrated cuisines

Lamb şiş kebab
Chicken şiş kebab
Stuffed aubergine (eggplant)
Chilli sauce
Prawn (shrimp) kebab
Lamb cutlet
Doner kebab

A selection of typical Turkish kebabs

Local Dishes and Specialities

Because of Istanbul's proximity to the sea, fresh fish is readily available and is a key ingredient on the city's menus. Since ancient times the Bosphorus has been known for its excellent fishing. In the winter months especially, there is a bounty of oil-rich fish, such as bluefish, bream, bonito tuna, sea bass, mullet and mackerel, waiting to be reeled in. From the Black Sea, Istanbul is also provided with a steady supply of juicy mussels and *hamsi*, a type of anchovy. Sweets are also popular and eaten throughout the day, not just after a meal. They are sold in shops, on stalls and by street vendors. Istanbul is renowned for its *baklava*, sweet pastries coated with syrup and often filled with nuts.

Turkish Delight

Midye dolması Mussels are stuffed with a spiced rice mixture, steamed and served with a squirt of lemon juice.

A splendid array of fruit, vegetables and dried goods in the Spice Bazaar

of France and China grew up. At the height of the Ottoman Empire, in the 16th and 17th centuries, legions of kitchen staff slaved away on the Sultan's behalf. Court cooks usually specialized in particular dishes. Some prepared soups, while others just grilled meats or fish, or dreamed up combinations of vegetables, or baked breads, or made puddings and sherberts. As Ottoman rule expanded to North Africa, the Balkans and parts of southern Russia, influences from these far-flung places crept into the Turkish imperial kitchens. Complex dishes of finely seasoned stuffed meats and vegetables, often with such fanciful names as "lady's lips", "Vizier's fingers" and the "fainting Imam", appeared. This imperial tradition lives on

in many of Istanbul's restaurants, where dishes such as *karnıyarık* (halved aubergines (eggplant) stuffed with minced lamb, pine nuts and dried fruit) and *hünkar beğendili köfte* (meatballs served with a smooth purée of smoked aubergine and cheese) grace the menu.

Fresh catch from the Bosphorus on a fish stall in Karaköy

Bazaar Culture

A visit to the market that spills out around Istanbul's Spice Bazaar (see p90) is an absolute must. A cornucopia of fine ingredients is brought here daily from farms that surround the city. Apricots, watermelons, cherries and figs sit alongside staple vegetables, such as peppers, onions, aubergines and tomatoes. Fine cuts of lamb and beef, cheeses, pickles, herbs, spices and honey-drenched pastries and puddings are also on offer.

KNOW YOUR FISH

The profusion of different species in the waters around Istanbul makes the city a paradise for fish lovers:

Barbunya Red mullet

Çupra Sea bream

Dilbalığı Sole

Hamsi Anchovy

Kalamar Squid

Kalkan Turbot

Kefal Grey mullet

Kılıç Swordfish

Levrek Sea bass

Lüfer Bluefish

Midye Mussels

Palamut Bonito tuna

Uskumru Mackerel

İmam bayıldı Aubergines, stuffed with tomatoes, garlic and onions, are baked in the oven until meltingly soft.

Levrek pilakisi This stew is made by simmering sea bass fillets with potatoes, carrots, tomatoes, onions and garlic.

Kadayıf Rounds of shredded filo pastry are stuffed with nuts and doused with honey to make a sumptuous dessert.

Mezes

As in many southern European countries, a Turkish meal begins with a selection of appetizing starters known as *mezes*, which are placed in the middle of the table for sharing. In a basic *meyhane* restaurant, you may be offered olives, cheese and slices of melon, but in a grander establishment the choice will be enormous. Mainly consisting of cold vegetables and salads of various kinds, *mezes* can also include a number of hot dishes, such as *börek* (cheese pastries), fried mussels and squid. *Mezes* are eaten with bread and traditionally washed down with *rakı* (a clear, anise-flavoured spirit).

Humus with *pide* bread

Zeytinyağli enginar (artichokes)

Çoban salatasi (tomato, red onion and cucumber salad)

Ayşe fasulye (green beans with tomato sauce)

Kavun with beyaz peynir (melon with a creamy, feta-like cheese)

Yaprak dolması (stuffed vine leaves)

Tarama (a dip made with cod's roe, garlic and olive oil)

Turkish Breads

Bread is the cornerstone of every meal in Turkey and comes in a wide range of shapes and styles. Besides *ekmek* (crusty white loaves) the other most common types of Turkish bread are *yufka* and *pide*. *Yufka*, the typical bread of nomadic communities, is made from thinly rolled sheets of dough which are cooked on a griddle, and dried to help preserve them. They can then be heated up and served to accompany any main meal as required. *Pide* is the type of flat bread that is usually served with *mezes* and kebabs in restaurants. It consists of a flattened circle or oval of dough, sometimes brushed with beaten egg and sprinkled with sesame seeds or black cumin, that is baked in an oven. It is a staple during many religious festivals. In the month of Ramadan, no meal is considered complete without *pide*. Another popular bread is *simit*, a crisp, ring-shaped savoury loaf that comes covered in sesame seeds.

A delivery of freshly baked *simit* loaves

What to Drink in Istanbul

The most common drink in Istanbul is tea (çay), which is normally served black in small, tulip-shaped glasses. It is offered to you wherever you go: in shops and bazaars, and even in banks and offices. Breakfast is usually accompanied by tea, whereas small cups of strong Turkish coffee (kahve) are drunk mid-morning and also at the end of meals. Cold drinks include a variety of fresh fruit juices, such as orange and cherry, and refreshing syrup-based sherbets. Although Turkey does produce its own wine and beer, the most popular alcoholic drink in Istanbul is rakı, which is usually served to accompany mezes.

Fruit juice seller

Soft Drinks

Bottled mineral water (su) is sold in corner shops and served in restaurants everywhere. If you are feeling adventurous, you may like to try a glass of ayran, salty liquid yoghurt. Boza, made from bulgur wheat, is another local

Vişne suyu   Ayran

drink to sample (see p94). There is always a variety of refreshing fruit and vegetable juices available. They include cherry juice (vişne suyu), turnip juice (şalgam suyu) and şıra, a juice made from fermented grapes.

Alcoholic Drinks

The national alcoholic drink in Turkey is rakı – "lion's milk" – a clear, anise-flavoured spirit, which turns cloudy when water is added. It is drunk with fish and mezes. The Turkish wine industry produces some good reds and whites, served in many restaurants. Doluca and Kavaklıdere are two of the leading brands. Foreign and imported wines are widely available at high prices. Turkey's own Efes Pilsen beer is widely sold. Note that alcohol is not served in some of the cheaper restaurants and kebab houses.

Rakı   Beer   Red wine   White wine

Coffee and Tea

Turkish coffee (kahve) is dark and strong and is ordered according to the amount of sugar required: az (little), orta (medium), or çok (a lot). You may have to ask for it especially, as some restaurants may give you instant coffee. The ubiquitous drink is tea (çay). It is served with sugar but without milk, and in a small, tulip-shaped glass. Apple (elma), is the most popular flavour, but there are also linden (ıhlamur), rosehip (kuşburnu) and mint (nane) teas.

Traditional samovar for tea

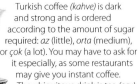

Apple tea   Linden tea

Turkish coffee is a very strong drink and an acquired taste for most people.

Sahlep is a hot, winter drink made from powdered orchid root.

Where to Eat and Drink

Seraglio Point

Hocapaşa Pidecisi $
Turkish Pizza **Map** 5 D2
19 Hocapasa Sok, Sirkeci
Tel (0212) 512 09 90
Pide, best described as a long,
chewy Turkish pizza, is the
speciality. The one with mince is
deliciously spicy, and can come
with or without an egg in it.

Şehzade Erzurum Cağ Kebabı $
Kebab **Map** 5 D1
3A Hocapaşa Sok, Sirkeci
Tel (0212) 520 33 61
This unassuming place serves
up a delicious alternative to the
doner *kebab*, which hails from
the eastern city of Erzurum. The
meat is laterally skewered before
being served. Few items on
the menu. Try the tasty marinated lamb.

Café Mese $$
Café **Map** 5 E2
27 Hudavendigar St, Sirkeci
Tel (0212) 519 18 00
Pastas, desserts, coffees and
pints of beer (hard to find in
the old city) are popular choices
at this friendly café. Close to
the train station and tram lines.

Can Oba $$
Turkish Fusion **Map** 5 D1
10 Hocapaşa Sok, Sirkeci
Tel (0212) 522 12 15
A relative newcomer to the
Sirkeci restaurant scene,
chef Can Oba trained abroad
before returning to set up his
own place. While there are
few tables at his restaurant, the
imaginatively prepared dishes
make sure there's always a
crowd here.

DK Choice

Imbat $$
Aegean **Map** 5 D2
34 Hudavendigar Cad, Sirkeci
Tel (0212) 520 71 91
Popular Aegean restaurant
atop the Orient Express Hotel.
Reserving ahead is almost
essential, and is the best way
to secure a coveted Bosphorus-
facing spot on the terrace. The
succulent lamb is highly rated,
but the menu also caters to
vegetarians without compro-
mising on originality. Attentive
staff complete the picture.

Paşazade $$
Ottoman **Map** 5 D2
5A Ibn-i Kemal Sok, Sirkeci
Tel (0212) 513 37 57
Many restaurants purport to serve
Ottoman cuisine, but Pasazade
doesn't take this duty lightly. The
menu boasts hard to find dishes
– mahmudiye, a fruity chicken dish,
is one of them. The view from the
rooftop terrace is also a draw.

Karakol $$$
Turkish Fusion **Map** 5 F3
*Inside Topkapı Palace grounds,
next to Aya Irene*
Tel (0212) 514 94 94
Next to the 6th-century church,
Haghia Iren. Most of the seating
here is outside, but in winter,
patrons can sit in the recently
restored sentry post building.

Konyalı $$$
Kebab
Inside Topkapı Palace **Map** 3 F3
Tel (0212) 513 96 96
This upmarket restaurant has
many branches through the city.

Price Guide
Price categories include a three-course
meal for one, and all unavoidable extras
including service and tax.

$	under US$30
$$	US$30 to 60
$$$	over US$60

The Topkapı Palace branch
offers breathtaking views of
the Bosphorus, although guests
have to pay an admission fee.

Neyzade $$$
Meyhane **Map** 5 E2
5 Taya Hatun Sokak, Sirkeci
Tel (0212) 528 43 44
Nestled outside the wall of
the Topkapı Palace, Neyzade's
carefully chosen menu showcases
different regional Turkish cuisines.
Instead of trying to specialize in
all of them, the restaurant picks
a few dishes – *mezes*, soups and
kebabs – and does them well.

Olive Restaurant $$$
Ottoman **Map** 5 E2
*Hotel Yaşmak Sultan (top floor) ,18
Ebusuud Cad*
Tel (0212) 528 13 47
Elegant Ottoman-inspired cuisine,
along with sweeping views of the
Haghia Sofia, Topkapı Palace and
the Bosphorus from the terrace.

Orient Express Restaurant $$$
Meyhane **Map** 5 E1
Inside Sirkeci Train Station
Tel (0212) 522 22 80
Housed in the terminus building
of the Orient Express, the station
and restaurant are a fading
monument to a gentler age.
Not the best value *meyhane*, but
with tables spilling out onto the
station platform, its atmospheric
setting can't be beaten.

Gently lit interiors at Café Mese, Seraglio Point

Sarnıç $$$
Meyhane Map 5 F3
38 Sogukcesme Sok,
Sultanahmet
Tel (0212) 512 42 91
Dramatically set in a millennium-old Byzantine cistern from which it takes its name. Enjoy an evening meal in its brick and wrought-iron, candle-lit interior.

Sultanahmet
Doyuran Lokantası $
Lokanta Map 4 A5
10 Ördekli Bakkal Sok, Kumkapi
Tel (0212) 458 26 37
Eat like the locals and skip tourist fare in favour of the daily specials at Doyuran. Far from fancy, the home-made meals are filling and won't set you back by very much.

Fes Café $
Café Map 4 C3
25 Ali Baba Türbe Sok, Nuruosmaniye
Tel (0212) 526 30 70
Glamourous café in the streets around the bazaar. Fruit sherbets, coffees and modest lunch options in cool, retro surroundings.

Köfteci Ramiz $
Kebab Map 5 D3
Bab-ı Ali Cad, Himaye-i Ekfal
Sok 17, Fatih
Tel (0212) 527 13 40
Part of a chain. Specializes in meatballs. Clean and predictable with no alcohol – try the *ayran* instead.

Imren Lokantasi $
Lokanta Map 4 A5
Kadırga Liman Cad 81
Kumkapı, Fatih
Tel (0212) 638 11 96
Utilitarian, inexpensive and very popular for its tasty meals. Pick from a series of daily specials, but come early in the day for the widest selection.

DK Choice

Tarihi Sultanahmet
Köftecisi $
Traditional Map 5 E4
12 Divanyolu Cad
Tel (0212) 520 05 66
Along a strip of imitators, this is the most original. The *kofte*, or meatballs, have many famous admirers, whose comments are framed upon the walls. Eat your *kofte* with *pazi* or bean salad, and follow up with the semolina *helva* dessert. The menu may not be diverse, but whatever they do, they do well.

Glass and tile decor of Fes Café, Sultanahmet

Ahırkapı Balıkçısı $$
Meyhane Map 5 F5
46 Keresteci Hakkı Sok
Tel (0212) 518 49 88
A tiny neighbourhood fish restaurant, which caters to locals and tourists alike. Save room for the baked *helva* dessert.

Albura Kathisma $$
Kebab Map 5 F5
26 Akbıyık Cad
Tel (0212) 517 90 31
Waiters here seem less pushy than in other restaurants. A good range of meat and vegetarian dishes caters to all palettes.

Aloran Café & Restaurant $$
Traditional Map 5 F4
11 Adliye Sok, Cankurtaran
Tel (0212) 458 85 28
Try Turkish *mezes* and meats at this lesser known restaurant. Interesting flavours and reasonable prices.

Doy Doy $$
Traditional Map 5 D5
Sifa Hamami Sok 13
Tel (0212) 517 15 88
Doy Doy is a predictable and reasonable place for the uninitiated to try Turkish cuisine. It's worth hiking up four flights of stairs for the view from the terrace.

Dubb $$
Indian Map 5 F5
10 Incili Çavuş Sok
Tel (0212) 513 73 08
Popular Indian restaurant. The atmosphere here is jolly – dancing lessons are given on Saturdays.

Fuego Restaurant $$
Kebab Map 5 E3
15A, Incili Cavus Sok
Tel (0212) 531 36 97
A deceptively named restaurant serving not Spanish cuisine, but Turkish and Kurdish specials, backed by a well-stocked bar.

Karışma Sen Meyhane $$
Meyhane Map 2 A5
28–30 Kennedy Cad, Sahil Yolu,
Cankurtaran
Tel (0212) 458 00 81
A proper historical Istanbul *meyhane*, which started life as a nightclub in the 1930s. Serves a variety of *mezes*, fish as well as desserts.

Sultanahmet Fish House $$
Meyhane Map 3 E4
14 Prof K Ismail Gurkan Cad
Tel (0212) 527 44 45
Good choice for fish, with helpful and knowledgeable staff. Seasonal specials like salt-baked sea bass follow a range of *mezes*. There are a few *kebab* choices too, but the real emphasis is on seafood.

The North Shield $$
Pub Map 5 E4
Yerebatan Cad 13
Tel (0212) 444 93 32
It would be hard to claim that people come here for the food – most come for the cold beer, and the many screenings of football that invariably accompany it.

Vonalı Celal $$
Meyhane Map 5 F5
40 Kennedy Cad, Sahil Yolu,
Cankurtaran
Tel (0212) 516 18 93
The Vonalı Celal stands out among a string of restaurants looking out over the Marmara. It serves special Black Sea dishes along with more ubiquitous fish grills, but the real passion here is for pickles, which form the centrepiece of the menu.

For more information on types of restaurants *see page 191*

Amedros $$$
Kebab **Map** 5 D3
7 Hoca Rüstem Sok
Tel (0212) 522 83 56
Reliable restaurant serving
vegetable kebabs as well as stews
for two. The wide-ranging menu
includes Ottoman-inspired dishes.

Balıkçı Sabahattin $$$
Seafood **Map** 5 F4
Seyit Hasan Kuyu Sok 1,
Cankurtaran, Eminönü
Tel (0212) 458 18 24
Housed in a restored wooden
mansion near the Armada
hotel, this old Istanbul favourite
specializes in seafood. In summer,
diners spill out onto the
pretty garden.

Faros Hotel Restaurant $$$
International **Map** 5 D3
76 Divan Yolu Cad, Sultanahmet
Tel (0212) 518 83 88
Located on the top floor of the
Faros hotel, this restaurant has a
variety of international cuisine with
some Turkish-influenced dishes.

Giritli Restaurant $$$
Meyhane **Map** 5 F5
Keresteci Hakkı Sok, Cankurtaran
Tel (0212) 458 22 70
Cretan restaurant hidden in
a lovely courtyard down an alley.
The only option here is a good
value all-you-can-eat menu,
which includes limitless alcoholic
drinks and about 20 kinds of
meze. Book ahead.

Khorosani $$$
Kebab **Map** 5 D3
39/41 Ticarethane Sok
Tel (0212) 519 59 59
Visitors won't find bargain-
basement prices at Khorosani,
but they are serious about their
kebabs. The *Testi kebab* – a stew
made in a sealed urn, which is
broken open at the table – is a
popular choice here.

Mozaik Restaurant $$$
Turkish **Map** 5 E3
1 Incili Cavus Sok
Tel (0212) 512 41 77
Plenty of intimate corners in
this converted old house. Try the
meze platter for starters, or the
oven-baked seafood.

Patara Restaurant $$$
Meyhane **Map** 4 A5
13 Samsa Sok, Kumkapı
Tel (0212) 517 99 19
A number of set menu options
save guests from the hassle of
choosing dishes at Kumkapi's
Patara Restaurant. Book ahead
and they will also arrange a free
pick-up from your hotel.

Seasons Restaurant $$$
International **Map** 5 F4
Four Seasons Hotel, 1 Tevkifhane
Sok, Cankurturan
Tel (0212) 402 30 00
The restaurant at this converted
late-Ottoman prison is a popular
destination for high-end dining.
Enjoy the all-you-can-eat spread,
with everything from sushi to
antipasti to more traditional
Turkish choices.

Tria Elegance $$$
Kebab **Map** 5 F4
Akbiyik Cad 11
Tel (0212) 518 45 18
Pleasant restaurant where dishes
like seabass stew or lamb shank
with saffron are served against a
breathtaking rooftop view.

Bazaar Quarter

Aslan Restaurant $
Lokanta **Map** 4 C3
Vezirhan Cad 66, Çemberlitaş
Tel (0212) 513 76 10
A reliable *esnaf* or tradesman's
restaurant, serving the best in
Turkish comfort food. Vegetable
dishes and soups form the core
of the menu, but there are meat
options on offer as well. A good
place for lunch.

Aynen Dürüm $
Kebab **Map** 4 C3
29 Muhafazacılar Sok, near gate 20
of the Grand Bazaar
Tel (0212) 527 47 28
Useful bolt-hole for tasty kebabs
when on the go. Keeps bazaar
hours, so closes by early evening.

Bizim Mutfak $
Lokanta **Map** 5 D1
2 Şeyhülislam Hayri Efendi
Cad, Eminönü
Tel (0212) 522 78 46

Intimate dining at the well-reviewed
Amedros in Sultanahmet

Modern dining room tucked away
behind the New Mosque. Local
workers flock here at lunchtime
for a variety of soups, desserts,
meat and vegetable choices.

Borsa $
Traditional **Map** 5 D1
60–62 Yalıköşkü Han, Yalıköşkü
Cad, Eminönü
Tel (0212) 511 80 79
A clean, efficient family eatery
that serves breakfast, lunch and
dinner, and is never without a
throng of customers. Convenient
pit-stop for sightseers along the
Eminönü shoreline.

Can Restaurant $
Lokanta **Map** 4 B3
Sorguclu Han No 19–24, Kapalicarsi
Tel (0212) 511 91 53
An out-of-the-way lunch spot
where both bazaar workers and
shoppers come to get their fill of
hearty home-style cooking.The
meat broth thickened with egg
is worth the trip.

Çiğ Köfteci Ali Usta $
Café **Map** 5 D2
Mimar Vedat Sok, in the alley behind
Kral Kokoreç
Join the queue for a portion of *cig*
kofte (balls of a spicy mixture of
raw meat and tomato paste). Get
yours wrapped in crispy lettuce or
in a tub to take away.

Gaziantep Burç Ocakbaşı $
Kebab **Map** 4 B3
Parçacılar Sok 12, Kapalicarsi
Tel (0212) 527 15 16
This narrow bazaar restaurant
serves meat dishes from the
south-eastern region of Turkey,
which is famed for its flavourful
kebabs. Stuffed and dried vege-
tables are a delicious alternative
for vegetarian guests.

Kahve Dünyası $
Café **Map** 4 C3
Kızılhan Sok 18, Eminönü
Tel (0212) 520 02 04
Turkey's answer to Starbucks is
a good place to grab a coffee –
whether Turkish or otherwise.
It always comes with a sweet of
some kind, showing off the other
speciality of this chain: chocolates.

Kardeşler Pilav Evi $
Café **Map** 4 C1
Tahtakale Cad 48
Tel (0212) 514 63 62
A classic tradesman's lunch spot
with a humble menu consisting
of chicken, rice and chickpeas.
Wash everything down with *ayran*
(a salty yoghurt drink). Don't
come after dark though – things
pack up at 5:30pm.

Kral Kokoreç $
Kebab **Map** 5 D1
Büyük Postane Cad 54, Sirkeci
Tel (0212) 526 71 69
Serving only sandwiches of spicy but delicious grilled lamb innards, this place is not for the faint-hearted. However, those who try it will find themselves wooed by Istanbul's favourite hangover cure.

Makarna Sarayı $
International **Map** 4 C3
18 Vezirhan Cad, Çemberlitaş, Fatih
Tel (0212) 528 29 38
This busy café features a changing menu, with over ten kinds of pasta competing for attention. Falafel, juices and some daily Turkish specials can also be found here.

Nuruosmaniye Köftecisi $
Kebab **Map** 4 C3
Vezir Han Cad 73, Cemberlitas
Tel (0212) 526 71 69
Meatballs and beans are the staples here. Cheap, delicious and fulfilling – a great place to refuel on the way to the bazaar.

Ocakbası Dürüm Ve Kebap Salonu $
Kebab **Map** 5 D1
Hasırcılar Cad 62, Eminönü
Tel (0212) 526 32 29
Chicken or lamb grills are almost all there is at this pit-stop near the Spice Bazaar. Reasonable and delicious lunch options served on a platter or in a wrap.

Şark Kahvesi $
Café **Map** 4 B2
134 Yaglikcilar Cad, Kapalicarsi, Beyazit
Tel (0212) 512 11 44
All roads in the bazaar lead to Şark Kahvesi, or so it seems. Enjoy coffee and a game of backgammon.

Seref Buryan $
Traditional **Map** 2 A2
4 Itfaiye Cad, Husambey Mah, Fatih
Tel (0212) 635 80 85
A good choice among a strip of restaurants purveying delicious tandoori lamb from the Kurdish south-eastern region. *Perde pilavi*, a chicken and almond rice dish, and *mumbar*, a kind of stuffed sausage, are among the other options.

Havuzlu $$
Lokanta **Map** 4 B3
3 Gani Çelebi Sok, inside the Grand Bazaar
Tel (0212) 527 33 46
Because of its size, Havuzlu is a rare dining option in the Grand

Buffet spread at Nar Lokanta, Bazaar Quarter

Bazaar. It does not offer the best value but is nevertheless a pleasant sit-down restaurant in the centre of the bazaar.

Daruzziyafe $$$
Kebab **Map** 2 B3
6 Şifahane Sok, Süleymaniye
Tel (0212) 511 84 14
Located in the grounds of the recently restored Süleymaniye Mosque, this spacious, airy restaurant mostly caters to tour groups, but is a pretty setting for a meal.

Hamdi $$$
Kebab **Map** 4 C1
17 Kalçin Sok, Rüstem Paşa, Fatih
Tel (0212) 528 03 90
A multi-storey kebab emporium serving up meats from the spiced to the pistachioed to the aubergined. Book ahead for a seat that looks out at the mouth of the Bosphorus.

DK Choice

Nar Lokanta $$$
Lokanta **Map** 4 C3
Inside Armaggan store, 65 Nuruosmaniye Cad, 5th Floor
Tel (0212) 522 28 00
A special choice in the hit-and-miss culinary fringes of the bazaar. Nar makes a point of only using seasonal ingredients, and from these they manage to fashion 50 daily dishes. One option inside this glamorous tiled dining room is an open buffet of vegetable specials, made using their own brand of pressed olive oil. Has an extensive list of Turkish wines too.

Beyoğlu

Bambi Café $
Café **Map** 7 E4
2 Siraselviler Cad, Taksim
Tel (0212) 293 21 21
Although it might not look like much during the day, Bambi comes alive at night with patrons queuing around the block for their famous fast food. Quick, cheap and tasty.

By Corbaci Soup Bar $
International **Map** 7 D4
8 Yeniçarşi Cad, Galatasaray
Tel (0212) 244 51 69
With 30 kinds of soup a day from a revolving menu of 600, the restaurant is obviously serious about its soup. It stays open till 6pm on the weekend. Come here for a late night fix of tripe soup, a local hangover cure.

Café Grand Boulevard $
Café **Map** 7 D4
Hazzo Pulo Pasaji, 116 Hengecidi Sok, Istiklal Cad
Tel (0212) 293 34 46
This café makes a great spot to drink tea and play backgammon in the pleasant courtyard of Hazzopulo Pasaj.

Canım Ciğerim $
Kebab **Map** 7 D5
162 Istiklal Cad
Tel (0212) 243 10 05
Famous for its skewers of liver, this inexpensive restaurant is popular with locals and tourists alike. Get yours on the skewer or wrapped up with onions and greens. There is chicken and meat for the faint-hearted, and sweet cheesy *kunefe* for dessert.

For more information on types of restaurants *see page 191*

Modern dining area at the Culinary Institute in Beyoğlu

Datli Maya $
Lokanta   **Map** 7 E5
Türkgücü Cad 59/A, Cihangir
Tel (0212) 292 90 56
The latest project from eccentric
and exuberant chef, Dilara Erbay.
Housed in an old *simit* factory,
it has a menu of creatively
reimagined Turkish street food
staples – *durum* wraps, which
diners may encounter elsewhere,
but not the vegan version!

Fasuli $
Lokanta   **Map** 7 E5
6 Kiliçalıpasa Cad, Tophane
Tel (0212) 243 65 80
This Black Sea restaurant is
famous for the beans after
which it is named. Corn bread,
a cheesy fondue called *mihlama*
and healthy salads are executed
with aplomb.

Fürreyya $
Seafood   **Map** 7 D5
2b Serdari Ekrem Sok
Tel (0212) 252 48 53
Miniature restaurant that serves
excellent fish a stone's throw away
from the Galata Tower. Fish soups,
wraps, and sandwiches brimming
with caramelized onions come at
under 10 YTL. There are also more
elaborate plates of whitebait and
shrimp to choose from.

Güllüoğlu Baklavacısı $
Café   **Map** 3 E1
Katli Otopark Alti, Karaköy
Tel (0212) 293 09 10
Come to the *baklava* kings of
Turkey for the best example of
this delectable *filo* dessert.

İsmail Kebab $
Café   **Map** 7 E4
7 Hocazade Sok, Siraseviler Cad
Tel (0212) 252 34 87
Great place for cheap, crisp
and tasty Turkish *lahmacun*
pizzas. Roll them up with lemon
and salad.

İzi Burger $
International   **Map** 7 D5
8 Ensiz Sok, Asmalı Mescit
Tel (0212) 243 58 69
Cool burger joint of the kind that
wouldn't seem out of place in
London or New York. The menu
changes in response to requests,
which patrons can scrawl upon
the mirrored walls. Try the Hangover Burger which comes with a
delectable Bloody Mary sauce.

Namlı $
Lokanta   **Map** 3 E1
Rıhtım Cad, Katotopark Altı, Karaköy
Tel (0212) 293 68 80
This overflowing deli offers a
good introduction to an array
of Turkish flavours. Point and
pick what you like. The variety is
such that they even stock several
different kinds of *salgam suyu* –
a pickled turnip juice. Cheese
varieties aplenty!

Sabırtaşı $
Kebab   **Map** 7 D4
Floor 5, 122 Istiklal Cad
Tel (0212) 251 94 23
Family-run restaurant that is famous
for its menu centred around
manti (Turkish dumplings) and *icli
kofte* (minced meat *bulgur* parcels).

Saray Muhallebicisi $
Patisserie   **Map** 7 D4
173 Istiklal Cad
Tel (0212) 292 34 34
Less a restaurant than a five-storey
temple to dessert – 10 kinds of
baklava, milky puddings and cakes
are served here till 3 in the morning. Don't miss the *tavuk gogusu* –
a sweet milky pudding made
with boiled chicken.

Van Kahvaltı Evi $
Breakfast   **Map** 7 E5
Defterdar Yokusu 52A, Cihangir
Tel (0212) 293 64 37
Welcome to a cornucopia of
regional specialities at this hip

Kurdish breakfast joint. It is so
popular that there can be a long
wait to get in, but the management
usually ply guests with tea till
they can be seated.

Ada Café & Bookstore $$
International   **Map** 7 D5
Istiklal Cad 158
Tel (0212) 251 55 44
A bookshop-cum-café on Beyoglu's
main pedestrian thoroughfare.
Previously housing nothing but
books, some of the floor was
cleared to accommodate diners,
who nevertheless can still be
spotted perusing their new
purchases along with Italian
influenced pastas and salads.

Ara Kafe $$
Café   **Map** 7 D4
*Tomtom Mah, Tosbağa Sok 2,
Galatasaray*
Tel (0212) 245 41 05
Housed in the building where
photographer Ara Guler has his
studio, the décor as much as the
photographs on the wall at Ara
Kafe are a slice of old world Istanbul.
No alcohol is served, but Indian
teas and home-made lemonades
keep things rolling along.

Culinary Institute $$
Turkish Fusion   **Map** 7 D4
59 Meşrutiyet Cad, Asmalı Mescit
Tel (0212) 251 22 14
The dining room of a cookery
school, the Culinary Institute
serves a full monthly menu. Some
of the interesting twists on Turkish
favourites to be found here are
persimmon martini and dried
aubergine stuffed kebab, as well
as a few international meals.

Date $$
Turkish Fusion   **Map** 7 D5
*Asmali Mescit Mah, Ensiz Sok 1/B,
Asmalı Mescit*
Tel (0212) 243 81 27
Some of the large shared tables
may make it hard to indulge
in the romantic tete-a-tete it
promises, but Date boasts a
number of cosy corners too.
Try the samphire and scallops,
or the steak tartare.

Ficcin $$
Meyhane   **Map** 7 D4
Kallavi Sok 7/1–13/1
Tel (0212) 293 37 86
Circassian-influenced *meze* place
that comprises a series of venues
lining the same street. A worthy
dinner stop for small groups, away
from the chaos of Nevizade. Don't
miss the *cerkez tavuk*, a garlicky
chicken walnut dish. The restaurant's
eponymous meat pie is also hard
to find elsewhere.

Hacıbaba $$
Traditional   **Map** 7 E4
49 İstiklal Cad
Tel (0212) 244 18 86
Conveniently situated restaurant that serves traditional Turkish food, if visitors don't mind competing with tour groups. Open buffet with a big vegetarian selection, and kebab choices for the main courses.

Helvetia $$
Lokanta   **Map** 7 D5
Asmalı Mescit Mah, Gen Yazgan Sok 12
Tel (0212) 245 87 80
A vegetarian restaurant without being strictly vegetarian. A few choices for carnivores nestle alongside the day's specials. Pick from home-style vegetable gratins and olive-oil dishes, followed by aromatic herbal teas.

Jash $$
Meyhane   **Map** 7 F4
Pürletaş Mah, Cihangir Cad 9
Tel (0212) 244 30 42
This intimate *meyhane* serves Armenian *mezes*. But when the musicians move in with their accordions, things can get a bit raucous!

DK Choice

Kahve6 $$
Breakfast   **Map** 7 E5
Anahtar Sok 13, Cihangir
Tel (0212) 293 08 49
Kahve 6's name is a pun on the word 'breakfast', but the riffs on the best meal of the day don't end there. From poached eggs with a garlic sauce to the life-saver *simit* (a seeded bread ring served with all the essential Turkish breakfast jams, cheeses and olives), this Cihangir hang-out serves creative versions of old favourites.

Vibrant and colourful tables at Çok Çok Thai, Beyoğlu

Karaköy Lokantası $$
Lokanta   **Map** 3 E1
37 Kemankeş Cad, Karaköy
Tel (0212) 292 44 55
Beautiful tiled interior in this hip take on the *lokanta*. A popular lunch choice for business people in the area.

Kitchenette $$
International   **Map** 7 E3
Gümüşsuyu Mah, Tak-ı Zafer Cad 3, Taksim
Tel (0212) 292 68 62
A reliable chain of brasseries. Amongst their menus is one called 'fit-for-you', which counts the calories in your salmon and vegetables *en papillote*. There is also a kids' menu as well as burgers, breakfasts and *quesadillas* – the objective is to cater to all kinds of tastes.

Klemuri $$
Meyhane   **Map** 7 E4
2 Büyükparmakkapi
Tel (0212) 292 32 72
A friendly Laz *meyhane*. Besides serving dishes from Turkey's lush Black Sea region, the proprietors also curate cultural shows from the east, and sometimes host guest-cooks. The menu indicates vegan or vegetarian suitability, but there's plenty to satisfy a meat eater.

Şehir Meyhanesi $$
Meyhane   **Map** 7 D4
Kartal Sok 3/A
Tel (0212) 249 61 60
Şehir Meyhanesi doesn't feel the need to play up the nostalgic stereotype. The food, like marinated sea bass and grilled liver, is typical *meyhane* fare, but the crowd is hipper and younger than at many other eateries of its kind.

White Mill Café $$
International   **Map** 7 E5
13 Susam Sok, Cihangir
Tel (0212) 292 28 95

With a beautiful, expansive outdoor courtyard garden, this restaurant in the bohemian district of Cihangir is a popular destination for languid lunches.

Zencefil $$
Lokanta   **Map** 7 E4
Şht Muhtar Mah, 8 Kurabiye Sok
Tel (0212) 243 82 34
Pretty café in a glasshouse of a building. Mainly vegetarian dishes on offer, with some non-vegetarian options. A calm oasis away from the noise and traffic of Taksim's busier end.

5 Kat $$$
International   **Map** 7 E4
7 Soğancı Sok, Cihangir
Tel (0212) 293 37 74
Popular Cihangir restaurant and bar. The upbeat atmosphere and lovely views are more enticing than the food, although the *prix fixe* menu is useful for large parties.

Ca'd'oro Salt Restaurant and Café $$$
International   **Map** 3 D1
SALT Galata, Bankalar Cad
Tel (0212) 243 82 92
Housed in the newly-restored Ottoman Bank building next to SALT gallery and the research library. A purpose-built glass cube at the back has a small café menu, while an upstairs restaurant offers cuisine with Italian and Turkish influences. Views of Golden Horn.

Cezayir $$$
Turkish Fusion   **Map** 7 E4
12 Hayriye Cad, Galatasaray
Tel (0212) 245 99 80
Housed in the restored Italian Workers' Association. This elegant building has a dining room on the ground floor and a large garden downstairs. They also host events.

Çok Çok Thai $$$
International   **Map** 7 D4
51 Mesrutiyet Cad
Tel (0212) 292 64 96
Upmarket Thai restaurant with a hip ambience and friendly staff. The honey grilled salmon with mung bean salad is a winner.

La Mouette $$$
Turkish Fusion   **Map** 7 D5
18 Tomtom Kaptan Sok
Tel (0212) 292 44 67
Excellent new resturant, great for a special occasion. The degustation menu allows guests to sample a gamut of creative dishes.

For more information on types of restaurants *see page 191*

Convivial atmosphere at the popular Pierre Loti Coffee House, Eyüp

Litera Café $$$
International **Map** 7 D4
32 Yeni Carsi Cad
Tel (0212) 292 89 47
Café, bar and restaurant above the Goethe Institute that serves a wide variety of drinks and cocktails. Wonderful view from the rooftop.

Mikla $$$
Turkish Fusion **Map** 7 D4
The Marmara Pera Hotel, 15 Mesrutiyet Cad
Tel (0212) 293 56 56
Enjoy amazing aerial views of the city at this sprawling, chic restaurant. The fixed menu is reasonably priced and showcases updates of Turkish classics.

Münferit $$$
Turkish Fusion **Map** 7 D4
Yeni Çarşı Cad 19, Galatasaray
Tel (0212) 252 50 67
With an interior by local design team Autoban, this is a cool place to go to for both dinner and after-dinner dancing. Indoor and outdoor seating.

Ninja $$$
Japanese **Map** 7 F4
43 Inonu Cad, Gümüşsuyu
Tel (0212) 245 35 95
One of the first Japanese restaurants in Turkey, Ninja serves Japanese grills as well as noodles and sushi. There are small booths to seat private parties.

Sofyalı 9 $$$
Meyhane **Map** 7 D5
9 Sofyalı Sok
Tel (0212) 245 03 62
Proper old-fashioned Istanbul *meyhane*. The only thing that's changed in 50 years is the *rakı* list, which now also contains a wide selection of the newer boutique blends.

Yakup 2 $$$
Meyhane **Map** 7 D5
Asmalı Mescit Mah, Asmalı Mescit Cad 35
Tel (0212) 249 29 25
A *meyhane* with character, serving all the old favourites: *rakı* is consumed liberally here. Popular among locals.

Greater Istanbul

Ali Haydar $
Kebab **Map** 5 D5
Gümüşyüzük Sok 6, Samatya
Tel (0212) 584 21 62
This popular eatery features in its own popular Turkish soap series, *The Second Spring*. Set in an old Armenian neighbourhood, it has a hearty and well-priced menu of kebab dishes. On summer nights, find yourselves being serenaded by Samatya street musicians.

Egg & Burger $
International
Nispetiye Cad, Yıldızçiçeği Sok 2/E, Etiler
Tel (0212) 265 09 99
A pastiche American burger joint near Etiler's Akmerkez shopping centre. Be sure to try their house burger, which comes with caramelized onions as well as the eponymous egg. Busy lunch hour.

Fenerbahçe Büfe $
Café
Rahmi M Koç Museum, 5 Hasköy Cad
Tel (0212) 369 66 00
There's not much on the menu here besides tea with bread rings and white cheese – but that's not the point. Part of industrialist Rahmi Koc's eccentric collection, this café is housed in a retired Bosphorus ferry, and serves the kind of fare diners may have tasted on their way across.

Pastel $
Café
Cevdetpasa Cad 123, Bebek
Tel (0212) 265 01 45
Recently opened by a returning Turkish expat, Pastel is the answer to the prayers of a generation of sophisticated Turks brought up on *pattiserie* outside their shores, and for whom only a genuine opera cake or *mille feuille* will do. Light lunches are also offered.

DK Choice

Pierre Loti Coffee House $
Café
Gümüşsuyu Balmumcu Sok 1, Eyüp
Tel (0212) 581 26 96
Named after the French novelist and naval officer, the this is a modest tea spot famous for its spectacular views of the Golden Horn. Walk up the green slope from Eyup Mosque, or take the funicular to the top, crossing over the cemetery en route to the hill. Either way, on sunny days, the views are worth the trip, even if the rickety chairs and simple menu wouldn't be worth the detour on their own.

Yanyalı Fehmi Lokantası $
Traditional
Yaglikci Ismail Sok 1, Kadikoy
Tel (0216) 336 33 33
The encyclopedic menu belies this restaurant's unconventional appearance – but it showcases quality as well as breadth. The meatballs are delicious, and the saffron rice makes an intriguing change from plain old *pilav*. Save room for dessert.

Akasya $$
International
23 Nisan Cad, 49 Nizam Mah, Büyükada
Tel (0216) 382 10 50
Charming new restaurant on the island of Buyukada; offers an Italian-influenced menu featuring meat, pastas and gourmet dishes from around the world.

Akdeniz Hatay Sofrası $$
Traditional **Map** 1 B4
Ahmediye Cad 44, Fatih
Tel (0212) 444 72 47
A wonderful showcase of the Antakya region's flavourful cuisine. Try the sour minced meat, chickpea and pomegranate soup. Call ahead to sample the special chicken, which is stuffed with rice and spices and then salt-baked.

Aziyade Restaurant $$
Ottoman
Pierre Loti Tepesi, Eyüp
Tel (0212) 497 13 13
Magnificent views of the Golden Horn, an open buffet breakfast, followed by lunch and dinner. It also hosts events such as meetings and Ramadan dinners.

Baccim $$
Ottoman
Aytar Cad 14 Levent, Beşiktaş
Tel (0212) 283 87 44
An intriguing restaurant, near the financial district, specializing in a kind of traditional Turkish stew, with a garish gold leaf interior and occasional live *fasil* music.

Beymen Brasserie $$
International   **Map** 7 F1
Abdi İpekçi Cad 23/1, Nişantaşı
Tel (0212) 343 04 43
The menu at this elegant restaurant is predominantly French. On warm summer evenings, diners occupy the lovely outdoor tables.

Brasserie La Brise $$
French   **Map** 7 F1
Mim Kemal Öke Cad 11A, Nişantaşı
Tel (0212) 244 48 46
Authentically French menu with wines to match. The price tags on the alcohol are very much Turkish, however, and are liable to make your eyes water more than the onions.

bread & butter $$
Café   **Map** 7 F1
Mim Kemal Öke Cad 1/C, Nişantaşı
Tel (0212) 248 40 00
The smell of freshly baked breads and pastries tempts Nişantaşı's shoppers off the streets and into bread & butter. Salads and sandwiches are also on offer.

Büyük Çamlıca Yörük Çadırı $$
Kebab
Turistik Çamlıca Cad 34, Üsküdar
Tel (0216) 443 22 17
This tent café at the top of Camlica hill is a strange but invariably jolly experience. Try endless platters from the buffet, or explore the range of set menus. The highlight is the entertainment, which begins at night, to the delight of local families who come to join in the singing and dancing.

Çiya Kebap $$
Lokanta
48/B Güneşli Bahçe Sokak, Caferağa, Kadikoy
Tel (0216) 336 30 13

Çiya is a humble trio of restaurants along the Kadikoy street. They serve no alcohol, but a recent spate of press activity, including a *New Yorker* profile, means that the chef's encyclopedic menu is no longer the secret it once was. Guests here can sample dishes that don't exist anywhere else.

Fener Köşkü $$
Meyhane   **Map** 1 C1
Abdülezelpaşa Cad 311, Fener
Tel (0212) 621 90 25
Located next to the city walls, the decor here exactly reflects historical events. Drink *rakı* while enjoying a wide range of seafood dishes. Also listen to Greek and Turkish traditional music here.

Mabeyin $$
Kebab
7 Eski Kısıklı Cad, Burhaniye, Kısıklı
Tel (0216) 422 55 80
Delicious kebab restaurant in the hills above the Bosphorus Bridge. Try the *icli kofte*, a stuffed *bulgur* and chopped meat dumpling, which in this case comes laced with pistachios. Save space for a homemade *baklava* dessert.

Mahal $$
Ottoman
Kanyon AVM, Büyükdere Cad 185, Kat 1 B/169, Levent
Tel (0212) 353 51 53
Ottoman fast food is the unlikely staple of Mahal. The two branches are both good places to take a break from your shopping schedule. Be sure to try the *borek*, or traditional Turkish cheese pastry.

Malta Köşkü $$
Kebab   **Map** 9 D2
Yıldız Park, Beşiktaş
Tel (0212) 258 94 53

Hidden away in the gardens of Yıldız Palace, this late Ottoman mansion houses a restaurant that serves brunches, lunches, dinners and everything in between.

Mezzaluna $$
Italian   **Map** 7 F1
21 Mim Kemal Oke Cad, Nişantaşı
Tel (0212) 231 31 42
Istanbul's original Italian restaurant now has branches through the city – this one is where the shoppers of Nişantaşı go for pizzas.

Mythos $$
Meyhane
Inside Haydarpaşa station building, Rihtim, Kadıköy
Tel (0216) 337 09 79
Aegean *meyhane* that occupies a nostalgic corner of Haydarpaşa train station. Its high ceilings and tiled interior form a pretty backdrop to some unusual *meyhane* fare: the sardines marinated in capers and orange peel are unique.

Nusr-Et $$
Kebab
Bebek Mah, Manolya Sok 244–1, Bebek
Tel (0212) 265 45 02
Try the mouthwatering steaks and burgers or rarer cuts at this popular steakhouse. Great for meat lovers. Completing the menu are American-style desserts.

Paper Moon $$
Italian
Adnan Saygun Cad, Akmerkez, Residence Entrance No 224, Akmerkez AVM-Etiler
Tel (0212) 282 16 16
Perhaps more high-end than it has the right to be, this long-established Italian restaurant is not cheap, but still continues to draw in a jet-setting crowd.

Outdoor tables at bread & butter, Greater Istanbul

For more information on types of restaurants *see page 191*

Park Şamdan
International $$
Map 7 F1
18 Mim Kemal Öke Cad, Nişantaşı
Tel (0212) 225 07 10
Continental as well as Turkish
food in an upmarket bistro
environment. Set amid luxury
hotels and art galleries, this has
long been a fashionable spot
for the glitterati of Nişantaşı.

Sıçanlı Meyhane
Meyhane $$
Hurşit Efendi Sok 6, Çınaraltı, Emirgan
Tel (0212) 277 63 03
A notorious *fasil* venue: a
restaurant offering not just *mezes*,
but also singing and dancing –
and lots of it. This traditional
music form, often associated
with belly dancing, is a boisterous
affair, so don't come expecting
to sit quietly in a corner.

Zanzibar
Turkish Fusion $$
*Cemil Topuzlu Cad 102–A,
Caddebostan*
Tel (0216) 385 64 30
Zanzibar is not a traditional Turkish
restaurant, because the plates
here are not for sharing. But when
your chocolate cheesecake or
grilled seabass fillet is this deli-
cious, why would diners want to
share? This branch is housed in
an ornate Ottoman mansion.

360 East
Turkish Fusion $$$
31 Albay Faik, Sozdener Cad, Kadikoy
Tel (0216) 542 43 50
The upmarket 360 chain has now
opened an expansive dinner and
nightclub in Istanbul's Moda
neighbourhood. The boat ride
over is part of the fun, as are the
views of the old city. The programme of events sees international
DJs and musicians passing through.

Asitane
Ottoman $$$
Map 1 B1
6 Kariye Camii Sok, Edirnekapı
Tel (0212) 635 79 97
A well-researched menu of
Ottoman palace cuisine at this
smart restaurant. Each dish comes
with expansive notes. Combine a
meal here with a trip to the beau-
tiful, mosaic-filled Kariye Museum.

Beyti
Kebab $$$
8 Orman Sok, Florya
Tel (0212) 663 29 90
A pilgrimage site for meat-lovers,
as might be expected if the
patron is the only living Turk to
have a kebab named after him.
The portions are enormous, so
a mixed grill might give a better
chance of trying a range of tastes.

The ultra modern and stylish 360 East, Greater Istanbul

Delicatessen
International $$$
Map 7 F1
*Mim Kemal Oke Cad19/1,
Nişantaşı, Harbiye*
Tel (0212) 225 06 04
One of the Nişantaşı restaurant
scene's swankier venues: not
content with flogging fish salads
and burgers, it has even expanded
into a range of homeware. Good
wine list.

Divan Lokanta
Turkish Fusion $$$
Map 7 F3
Asker Ocağı Cad, 34367, No 1 Şişli
Tel (0212) 315 55 00
An Istanbul landmark for more
than 50 years. Having undergone
renovation, it now boasts a range
of new restaurants, including this
venue for high-end Turkish cuisine.
Sensitively executed glass sculptures by Robert du Grenier feature
throughout, while service is
diligent and attentive.

Hünkar
Lokanta $$$
Map 7 F1
Mim Kemal Oke Cad 21, Nişantaşı
Tel (0212) 225 46 65
Meat dishes like *hunkar begendi*
(meat chunks on top of aubergine
mash) are popular, but there are
also a great number of vegetarian
options to try at this upmarket
tradesman's restaurant.

Müzede Changa
Turkish Fusion $$$
42 Sakıp Sabancı Cad, Emirgan
Tel (0212) 323 09 01
Inventive fusion cuisine in the
leafy surroundings of the Sabanci
Museum. Try grilled octopus with
black olive paste and caper-berry
sauce, or clove flavoured Turkish
meatballs. There is a shuttle from
the museum to the restaurant.

Tahtasaray
Meyhane $$$
*4 Levent Meşeli Sok 25,
Dördüncü, Levent*
Tel (0212) 283 85 85

In the business district of
Levent, packed with devoted
patrons who come here for
the *mezes* and meats on offer.
Hot starters, like a thin hazelnut
and mince pizza, are part of
Tahtasaray's appeal.

Ulus 29
Turkish Fusion $$$
1 Yol Sok, Kuruçeşme
Tel (0212) 358 29 29
Set in the hills overlooking
the Bosphorus Bridge, Ulus
29 was the closest Istanbul
dining got to haute and even
molecular cuisine for many
years. The excellent sommelier
has put together a list that
champions new Turkish grapes
to match the wonderful fine
dining experience.

The Bosphorus

Aşşk Kahve
Café $
*Muallim Naci Cad 64/B,
Kurucesme, Besiktas*
Tel (0212) 265 47 34
Assk's encyclopedic menu
manages to cover everything
from breakfast to bellinis, but
all its dishes are infused with
a sense of fun. On the Bosphorus
coast by Kurucesme, it has a
great location as well.

Asude
Lokanta $
*4 Perihan Abla Sok,
Kuzguncuk, Üsküdar*
Tel (0216) 334 44 14
Crowded, family-run lunch spot
with a few revolving specials. On
Monday, the speciality is home-
made Turkish *ravioli* with a garlic
yoghurt sauce.

Çengelköy Börekçisi
Café $
26 Çengelköy Cad, Çengelköy
Tel (0216) 318 34 68

This store serves tasty and filling *boreks*, or savoury pastries, of all description. While it has expanded into other parts of the city, this one is the original.

Çengelköy Kokoreççisi Mehmet Erözcan $
Café
15 Halk Cad, Çengelköy
Tel (0216) 318 76 56
Delicious spot to sample *kokoreç*, or grilled and spiced lamb's intestines. Get your portion stuffed into a sandwich in this kitschily decorated family-run café.

Kanaat $
Lokanta
9 Selmanipak Cad, Üsküdar
Tel (0216) 341 54 44
A good choice in Üsküdar for its wide range of olive oil dishes and meat lunch specials. Cold yoghurt and cucumber soup for starters and milky pudding for dessert are tasty options.

Ortaköy Mantı Evi $
Lokanta **Map** 9 F2
3 Değirmenci Sok, Ortaköy
Tel (0212) 261 45 50
Purveyors of delicious *manti*, or Turkish *ravioli* served in a garlicky yoghurt sauce.

Pide Ban $
Lokanta
23 Dereboyu Cad, Sariyer
Tel (0212) 242 42 39
Traditional cuisine from the Black Sea region. Huge range of *pide* on offer, and an extensive menu of vegetable dishes and meats from the grill.

Adem Baba Balık $$
Meyhane
2 Satışmeydanı Sok, Arnavutköy
Tel (0212) 263 29 33
Fun fish restaurant filled with fishing memorabilia. Expect all the usual *meyhane* repast, except without alcohol.

House Café $$
International **Map** 9 F3
1 Salhane Sok, Ortaköy
Tel (0212) 227 26 99
This chic restaurant is such an Istanbul institution that it even has its own radio station. Enjoy tasty pastas, pizzas and fresh lemonade alongside live beats.

İncir Altı $$
Meyhane
4 Arabacılar Sok, Beylerbeyi
Tel (0216) 557 66 86
Particularly nice, secret-walled garden offering old-fashioned Istanbul *mezes*.

Kıyı Fish Restaurant $$
Meyhane
Kefelikoy Cad 126, Tarabya
Tel (0212) 262 00 02
Although there is no outdoor seating at this long-established fish restaurant, in the summer, large glass panels open out into the fresh air.

Kosinitza $$
Meyhane
2 Bereketli Sok, Kuzguncuk, Üsküdar
Tel (0216) 334 04 00
While most Istanbul restaurants serve their fish plain and grilled, here, they think a bit more about combinations of flavours – so patrons are just as likely to find an elegantly spiced fish stew as a plain grilled offering.

Ortaköy Sefarad $$
Meyhane **Map** 9 F2
21 Muvakkit Sok, Ortaköy
Tel (0212) 261 29 83
Jolly, traditional *meyhane* away from this waterside neighbourhood's worst tourist traps.

Suna'nın Yeri $$
Meyhane
4 Kandilli İskele Cad, Kandilli
Tel (0216) 332 32 41
Unpretentious fish restaurant on the waterside. Located in the shadow of a mosque, it has no wine list as such, but ask around and guests might be surprised by what they can have brought to their table.

Tike $$
Kebab **Map** 8 C4
19 Beylerbeyi iskele Cad, Beylerbeyi
Tel (0216) 422 69 37
Tike is justly famous for its kebabs. Multiple branches exist in the city; this one is a good excuse to visit the quiet Bosphorus neighbourhood of Beylerbeyi.

Angel Salacak $$$
Meyhane
46 Salacak Sahil Yolu, Üsküdar
Tel (0216) 553 04 26
A smart *meyhane*, which looks out towards Seraglio Point. Creative fish *mezes* are a big draw here, as well as salt-baked John Dory, which is wheeled to your table girded by blue flames.

Balıkçı Kahraman $$$
Meyhane
15 Iskele Cad, Rumeli Kavağı
Tel (0212) 242 64 47
Although this restaurant doesn't have a seafront, it is still packed to the rafters on evenings and weekends. The reason? Crowds from the city are drawn to Kahraman's famous turbot, cooked in a clay-lined oven.

Boğaziçi Borsa $$$
Turkish Fusion **Map** 7 F1
Lütfi Kırdar complex, Harbiye
Tel (0212) 232 42 01
A grand restaurant set in the rolling hills of Lütfi Kırdar. Ideal for business lunches or fancy dinners. Everything tastes exquisite, and meat dishes feel less greasy than in Anatolian cuisine elsewhere.

Fish Var Balıkçı $$$
Meyhane
26 İstinye Cad, İstinye
Tel (0212) 277 25 82
A popular fish restaurant near the water on the İstinye inlet, serving a wide range of fresh fish dishes, but no alcohol.

Hanedan $$$
Meyhane
27 Çigdem Sok, Beşiktaş
Tel (0212) 259 40 17
Next to the Besiktas boat terminal, this popular place is really five restaurants in one. One floor focuses on meat, the other on fish, while there is a bar on the ground floor. Rakı is popular throughout!

Spectacular sea view from the House Café in Ortakoy, The Bosphorus

For more information on types of restaurants *see page 191*

Istanbul Modern $$$
Turkish Fusion **Map** 7 F5
*Antrepo No 4, Liman İşletmeleri
Sahası, Meclis-i Mebusan Cad, Karaköy*
Tel (0212) 334 73 00
The dining room of the museum is
a great place to sip a cocktail and
sample a varied menu, while
enjoying stunning views of the
Bosphorus and the old city.

Kızkulesi $$$
International **Map** 10 A3
Kizkulesi, the Maiden's Tower
Tel (0216) 342 47 47
Situated right in the middle of
the Bosphorus on a landmark
site, this restaurant boasts a
unique view – though there
is a surcharge! Boats leave from
Kadikoy or Kabatas.

Lacivert $$$
Meyhane
57 Körfez Cad, Anadolu Hisarı
Tel (0216) 413 37 53
Set practically under the second
Bosphorus bridge, this *meyhane's*
waterside location served as a
set for Turkish films of the 1970s.
Seafood is the focus.

Lucca $$$
International
Cevdetpaşa Cad 51 B, Bebek
Tel (0212) 257 12 55
Trendy and informal celebrity
hangout that serves a range of
modern fusion cuisine.

Sur Balık $$$
Seafood
52 Arnavutköy Cad, Bebek
Tel (0212) 257 27 43
Fine dining option with excellent
views of the Bosphorus. A great
place for lovers of seafood. Set
in Körükçü Yalısı, the beautiful
150-year-old summerhouse,

Diners enjoying a meal at Istanbul
Modern, The Bosphorus

which is said to be among the
best examples of Ottoman
civilian architecture.

Takanik Balik $$$
Meyhane
87 Birinci Cad, Arnavutköy
Tel (0212) 263 83 46
Pickles and fresh fish form the
main dishes at this dependable,
delicious fish restaurant. No
alcohol is served.

DK Choice

Tapasuma $$$
Turkish Fusion
43 Kuleli Cad, Çengelköy
Tel (0216) 401 13 33
Tapasuma plays with great
originality on the links between
tapas and *meze*. The result is an
ingenious tableau of flavours.
The restored distillery that
houses the restaurant is owned
by a pair of architects, whose
eye for detail is evident in the
elegant decor. Guests can make
their own way over to Çengelköy,
or can go in the restaurant's boat.

Villa Bosphorus Beylerbeyi $$$
Meyhane
18 Iskele Cad, Beylerbeyi
Tel (0216) 318 68 10
Lovely waterside fish restaurant
in the former fishing village
neighbourhood of Beylerbeyi.

Beyond Istanbul

Ciğerci Kazım ve Ilhan Usta $
Kebab
*Balıkpazarı, Osmaniye
Cad 43, Edirne*
Tel (0284) 212 12 80
With a menu of liver, vegetable
side dishes and not much else,
this is a quick, cheap and tasty
dining option. Their method of
cooking crispy liver turns out to
be quite outstanding. Twelve
kinds of breakfast are also on offer.

**Doyum Pide ve Kebab
Restaurant** $
Café
*Demircioğlu Cad, Cumhuriyet
Meydanı, Çanakkale*
Tel (0286) 217 48 10
Functional café that serves not
just *pide*, but a range of kebabs
as well. It is worth saving room
for *kadayıf*, the shredded
pastry dessert.

Tahmis Köftecisi $
Kebab
*Sabuni Mah, Tahmis Çarşısı
No 6, Edirne*
Tel (0284) 213 30 92

The menu here is sparse – expect
meatballs, beans and soup. That's
basically it, but the meatball
speciality of this small Edirne
eatery is cooked to such perfection
that it's hard to complain.

DK Choice

Burç Beach $$
Café
*Bogazici Universitesi Gumusdere
Mevki, Saritepe Campus, Kumkoy
(Kilyos) Koyu, Sariyer*
Tel (0212) 203 02 36
The café at Burç Beach is, of
course, not the main attraction
– that would be the long white
sands, which visitors flock to
for kitesurfing, volleyball and
sunbathing. In summer, there
are plenty of snack options at
this eatery on the sands to keep
patrons fuelled all day, with
occasional concerts adding to
the carnival atmosphere.

Çamlık Motel $$
Meyhane
Göl Sahil Yolu, İznik
Tel (0224) 757 13 62
Set amid pine trees near the lake,
this pleasant restaurant serves an
extensive range of *mezes*. Locally
caught catfish is a speciality.

Dalia Beach Club $$
Meyhane
*Kilyos Yolu, Üzeri Dalyan
Mevkii, Demicíköy*
Tel (0212) 204 03 68
Quieter than Burç Beach, Dalia is
a resort with more of a family feel
to it, as well as a fish restaurant.

Erol Balık $$
Meyhane
*Arnavutkoy Balikci Barinagi Karsisi,
Mudanya, Bursa*
Tel (0224) 544 66 30
Erol is not in the centre of Bursa,
but the trip is worth it for the
reasonably priced fish dishes
in a small family-run restaurant.
Delectable hot fish starters.

Halit Balik $$
Meyhane
Sahilyolu Cad 7, Hereke, Kocaeli
Tel (0262) 511 34 34
The set menu with five courses
and coffees, is very reasonable
for large groups. Even a la carte,
the seasonal fish selection and
waterfront setting make it
worth it.

Hünkar Köşkü Sosyal Tesisi $$
Ottoman
*Mollaarap Mah, Sabiha Gökçen
Sok 2, Bursa*
Tel (0224) 800 20 70

Informal dining area in the Westside Café and Bistro, Beyond Istanbul

An Ottoman-inspired menu at this restaurant, housed in premises built more than 160 years ago by Sultan Abdulmecid. Today, the view has been altered by the addition of skyscrapers, but the terrace still makes a good vantage point.

Ilhan Restaurant $$
Meyhane
Liman Ici Balikhane Sok 2, Gelibolu
Tel (0286) 566 11 24
Fish restaurant right on the Gallipoli Pier, notable not just for its reliable seasonal fish dishes and its great view but also for the friendliness of its staff.

İskele Balik $$
Meyhane
Iskele Meydanı No 2/1, Rumeli Kavağı
Tel (0212) 242 22 73
Located conveniently near the ferry terminal at the mouth of the Black Sea, this is a pleasant, casual fish restaurant for a leisurely summer lunch before exploring the castle up on the hill.

Kitap Evi $$
International
Burc Ustu 21, Tophane, Bursa
Tel (0224) 225 41 60
An elegantly restored Ottoman mansion, which used to be a bookshop with an adjoining café. The place is now a hotel, but it retains its former charm in a pleasant garden seating area. The menu features salads, pastas and sandwiches.

Lalezar $$
Kebab
Karaağaç Mahallesi, Lozan Cad 6, Edirne
Tel (0284) 223 06 00
With a children's playground and a ballroom, Lalezar has it set when it comes to catering for grand events – but there is much in their

excellent kebab selection and serene riverside location that will also appeal to the more casual Edirne diner.

Saki Rum Meyhanesi $$
Meyhane
Eski Mudanya Yolu 25, Bademli Girisi, Bursa
Tel (0224) 549 02 89
The leafy and spacious setting sets this place apart. Whether the grilled octopus and beef steaks are actually Greek is open to question, but the menu does not disappoint. A fish or meat set menu for groups of six or above is an economical choice that ensures countless dishes and unlimited local booze.

Yalova Liman Restaurant $$
Meyhane
Entrance at Gümrük Sok 7, Çanakkale
Tel (0286) 217 10 45
Overlooking Canakkale harbour, and brimming with character. Popular with locals who come for the stews and soups at lunch, and then fill the place again for more formal fish, steaks and grills in the evening.

Yoros Café Restaurant $$
Meyhane
Feneryolu Cad, Yoros Kalesi Yanı, Anadolu Kavağı, Beykoz
Tel (0216) 320 20 56
Fish and *meze* form a menu that guests can enjoy seated atop the castle hill, while taking in sweeping views of the Bosphorus. However, the trek up the hill is not for the faint-hearted.

Yusuf Restaurant $$
Kebab
Kültür Park, Bursa
Tel (0224) 234 49 54
Yusuf serves some of the city's tastiest food. Locals flock here for the lamb *tandir* (lamb baked

in a clay oven). There is a huge choice of *mezes*, grills, vegetarian dishes – and football screens, which keep the place packed.

Balıkçı Yaşar Restaurant $$$
Meyhane
Opp the Piri Reis fountain, Atatürk Cad 333, Çanakkale
Tel (0286) 218 04 41
Near the university campus, this is one of the best local venues at which to enjoy excellent fish. *Meze* and salad choices are vast, but leave room for the traditional quince and pumpkin desserts. Wide selection of rakıs.

Gizli Bahçe Restaurant $$$
Meyhane
Sazgeyin Mevkii Kopru Yani No 1, Agva, Sile
Tel (0216) 721 72 23
A secluded lunch spot in the village of Agva. Worth the detour, not just for the menu, which has specialities like *hodan* or *ebegumeci* (a kind of boiled marrow), but also because between the boats, the hammock area and children's amusements, there are enough activities to fill the day.

Kebabçı Iskender $$$
Kebab
Tayyare Kültür Merkezi Yanı, Atatürk Cad 60, Bursa
Tel (0224) 221 10 76
This place has a worthy claim to being the home of *iskender kebap*, a delicious take on the *doner kebab* whose peculiarity is the soft bread layer below the meat and the lashings of tomato, yoghurt and melted butter above.

Leonardo Restaurant $$$
International
Köyiçi Sok 32, Polonezköy
Tel (0216) 432 30 82
With a menu of French, Polish and Austrian cuisine, Leonardo seems to be becoming more popular with time. Set in lush garden surroundings, it gets very crowded on weekends, when the buffet brunch is served and guests flock here to use the pool.

Westside Café and Bistro $$$
American
Istanbul Cad, Telekom Sok, Arcadium Carsisi No 3/7, Kemerburgaz
Tel (0545) 328 93 78
Everything from hamburgers to pancakes with maple syrup and that rarest of Istanbul culinary experiences – bacon – can be found on the menu at this Californian restaurant.

For more information on types of restaurants *see page 191*

Light Meals and Snacks

Eating on the streets is a part of life in Istanbul. You cannot go far without coming across a café, street stall or pedlar selling snacks to appease the hunger of busy passers-by. Savoury snacks like kebabs, *lahmacun*, *pide* and *börek* (see pp190–5) are eaten at any time of day, as are sweets and puddings. On every street corner you will find a *büfe* or *simit sarayı* (sandwich kiosk). If you want to sit down, try a traditional *kahve*, or one of the increasing number of European-style cafés in the more affluent and cosmopolitan parts of Istanbul. There are also dozens of American-style restaurants in the city, selling hamburgers, pizzas and other types of fast food.

Street Food

A common sight on the streets of Istanbul is the seller of *simits* – chewy bread rings coated with sesame. The traditional *simit*-seller (*simitçi*) carries his fare on his head on a wooden tray; better-off ones push a glass-fronted cart from which they also sell *poğaça* (flaky pastry filled with cheese or mince), *su böreği* (filled layered pastry), *açma* (a fluffy *simit* shaped like a doughnut) and *çatal* (sweeter, eye-shaped *simits* without sesame seeds). They are all best eaten fresh.

During the summer street vendors sell grilled or boiled corn on the cob (*mısır*), generously sprinkled with salt. In winter they sell roast chestnuts (*kestane*).

Kağıt helvası, a sweet, is another summer snack. *Kağıt* means "paper", and the thin, crumbly layers of pastry filled with sugar melt in your mouth. Street food in Ortaköy is dominated by *Kumpir*, baked potatoes smothered with every imaginable topping.

Sandwich and Pastry Shops

Delicious sandwiches are on sale from small kiosks or *büfes*, usually near bus stops. They include inexpensive thin, toasted sandwiches (*tost*) and hot dogs (*sosisli sandviç*).

The snack bars of Ortaköy (see p124) specialize in pastries from southern Turkey like *gözleme* and *dürüm*. Both consist of thin layers of bread, grilled on a hot sheet of iron and stuffed with meat, cheese and vegetables. *Dürüm* bread is cooked first, then stuffed and rolled, while *gözleme* is cooked with the ingredients inside, then folded over in a triangle.

Fish

Fish sandwich sellers offer delicious grilled or fried fresh fish inside a large piece of bread. *Midye tava* (fried mussels), dressed with ground hazelnuts, garlic and oil, are also served inside bread or on a stick.

Fish and mussel sandwiches are sold at the Galatasaray Fish Market in Beyoğlu (see p214). Here you can also buy *midye dolma*, mussels stuffed with pine nuts, rice and currants (see p192). However, be vigilant when purchasing food that may have had a long street life, particularly in the summer months.

Kahvehanes

The typical Turkish café, *kahvehane* (or *kahve*), is a male-dominated local coffee shop. The original Ottoman name, *kıraathane*, means "a place to read", but such cafés are more a place where men play backgammon and cards, puff on a nargile (bubble pipe) and drink endless cups of coffee and tea. No alcoholic drinks or food are served.

In tourist areas like Beyazıt and Sultanahmet, however, female foreigners will be welcome in *kahves* and, although they may be stared at, they will not be disturbed. **Çorlulu Ali Paşa Medresesi** (see p98) is a *kahve* popular with artists and students. The **Basilica Cistern Café** offers a cooling retreat in an unusual setting although you have to pay to get into the cistern (see p78). **Café Kafka** is frequented by academics and intellectuals. They serve delicious coffee, cake and snacks in a convivial atmosphere. In Eyüp (see p122) the **Pierre Loti Café** is another traditional *kahve*. Decorated with memorabilia and antique wall tiles, it serves good apple tea and claims to have been the haunt of Pierre Loti. **İsmail Ağa Café**, by the waterside in Kanlıca (see p143), is famous for delicious yoghurt.

Next to the Bebek ferry jetty (see p140) is **Bebek Kahvesi**. This café is a favourite with students and middle-class families who read their Sunday newspapers on the terrace while enjoying the breeze of the Bosphorus.

Patisseries and Pudding Shops

The best patisseries are in two Beyoğlu hotels: the Divan and Pera Palas (see p106). **Divan** is known for its chocolates. **Patisserie de Pera** retains its charm with period decor, classical music and tasty biscuits. It has a good selection of English teas. **İnci Patisserie** is famous for its excellent profiteroles and baklava. Despite its run-down appearance, it is always busy.

Next to the Taksim hotel (see p189), **Gezi Istanbul Café** sells handmade confectionery such as truffles and rich torte.

Pudding shops (*muhallebici*) sell traditional sweet milk puddings. **Sütiş Muhallebicisi** is a long-established chain.

Ice Cream Shops

Itinerant ice cream vendors are a common sight in residential districts in the summer. Turkish ice cream (*dondurma*) is thick and very sweet. It comes in milk chocolate and fruit varieties and is served in cones. One of the best places to eat ice cream is **Mado**, which has several outlets. Also try **Mini Dondurma** in Bebek.

European-style Cafés

European-style cafés serving light meals such as salads, croque monsieur, omelettes and crepes are now common in Istanbul. Sweets usually include cheesecake, chocolate brownies, tiramisu and ice cream in summer.

The best are around Taksim and İstiklal Caddesi in Beyoğlu (see pp104–5). The elegant, late 19th-century **Lebon** serves savoury dishes such as vol-au-vents, as well as sumptuous Viennese cakes. **Leyla**, opposite the Tünel underground exit, is a popular meeting place for local media types.

Sultanahmet has a few chic, designer cafés. The **Lale Restaurant**, a hippie spot in the 1970s, now serves inexpensive casseroles and grilled chicken, as well as Turkish milk puddings.

Zanzibar, in the smart shopping district of Nişantaşı, is popular with a stylish young clientele. It serves dishes such as vegetable grill, Waldorf salad and toast provençale. Also in Nişantaşı is the **Next Café**, which offers European-style cakes and pies as well as savoury dishes such as *börek*.

The area around Ortaköy (see p124), with its market, many craft shops and a good nightlife scene, is a haven of street food and light snacks.

Further up along the shores of the Bosphorus, in Rumeli Hisarı (see p142), there is an exclusive English café called **Tea Room**. Decorated in a colonial style, it serves scones and, of course, a variety of English teas.

Among a new generation of internet cafés (see p235) springing up in the city, one of the best is **Antique**.

Cafés are now beginning to open on the Asian side, too. One of the most interesting is **Kadife Chalet** near Moda. Housed in a 19th-century wooden building, it offers home-made cakes and dishes made with home-grown ingredients, as well as a range of herbal teas.

Bars

Despite the Islamic edict against alcohol, there are plenty of bars in Istanbul. The majority of the city's fashionable cafés turn into bars in the evening, signalled by a change of music from soft tunes to loud pop. It is possible just to sit with a drink, but for those who wish to have food, many serve pasta, steaks, grills and salads at the bar. Even bars that are not cafés during the day will serve snacks.

Pano Şaraphanesi is one of several historic wine houses found in the back streets of Beyoğlu which serve wine by the glass or bottle in convivial surroundings. A few hotel bars, such as **City Lights** at the Ceylan Intercontinental hotel (see p189), offer more elaborate dishes. Other bars, like **Zihni's**, have restaurant sections. Many bars feature live bands playing rock or jazz music. For further details see page 221.

DIRECTORY

Kahvehanes

Bebek Kahvesi
Cevdetpaşa Cad 137,
Bebek.
Tel (0212) 257 54 02.

Café Kafka
Yeni Çarşı Cad 26/1,
Galatasaray.
Map 7 D4.
Tel (0212) 245 19 58.

Çorlulu Ali Paşa Medresesi
Yeniçeriler Cad 36,
Çemberlitaş.
Map 2 C4 (4 B3).
Tel (0212) 528 37 85.

İsmail Ağa Café
Simavi Meydanı, Kanlıca.

Pierre Loti Café
Gümüşsuyu Karyağdı Sok 5 (inside Eyüp cematery),
Eyüp. **Tel** (0212) 581 26 96.

Patisseries and Pudding Shops

Divan
Cumhuriyet Cad 2,
Elmadağ. **Map** 7 F3.
Tel (0212) 231 41 08.

Gezi Istanbul Café
İnönü Cad 5/1, Taksim.
Map 7 F4.
Tel (0212) 292 53 53.

İnci Patisserie
İstiklal Cad, Mis Sok 18,
Beyoğlu.
Map 7 E4.
Tel (0212) 293 92 24.

Patisserie de Pera
Pera Palas Hotel,
Meşrutiyet Cad 98–100,
Tepebaşı.
Map 7 D5.
Tel (0212) 251 45 60.

Sütiş Muhallebicisi
Sıraselviler Cad 9/A,
Taksim.
Map 7 E4.
Tel (0212) 252 82 68.

Ice Cream Shops

Mado
Osmanzade Sok 26,
Ortaköy. **Map** 9 F3.
Tel (0212) 227 38 76.

Mini Dondurma
Cevdetpaşa Cad 107,
Bebek.
Tel (0212) 257 10 70.

European-style Cafés

Antique
Kutlugün Sokak 51,
Sultanahmet. **Map** 3 E4.
Tel (0212) 517 67 89.

Kadife Chalet
Kadife Sok 29, Kadıköy.
Tel (0216) 347 85 96.

Lale Restaurant
Divanyolu Cad 6,
Sultanahmet.
Map 3 E4 (5 E4).
Tel (0212) 522 29 70.

Lebon
Richmond Hotel, İstiklal
Cad 445, Beyoğlu.
Map 7 D5.
Tel (0212) 252 54 60.

Leyla
Tünel Meydanı 186,
Beyoğlu. **Map** 7 D5.
Tel (0212) 245 40 28.

Next Café
Ihlamur Yolu 3–1,
Nişantaşı. **Map** 7 D5.
Tel (0212) 247 80 43.

Tea Room
Yahya Kemal Cad 36A,
Rumeli Hisarı.
Tel (0212) 257 25 80.

Zanzibar
Teşvikiye Cad 43–57,
Reassürans Çarşısı No.60,
Teşvikiye. **Map** 8 A2.
Tel (0212) 233 80 46.

Bars

City Lights
Ceylan Inter-Continental
Hotel, Asker Ocağı Cad 1,
Taksim.
Map 7 F3.
Tel (0212) 231 21 21.

Pano Şaraphanesi
Hamalbaşı Cad, Beyoğlu.
Map 7 D4.
Tel (0212) 292 66 64.

Zihni's
Muallim Naci Cad 119,
Ortaköy.
Map 9 F2.

SHOPPING IN ISTANBUL

Istanbul's shops and markets, crowded and noisy at most times of the day and year, sell a colourful mixture of goods from all over the world. The city's most famous shopping centre is the Grand Bazaar and there are many other bazaars and markets to browse around *(see pp214–15)*. Turkey is a centre of textile production, and Istanbul has a wealth of carpet and fashion shops. If you prefer to do all your shopping under one roof, head for one of the city's modern shopping malls which offer a variety of international and Turkish brand goods. Wherever you shop, be wary of imitations of famous brand products – even if they appear to be of a high standard and the salesman maintains that they are authentic. Be prepared to bargain where required: it is an important part of a shopping trip.

Brightly decorated candle lanterns in the Grand Bazaar

Opening Hours

Shops are open, in general, from 9am to 8pm Monday to Saturday; open-air markets from 8am onwards. Large shops and department stores open slightly later in the morning. The Grand Bazaar and Spice Bazaar open their gates at 8:30am and close at 7pm. Big shopping malls open from 10am to 10pm seven days a week. Shops do not close for lunch, although a few small shops may close briefly at prayer times, especially for the midday prayers on Fridays. Most shops close for the religious holidays of Şeker Bayramı and Kurban Bayramı, but remain open on national holidays *(see pp46–9)*.

How to Pay

Most shops that cater to tourists will be happy to accept foreign currency. If you can pay in cash, you can usually get a discount. Exchange rates are often displayed in shops and also appear in daily newspapers.

Credit cards are widely accepted (except in markets and smaller shops) and most vendors do not charge a commission. Resist any attempts to make you pay a small compensatory commission. It is not unusual to be asked to draw the money out from a bank on your card. Very few shops now accept travellers' cheques. Cash and haggling are expected in the markets and bazaars. Start by offering half the asking price. In rural markets merchants may accept foreign currency.

VAT Exemption

If you spend at least 118 TL in one shop, you can claim back VAT (known as KDV in Turkey), which is 18 per cent. More than 2,200 retail outlets display the Tax Free Shopping logo. The retailer will give you a Global Refund Cheque, which you should then present to the customs officials with your invoices and purchases for a cash refund when leaving Turkey.

Fezes for sale on street stall

Sizes and Measures

Turkey uses continental European sizes for clothes and shoes. Food and drink are sold in metric measures. This book has a conversion chart on page 227.

Buying Antiques

Before purchasing antique items, it is important to know what can and cannot be taken out of Turkey. The rule is that objects which are over 100 years old may be exported only when a certificate stating their age and granting permission to remove them from the country has been issued by the relevant authority. Museums issue these certificates, as does

Turkish delight and boiled sweets, sold by weight at market stalls

Antiques shop in Çukurcuma

the Ministry of Culture in Ankara, who will also undertake to authenticate the correct age and value of an object, if necessary. The shopkeeper from whom you bought your goods will often know which museum will be authorizing your purchases for export. In theory, a seller should already have registered with a museum all goods for sale that are over 100 years old. In practice, sellers usually only seek permission after a particular item has been sold. In the past, antiques could be removed from Turkey without a certificate. Although this has changed, the export of antiques is not forbidden, as some believe. If the proper authorities permit your purchase to be exported, you can either take it with you or send it home, whether or not it is over 100 years old. Do take note, however, that taking antiques out of Turkey without proper permission is regarded as smuggling, and is a punishable offence.

Van cats and Kangal dogs have recently been included in this category.

Shopping Malls and Department Stores

Istanbul's modern shopping malls are popular for their entertainment as well as their shopping facilities. They have multiscreen cinemas, food courts selling fast food and chic cafés, and hundreds of shops.

Akmerkez in Etiler is an ultra-modern skyscraper where leading Turkish fashion companies and outlets for famous international names can be found. The glass-ceilinged **Istinye Park**, on Istinye Bayırı Caddesi, houses 300 stores and a 12-screen cinema within its indoor and outdoor space. **Galleria**, next to the yacht marina in Ataköy, offers a wide range of well-known clothes stores, including a branch of the French department store, Printemps, and an ice rink (see p222). **Kanyon**, in Levent, boasts 160 stores, a cinema, gourmet restaurants and a fitness centre. The mall is anchored by a Harvey Nichols.

International boutiques and local Turkish shops in Akmerkez

Seasonal Sales

Clothes shops are the main places for seasonal sales (indirim), although department stores and a number of speciality shops also have them. They begin in June or July and continue to the end of September. The winter sales start as soon as New Year shopping is over in early January and continue until mid-April. There are no sales in bazaars – every day of the year offers bargains depending on your haggling skills.

How to Bargain

In up-market shops in Istanbul, bargaining is rarely practised. However, you will probably do most of your shopping in the Grand Bazaar and the shops located in or around the old city (Sultanahmet and Beyazıt). In these places haggling is a necessity, otherwise you may be cheated. Elsewhere you can try making an offer but it may be refused.

Bazaar shopkeepers, characterized by their abrasive insistence, expect you to bargain. Always take your time and decide where to buy after visiting a few shops selling similar goods. The procedure is as follows:

• You will often be invited inside and offered a cup of tea. Feel free to accept, as this is the customary introduction to any kind of exchange and will not oblige you to buy.
• Do not feel pressurized if the shopkeeper turns the shop upside down to show you his stock – this is normal practice and most salesmen are proud of their goods.
• If you are seriously interested in any item, be brave enough to offer half the price you are asked.

Haggling over the price of a rug

• Take no notice if the shopkeeper looks offended and refuses, but raise the price slightly, aiming to pay a little more than half the original offer. If that price is really unacceptable to the owner he will stop bargaining over the item and turn your attention to other goods in the shop.

Where to Shop in Istanbul

Istanbul is home to a vast range of shops and bazaars. Often shops selling particular items are clustered together, competing for custom. The Grand Bazaar *(see pp100–101)* is a centre for carpets and kilims, gold jewellery and leather jackets, as well as every type of handicraft and souvenir. Nişantaşı and İstiklal Caddesi on the European side, and Bağdat Caddesi on the Asian side, have a good range of clothes and shoe shops. The best choices for food are the Spice Bazaar *(see p90)* and the Galatasaray Fish Market *(see p215)*.

Carpets and Kilims

One of the best places to buy carpets and kilims in Istanbul is in the Grand Bazaar *(see pp100–1)*, where **Şişko Osman** has a good range of carpets. **Nakkaş** offers a range of quality carpets and kilims in a huge variety of sizes, colours and patterns. The **Arasta Bazaar** *(see p73)* has many kilim shops, and **Hazal Halı**, in Ortaköy, is run by a wonderfully professional lady who knows the history of almost all of the carpets.

Fabrics

As well as rugs, colourful fabrics in traditional designs from all over Turkey and Central Asia are widely sold. **Sivaslı Yazmacısı** sells village textiles, crocheted headscarves and embroidered cloths. Centrally located behind the Blue Mosque, **Khaftan**

Brightly coloured Central Asian *suzani* wall hangings

offers a wide selection of traditional Ottoman textiles. The antiques dealer **Aslı Günşiray** sells both original Ottoman and reproduction embroidered cloths.

Jewellery

Istanbul's substantial gold market centres on Kalpakçılar Caddesi in the Grand Bazaar. Here gold jewellery is sold by weight, with a modest sum added for craftsmanship, which is generally of good quality. The daily price of gold is displayed in the shop windows. Other shops in the Grand Bazaar sell silver jewellery, and pieces inlaid with precious stones.

Icons for sale in the Grand Bazaar

Urart stocks collections of unique gold and silver jewellery inspired by the designs of ancient civilizations. **Antikart** specializes in restored antique silver jewellery made by Kurds and nomads in eastern Turkey.

Leather

Turkish leatherwear, while not always of the best quality hides, is durable, of good craftsmanship and reasonably priced. The Grand Bazaar is full of shops selling leather goods. **B B Store**, for example, offers a good range of ready-to-wear and made-to-order garments. **Meb Deri** sells designer handbags and small leather goods, and **Desa** has classic and fashionable designs.

Antiques and Books

The best area for antiques is Çukurcuma *(see p109)*, in the backstreets of Beyoğlu. Shops worth a visit are **Aslı Günşiray**, **Antikhane** and **Antikarnas** for their Turkish, Islamic and Western stock. A vast array of Ottoman antique brassware, furniture and pottery, including Turkish coffee cups and vases, are sold in the Grand Bazaar.

The antiquarian bookshops, such as **Librairie de Pera** sell old postcards and prints. One of the very best shops for new books is **Galeri Kayseri**, which sells a wide selection of English-language titles.

Handicrafts and Souvenirs

All types of Turkish arts and crafts can be found in the Grand Bazaar. Ideal gifts and souvenirs include

embroidered hats, waistcoats and slippers, mother-of-pearl inlaid jewellery boxes, meerschaum pipes in the shape of heads, prayer beads made from semi-precious stones, alabaster ornaments, blue-eye charms to guard against the evil eye, nargiles (bubble pipes) and reproductions of icons. At the **Istanbul Crafts Centre** *(see p78)*, watch the traditional art of calligraphy being practised. **Rölyef** in Beyoğlu, the **Book Bazaar** *(see p96)*, **Artrium** and **Sofa** also sell antique and reproduction calligraphy, as well as *ebru* (marbled paintings) and reproductions of Ottoman miniature paintings.

Pottery, Metal and Glassware

Hundreds of shops in the Grand Bazaar are stocked with traditional ceramics, including many pieces decorated with exquisite blue-and-white İznik designs *(see p163)*. Other types of pottery come from Kütahya – distinguished by its free style of decoration – and Çanakkale *(see p172)* – which uses more modern designs, often in yellows and greens. To purchase a modern piece of Kütahya ware, visit **Mudo Pera** which stocks a collection by Sıtkı Usta, a master of Kütahya pottery. Most museum shops also have a good range of pottery for sale, including reproduction pieces.

The Grand Bazaar and the Arasta Bazaar *(see p215)* are centres of the copper and brass trade and offer a huge selection to the browsing visitor. For glassware, **Paşabahçe**, the largest glass manufacturer in Turkey, creates delicate

çeşmibülbül vases (decorated with blue and gold stripes) and Beykoz-style ware (with gilded decoration).

Food, Drink, Herbs and Spices

The Spice Bazaar *(see p90)* is the place to buy nuts (especially pistachios) and dried fruits, herbs and spices, jams and the many types of herbal tea produced in Turkey. These include sage *(adaçayı)*, linden

(ıhlamur) and camomile *(papatya)*. However, other foods can be bought here as well, including such luxuries as caviar. Another place with a wide variety of good quality herbs, jams, teas and spices is the Galatasaray Fish Market.

Several shops specialize in particular foods. **Şekerci Hacı Bekir** is renowned for its delectable Turkish delight and baklava. Also popular is **Bebek Badem Ezmesi**, on the Bosphorus, widely acclaimed for its pistachio and almond fondants. Over the course of more than a century in business, **Kurukahveci Mehmet Efendi** *(see p88)* has become the best known producer of Turkish coffee. The quintessential Turkish spirit, rakı *(see p195)*, can be bought in any grocery store.

Pickled fruits and vegetables, sold in markets and on street stalls

DIRECTORY

VAT Exemption

Global Refund
Teşvikiye, Ferah Sokak 19/A-2.
Tel (0212) 232 11 21.
🌐 globalrefund.com

Shopping Malls

Akmerkez
Nispetiye Cad, Etiler.
Tel (0212) 282 01 70.

Galleria
Sahil Yolu, Ataköy.
Tel (0212) 559 95 60.

Istinye Park
Istinye Bayırı Cad 73, Sarıyer.
Tel (0212) 345 55 55.

Kanyon
Büyükdere Cad 185, Levent.
Tel (0212) 353 53 00.

Carpets and Kilims

Hazal Halı
Mecidiye Köprüsü Sok 27–9, Ortaköy. **Map** 9 F3.
Tel (0212) 261 72 33.

Nakkas
Nakilbent Sok 33, Sultanahmet. **Map** 3 D5 (5 D5). **Tel** (0212) 516 52 23.

Şişko Osman
Halıcılar Cad 49, Grand Bazaar. **Map** 2 C4 (4 B3).
Tel (0212) 528 35 48.

Fabrics

Khaftan
Nakilbent Sok 32, Sultanahmet. **Map** 3 D5 (5 D5). **Tel** (0212) 458 54 25.

Sivaslı Yazmacısı
Yağlıkçılar Sok 57, Grand Bazaar. **Map** 2 C4 (4 B3).
Tel (0212) 526 77 48.

Jewellery

Antikart
İstiklal Cad 207, Beyoğlu.
Map 7 D4.
Tel (0212) 252 44 82.

Urart
Abdi İpekçi Cad 18/1, Nişantaşı. **Map** 7 F1.
Tel (0212) 246 71 94.

Leather

B B Store
Gani Çelebi Sok 4–6, Grand Bazaar.
Map 2 C4 (4 B3).
Tel (0212) 527 53 38.

Desa
İstiklal Cad 140, Beyoğlu.
Map 7 D4.
Tel (0212) 243 37 86.

Meb Deri
Abdi İpekçi Cad 14/2, Nişantaşı. **Map** 1 C1.
Tel (0212) 225 56 80.

Antiques

Antikarnas
Faik Paşa Yok 15, Çukurcuma. **Map** 7 E4.
Tel (0212) 251 59 28.

Antikhane
Faik Paşa Yok Restohan 41, Çukurcuma. **Map** 7 E4.
Tel (0212) 251 95 87.

Aslı Günşiray
Çukurcuma Cad 72–74, Çukurcuma. **Map** 7 E4.
Tel (0212) 252 59 86.

Books

Galeri Kayseri
Divanyolou Caddesi 11, Sultanahmet. **Map** 3 D4.
Tel (0212) 516 3366.

Librairie de Pera
Galip Dede Cad 22, Tünel.
Map 7 D5.
Tel (0212) 252 30 78.

Handicrafts

Atrium
9th floor, Swissôtel, Maçka. **Map** 8 A4.
Tel (0212) 2559 02 28.

Rölyef
Emir Nevruz Sok 16, Beyoğlu. **Map** 7 D4 (4 C3).
Tel (0212) 244 04 94.

Sofa
Nuruosmaniye Cad 42, Cağaloğlu. **Map** 3 D4 (4 C3). **Tel** (0212) 527 41 42.

Pottery, Metal and Glassware

Mudo Pera
İstiklal Cad 401, Beyoğlu.
Map 7 D5.
Tel (0212) 251 86 82.

Paşabahçe
İstiklal Cad 314, Beyoğlu.
Map 7 D5.
Tel (0212) 244 05 44.

Food

Bebek Badem Ezmesi
Cevdetpaşa Cad 238/1, Bebek.
Tel (0212) 263 59 84.

Kurukahveci Mehmet Efendi
Tahmis Cad 66, Eminönü.
Map 3 D2.
Tel (0212) 511 42 62.

Şekerci Hacı Bekir
Hamidiye Cad 83, Eminönü. **Map** 3 D3.
Tel (0212) 522 06 66.

Istanbul's Markets

Whether you want to lose yourself in the aromas of exotic spices, rummage for old prints and miniatures among secondhand books, hunt for souvenirs or just shop for food, you will find a market or bazaar catering to your tastes somewhere in Istanbul. An obvious first stop is the Grand Bazaar, but several others are well worth visiting for their more specialized produce and their atmospheric settings. Every neighbourhood in Istanbul has its own open-air market on a specific day of the week. At these markets, crowded with budget-conscious housewives, you will find a huge variety of merchandise at the cheapest possible prices.

Şişli Feriköy
Organic Market

Galatasaray Fish Market
The best fish market in Istanbul runs along a historic alleyway. Constantly sprinkled with water to keep them cool, fresh fish from the Sea of Marmara and elsewhere lie waiting to be sold *(see p105).*

İSTİKLAL

Golden Horn

ABÜLEZEL PAŞA

ŞİR

NEC

MACAR KARDEŞLER CAD

VATAN CADDESİ

ATATÜRK BULVARI

ORDU CADDESİ

Wednesday Street Market
One of Istanbul's colourful neighbourhood markets, the Wednesday market, is next to the Fatih Mosque *(see p115)* and sells everything from fresh produce and household goods to bulbs and seeds.

Spice Bazaar   Arasta Bazaar

Book Bazaar
Next to the Grand Bazaar, the Book Bazaar (Sahaflar Çarşısı) offers a wealth of printed matter in various languages, from tourist guides to academic tomes and old magazines *(see p96).*

Grand Bazaar
The largest market in the world, the Grand Bazaar contains about 4,000 shops. In this roofed labyrinth of passages you can find every commodity associated with Turkey, from costly jewellery to basic foodstuffs. It has operated for hundreds of years *(see pp100–1).*

Şişli Feriköy Organic Market
Istanbul's first organic fruit and vegetables market is open every Saturday in Feriköy.

Ortaköy Flea Market
Every Sunday the main square of Ortaköy is filled with stalls selling souvenirs to suit every budget, from junk to fine jewellery and original Turkish handicrafts (see p124).

BARBAROS BULVARI

ÇIRAĞAN CADDESİ

0 metres 500
0 yards 500

Bosphorus

PAŞA LİMANI CADDESİ

ÜSKÜDAR-HAREM SAHİL YOLU

GÜNDOĞUMU CAD

TIBBİYE CADDESİ

Kadıköy Street Market
The main market for food on the Asian side of the city can be found in Kadıköy Square, behind the post office.

Sea of Marmara

Spice Bazaar
The Spice Bazaar is an exotic trading house for dried herbs, spices and other foodstuffs (see p90).

Arasta Bazaar
Converted Ottoman stables are the setting for this bazaar below the Blue Mosque (see pp80–81). Carpets (see pp218–19) are the main items touted, but handicrafts and jewellery are also on sale (see p73).

What to Buy in Istanbul

With its endless bazaars, markets, shops and stalls, Istanbul is a souvenir hunter's paradise. If you are seeking a bargain, jewellery and leather can be worth investing in. For something typically Turkish, there is a wide selection of ceramics and copperware based on the designs of traditional Ottoman handicrafts and arts. The city's antique shops *(see p212)* are also worth a visit. Istanbul is possibly most famous for its carpets and kilims *(see pp218–19)*, but check the quality before you buy.

Copperware

Antique copperware can be very expensive. Newer items, however, are also available, at more affordable prices.

Copper goblets

Antique copper water ewer

Pipes

Classic nargiles (bubble pipes) are still used by older Turkish men. They make attractive ornaments even if you do not smoke.

Jewellery

Jewellery includes pendants made from gold, silver, semi-precious stones and other materials. A simple blue glass eye is said to ward off evil.

Blue glass-eye pendants

Ceramics

Ceramics form a major part of Turkey's artistic tradition. The style varies according to the area of origin. Blue and white pottery is in the İznik style *(see p163)*; other areas of production include Kütahya and Çanakkale *(see p172)*.

Colourful Kütahya ware

Green jugs from Çanakkale

Blue and white decorated plate

İznik-style tile

Miniatures

Istanbul has a history of miniature painting, examples of which can be seen in the city's museums, especially Topkapı Palace *(see p59)*. These tiny works of art, often depicting the sultan at court, were once bound in books. Those for sale are copies of originals.

Miniature from the Grand Bazaar

Box inlaid with mother-of-pearl

Box with painted scenes on bone inlay

Handicrafts

Jewellery boxes crafted from wood or bone, alabaster figurines and other hand-made ornaments make unusual souvenirs.

Textiles

Hand-woven cloths, including ikat work (where the cotton is dyed as it is woven), fine embroidery and knits are just some of the range of textiles that can be bought.

Embroidered scarves, known as *oyalı*

Cotton ikat work

Glassware

This elegant jug is an example of the blue and white striped glassware, *çeşmibülbül*, made in the Paşabahçe works *(see p149)*.

Çeşmibülbül jug

Local Delicacies

Delicious sweets such as halva, Turkish delight and baklava are very popular. A huge range of fragrant spices, dried fruit and nuts are sold loose by weight in the city's bazaars.

Halva

Nuts in honey

Turkish delight

Mulberries

Sunflower and pumpkin seeds

Chickpeas

Dried red peppers and aubergines

Apricots

Almonds

Pistachio nuts

Turkish Carpets and Kilims

The ancient skill of weaving rugs has been handed down from generation to generation in Turkey. Rugs were originally made for warmth and decoration in the home, as dowry items for brides, or as donations to mosques. There are two main kinds of rug: carpets (halı), which are knotted, and kilims, which are flat-woven with vertical (warp) and horizontal (weft) threads. Many foreign rugs are sold in Istanbul but those of Turkish origin come in a particularly wide range of attractive colours. Most of the carpets and kilims offered for sale will be new or almost new; antique rugs are rarer and far more expensive.

A carpet may be machine-made or handmade. Fold the face of the rug back on itself: if you can see the base of the knots and the pile cannot be pulled out, it means that it is handmade.

Carpets are made using three different combinations of material: wool on wool, silk on silk, or wool on cotton.

Weaving a Carpet
Wool for rugs is washed, carded, spun and dyed before it is woven. Weaving is a cottage industry in Turkey; the women weave in winter leaving the summer months for farming duties.

Carpet
This reproduction of a 16th-century Uşak carpet is known as a Bellini double entrance prayer rug.

Rug-making Areas of Western Turkey

The weaving industry in Turkey is concentrated into several areas of production, listed below. Rug designs are traditional to their tribal origins, resulting in a wide range of designs and enabling the skilled buyer to identify the area of origin.

Carpets
① Hereke
② Çanakkale
③ Ayvacık
④ Bergama
⑤ Yuntdağ
⑥ Balıkesir
⑦ Sındırgı
⑧ Milas
⑨ Antalya
⑩ Isparta

Kilims
⑪ Denizli
⑫ Uşak

Carpets and Kilims
⑬ Konya

Indigo

Madder

Camomile

Dyes

Before chemical dyes were introduced in 1863, plant extracts were used: madder roots for red; indigo for blue; and camomile and other plants for yellow.

The "prayer design" is inspired by a mihrab, the niche in a mosque that indicates the direction of Mecca *(see p40)*.

The tree of life motif at the centre of the kilim is symbolic of immortality.

Kilim
Kilims are usually made using the slit weave technique by which a vertical slit marks a colour change.

The width of a rug is limited by the size of the loom. Most rugs are small because a large loom will not fit into a village house.

Buying a Rug

Before you buy a rug, look at it by itself on the floor, to see that it lies straight – without waves or lumps. Check that the pattern is balanced, the borders are of the same dimensions, and the ends are roughly the same width. The colours should be clear and not bleeding into one another. Bargaining is essential *(see p211)*, as the first price given is likely to be at least 50% higher than the seller really expects.

Buying a good quality old rug at a reasonable price, however, is a job for an expert. The age of a rug is ascertained from its colour, the quality of the weaving and the design. Check the pile to make sure that the surface has not been painted and look for any repairs – they can easily be seen on the back of the rug. Restoration of an old carpet is acceptable but the repair should not be too visible. Make sure the rug has a small lead seal attached to it, to prove its authenticity and that it may be exported, and ask the shop for a receipt.

Kilim pieces are used to make a variety of smaller craft objects, also for sale in carpet shops.

Burdock motif

Chest motif

Motif from wolf track, crab or scorpion

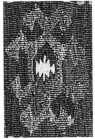

Modern motif of a human figure

Motifs

The recurring motifs in rugs – some of them seemingly abstract, others more figurative – often have a surprising origin. For instance, many are derived from marks that nomads and villagers used for branding animals.

ENTERTAINMENT IN ISTANBUL

Istanbul offers a great variety of leisure pursuits, ranging from arts festivals, folk music and belly dancing to sports centres and nightclubs. The main event in the cultural calendar is the series of festivals organized by the Istanbul Foundation for Culture and the Arts *(see pp46–9)*. The festivals take place between March and November, and always draw international performers and large audiences. Throughout the year, traditional Turkish music, opera, ballet, Western classical music and plays are performed at the Lütfi Kırdar Kongre Merkezi (Istanbul Convention & Exhibition Centre, ICEC), the Cemal Reşit Rey Concert Hall (CRR), Haghia Eirene and other venues around the city. Beyoğlu is the main centre for entertainment of all kinds. This area has the highest concentration of cinemas in the city as well as several cultural centres, both Turkish and foreign. In the evening the bars and cafés here play live music. Ortaköy, on the European shore of the Bosphorus, is another popular venue where, on summer nights, dining, music and dancing continue into the small hours of the morning.

Copies of *The Guide*, a good source for information on entertainment in Istanbul

Entertainment Guides

Istanbul has a bi-monthly entertainment and listings magazine in English called *The Guide*. This publishes the programmes of the ICEC and CRR, and information on other cultural events, as well as bars and nightclubs around the city. *The Guide* is sold at the larger, central newsagents and book shops. The English-language newspaper *Turkish Daily News*, available from newsstands, also has information on entertainment in Istanbul.

Lists of events taking place at individual theatres and cultural centres (including those attached to foreign consulates) can be obtained from tourist information offices *(see p229)*.

The Turkish Airlines in-flight magazine, *Skylife*, has details of major events, and the daily Turkish newspaper *Hürriyet* has listings in Turkish.

Booking Tickets

Tickets for performances at the Lütfi Kırdar Kongre Merkezi (ICEC) and Cemal Reşit Rey Concert Hall can be purchased one week in advance from their box offices. Perhaps one of the fastest and most convenient ways to book and pay for tickets to any event is through **Biletix**. **Vakkorama** department store and **Galleria, Akmerkez** and **Capitol** shopping centres sell tickets for large pop and jazz concerts, and also for performances at the Cemal Reşit Rey Concert Hall.

Late-night Transport

The last late-night buses and dolmuşes leave at midnight from Taksim, which is close to many entertainment venues. Taxis run throughout the night. During the music festivals in June and July there is a special bus service which runs between show venues and central parts of Istanbul.

Festivals

Five arts festivals, four annual and one biennial, are organized by the Istanbul Foundation for Culture and the Arts. The Film Festival runs from March to April every year, the Theatre Festival is in May and June, the Music and Dance Festival – the original and biggest festival – is in June and July and the Jazz Festival is in July. The biennial Fine Arts Festival takes place in the autumn. Tickets for all these festivals can be bought over the phone from the **Istanbul Festival Committee**, which also has programme details, and from the venues.

The Yapı Kredi Arts Festival, Akbank Jazz Festival and Efes Pilsen Blues Festival are also in the autumn *(see p48)*.

Western Classical Music and Dance

Every season the Istanbul State Opera and Ballet companies, State Symphony Orchestra and State Theatre perform a wide repertoire of classical and modern works. The companies share the same venue: the **Lütfi Kırdar Kongre Merkezi**. Early booking is essential for shows here. The **Cemal Reşit Rey Concert Hall** stages concerts of Western classical music as well

Classical concert in the church of Haghia Eirene *(see p62)*

Folk dancing at Kervansaray, a long-established venue

as hosting a wide variety of music and dance groups from all over the world. Concerts, operettas and ballets are also performed at smaller venues throughout the city.

Laser disc screenings of opera, ballet and classical music performances are held most days at 2pm and 6pm at the **Aksanat Cultural Centre**. It also sometimes stages live plays and music recitals.

Rock Music and Jazz

Istanbul has an increasing number of bars and clubs playing good live music. **Hayal Kahvesi** is a bar dedicated to jazz, rock and blues by groups from Turkey and abroad. It also has an outdoor summer branch next to the Bosphorus in Çubuklu. The **Q Jazz Bar**, located in the Hôtel Les Ottomans, is an exclusive jazz bar which regularly invites well-known performers. Further up the Bosphorus, in Ortaköy, the **Rock House Café** is an imitation of the famous Hard Rock Café. It has live bands on certain nights of the week.

In the city centre, **Kemancı** features live rock and heavy metal performers. In **Sappho** they play softer, more sophisticated jazz and quality

Turkish pop music. Other venues for popular Turkish music are **Tribunal** and **Vivaldi**, while at **Mojo** they play Turkish pop with strong folk music influences.

Nightclubs

The luxurious, summer-only **Club 29** is probably the most glamorous nightclub in Istanbul. It has a restaurant, swimming pool and torch-lit garden with glorious views of the Bosphorus. Every half-hour a boat ferries guests to and from İstinye on the European side. The bar becomes a disco after midnight. **Reina**, also open in summer only, is the city's biggest nightspot, with a large dancefloor right beside the Bosphorus, as well as several bars and restaurants. **Blackk** is a high-end club replete with lavish decoration and jaw-dropping lighting and sound systems. Uniquely for Ortaköy, it offers a fantastic view of the Bosphorus. There is also a restaurant/lounge on the upper floor. **Supperclub** hosts a talented line-up of local and international DJs and shows atmospheric movies.

Avoid the seedier-looking clubs in Beyoğlu, as these have been known to coerce clients into paying extortionate bills.

Musicians at the Jazz Festival

Traditional Turkish Music and Dance

Traditional Turkish music is regularly performed at the Cemal Reşit Rey Concert Hall. This includes Ottoman classical music, performed by an ensemble of singers and musicians, mystical Sufi music and folk music from various regions of Turkey. In summer, recitals of Turkish music are occasionally organized in the Basilica Cistern *(see p78)*, which has wonderful acoustics. The Sultanahmet Tourist Office *(see p229)* has details.

Fasıl is a popular form of traditional music best enjoyed live in *meyhanes* such as **Ece, Istanbulin Dinner Show** and **Asır Rest**. It is usually performed by gypsies on instruments which include the violin, *kanun* (zither), *tambur* and *ut* (both similar to the lute).

Belly dancing is performed mainly in nightclubs. Though often underrated, the sensuous movements of the female dancers are considered an art. Many clubs and restaurants stage belly dancing together with Turkish folk music and dance. Dinner is often included in the show. One of the best venues is the restaurant in the **Galata Tower** *(see p107)*. Other venues featuring top performers are **Kervansaray, Orient House** and **Manzara**.

A folkloric whirling dervish troupe gives a public perform-ance at the Mevlevi Monastery *(see p106)* once a month.

The traditional *ut*, a lute-like instrument played in *fasıl* music

Cinemas

The latest foreign films are on general release in Istanbul at the same time as other European countries. They are screened in their original languages with Turkish subtitles.

Most of the city's cinemas are on İstiklal Caddesi. **Nişantaşı Citylife**, **AFM Fitas** and **Atlas** tend to show art-house films. There are also numerous cinemas in Kadıköy, on the Asian side, while all the main shopping centres (like Nişantaşı Shopping Mall) have multi-screen cinemas.

The first screening of the day is half-price, and many cinemas offer tickets at half-price all day on Wednesdays. Students with a valid card are entitled to a discount for all showings. There is usually an interval.

Theatre

Plays by Turkish and international playwrights are staged in Istanbul's theatres, but only in Turkish. A popular company is the Istanbul State Theatre. They perform at theatres across the city, such as at the Cevahir stage in the Cevahir Shopping and Entertainment Centre in Şişli, the Küçük Sahne in Beyoğlu and the Üsküdar stage in Paşa Limanı.

Health Clubs and Sports Centres

All the main five-star hotels have good swimming pools and welcome non-residents for a daily fee. Health clubs such as the **Vakkorama Gym**, the **Alkent Hillside Club** and the **Cihangir Sports Center** can also be used by non-members for a daily fee.

At the edge of the Belgrade Forest, the **Kemer Country Riding and Golf Club** has stables and a 9-hole golf course. It also offers riding and golf lessons. For ice-skaters, the rink in the **Galleria** shopping centre *(see p211)* is open to the public after 7pm. Skates are available for hire. Yoga and detox centres,

such as **Cihangir Yoga**, are cheaper than in the rest of Europe and are very popular.

Spectator Sports

Football has a large following in Turkey. The three Istanbul teams, **Beşiktaş JK**, **Fenerbahçe SK** and **Galatasaray AS**, all compete at international level and play in Istanbul most Sundays. Horse racing takes place at **Veli Efendi Hipodromu** racecourse between 14 April and 31 October, on Wednesdays, Fridays and at weekends. In summer there are yacht regattas in the Sea of Marmara *(see p47)*. For an unusual spectator sport, head to Edirne at festival time, to see the grease wrestling *(see p156)*.

Galatasaray team logo

Beaches

The best place to swim, water-ski and windsurf in Istanbul is the Princes' Islands *(see p161)*. Yörükali Plajı, on Büyükada, is a public beach, but it is safe to swim anywhere around the islands.

There are large beaches at Kilyos *(see p160)* and Gümüşdere on the Black Sea, about 30 minutes' drive from central Istanbul, and Şile *(see p160)*. The Black Sea can be rough at times, however, with big waves and dangerous undercurrents, so always exercise caution on these beaches. The Marmara Islands *(see p171)*, are also popular for their beaches.

Children

Little in Istanbul has been designed with children in mind. Nevertheless, there are many things to interest children and increasingly activities and sights that will attract them.

However, children are welcome and will be made a fuss of almost everywhere they go. With a little thought you can find plenty of things for children to do.

The Archaeological Museums *(see pp64–7)* has a special children's section tracing the history of mankind, with a medieval castle and a Trojan horse to climb on.

The **Turkuazoo Aquarium** at Forum Istanbul shopping centre *(see p211)* is open daily and boasts an 80 metre (262 ft) underwater tunnel.

There are parks at Yıldız *(see pp126–7)* and Emirgan *(see p143)*. Another park near Emirgan, the **Park Orman**, is a family complex situated in woods, with picnic areas, a swimming pool and a theatre. **Miniatürk** in Sütlüce, on the edge of the Golden Horn, boasts an extensive model village of miniature replicas of Turkey's cultural landmarks, as well as restaurants, shops and a pool. On the Princes' Islands, where there are no cars, children can cycle safely, or take a tour in a horse-drawn carriage. The **Toy Museum** in Göztepe is the first of its kind in Turkey. In Darica, 28 miles (45 km) from Istanbul, the **Faruk Yalçın Zoo** has exotic animals in natural habitats.

A theme park near Istanbul

DIRECTORY

Booking Tickets

Akmerkez
Nispetiye Cad, Etiler.
Tel (0212) 282 01 70.

Biletix
Tel (0216) 556 98 00.
Ⓦ biletix.com

Capitol
Mahir İz Cad, Altunizade.
Tel (0216) 554 77 77.

Galleria
Sahil Yolu, Ataköy.
Tel (0212) 559 95 60.

Vakkorama
Abdi İpekçi Cad 29,
Nişantaşı. **Map** 7 E4.
Tel (0212) 224 31 72.

Festivals

**Istanbul Festival
Committee**
Tel (0212) 334 07 00.
Ⓦ istfest.org

Western Classical Music and Dance

**Aksanat Cultural
Centre**
İstiklal Cad 16, Taksim.
Map 7 D4.
Tel (0212) 252 35 00.

**Cemal Reşit Rey
Concert Hall (CRR)**
Darülbedayi Cad, Harbiye.
Map 7 F1.
Tel (0212) 231 54 97.

**Lütfi Kırdar Kongre
Merkezi (ICEC)**
Gümüş Cad 4, Harbiye.
Map 7 F1.
Tel (0212) 373 11 00.

Rock Music and Jazz

**Hayal Kahvesi
(Beyoğlu)**
Büyükparmakkapı Sok 19,
Beyoğlu. **Map** 7 E4.
Tel (0212) 244 25 58.

**Hayal Kahvesi
(Çubuklu)**
Burunbahçe Mevkii,
Çubuklu. **Open** May–Oct.
Tel (0216) 413 68 80.

Kemancı
Sıraselviler Cad 69/1–2,
Taksim. **Map** 7 E4.
Open May–Jun.
Tel (0212) 251 27 23.

Mojo
Büyük Parmakkapi Sok,
Beyoğlu.
Map 7 E4.
Tel (0212) 243 29 27.
Ⓦ mojobeyoglu.net

Q Jazz Bar
Hôtel Les Ottomans,
Muallim Naci Cad 168,
Kuruçeşme.
Map 9 F2.
Tel (0212) 359 15 82.

Rock House Café
Princess Hotel, Dereboyu
Cad 36–8, Ortaköy.
Map 9 F2.
Tel (0212) 227 60 10.

Sappho
İstiklal Cad, Bekar Sok 14,
Beyoğlu.
Map 7 E4.
Tel (0212) 245 06 68.

Tribunal
Muammer Karaca Çıkmazı
3, Beyoğlu.
Map 7 D5.
Tel (0212) 249 71 79.

Vivaldi
Büyükparmakkapı Sok
29/1, Taksim.
Map 7 E4.
Tel (0212) 293 25 99.

Nightclubs

Blackk
Muallim Naci Cad 71,
Ortaköy.
Map 9 F2.
Tel (0212) 236 72 56.
Ⓦ blackk.net

Club 29
A. Adnan Saygun Cad,
Ulus Parki içi, Ulus.
Tel (0212) 358 29 29.
Ⓦ club29.com

Reina
Muallim Naci Cad 44,
Kuruçeşme.
Map 9 F2.
Tel (0212) 259 59 19.
Ⓦ reina.com.tr

Supperclub
Muallim Naci Cad 65,
Ortaköy.
Map 9 F2.
Tel (0212) 261 19 88.
Ⓦ supperclub.com

Traditional Turkish Music and Dance

Ece
Tramvay Cad 104,
Kuruçeşme.
Tel (0212) 265 96 00.

Galata Tower
Galata-Tünel. **Map** 3 D1.
Tel (0212) 293 81 83.

Hasır
Beykoz Korusu, Beykoz.
Tel (0216) 322 29 01.

**Istanbulin Dinner
Show**
Cumhuriyet Cad, Cebel
Topu Sokak 2, Harbiye.
Tel (0212) 291 84 40.
Ⓦ istanbulin.org

Kervansaray
Cumhuriyet Cad 52/A,
Harbiye. **Map** 7 F2.
Tel (0212) 247 16 30.

Manzara
Conrad Hotel, Yıldız Cad,
Beşiktaş. **Map** 8 C3.
Tel (0212) 227 30 00.

Orient House
Tiyatro Cad 27, next to
President Hotel, Beyazıt.
Map 2 C4 (4 A4).
Tel (0212) 517 61 63.
Ⓦ orienthouseistanbul.
com

Cinemas

AFM Fitas
İstiklal Cad 24, Beyoğlu.
Map 7 E4.
Tel (0212) 251 20 20.

Atlas
İstiklal Cad 209, Beyoğlu.
Map 7 D4.
Tel (0212) 252 85 76.

Nişantaşı Citylife
Nişantaşı Shopping Mall,
Teşvikiye Cad 162. **Map** 8
A2. **Tel** (0212) 373 35 35.

Health Clubs and Sports Centres

Alkent Hillside Club
Alkent Residential
Complex, Tepecik Yolu,
Etiler. **Tel** (0212) 257 78 22.

**Cihangir Sports
Center**
Sıraselviler Cad 118, Mavi
Plaza, Cihangir. **Tel** (0212)
245 12 55.

Cihangir Yoga
Meclisi Mebusan Yokuşu
51, Cihangir.
Tel (0539) 572 84 37.
Ⓦ cihangiryoga.com

**Kemer Country Riding
and Golf Club**
Göktürk Beldesi,Uzun
Kemer Mevkii, Eyüp.
Tel (0212) 239 70 10.

Vakkorama Gym
Osmanlı Sok 13, Taksim.
Map 7 E4.
Tel (0212) 251 15 71.

Spectator Sports

Beşiktaş JK
Spor Cad 92, Beşiktaş.
Map 8 A4.
Tel (0212) 227 87 80.

Fenerbahçe SK
Fenerbahçe Spor Kulübü,
Kızıltoprak, Kadıköy.
Tel (0216) 345 09 40.

Galatasaray AŞ
Hasnun Galip Sok 7,
Galatasaray.
Map 7 E4.
Tel (0212) 305 19 05.

**Veli Efendi
Hipodromu**
Türkiye Jokey Kulübü,
Osmaniye, Bakırköy.
Tel (0212) 543 70 96.

Children

Faruk Yalçın Zoo
Tuzla Cad, Darica.
Tel (0212) 265 99 65.

Miniatürk
İmrahor Cad, Sütlüce.
Tel (0212) 222 28 82.
Ⓦ miniaturk.com.tr

Park Orman
Fatih Çocuk Ormanı,
Maslak Cad, Maslak.
Tel (0212) 285 95 47.

Toy Museum
Dr. Zeki Zeren Sokak 17,
Göztepe.
Tel (0216) 359 45 50.

Turkuazoo Aquarium
Bayrampaşa.
Tel (0216) 640 27 40.
Ⓦ turkuazoo.com

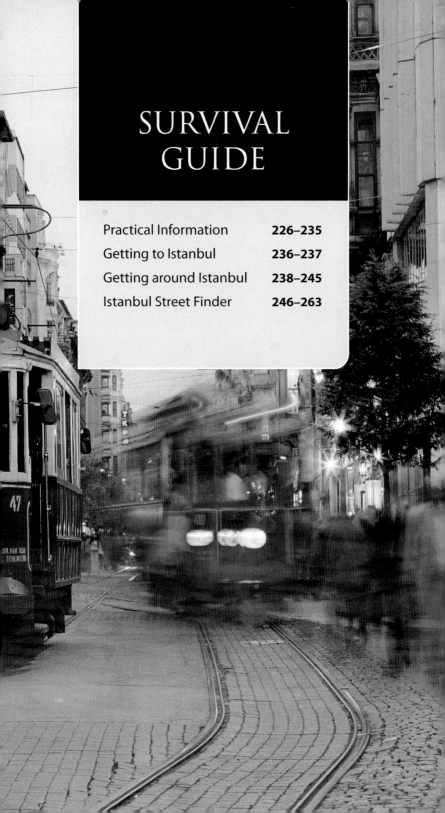

SURVIVAL GUIDE

PRACTICAL INFORMATION

Rapidly expanding Istanbul has the transport, banking and medical facilities of any large modern city. However, in remoter suburbs of the city, and less-visited parts of the Bazaar Quarter, banks and ATM machines may be thin on the ground, so it is worth carrying a day's supply of Turkish lira. It also makes sense to carry the Istanbul Card travel pass *(see p241)*, a mobile phone and/or phone card. Certain aspects of Turkish culture may seem strange to the foreign visitor, especially if you have never travelled in a Muslim country. It is not considered rude to stare and foreigners are objects of attention in quarters less visited by tourists. *Istanbullu* (Istanbul residents) are subject to the same pressures as any modern urban dweller, but in general are friendly and hospitable, and appreciate any effort to show respect for their traditions.

When to Go

With its hot, humid summers and cold, wet winters, Istanbul is best visited in May and June or September and October, when the weather is usually warm and sunny enough to enjoy open-air cafés but not too hot to explore on foot. This said, mid-summer temperatures seldom exceed 30°C (86°F) and sightseeing is manageable if you avoid walking around in the midday heat. Bear in mind that you will need to be suitably dressed (shoulders and knees must be covered) when visiting mosques *(see p227)*. The city is at its least busy (and best value) in winter, and the sights are all the better for the lack of crowds. However, fog and rain may be encountered so take a coat and umbrella.

Tourists on the steps of Dolmabahçe Palace on a sunny day

◄ Trams plying in a busy street in Beyoğlu

Customs Information

Only airports and main road entry points offer a full customs service. At major ports or marinas, customs hours are 8:30am–5:30pm on weekdays. Outside these hours a fee must be paid to consult a customs official. You can buy duty-free items at the airport on entering the country. Visitors over 18 years old can bring in generous amounts of coffee, perfume (5 bottles), spirits (5 litres/180 fl oz) and cigarettes (500). There is no limit on the amount of foreign currency or Turkish lira you can bring in. The maximum when leaving is US$5,000 (or Turkish lira equivalent). In practice, this is rarely enforced.

Turkey is very strict with regard to illegal drugs. Sniffer dogs are used at Atatürk and Sabiha Gökçen airports. You need to have a permit to export antiquities *(see p210)*.

Visas and Passports

Visitors to Turkey should have a full passport with at least six months validity. Overstaying your visa incurs a fine, which escalates rapidly. Citizens of the following countries require visas, paid for in hard currency at the point of entry into Turkey: UK (£10), Canada (US$60), Australia (US$20), USA (US$20) and Ireland (€10). Most tourist visas are issued for three calendar months. Citizens of some countries must apply for a visa before arrival. The process is more complicated if you arrive by sea. Requirements can and do change, so for up-to-date information contact the Turkish consulate in your country or visit www.mfa.gov.tr.

Travellers outside the tourist information office in Sirkeci

Tourist Information

The sign for a tourist information office is a white "i" on a green background in a white box. The offices themselves are named in English and Turkish. They rarely have much printed information to give out but the main office in Sultanahmet Square, in particular, will be able to answer questions on all aspects of your stay in Istanbul. Edirne, Bursa, İznik and Çanakkale have offices near the town centre. Most information offices are open 9am–5pm, Mon–Sat. Some stay open later in summer, while the one in the arrivals terminal of Atatürk airport is open 24 hours daily.

Admission Fees and Opening Hours

Entry fees to Istanbul's major monuments and museums are comparable to elsewhere in Europe, although smaller, less well known establishments are considerably cheaper. In some monuments there is an additional charge for a special section, for example the Harem in Topkapı Palace *(see pp56–61)*.

Most sights are closed one day a week, usually Monday or Tuesday. Exhibits in the most-visited museums are generally labelled in Turkish and English. Museum opening times are usually 8:30 or 9am to 5 or 6pm, with a break for lunch in smaller establishments. Remember that it is best to avoid mosques at prayer times *(see below)*.

Shops open from 8:30 or 9am to 7 or 8pm *(see p210)*. For information on opening times of banks and exchange offices *(döviz) see page 232*.

Public offices are closed on Saturdays and Sundays, and some shops on Sundays, although shopping malls, supermarkets and small grocers' are invariably open seven days a week.

Etiquette

In Istanbul around 10 per cent of women cover their arms, legs and heads in public. Residents of devout areas such as Fatih *(see pp112–15)* may be offended at exposed limbs in the street. In areas like Beyoğlu *(see pp103–9)* most Turkish women dress as they choose and visitors can do the same, except when visiting a mosque *(see below)*.

Although areas like Beyoğlu are lined with bars and restaurants, most Turks drink alcohol in moderation, and overt drunkenness and rowdiness are frowned upon. Visitors who transgress the law while intoxicated will get little sympathy.

Wearing the veil, a matter of personal choice for Turkish women

The venerable Blue Mosque *(see pp80–81)*

Traditional rules of etiquette and hospitality are still an important aspect of Turkish society. Always show respect for Atatürk *(see p33)*, whose picture you will see often.

Discreet gay and lesbian visitors are unlikely to experience problems and Istanbul has a lively gay scene, though overt displays of affection are best kept to a minimum.

Since 2009 smoking has been prohibited in all enclosed spaces, including government offices, public transport, restaurants, bars and even *nargile* cafés, establishments devoted to smoking the traditional water pipe.

Visiting Mosques

Although large mosques are open all day, closing after last prayers in the evening, smaller ones open only for the five daily prayer times *(namaz)*. At these mosques it may be difficult to gain entrance outside prayer times unless there is a caretaker around to open up for you. Non-Muslims should try not to enter any mosque during prayers.

The times of prayer change throughout the year according to sunrise and sunset. They are displayed on a board either outside or inside the mosque, but are always signalled by the call to prayer *(ezan)* from a loudspeaker that is fixed to

the minaret of the mosque. When visiting a mosque women and men should dress appropriately. Most mosques in Istanbul have a prominent notice outside, in English, noting the entry requirements: cover your head (women) and bare shoulders (both sexes); no skirts above the knee or shorts; remove shoes. Some mosques provide shawls to cover head, arms and shoulders. Shoes are usually left on racks in the entryway, but you may prefer to carry them with you as theft is not unknown. Some mosques provide elasticated plastic bags to slip over your shoes instead of removing them. Make as little noise as possible inside and show consideration for anyone who is praying there.

Taxes and Tipping

The rate of VAT (KDV in Turkish) varies between 1 and 23 per cent, though the most common rate is 18 per cent. It is included in hotel prices as well as in the purchase price of most goods and services.

A service charge of 10 to 15 per cent is usually charged in upmarket and licensed restaurants and cafés, and it is customary to tip the waiters here a further 5 per cent. Waiters working in more basic establishments will also appreciate a gratuity.

Language

As a rule, Turks will make every effort to communicate with foreigners. In areas frequented by tourists it is easy to find English-speakers, but it is worth making an effort to learn a few words and phrases in Turkish. The Phrase Book on pages 279–80 is a useful place to start.

Public Conveniences

Public toilets are thin on the ground in Istanbul, usually located in prominent underpasses and at transport terminals. Entrances are marked *Bay* for men and *Bayan* for women. The attendant sitting outside, whom you pay on exit (a sign generally shows the charge), may supply toilet paper, but it is a good idea to carry tissues with you. Fortunately, virtually every mosque (of which there are many) has facilities attached for both men and women. Like public toilets, there is usually an attendant and a small fee is charged.

If you are reluctant to use the squat toilets generally found in public and mosque facilities, you can ask to use the modern flush-style toilets in most restaurants, hotels or cafés. Museums and major sights all have toilets and, outside the city, motorway service areas have excellent, free washroom facilities.

Travellers with Special Needs

Istanbul has few facilities for disabled people and the poor state of the streets can make it difficult to get around. Few mosques allow wheelchairs, and very few museums have disabled access. Toilets with special facilities are also very rare. Conversely, museum staff and the public will go to great lengths to assist with entry to buildings, and there are some low-level public telephones and special access buses *(see p239)*. Trams are accessible to wheelchair users, although

Sign for a public toilet

accessing some of the underground stations will be difficult. Other stations have platforms with gentle ramps from street level *(see p240)*.

The **Turkish Tourist Office** in London publishes a guide to facilities for the disabled in Turkey. This contains specific details of hotels as well as general information.

The **Turkish Association for the Disabled** (Türkiye Sakatlar Derneği) helps disabled people living in Istanbul, and can arrange bus tours around the city for small groups of disabled tourists.

Women Travellers

Women travelling in Turkey may receive unwelcome attention from men, but are rarely in danger of physical attack. To avoid harassment, dress respectably and look purposeful when walking around. Avoid being out alone at night. Traditional cafés *(see pp208–9)* tend to be male preserves, while restaurants often have a section reserved for women and families *(see p191)*.

The Beyoğlu area of Istanbul, along with many of the more prosperous suburbs, is a different proposition, and women can and do go out and about without male company, even at night.

Students outside the Moorish-style gateway of Istanbul University

Students

Apart from a small discount on inter-city trains, an ISIC card is of little use in Turkey. Budget accommodation is easy to find. In July and August you can get a bed in a student dormitory through the Sultanahmet tourist information office. There are also a few youth hostels *(see p185)*, and some cheap hotels and guesthouses in the city centre *(see pp186–9)*.

Photography

Museums do not usually charge visitors for using cameras, but there is often a charge for the use of a video camera. Flash is forbidden in most museums, as are tripods. Some mosques do not permit the use of a flash, but discreet photography is

Groups of friends socializing at a café in Beyoğlu

usually allowed. It is polite to ask permission before taking photographs of people.

Time

Turkey is 3 hours ahead of GMT in summer (March–October) and 2 hours ahead for the rest of the year.

Electricity

As in Europe, the electric current is 220V AC. Plugs have two round pins and adaptors are readily available in Turkey.

Conversion Chart

Imperial to Metric
1 inch = 2.54 centimetres
1 foot = 30 centimetres
1 mile = 1.6 kilometres
1 ounce = 28 grams
1 pound = 454 grams
1 pint = 0.6 litres
1 gallon = 4.6 litres

Metric to Imperial
1 centimetre = 0.4 inches
1 metre = 3 feet, 3 inches
1 kilometre = 0.6 miles
1 gram = 0.04 ounces
1 kilogram = 2.2 pounds
1 litre = 1.8 pints

Colourful display of fruit and vegetables at a market stall

Responsible Tourism

Traditionally, recycling is carried out by members of the Roma community who, pulling hand-carts fitted with giant sacks, scavenge through the large waste-bins left out on the street for collection. Plastics, paper, metal and glass are sold to private operators for recycling. Some Turks help by leaving recyclable materials next to bins rather than putting them in – visitors could do the same.

Environmental awareness in Turkey is improving, with municipality-controlled recycling bins beginning to appear on the streets of Istanbul and other cities. Visitors should make use of these when available.

Electricity is expensive, so many Turks use solar-energy systems for their hot-water needs. If you are serious about energy conservation, check that your proposed accommodation has a system installed. For the same reason low-energy light bulbs have caught on in a big way here.

Street markets are abundant in Istanbul (see pp214–215) and buying from them reduces the amount of packaging – try the Wednesday market (Çarşamba Pazarı) in Fatih.

DIRECTORY

Consulates

Australia
Asker Ocağı Cad 15, Elmadağ-Taksim. **Map** 7 F3. **Tel** (0212) 243 13 33.

Canada
İstiklâl Cad 189/5, Beyoğlu. **Map** 7 D4. **Tel** (0212) 251 98 38.

New Zealand
İnönü Cad 48/3, Taksim. **Map** 7 F4. **Tel** (0212) 244 02 72.

United Kingdom
Meşrutiyet Cad 34, Tepebaşı. **Map** 7 D4. **Tel** (0212) 334 64 00.

United States
Kaplıcalar Mevkii 2, İstinye. **Tel** (0212) 335 90 00.

Tourist Information

Atatürk Airport
International Arrivals Hall. **Tel** (0212) 465 31 51.

Hilton Hotel Arcade
Cumhuriyet Cad, Elmadağ. **Map** 7 F2. **Tel** (0212) 233 05 92.

Karaköy International
Maritime Passenger Terminal (Terminal 2). **Map** 3 E1. **Tel** (0212) 249 57 76.

Sirkeci Station
Sirkeci İstasyon Cad, Sirkeci. **Map** 3 E3 (5 E1). **Tel** (0212) 511 58 88.

Sultanahmet Square
Divanyolu Cad 3, Sultanahmet. **Map** 3 E4 (5 E4). **Tel** (0212) 518 18 02.

Religious Services

Anglican Christ Church
Serdar-ı Ekrem Sok 82, Tünel. **Map** 7 D5. **Tel** (0212) 251 56 16.

Greek Orthodox St George's Cathedral
Sadrazam Ali Paşa Cad 35, Fener. **Tel** (0212) 525 21 17.

Jewish Neve Shalom Synagogue
Büyük Hendek Cad 61, Şişhane. **Map** 6 C5. **Tel** (0212) 293 75 66.

Presbyterian All Saints Church
Yusuf Kamil Sok Paşa 10, Moda. **Map** 3 D5 (4 C5). **Tel** (0216) 449 39 74.

Roman Catholic St Anthony of Padua
İstiklâl Cad 325, Galatasaray. **Map** 7 D4. **Tel** (0212) 244 09 35.

Travellers with Special Needs

Turkish Association for the Disabled
Tel (0212) 521 49 12.
W tsd.org.tr

Turkish Tourist Office
170–73 Piccadilly, London W1V 9DD, UK. **Tel** (020) 7839 7778.

Personal Security and Health

Istanbul is safer than many other European cities, and visitors rarely encounter violence. It is, however, a fast-growing city with huge disparities between rich and poor, and burglary, pickpocketing and petty theft are all on the rise. Keep an eye on your valuables in crowded areas and do not wander the streets late at night on your own. The standard of health care in the city is very good, with excellent private hospitals. For minor complaints, pharmacists will be able to provide advice.

Police

There are several police forces in Turkey. The Security Police (*Emniyet Polisi*), the city's main force, wear dark-blue uniforms and caps, and pale-blue shirts. The Tourist Police (*Turizm Polisi*) is a branch of the *Emniyet Polisi*. Most officers have some knowledge of one or two European languages. The Tourist Police station in Sultanahmet, opposite the Basilica Cistern (*see p78*), is open 24 hours daily, and has an English–Turkish translator available 8:30am to 5pm Monday to Friday.

The Dolphin Police (*Yunus Polisi*) is a rapid-reaction branch of the *Emniyet Polisi*. Dolphin officers ride motorbikes and wear black biking leathers with a red stripe.

The Traffic Police (*Trafik Polisi*) wear the same blue uniform as the *Emniyet Polisi* but with a white belt, hat and gloves. Officers patrol the streets in black and white cars equipped with loudspeakers.

The navy-blue-uniformed Market Police (*Zabıta*) is a municipal police force, which patrols bazaars and other areas of commerce.

The Military Police (*Askeri İnzibat*) controls Turkey's many conscripts and officers wear an army uniform and white helmet bearing the abbreviation "As İz". The Gendarme (*Jandarma*) polices rural areas.

Dolphin Motorbike Police badge

What to be Aware of

When looking after your personal safety use common sense as you would in any large city. Be alert for pickpockets, particularly at markets, as well as on public transport and at termini. Keep your cash in a money-belt and other valuables, such as cameras and mobile phones, well out of sight. Carry bags on your front with the strap worn across your shoulder. In the event of any trouble, shout *"imdat"* (help) to alert fellow passengers or officials. If necessary contact the Tourist Police. Women travelling alone or in groups without a male escort may need to take extra care. After dusk, avoid the areas bordering the old city walls as muggings have taken place here. The Tarlabaşı neighbourhood of Beyoğlu is notorious for petty theft, drug-dealing and prostitution, and Taksim Square, especially around the Tarlabaşı Bulvarı exit, can be unsavoury at night.

Do not leave valuables in your hotel room (use the hotel safe), and remember that Turkish law requires that you carry ID, preferably your passport (or at least a photocopy of it), at all times. Official tourist guides all carry photo ID around their necks – avoid any who do not. Finally, make sure your taxi driver turns on his meter before setting off.

In an Emergency

For emergency telephone numbers see the directory opposite. If your condition is serious or life-threatening you should be treated automatically, but carry your insurance details with you to prove your ability to pay. The state-run **Taksim Ilkyardım Hastanesi** (Taksim Emergency Hospital) has a decent reputation. The American and German hospitals listed in the directory have emergency dental practitioners.

Lost and Stolen Property

Turks are generally very honest and will go to great lengths to return lost property. It is worth returning to the last place the item was seen, or going to the Tourist Police. Property left on public transport can be reclaimed from **IETT Buses**. If you have anything stolen, contact the

Security policeman   Traffic policeman   Dolphin policeman

Fire engine

Turkish Security Police *(Emniyet Polisi)* car

State ambulance

Tourist Police. In order to make an insurance claim, you will need to give (and sign) a statement, preferably at the Tourist Police station in Sultanahmet.

Hospitals and Pharmacies

The Turkish health system has public and private hospitals. Both are usually well equipped but state-owned hospitals can be overcrowded and bureaucratic. Private establishments tend to be more efficient and more comfortable, have a higher proportion of English-speaking doctors, and some run their own ambulance services.

There are also a number of public clinics *(poliklinik)* all over the city offering treatment for minor ailments, as well as private general practitioners *(tibbi doktorlar)* offering the same services. The first port of call with a minor complaint, however, should be a pharmacy *(eczane)*.

Sign for a state hospital in Şişli

Typical sign for a pharmacy in Istanbul

Pharmacists are well-trained, many speak some English and antibiotics can be purchased without a prescription. Outside opening hours, the address of the nearest *nöbetçi eczane* (duty pharmacist) is usually posted in the pharmacy window.

Minor Hazards

Before leaving, make sure that your basic inoculations (diphtheria, polio, typhoid and tetanus) are all up-to-date. Check with your doctor about hepatitis A and hepatitis B vaccinations.

Do not drink tap water (bottled water is readily available everywhere), and exercise care when choosing restaurants and meals. Avoid anything that has been standing around, especially seafood, and only eat salads in more upmarket restaurants.

Some travellers to Turkey experience stomach upsets, often as a result of the amount of oil used in cooking or from drinking tap water. Stick to a bland diet for a few days, eating only bread, yoghurt and rice. Drink lots of fluids and keep alcohol intake to a minimum. Should you suffer from stomach troubles, remedies available from pharmacies include Lomotil, Ge-Oral (oral rehydration salts) and Buscopan. If you are still unwell after 24 hours it is almost certainly some kind of food-poisoning and antibiotics will be required.

Mosquitoes can be a minor irritant, so bring some repellent from your home country or buy a plug-in locally.

Travel and Health Insurance

The state health system in Turkey has few reciprocal agreements with other countries and private hospital costs are high, so be sure to take out travel and medical insurance before you leave.

DIRECTORY

Emergency Numbers

Ambulance
Tel 112.

Fire Service
Tel 110.

Hospital Call Line
Tel (0212) 444 09 11.

Police
Tel 155.

Tourist Police
Yerebatan Cad 6, Sultanahmet.
Map 3 E4.
Tel (0212) 527 45 03 or 528 53 69.

Lost Property

IETT Buses
Tünel, Beyoğlu. **Map** 7 D5.
Tel (0212) 245 07 20 ext 3205.

Hospitals and Pharmacies

American Admiral Bristol Hospital
Güzelbahçe Sok 20, Nişantaşı.
Map 8 A2. **Tel** (0212) 444 37 77.

Ayasofya Eczanesi
Divanyolu Cad 28, Sultanahmet
Map 3 D4. Tel (0212) 513 72 15.

Cerrahpaşa Hospital
Koca Mustafa Paşa Cad, Fatih.
Map 1 C5. Tel (0212) 414 30 00.

European (Avrupa) Hospital
Mehmetçik Cad, Cahit Yalçın Sok 1, Mecidiyeköy.
Map 8 A1.
Tel (0212) 212 88 13.

German Hospital
Sıraselviler Cad 119, Taksim.
Map 7 E4. **Tel** (0212) 2448 26 18

İstiklâl Eczanesi
İstiklâl Cad 423, Beyoğlu
Map 7 D4. **Tel** (0212) 2448 26 18.

Taksim İlkyardım Hastanesi
Sıraselviler Cad 1, Taksim.
Map 7 E4. **Tel** (0212) 252 4300.

Banking and Currency

There is no limit to the amount of currency (foreign or Turkish) you can bring into Turkey. In January 2005, after decades of sky-rocketing inflation, the New Turkish Lira (*Yeni Türk Lirası* or YTL) was introduced, and the many zeros that humbled the old currency were eliminated. Four years later, having successfully combated inflation (which had run at some 10 per cent), the government deleted the *Yeni* (New) and the nation's currency reverted to the Turkish Lira. The lira fared well in the 2009 economic meltdown, holding or increasing in value against most currencies. Visitors will have few problems paying for most things by credit card, using ATMs or making their usual banking transactions.

Cash dispenser with instructions in a range of languages

Banks and Bureaux de Change

Most private banks, such as Garanti and Yapıkredi, are open 9am–5pm Mon–Fri and some bigger branches also offer limited Saturday opening. State banks, such as Ziraat, close 12:30–1:30pm. Banks can be found in all main areas, on Divanyolu Caddesi in Sultanahmet and on İstiklâl Caddesi in Beyoğlu. The İş Bankası at Atatürk airport is open 24 hours daily. Apart from Turkish banks, there are many foreign banks like Citibank and HSBC, with familiar logos and services.

Most banks have an automated queuing system. Take a numbered ticket from the dispenser (for currency exchange there is usually a button marked *döviz*) and wait for your number to flash up on screen.

Several Turkish banks have outlets at airports, offering a full range of banking services. With modest inflation, there

is no need to worry about exchanging foreign currency at the most beneficial time. Exchange offices (*döviz*) still exist, but not in the numbers they once did. Well-established offices include **Bamka Döviz** in Taksim and **Çetin Döviz** on İstiklâl Caddesi. *Döviz* are open for longer hours than banks, and also on Saturdays, but the exchange rate is often better in banks.

ATMs

ATMs are found outside all banks and near major tourist, business and shopping areas. They accept most debit cards, allowing you to withdraw the equivalent of about £250 daily. There is an English-language option on every machine. You can also use some credit cards such as MasterCard and Visa. It is worth remembering that using a debit or credit card at an ATM involves a fee.

Traveller's Cheques and Credit Cards

Credit and debit cards, along with ATMs, have made traveller's cheques almost obsolete. Travellers are advised not to bring them into Turkey because they are difficult to cash. If you need to have large sums of money to hand, consider using a money-order *(havale)* service such as Western Union. They have an association with the Turkish Post Office (PTT – *see p235*) and some banks. This is a safe and speedy, although expensive, way to transfer money.

Credit cards, such as VISA and MasterCard, and, to a lesser extent, American Express and

DIRECTORY

Banks and Bureaux de Change

Bamka Döviz
Cumhuriyet Cad 23, Taksim.
Map 7 E3. **Tel** (0212) 253 70 00.

Çetin Döviz
İstiklal Cad 39, Beyoğlu.
Map 7 E4. **Tel** (0212) 225 64 28.

Ziraat Bankası
Yeniçeriler Cad 55, Beyazıt
Map 2 C4 (4 B3).
Tel (0212) 517 06 00.

Credit Cards

American Express
Tel (0212) 444 25 25.

Diners Club, VISA, MasterCard and Eurocard
Tel (0212) 225 00 80.

A branch of HSBC in Istanbul

Diners Club are universally accepted in hotels, shops and restaurants. Smaller restaurants and grocery stores, however, may not accept card payment. A number of debit cards issued by international banks, such as HSBC and Citibank, are also accepted, but check before leaving that your card is valid internationally. Ensure you know your PIN number because swipe readers use chip and PIN protocol. It is also a good idea to inform your bank of your travels so that they expect your card to be used in Turkey.

There is no commission on paying with credit cards, though many hotels offer discounts for paying with cash *(see p184)*. If you buy an airline ticket from a travel agent however, they will charge about 3 per cent commission.

Currency

The Turkish currency is known as the Turkish Lira (TL) or, more officially (as your credit card statement will show), TRY. A symbol for the currency was introduced in 2012. The sub-division of the lira is the kuruş, with 100 kuruş equalling 1 lira. The lowest denomination note is 5 TL, the highest 200 TL. If you are given one of the old YTL notes, which ceased to be legal tender on 1 January 2009, do not be concerned because it can still be exchanged at a state bank. Beware that some Turks, out of habit, still talk in old, hyper-inflated lira terms, asking *bir milyon* (one million) for a glass of tea (1 lira). You are allowed to take up to US$5,000 out of Turkey in cash.

Banknotes

Turkish banknotes come in six denominations: 200 TL, 100 TL, 50 TL, 20 TL, 10 TL and 5 TL, and each denomination has its own distinctive colour. All the notes display the head of Atatürk on the front, with other Turkish notables on the reverse. Those shown here are 50 TL, 20 TL, 10 TL and 5 TL.

50 lira

20 lira

10 lira

5 lira

Coins

Coins are in denominations of 5 kuruş, 10 kuruş, 25 kuruş and 50 kuruş, and 1 lira (100 kuruş). All coins feature Atatürk on one side.

| 1 lira | 50 kuruş | 25 kuruş | 10 kuruş | 5 kuruş |

Communications and Media

All major cities in Turkey enjoy easy access to efficient high-speed Internet and broadband connections. Internet cafés abound, though they are now being challenged by an ever-increasing number of places offering wireless connection. The formerly state-owned company, Türk Telekom, has a monopoly on all fixed-line telecommunications.

Post offices are clearly identified by the letters PTT and, although slow, the postal service is fairly reliable. Making phone calls from counter-top metered phones within a PTT building is economical, and many change foreign currency and offer the Western Union service for sending and receiving money.

Dozens of Turkish papers vye for readers' attention, ranging from the pro-Islamic to the staunchly secular, and all persuasions in between. Satellite TV has revolutionized the country's once staid, parochial broadcasting, and many foreign-language channels are widely available.

International and Local Telephone Calls

Istanbul has two area codes, 0212 (European side) and 0216 (Asian side). When calling a number within the same area, it is not necessary to use the code. When calling the European side from the Asian, you must prefix the number with 0212; use the prefix 0216 when calling the Asian side from the European.

To call another city in Turkey, use the appropriate area code, for example 0224 for Bursa. To make an international call from Turkey, dial 00 followed by the code for the country, eg: Australia: 61; US and Canada: 1; New Zealand: 64; Republic of Ireland: 353 and UK: 44.

Mobile Phones

Mobile (cell) phones are essential items in modern Turkey. The market is dominated by three players – **Turkcell**, **Vodafone** and **Avea**. Most visitors with a roaming facility can use their existing mobile phone as they would at home because Turkey uses the standard 900 or 1800 MHz frequencies. Most North American phones are not compatible with the Turkish system and will not work here.

Requiring only a few formalities, visitors have a flexible option of purchasing prepaid SIM cards from local mobile operators. There are numerous outlets around Sirkeci Station in Eminönü. The SIM card can be slipped into your own phone, but the phone will need to be unlocked first in order for the SIM to work. Calls made using a locally bought SIM are considerably cheaper than using your roaming facility. Be aware that the cards self-cancel after two weeks.

Public Telephones

Telephone calls in Istanbul can be made from public phone boxes, post offices (PTT) and Türk Telecom (TT) centres using phonecards. The Alokart, with its scratch-off code, allows you to make calls from any landline in Turkey. Chipped Türk Telekom Kontörlü cards are available in units of 50, 100, 200 and 350. Both can be purchased at PTT and TT centres and, for an additional charge, from street sellers and kiosks.

Chipped Türk Telekom Kontörlü
prepaid phonecard

Internet Access

Istanbul has plenty of Internet cafés, although they are in short supply in the major tourist hub of Sultanahmet. Internet cafés charge, very modestly, by the hour, but you can usually negotiate a half-hour rate for minimal usage. The Turkish keyboard can be frustrating to use so ask for help. Look out for the dotless Turkish "i", for example, which will render web and email addresses invalid if used inadvertently. The "@" sign is usually made by pressing the "alt" and "q" keys at the same time.

Wireless Internet (Wi-Fi) connection is now found in many hotels and guesthouses and, although some luxury hotels charge, it is usually free. Most hotels also have fixed terminals where you can check your mail. Many cafés in the city now offer wireless connection free of charge. VOI (voice-over-Internet)

Public telephone boxes in Istanbul

Woman using free Wi-Fi point in a street in Istanbul

protocol permits you to make phone calls anywhere in the world from a computer providing you have the right software installed and all the necessary adaptors and hardware.

Postal Services

Post offices are found throughout Istanbul. There are large branches, with a full range of postal services, in **Sirkeci**, **Taksim** and **Karaköy**. Other locations are marked on the Street Finder (see pp238–48). Opening hours are usually 8:30am–5:30pm Monday to Friday and 8:30am–noon on Saturday. Stamps are only available from post offices.

Letters and postcards can be handed over the counter at post offices or posted in letter boxes, which are yellow and labelled **PTT**. Common signs indicating which box or slot to put your letter in are: Şehiriçi (local), Yurtiçi (domestic) and Yurtdışı (international).

Use air mail (uçak ile) when posting items abroad as surface post is slow. If you want to send a parcel by surface mail, use registered (kayıtlı) post. The contents of a package must be inspected at the post office, so take tape with you to seal your parcel at the counter. Letters and postcards to the rest of Europe take around a week, but may take twice as long to reach other continents. A recorded

delivery service (called APS) is available from post offices, with delivery in three days within Turkey. Local courier companies such as **Aras Kargo** and **Yurtiçi Kargo** will deliver letters and parcels in Turkey in a day or so at a comparable price.

Poste restante mail should be addressed with the recipient's name, then: poste restante, Büyük Postane, Büyük Postane Caddesi, Sirkeci, Istanbul, Turkey. A nominal fee is payable on collection of the mail.

Newspapers and Magazines

Turkey has two English-language daily papers, the liberal, pro-Islamic *Today's Zaman* and the nationalist, secular *Hürriyet Daily News*. Both give round-ups of Turkish and foreign news. Foreign newspapers and magazines can be obtained from newsstands wherever there are substantial numbers of tourists or foreign residents. One of the most convenient outlets is located at the İstiklâl Caddesi exit of the Tünel underground funicular railway (see p241). For current events listings try *The Guide* (see p220), which also has good features on Istanbul and Turkish culture. It is available from larger newsagents and book shops.

Newspaper stand outside the Topkapı Palace

Television and Radio

Satellite TV has blossomed in Turkey, with dozens of channels vying for viewers. Widely available foreign news channels include BBC World, CNN and Al Jazeera, with English-language entertainment provided by CNBCE, E2, BBC Entertainment and MTV. For foreign sports, look out for Eurosport and Spormax. Most hotels receive global satellite TV but check before booking if you particularly want foreign channels.

The state-owned TRT (Türk Radyo ve Televizyon) has 16 television channels and 14 radio stations. TRT3 radio (FM 88.2) broadcasts news bulletins in English, French and German.

DIRECTORY

Mobile Phones

Avea
Tel 444 15 00.
Ⓦ avea.com.tr

Turkcell
Tel 444 05 32.
Ⓦ turkcell.com.tr

Vodafone
Tel 444 05 42.
Ⓦ vodafone.com .tr

Postal Services

Aras Kargo
Alayköşku Cad 2.
Map 3 E4 (5 E3).
Ⓦ araskargo.com.tr

PTT
Karaköy: Kürekçiler Cad 25–7.
Map 3 D1.
Sirkeci: Büyük Postane Cad 1.
Map 5 D1.
Sultanahmet: Ayasofya Meydanı Cad 1.
Map 3 E4.
Taksim: Taksim Square.
Map 7 E3.
Ⓦ ptt.gov.tr

Yurtiçi Kargo
Meşrutiyet Cad 102.
Map 7 D4.
Ⓦ yurticikargo.com

GETTING TO ISTANBUL

The easiest way to reach Istanbul is to fly to one of the city's two international airports, Atatürk Airport, on the European side of the city, or Sabiha Gökçen on the Asian side. Turkish Airlines (THY) offers regular, direct flights from more than 100 destinations worldwide. Several major European carriers, such as Lufthansa and KLM, also fly direct to Istanbul. Most carriers fly into Atatürk Airport, but many budget and charter firms use Sabiha Gökçen. Coaches and trains also offer frequent and well-established services between Istanbul and several European capitals. There are no direct ferry sailings from Europe, although cruises of the Aegean and Mediterranean usually include a one-day stopover in Istanbul.

Planes parked at Atatürk Airport

Arriving by Air

Turkey's main international airline, **Turkish Airlines** (THY), has direct flights to Istanbul from all major cities in Europe and some in Asia. **Lufthansa**, **KLM** and **British Airways** all have at least one flight daily to Istanbul.

A number of budget airlines also serve Istanbul's airports. These include **easyJet**, which connects the UK with Sabiha Gökçen airport, and the Turkish carrier **Pegasus**, which flies into both Istanbul airports from the UK and several European cities. German/Turkish carrier **Sunexpress** serves Sabiha Gökçen airport from many northern European countries.

Turkish Airlines flies direct to Istanbul from Chicago and New York, and **Delta Airlines**, among others, also has regular direct flights from New York. **American Airlines**, **Qatar Airways** and several other international carriers serve the city, but not always directly.

Atatürk Airport

Istanbul's **Atatürk Airport** (Atatürk Hava Limanı) lies 25 km (16 miles) west of the city centre in Yeşilköy. Its huge international (Dış Hatları) terminal and separate domestic (İç Hatları) terminal are internally connected by a series of moving walkways; the journey between them takes about 5 minutes.

The international terminal has all the facilities you would expect, including 24-hour banking, car hire outlets, tourist information and a hotel reservation desk. Allow at least 2 hours to check in for departures from busy Atatürk Airport.

Taxis (see p238) wait outside the arrivals hall of the international terminal. The fare to Taksim or Sultanahmet will be about 40 TL.

The airport bus is a cheaper way of getting to the city centre. Buses depart every half-hour between 4am and 1am, take 30–40 minutes and cost 10 TL. The bus stop, marked "Havaş", is situated outside the main doors of the arrivals hall. Stops include Aksaray, (from where tram/taxis run to Sultanahmet), and it terminates in Taksim Square (see p109).

By far the most economical way to the city centre is by light railway (hafif metro) and tramway. Buy two tokens (jeton) at the airport terminus of the light railway and take the train to Zeytinburnu. Here use the second token and change to the tramway, which runs into Sultanahmet and across the Golden Horn to Karaköy (for Taksim/Beyoğlu).

Sabiha Gökçen Airport

Many domestic carriers and budget international airlines use **Sabiha Gökçen Airport**. Set in the suburbs of Asian Istanbul, 32 km (20 miles) southeast of the city centre, it has car hire outlets, banks, duty free shops and cafés.

A taxi ride to Taksim takes 1 hour and costs about 95 TL. Havaş buses travel to Taksim half-hourly between 4am and midnight. The 1-hour journey costs 13 TL.

The cheapest option is to take the I.E.T.T. (see p239) E3 bus to IV Levent, then the metro to Taksim. Alternatively, take the E10 bus to Kadıköy and the ferry across the Bosphorus to Eminönü (for Sultanahmet). The E3 operates every 15 minutes between 6am and 11:10pm; the E10 runs very frequently between 5am and 3:30am.

The magnificent exterior of Sirkeci Station in Eminönü

Arriving by Rail

The Orient Express (see p68) no longer runs as far as Istanbul. The best overland route, which takes two days, is from Munich via Vienna, Budapest and Bucharest. Information can be obtained on **The Man in Seat 61** website, but bookings are best done via **European Rail Ltd**.

Istanbul has two main-line stations. Trains from Europe arrive at **Sirkeci Station** (see p68), while those from Anatolia and Middle Eastern cities terminate at **Haydarpaşa Station** (see p135), linked by ferry to the European side. This station is closed for renovation.

Motorway sign showing Turkish and European road numbers

Arriving by Coach

The Turkish coach companies **Ulusoy** and **Varan** operate direct services from several European cities to Istanbul, with tickets available online. Ulusoy coaches depart from Munich and Thessalonica among other European cities, while Varan coaches depart from Berlin, Prague and Vienna. For services from the UK, contact **Eurolines**.

Coaches arrive at Esenler coach station (otogar), 10 km (6 miles) northwest of Istanbul city centre. Esenler is also the main terminal for domestic connections (see p244). Coach companies usually operate a courtesy minibus to the city centre. If not, take the light railway (hafif metro, see pp240–41) from the otogar to Aksaray, or the I.E.T.T. 91 bus to Eminönü, or 830 bus to Taksim.

Arriving by Car

Drivers bringing cars into Turkey must show registration documents and a valid driving licence at the port of entry. Your passport will be stamped to show you have brought in a vehicle, and you cannot leave the country without it. You will also be issued a certificate by the Turkish customs authorities and this should be carried at all times, together with your driving licence and passport. You must have a Green Card (available from your insurance company) if arriving from Europe, and appropriate insurance. A fire extinguisher, a first-aid kit and two hazard warning triangles are mandatory. Driving in Istanbul is very taxing and public car parks (otopark or katlıotopark) are scarce and often full.

The Bosphorus Bridge, one of two major road bridges

DIRECTORY

Arriving by Air

American Airlines
Tel (1 800) 433 7300 (US).
W aa.com

British Airways
Tel (0870) 850 9850 (UK).
W britishairways.com

Delta Airlines
Tel (0800) 414 767 (UK).
Tel (404) 765 5000 (US).
W delta.com

EasyJet
Tel (0871) 244 2366 (UK).
W easyjet.com

KLM
Tel (0871) 222 740 (UK).
Tel (1 866) 434 0320 (US).
W klm.com.tr

Pegasus Airlines
Tel (0845) 0848 980 (UK).
W flypgs.com

Qatar Airways
W qatarairways.com

Sunexpress
W sunexpress.com

Turkish Airlines (THY)
W turkishairlines.com

Airports

Atatürk Airport
Tel (0212) 444 08 49.
W ataturkairport.com

Sabiha Gökçen Airport
Tel (0216) 585 50 00.
W sgairport.com

Arriving by Rail

European Rail Ltd
W raileurope.com

Haydarpaşa Station
Tel (0216) 336 04 75.

The Man in Seat 61
W seat61.com

Sirkeci Station
Tel (0212) 527 00 50.

Arriving by Coach

Eurolines
Tel (08717) 818181-UK.
W eurolines.com

Ulusoy
Tel (0212) 444 18 88.
W ulusoy.com.tr

Varan
Tel (0212) 444 89 99.
W varan.com.tr

GETTING AROUND ISTANBUL

Central areas are well served by light railway, metro and tram lines. Buses and dolmuşes provide city-wide transport, but roads and vehicles are very crowded at rush-hour times. Ferries and water taxis ply the Bosphorus and, to a lesser extent, the Golden Horn. The massive Marmaray Project, scheduled for completion in 2017, will link the European and Asian sides of the city by an underwater tunnel and create more than 70 km (43 miles) of suburban rail line, with the city centre sections running underground. See the map inside the back cover for more information on Istanbul's ever-expanding public transport network.

Visitors strolling in front of the serene Blue Mosque *(see pp80–81)*

Green Travel

It is possible to walk between many of Istanbul's major sights *(see below)*, and the vast majority of the further-flung points of interest can be easily reached by public transport. Sadly, due to traffic congestion and lack of cycle routes, few people brave the city by bicycle.

Some of the city's buses use natural gas, as do most taxis, and the Metrobuses *(see p239)* have fuel-efficient, environmentally friendly hybrid engines.

Walking

The development of semi-pedestrianized zones, such as İstiklâl Caddesi and central Sultanahmet, and walking/jogging routes on the shores of sections of the Sea of Marmara and Bosphorus, has made it possible to walk with ease around some parts of Istanbul. Quieter areas of the city, like Eyüp *(see pp122–3)* and parts of Fatih, Fener and Balat

(see pp112–15) have relatively little traffic. For specialist tour companies offering walking tours around the city see page 229.

Bear in mind that traffic only stops at pedestrian crossings controlled by lights, and always make use of pedestrian overpasses and underpasses on main roads.

Istanbul, like any city, has parts that should be avoided *(see p230)*. If you are planning to walk in areas off the usual tourist track seek local advice, take extra care and do not walk in unfamiliar streets after dark.

Taxis

Taxis are ubiquitous in Istanbul. Fares are cheap in relation to other major European cities

Sign for a pedestrian underpass

and cabs operate day and night. They can be hailed in the street or found at taxi ranks *(see pp246–56)*. Hotel and restaurant staff can always phone for a taxi.

Cabs are bright yellow, with the word "taksi" on a sign on the roof. They take up to four passengers. The fare is charged according to a meter. If you cross the Bosphorus Bridge the bridge toll will be added to the fare. The driver will not expect a tip unless he has helped you load luggage, but it is usual to round up the fare to the nearest convenient figure.

Most taxi drivers speak little, or no, English. They may not be familiar with routes to lesser-known sights, so carry a map and have the name of your destination written down.

Taxis queueing for customers at a ferry port

A Plan Tours sightseeing bus

Dolmuşes

Dolmuşes are shared minibuses with fixed routes. The name derives from the Turkish word *dolmuş* ("stuffed" or "full"), and drivers usually wait until every seat is taken before setting off. Dolmuşes run throughout the day until mid-evening, and later on busy routes.

Points of origin and final destinations are displayed in the front windows. Fares generally range between 3 and 6 TL, and you pay by handing your money to the driver or another passenger to pass forward. To stop the vehicle, simply say to the driver "*inecek* (pronounced *eenejek*) *var*" ("somebody wants to get out").

Dolmuş stops are marked by a blue sign with a black "D" on a white background. From Taksim, destinations include Aksaray, Beşiktaş, Kadıköy and Topkapı, and vehicles depart from the Taksim end of Tarlabaşı Bulvarı, and where İsmet İnönü Caddesi exits Taksim.

Getting around by Bus

Inner-city buses are operated by two companies, both under municipal jurisdiction. **I.E.T.T.** (Istanbul Omnibus company) buses are red and the environmentally friendly ones (*yeşil motor*) are green and run on natural gas. Özel Halk (public) buses are mainly light blue and/or green. For a map of useful bus routes see the pull-out map.

I.E.T.T. buses accept only the Istanbul Card travel pass (see p241). The pass can be purchased from main bus departure centres, newsagents, kiosks and private vendors near bus shelters. Cheaper weekly and 15-day passes are available at major bus depots.

If you cross either of the Bosphorus bridges, expect to pay double fare.

You enter at the front of the bus and exit by the rear doors. Push the button above the door or attached to the railings to alert the driver that you wish to alight at the next stop. A list of stops is displayed on the side of buses or on a video screen. Most buses run from 6am until 10 or 11pm.

The large Metrobuses run on dedicated lanes. The first line completed is of little interest to visitors, but a line planned between Edirnekapı and Vezneciler will link the city walls with the Bazaar Quarter.

Useful Bus Routes

15 Üsküdar – Beykoz
15/A Beykoz – Anadolu Kavağı
22 Kabataş – İstinye
25/A Hacıosman Metro – Rumeli Kavağı
28 Edirnekapı – Beşiktaş
28/T Topkapı – Beşiktaş
37/E Eminönü – Edirnekapı
40 Taksim – Sarıyer
80 Eminönü – Yedikule
81 Eminönü – Yeşilköy
86/V Vezneciler – Edirnekapı

Guided Tours

Several tour operators run special-interest tours of Istanbul, as well as general guided tours of the city and further afield. **Plan Tours** has a variety of tours, including trips to Gallipoli, Troy and Bursa, Jewish heritage tours, and private yacht cruises along the Bosphorus (see pp146–51). Companies running city tours include **Backpackers Travel**, **Fest Travel** and **Turista**. For more companies offering trips outside Istanbul see page 245.

If you are approached by people offering their services as tour guides, make sure you see their photo ID, make it clear what you want to see and agree a fee. If you have little time, or do not wish to travel by public transport, it may be worth negotiating a private tour or visit to a sight with a taxi driver. This is best done through your hotel.

DIRECTORY

Taxi Complaints

Tel (0212) 325 15 15.

Getting around by Bus

I.E.T.T. (Istanbul Omnibus Company)
Erkan-ı Harp Sok No. 4, Beyoğlu.
Map 7 D5.
Tel (0800) 211 60 68, (0800) 211 61 20. iett.gov.tr

Guided Tours

Backpackers Travel
Yeni Akbıyık Cad 22, Sultanahmet.
Map 3 D4 (5 D3).
Tel (0212) 638 63 43.
w **backpackerstravel.net**

Fest Travel
Barbaros Bulvarı, 74/20, Beşiktaş.
Map 8 C2.
Tel (0212) 216 10 36.
w **festtravel.com.tr**

Plan Tours
Cumhuriyet Cad 83/1, Elmadağ.
Map 7 F3.
Tel (0212) 234 77 77.
w **plantours.com**
Sultanahmet Office (across from Haghia Sophia):
Map 3 E4 (5 E4).
Tel (0212) 458 18 00.

Turista Travel
Divanyolu Cad 16, Sultanahmet.
Map 3 D4 (5 D4).
Tel (0212) 518 65 70.
w **turistatravel.com**

Getting around by Metro, Tram and Train

Rail transport in Istanbul is becoming ever more efficient. The Marmaray Project will revolutionize public transport in the city. Much of the present slow and scruffy suburban rail network is being upgraded and will disappear underground, and the Asian and European sides of the city will be connected by an underwater train, while Beyoğlu will be linked to the old city by Metro, with a tunnel running under the Golden Horn.

To access the tramway purchase a token (*jeton*), which operates the turnstile (these also accept the Istanbul Card travel pass).

Trams travel on the right-hand side of the street, so be sure to stand on the correct platform. Trams are frequent, running every 5 minutes between 6am and midnight.

A tram on Istanbul's modern tramway system

Tramway

Istanbul's tramway system is modern and efficient, but it can be very crowded at peak times. Run by the **Istanbul Transportation Co.**, the line travels from Zeytinburnu (where it connects with the

hafif metro (light railway) coming in from Atatürk Airport) through Aksaray and Sultanahmet. The line then crosses the Galata Bridge (*see inside back cover*) and continues to Kabataş, offering plenty of sightseeing spots along the way.

Light Railway and Metro

The light railway (*hafif metro* in Turkish) runs east into the city centre from Atatürk Airport, with a few sections underground. It operates between 6am and 12:30am. The key stops are Zeytinburnu (for connecting to the tramway) and Otogar, for the inter-city bus station. The Aksaray stop connects to the tramway but it involves a short walk. This can be awkward with luggage because there is a bridge.

The Istanbul Metro is a true underground. It runs from Yenikapı, across the Golden

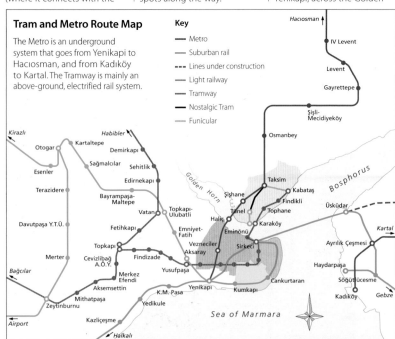

Tram and Metro Route Map

The Metro is an underground system that goes from Yenikapı to Hacıosman, and from Kadıköy to Kartal. The Tramway is mainly an above-ground, electrified rail system.

Key

— Metro
— Suburban rail
--- Lines under construction
— Light railway
— Tramway
■ Nostalgic Tram
— Funicular

Horn to the Hacıosman station, and from Kadıköy to Kartal on the Asian side, between 6:15am and 12:30am. The Metro is clean, well run and the cars are air-conditioned.

Journey tokens, purchased on entry, operate the turnstiles for both the light railway and the Metro. Alternatively, you can use an Istanbul Card.

Turkish Railways sign on the side of a train

Cable Cars and Funiculars

A cable car connects the shores of the Golden Horn in Eyüp with the Eyüp cemetery and tea gardens, and runs between 8am and 10pm daily. There is also a cable car in Maçka Park, which is open from 8am to 8pm daily.

Inaugurated in 1875, the Tünel is a French-built underground railway. It climbs steeply from Karaköy to Tünel Square in Beyoğlu, where it connects with the period tram on İstiklâl Caddesi. The Karaköy station is set back from the main road just off the Galata Bridge (see p91). The Tünel closes at 9pm. A useful modern funicular links Taksim Square with the ferry terminal at Kabataş from 6am to midnight.

The Nostalgic Tram

The Nostalgic Tram (Nostaljik Tramvay) covers a distance of just over 1 km (just under 1 mile) along İstiklâl Caddesi from Tünel to Taksim Square. On the Asian side, the tram runs from Kadıköy along Bahariye Caddesi to Moda. Both run from 7am to 8pm. The trams are the original early-20th-century vehicles, taken out of service in 1966 but revived in 1989. The ticket collectors wear period costume. The Istanbul Card can be used on both.

Suburban Trains

Suburban trains (banliyö) run beside the Sea of Marmara between Sirkeci and Halkalı (on the European side). Useful stops are Yedikule (for Yedikule Museum, see p117) and Ataköy (for Galleria mall, see p211).

As part of the undergoing Marmaray Project an undersea rail tunnel has been constructed to link Yenikapi across the Bosphorus Strait to Üsküdar and Ayrılık Çeşmesi on the Asian side. This has made Yenikapi a major hub station as it connects to the metro as well as the light rail.

Another line runs from Haydarpaşa to Gebze via Bostancı, one of the ferry piers for the Princes' Islands.

Suburban trains accept only the Istanbul Card and tokens. They start daily at 6am and stop at 11:30pm. For further information on the rail network, see the map inside the back cover.

Istanbul Card

The Istanbul Card is a travel pass that can be used on the entire public transport

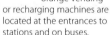

Istanbul Card

DIRECTORY

Tramway

Istanbul Transportation Co.
Tel (0212) 568 99 70.
W istanbul-ulasim.com.tr

system in Istanbul: light railway, tramway, Metro, suburban trains, city buses, ferries, motor boats and sea buses. It is a pre-paid and rechargeable contactless smartcard. The card can be bought from main bus stations and other public transport ticket offices.

When purchasing an Istanbul Card, you pay for a number of units in advance and a refundable 6 TL deposit for the card itself. The card can be topped up at any time. The distinctive orange vending or recharging machines are located at the entrances to stations and on buses.

To use, place the Istanbul Card in the proximity of a fare point, on a turnstile or boarding point, and the amount due will be automatically deducted.

Nostalgic Tram travelling along İstiklâl Caddesi in Beyoğlu

Getting around by Boat

The most pleasant and relaxing means of getting around Istanbul is by the innumerable water-borne craft which ply the Bosphorus between the European and Asian sides. These range from water taxis and small, privately operated ferries to larger ferries and high-speed catamarans. As well as being a relatively fast way to get around, a ride on a boat will also provide some great views of the city.

Old ferries at Karaköy, from which ferries run to Haydarpaşa and Kadıköy

Ferries

A constant traffic of ferries crosses the Bosphorus and the Golden Horn, run by the **Istanbul Sea Bus Company (İDO)**. Private steam ferries, called *vapur*, are run by

Şehirhatları The principal ferry terminus on the European side is at Eminönü *(see p89)*, just east of the Galata Bridge. Destinations served from here, clearly labelled on the relevant boarding halls at each pier, include Kadıköy, Haydarpaşa and Üsküdar on the Asian shore. There is also a pier marked "Boğaz Hattı" for the Bosphorus cruises *(see p243)*, and another labelled "Harem" for car ferries to Asian Istanbul. On the west side of the Galata Bridge is the pier for ferries up the Golden Horn (Haliç Hattı).

Another main terminus is Karaköy, opposite Eminönü, from which ferries run to

Passengers disembarking from a ferry, a popular mode of travel

Haydarpaşa and Kadıköy. The international dock, where cruise liners berth, is also here.

There are ferries from Eminönü to Kadıköy between 7am and 11pm, and from Eminönü to Üsküdar between 6am and 11:30pm, departing every 15 minutes or so. Other services are less frequent. If you want to explore independently using ferries, especially to hop between the villages along the Bosphorus, you will need to arm yourself with a timetable *(see p243)*.

Ferry and Sea Bus Route Map

There are numerous ferry and sea bus services departing daily from Eminönü and the other ports. In addition, a number of smaller, privately operated motor boats serve the same destinations.

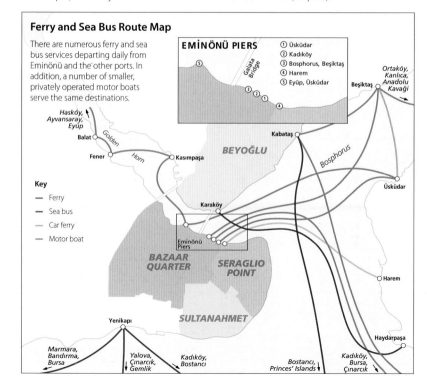

EMİNÖNÜ PIERS
① Üsküdar
② Kadıköy
③ Bosphorus, Beşiktaş
④ Harem
⑤ Eyüp, Üsküdar

Galata Bridge

Ortaköy, Kanlıca, Anadolu Kavağı

Beşiktaş

Hasköy, Ayvansaray, Eyüp

Balat
Golden Horn

Fener

Kasımpaşa

Kabataş

BEYOĞLU

Bosphorus

Üsküdar

Key
— Ferry
— Sea bus
— Car ferry
— Motor boat

Karaköy

Eminönü Piers

BAZAAR QUARTER

SERAGLIO POINT

Harem

SULTANAHMET

Yenikapı

Haydarpaşa

Marmara, Bandırma, Bursa

Yalova, Çınarcık, Gemlik

Kadıköy, Bostancı

Bostancı, Princes' Islands

Kadıköy, Bursa, Çınarcık

Sea Buses

The modern, Swedish-built catamarans which are known as sea buses *(deniz otobüsü)* are run by İDO. Their interiors resemble aircraft cabins, with long rows of comfortable, reclining seats, piped music and air-conditioning. Sea buses are considerably faster and more comfortable than ferries, but cost three times as much.

The most useful route is to the Princes' Islands *(see p161)*, with 6–12 departures daily. For destinations outside Istanbul *see pp244–5*.

One of the many ferries operating on the Bosphorus

Motor Boats

A number of companies, including **Dentur** and **Turyol**, operate motor boats which cross the Bosphorus and Golden Horn at various points, and run up the Bosphorus. These routes are also served by Şehirhatları ferries and although cheaper, they are less frequent. Motor boats accept only the Istanbul Card travel pass or a *jeton* token.

Water Taxis

Water taxis are the latest addition to the city's waterborne transport scene. There are 27 designated docks across the city. To book a water taxi either phone or reserve online. They operate a shared rate system for the 10-seater craft, and are very reasonably priced when shared.

Water taxi on its way along on the Bosphorous

The Bosphorus Trip

Şehirhatları runs daily ferry excursions up the Bosphorus *(see pp138–51)*. Although prices have increased steeply, they are still reasonable. Light refreshments are served but no meals. They get crowded in the summer,

especially at weekends, so arrive early to book your ticket and to ensure that you get a deck seat with a view. You should retain your ticket during the journey, as you must show it on the return trip. You can disembark at any pier along the way, boarding the next ferry that comes along with the same ticket; but if you make a second stop you will need to buy a new ticket to continue your journey. Şehirhatları also offers a trip from Kadıköy in summer at weekends only.

There are several alternatives to the official trip. The small private boats that leave Eminönü just after the Şehirhatları ferry sails in the summer months only go halfway up the straits and do not stop on the way. Alternatively you can book a private cruise through a reputable company, such as **Hatsail Tourism**.

Tickets & Timetables

For ferries and sea buses, buy a flat-fare token *(jeton)* from the booth *(gişe)* at the pier or from one of the unofficial street vendors who sit nearby and sell them at slightly higher prices. Ferry fares cost 3 TL, while those for sea buses to the Princes' Islands are 9 TL. You can use *jetons* for all local trips. Better still, use an Istanbul Card, which makes

boarding quicker and offers a discounted fare. Tickets for the Bosphorus trip cost 20 TL and you cannot use the Istanbul Card for it.

To enter the pier, put the *jeton* into the slot beside the turnstile, and then wait in the boarding hall for a boat.

İDO

İDO logo

A schedule of sailing times is on view at each pier and a copy of the timetable *(tarife)* can usually be bought at the ticket booth.

DIRECTORY

Ferries and Sea Buses

Istanbul Sea Bus Co. (İDO)
Tel (0212) 444 44 36.
ido.com.tr

Şehirhatları
Tel (0212) 444 18 51.
sehirhatlari.com.tr

Motor Boats

Dentur
Tel 444 63 36.
denturavrasya.com

Turyol
Tel (0212) 251 44 21.
turyol.com

Water Taxis

Deniz Taksi
Tel 444 44 98. deniztaksi.com

Private Cruises

Hatsail Tourism
Tel (0212) 241 62 50.
hatsail.com

Travelling Beyond Istanbul

The best way to reach nearby towns and cities from Istanbul is by coach. Further-flung destinations can be reached either by coach or air. A great number of coach companies operate in Turkey, but it is worth paying extra to travel with a reputable company. Many Turkish cities are served by domestic flights from both Atatürk and Sabiha Gökçen airports and fares are competitive. Trains serve fewer destinations and, aside from the fast train between Eskişehir and Ankara, are painfully slow. For destinations across the Sea of Marmara, ferries and sea buses are a relaxing means of transport.

High-speed sea bus on the Bosphorus

Intercity Coaches

The main coach station (Otogar) for both domestic and international destinations is at Esenler, 14 km (9 miles) northwest of the city centre. There is another at Harem, on the Asian side of the Bosphorus. Both are scruffy and poorly maintained, but all coach companies have city centre branches where you can buy tickets, and they run shuttle services to collection points near the motorway, so you will probably not need to use them.

You must make a booking for all coach journeys. Most companies accept credit cards. Varan and Ulusoy (see p237), the two most reputable bus companies, take bookings and issue tickets from their city centre offices. They operate services between main centres such as Ankara, Antalya and İzmir, as well as to destinations along the Black Sea coast. **Kâmil Koç** has a service to Bursa. The journey goes via Gebze, boarding the ferry to Yalova and takes about 4 hours. **Çanakkale Truva Seyahat** is the best company to use for getting to Gelibolu

(Gallipoli), which takes about 5 hours, or Çanakkale, which takes about 6 hours. **Metro Turizm** is a large and reliable coach company that runs regular schedules to many destinations outside Istanbul. Single passengers will usually be seated next to someone of the same sex. Couples can sit together. Refreshments are served free of charge, and there are frequent rest and meal stops. The better companies have some buses with single seats, offer free Wi-Fi and have TVs in the back of the seats. As an example, the fare for the 450-km (280-mile) journey between Istanbul and Antalya is 75 TL with a premium company.

Air Travel

Flying makes sense in Turkey if you wish to visit distant cities such as Antalya, İzmir, Kayseri (for Cappadocia), Trabzon or Van. Several companies compete on the same routes, so prices are very reasonable (starting from 70 TL) if booked early. **Anadolujet** and **Sunexpress** fly only from Istanbul's Sabiha Gökçen Airport. **Atlas Jet** and **Onur Air** use Atatürk Airport,

while **Pegasus** and **Turkish Airlines** use both. Turkish Airlines have flights to both Bursa and Çanakkale if you are pressed for time.

Sea Buses and Ferries

High-speed ferries (hızlı feribot) and sea buses (deniz otobüsü) are a convenient means of travelling long distances from a city surrounded by water. Run by **İDO** and **Şehirhatları** (see p242), they are good value; cars are also carried on some high-speed ferry routes.

For Bursa, take the twice-daily high-speed ferry from Yenikapı to Güzelyalı (90 minutes), or the sea bus from Kabataş to Güzelyalı (2 hours via Kadıköy), then a bus into Bursa. Alternatively, take the high-speed ferry (seven daily; 1 hour 10 minutes) to Yalova, from where it is 1 hour by bus to Bursa. From Yalova, regular minibuses serve İznik (1 hour). Sea buses also travel to the Marmara Islands from Yenikapı.

Trains to Edirne

The daily train to Edirne from Sirkeci Station (see p68) takes 6 hours, twice the length of time taken by coach. Advance reservations can be made at the railway stations in either city, or in certain travel agencies displaying the **TCDD** (Turkish State Railways) sign. Bursa, Çanakkale and İznik are not on the rail network.

Café at Istanbul's architecturally interesting Sirkeci Station

Car Hire and Road Travel

Turkey's comprehensive intercity coach and air network means that a car is not necessary for travelling to other cities. If you wish to drive, car hire companies including **Avis**, **Budget** and **Sixt** have both airport and city centre offices. You do not need an international driving licence, just your normal one. Turkish roads are hazardous because of fast, reckless driving. Traffic drives on and gives way to the right, even on roundabouts. The Turkish Touring and Automobile Club (Türkiye Turing ve Otomobil Kurumu, or **TTOK**), can give visiting motorists advice on driving in Turkey, as well as offering assistance with breakdowns, accidents and insurance. It has reciprocal agreements with the British AA and RAC.

Horse-drawn carriage (phaeton) on Büyükada

and offer an efficient and hassle-free method of simplifying your travel arrangements.
Reputable tour operators with English-speaking guides include **Plan Tours**, **Turista Travel** and **Türk Expres**. All offer classical, biblical and heritage tours in Istanbul as well as to regions throughout Turkey. Some companies offer personalized tours all over Turkey. Plan Tours also operates a double-decker bus tour around Istanbul. **CARED** (Çanakkale Tour Guide Association) can provide tour guides who speak many languages.

Car rental company logos

Day Trip Tours

A number of companies offer day trips from Istanbul to the Princes' Islands, the Dardanelles, Bursa and villages on the Black Sea. These are often good value

Local Transport Outside Istanbul

The main means of public transport in both Bursa and Edirne is the dolmuş. These are either minibuses or saloon cars, with the destination displayed on signs on the roof. If you stay in the centre of either

city and are moderately fit, you will find that all of the major sights are within easy walking distance.
In Bursa city centre, Heykel, at the eastern end of Atatürk Caddesi, is the main dolmuş terminus. From there you can get dolmuşes to most other parts of the city. There is also an efficient bus service and a metro.
Edirne is much smaller than Bursa, and the public transport system is not as comprehensive. To get from the coach station to the town centre, a distance of 2 km (1 mile), take a Merkez–Garaj minibus dolmuş, or a taxi.
There are no motor vehicles on the Princes' Islands. On Büyükada and Heybeliada phaeton carriages can be hired.

DIRECTORY

Intercity Coaches

Çanakkale Truva Seyahat
Tel (0212) 444 00 17.
🔳 truvaturizm.com

Kâmil Koç
Tel (0212) 444 05 62.
🔳 kamilkoc.com.tr

Metro Turizm
Tel (0212) 444 34 55.
🔳 metroturizm.com.tr

Air Travel

Anadolujet
Tel 444 25 38.
🔳 anadolujet.com.tr

Atlas Jet
Tel (0850) 222 00 00.
🔳 atlasjet.com

Onur Air
Tel (0850) 210 66 87.
🔳 onurair.com.tr

Pegasus Airlines
Tel (0850) 260 07 37.
🔳 flypgs.com

Sunexpress
Tel 444 07 97.
🔳 sunexpress.com

Turkish Airlines (THY)
Tel 444 08 49.
🔳 turkishairlines.com

Ferries

İDO
Tel (0212) 444 44 36.
🔳 ido.com.tr

Şehirhatları
Tel (0212) 444 18 51.
🔳 sehirhatlari.com.tr

Kabataş Pier
Tel (0212) 249 15 58.

Yenikapı Pier
Tel (0212) 516 12 12.

Trains

TCDD
🔳 tcdd.gov.tr

Car Hire and Road Travel

Avis
Tel 444 28 47.
🔳 avis.com.tr

Budget
Tel (0212) 663 08 58.
🔳 drivebudget.com

Sixt
Tel (0212) 215 24 19.
🔳 sixt.com/car-rental/turkey

TTOK
I. Oto Sanayi Sitesi Yanı, Seyrantepe Yolu, IV Levent.

Tel (0212) 282 81 40.
🔳 turing.org.tr

Day Trip Tours

CARED
Tel (0286) 213 90 40.
🔳 cared.org.tr

Plan Tours
Cumhuriyet Cad 83/1, Elmadağ. **Map** 7 F3.
Tel (0212) 230 22 72.
🔳 plantours.com

Turista Travel
Divanyolu Cad 16, Sultanahmet. **Map** 3 D4 (5 D4). **Tel** (0212) 518 65 70.
🔳 turistatravel.com

Türk Expres
Cumhuriyet Cad 47/1, Taksim. **Map** 7 E3.
Tel (0212) 235 95 00.
🔳 turkexpres.com.tr

STREET FINDER

The map references that are given throughout this guide refer to the maps on the following pages only. Some small streets with references may not be named on the map. References are given for hotels *(see pp182–9)*, restaurants *(see pp190–207)*, shops *(see pp210–19)* and entertainment venues *(see pp220–23)*. The map below shows the area covered by the ten maps and the key lists the symbols used. The first figure of the reference tells you which map page to turn to; the letter and number indicate the grid reference. For an overview of Greater Istanbul see pages 110–11. The map on the inside back cover shows public transport routes.

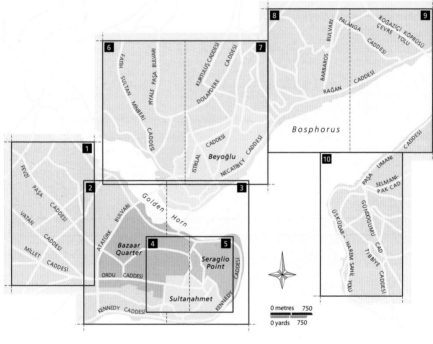

Key To Street Finder

- ▢ Major sight
- ▢ Place of interest
- ▢ Other building
- 🛥 Ferry boarding point
- 🛥 Sea bus boarding point
- 🚆 Railway station
- Ⓜ Metro / light rail station
- 🚇 Underground funicular stop
- 🚎 Tram stop
- 🚠 Cable car station
- 🚌 Main bus stop
- Ⓓ Dolmuş terminus
- ℹ Tourist information

- 🏢 Police station
- 🛁 Turkish baths
- Ⓒ Mosque
- ✡ Synagogue
- ✝ Church
- ✚ Hospital
- ▦ Railway line
- — Tram line
- ▤ Motorway
- Pedestrian tunnel
- — City walls

Scale of Maps 1–3 & 6–10

```
0 metres      250
0 yards       250
```

Scale of Maps 4 & 5

```
0 metres      200
0 yards       200
```

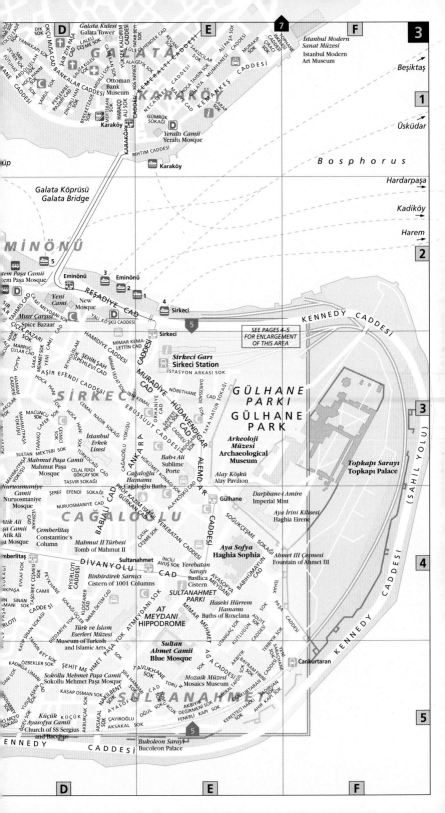

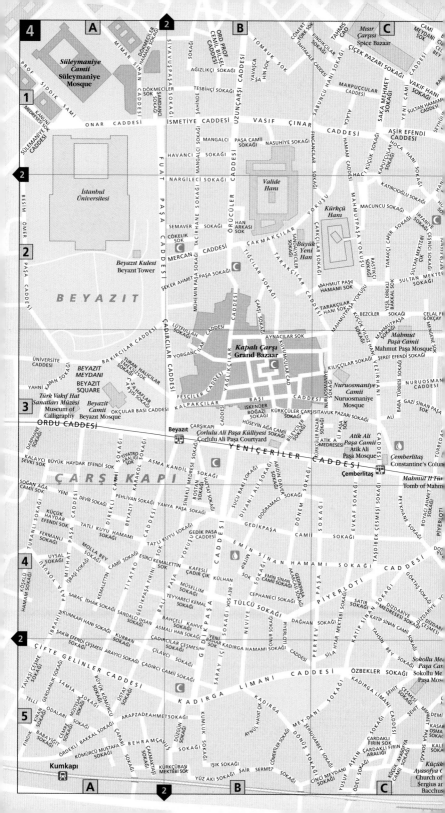

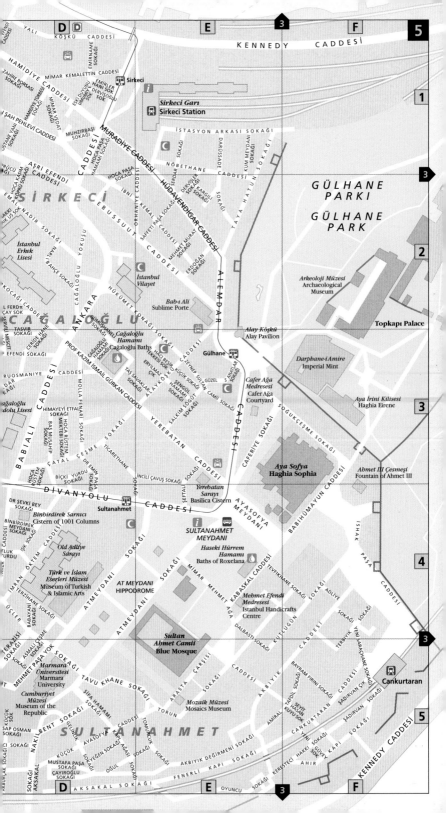

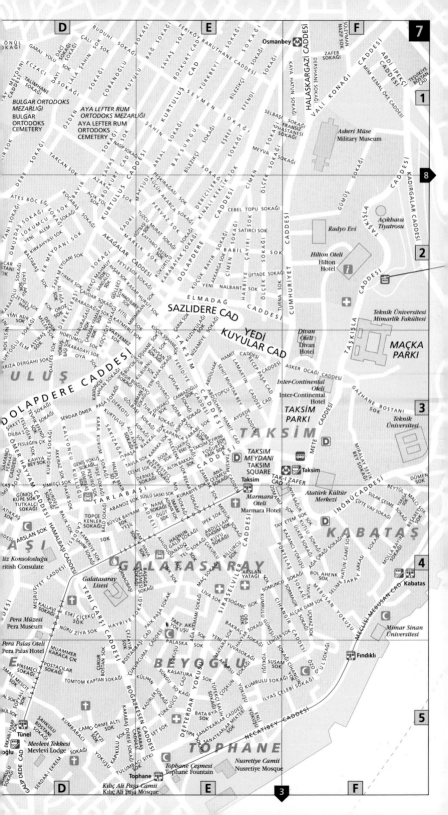

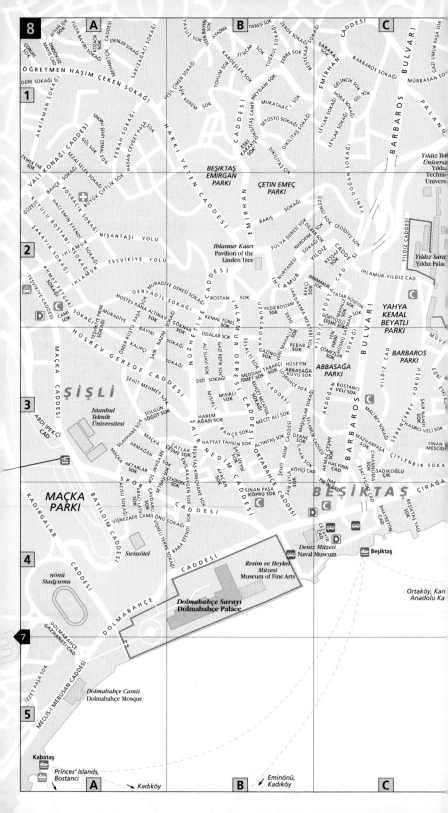

D **E** **F**

ZİNCİRLİKUYU YOLU

BESTEKAR ŞEVKİ

RUHL BAĞDADİ

BEY SOK

İTRİ SOKAĞI

ŞEYH ŞAMİL

İTRİ SOKAĞI

DELLALZADE SOKAĞI

MUSTAFA İZZET EFENDİ SOKAĞI

ŞİKTAŞ BOĞAZİÇİ KÖPRÜSÜ BAĞLANTI YOLU

CADDESİ

SAKAYOLU DERE SOKAĞI

VARNALI SOKAĞI

ÇAYIRLI SOK

AMBARLI DERE SOKAĞI

LEYLEK YUVASI SOKAĞI

TAVUK SOKAĞI

BOĞAZİÇİ KÖPRÜSÜ

ÇAMLIK KUYU SOK

AYAYDIN SOK

ORTAKÖY DERE BOYU CADDESİ

BK UYU SOK

CUDİ ÇK

1

ZİNCİRLİKUYU YOLU KURUÇEŞ ME KİREÇHANE SOK

KAYPAKOĞLU SOK

ORTAKÖY SOKAĞI

URGANCI SOK

AMCA BEY

MANDIRA

REVANİÇİ SOK

RESAT AĞA SOKAĞI

SİRACI SOKAĞI

DUVARCI SOK

ŞAİR NECATİ SOKAĞI

KIZ SOKAĞI

C

ORTAKÖY MEZARLIĞI

ORTAKÖY CEMETERY

ÇEVİRMECİ

ORTAKÖY KABRİSTAN SOK

BESTEKAR AHMET

M KARACA SOK

ÇAĞAN SOK

CUDİ EFENDİ SOK

GÜLTEKİN SOKAĞI

LOZAN SOKAĞI

GÖKTEKİN

ARACI SOK

AYDINLIK SOK

ŞAİR NECATİ SOKAĞI

GÜRCÜ KIZI SOKAĞI

ORTAKÖY

GÜRCÜ KIZI SOK

GÜRCÜ KIZI YOLU

ÇEVRE YOLU

ŞAİR

Şale Köşkü
Sale Pavilion

Malta Köşkü
Malta Pavilion

PALANGA

ÇÖPUR AHMET SOK

ORTAKÖY KABRİSTAN SOK

FISTIKLI KÖŞK SOKAĞI

SARIBAL SOK

NAR SOKAĞI

KABALAK SOKAĞI

ALADOĞAN SOKAĞI

ŞEHİT NURİ PAMİR SOK

KUMBARACI BAŞ

HASRET SOK

TARÇIN SOK

HERÇAĞNOS

CİBİNLİK

TAŞBASAMAK SOKAĞI

KARAKAŞ SOK

AKTAR SOK

BÜLGÜRCÜ SOKAĞI

KIRMIZI

HOCANR

ESKİ BAHÇ

VATMAN SOK

D

2

YILDIZ PARKI
YILDIZ PARK

Çadır Köşkü
Çadır Pavilion

PALANGA CADDESİ

Yıldız Çini Fabrikası
Imperial Porcelain Factory

MUALLİM NACİ CADDESİ

D

Boğaziçi Köprüsü
Bosphorus Bridge

İstinye, Sariyer

ÇIRAĞAN CADDESİ

YAHYA EFENDİ SOK

C

Ortaköy 🚢

Ortaköy Camii
Ortaköy Mosque

3

Kanlica, Anadolu Kavaği

ALÇIK- AR SOK

CADDESİ

Çırağan Sarayı
Çırağan Palace

4

Beylerbeyi

B o s p h o r u s

5

Kuzguncuk 🚢

PAŞA LİMANI CADDESİ

İCADİYE CADDESİ

URYANİZADE SOK

BAMYACI SOK

MENTEŞ SOK

TUTSULU SOK

BEREKETLİ SOKAĞI

BİCAN EFENDİ SOKAĞI

MEŞRUTA SOK

BİKANCABAŞ SOK

C

D **E** **F**

Street Finder Index

In Turkish, Ç, Ğ, İ, Ö, Ş and Ü are listed as separate letters in the alphabet, coming after C, G, I, O, S and U respectively. In this book, however, Ç is treated as C for the purposes of alphabetization and so on with the other letters. Hence Çiçek follows Cibinlik as if both names began with C. Following standard Turkish practice we have abbreviated Sokaği to Sok and Caddesi to Cad. References in brackets refer to the enlarged section of the Street Finder (maps 4 and 5).

General Index

Acknowledgments

Dorling Kindersley would like to thank the following people whose assistance contributed to the preparation of this book:

Main Contributors

Rosie Ayliffe lived in Turkey for three years, during which time she worked as a freelance writer in Istanbul for the English-language weekly *Dateline Turkey* and as a tour guide travelling all over western Turkey. She is one of the authors of the *Rough Guide to Turkey*, and has also contributed to the *Rough Guide to France* and to Time Out's London guides.

Rose Baring is a travel writer who has spent many months exploring Istanbul. She is the co-author of *Essential Istanbul* (AA) and has also contributed to guides to Tunisia, and Moscow and St Petersburg.

Barnaby Rogerson has travelled, written and lectured extensively in the countries of the eastern Mediterranean. He is, with Rose Baring, co-author of *Essential Istanbul* (AA), and has contributed to several other AA and Cadogan guides. He is the author of *A Traveller's History of North Africa*.

Canan Silay worked for many years as the editor-in-chief of the English-language magazine *Istanbul, The Guide*. Previously, she had worked as a journalist with the Turkish daily newspaper *Hürriyet*. She has contributed to several books on Turkey, including Insight guides to Istanbul, Turkey and the Turkish coast.

Managing Editor Georgina Matthews
Managing Art Editor Annette Jacobs
Senior Managing Editor Vivien Crump
Deputy Art Director Gillian Allan

Additional Contributors

Ghillie Başan, Arzu Bolukbasi, Krysia Bereday Burnham, Professor Anthony A M Bryer, Jim Crow, José Luczyc-Wyhowska, Colin Nicholson, Venetia Porter, Dott. A Ricci, Professor J M Rogers, Sargasso Media Ltd, London, Suzanne Swan, Tina Walsh.

Additional Cartography

Robert Funnell, Emily Green, David Pugh, Lee Rowe (ESR Cartography Ltd).

Picture Research

Rachel Barber, Marta Bescos, Rhiannon Furbear, Susie Peachey, Ellen Root,Nikil Verma.

Revisions and Relaunch Team

Didem Mersin Alıcı, Gillian Andrews, Jasneet Arora, Lydia Baillie, Sonal Bhatt, Tessa Bindloss, Imogen Corke, Gary Cross, Mehmet Erdemgil, Isobel Finkel, Amy Harrison, Sally Hibbard, Rupanki Kaushik, Hasan Kelepir, Batur Kızıltuğ, Priyanka Kumar, Maite Lantaron, Jude Ledger, Francesca Machiavelli, Hayley Maher, Alison McGill, Sam Merrell, Ella Milroy, Mary Ormandy, Catherine Palmi, Reetu Pandey, Marianne Petrou, Mani Ramaswamy, Lee Redmond, Lucy Richards, Nicola Rodway, Azeem Siddique, Beverly Smart, Sands Publishing Solutions, Anna Streiffert, Rosalyn Thiro, Conrad Van Dyk, Nikhil Verma, Dutjapun Williams, Veronica Wood.

Proofreader

Stewart Wild.

Indexer

Hilary Bird.

Additional Photography

DK Studio/Steve Gorton, Lydia Evans, John Heseltine, Izzet Keriber, Dave King, Ian O'Leary, Fatih Mehmet Akdan, Clive Streeter.

Artwork Reference

Kadir Kir, Remy Sow.

Special Assistance

The Publisher would like to thank staff at museums, mosques, churches, local government departments, shops, hotels, restaurants and other organizations in Istanbul for their invaluable help. Particular thanks are also due to: Feride Alpe; Halil Özek, Archaeological Museum, Istanbul; Hamdi Arabacıoğlu, Association of Mevlevis, Istanbul; Veli Yenisoğancı (Director), Aya Sofya Museum, Istanbul; Nicholas Barnard; Ahmet Kazokoğlu, Bel Bim A.Ş., Istanbul; Poppy Body; Banu Akkaya, British Consulate, Istanbul; Vatan Ercan and Mine Kaner, Bursa Tourist Office; Hanife Yenilmez, Central Bank of the Republic of Turkey, London; Reverend Father Ian Sherwood, Christ Church, Istanbul; Father Lorenzo, Church of SS Peter and Paul, Istanbul; Münevver Ek and Muazzez Pervan, Economic and Social History Foundation of Turkey, Istanbul; Edirne Müze Müdürlüğü; Emin Yıldız, Edirne Tourist Office; Tokay Gözütok, Eminönü Belediyesi, Istanbul; Mohammet Taşbent, Eminönü Zabıta Müdürlüğü, Istanbul; Orhan Gencer, Protocol Department, First Army HQ, Istanbul; Robert Graham; Cengiz Güngör, Şevki Sırma and Mustafa Taşkan, Greater Istanbul Municipality; Hikmet Öztürk, İETT Genel Müdürlüğü, Istanbul; Bashir Ibrahim-Khan, Islamic Cultural Centre, London; İsmet Yalçın, İstanbul Balık Müstahsilleri Derneği; Nedim Akıner, İstanbul Koruma Kurulu; Sühela Ertürk Akdoğan and all staff of the Istanbul Tourist Offices; Abdurrahman Gündoğdu and Ömer Yıldız, İstanbul Ulaşım A.Ş.; Mark Jackson; Sibel Koyluoğlu; Semra Karakaşlı, Milli Saraylar Daire Başkanlığı, Istanbul; Akın Bavur and Recep Öztop, Cultural Department, Ministry of Foreign Affairs, Ankara; staff at the Edirne Müftülüğü and Eyüp Müftülüğü; Mehmet Sağlam and staff at the Istanbul Müftülüğü; Professor Kemal İskender, Museum of Painting and Sculpture, Istanbul; Öcal Özerek, Museum of Turkish and Islamic Arts, Bursa; Dilek Elçin and Dr Celia Kerslake, Oriental Institute, Oxford University; Kadri Özen; Dr İffet Özgönül; Cevdat Bayındır, Public Relations Department, Pera Palas Hotel; Chris Harbard, RSPB; Rosamund Saunders; John Scott; Huseyin Özer, Sofra; Ahmet Mertez and Gülgün Tunç, Topkapı Palace, Istanbul; Doctor Tüncer, Marmara Island; Mr U Kenan İpek (First Secretary), Turkish Culture and Tourism Office in London and Istanbul, Turkish Embassy, London; Orhan Türker (Director of International Relations), Turkish Touring and Automobile Club, Istanbul; Peter Espley (Public Relations Counsellor) and all staff at the Turkish Tourist Office, London; Mustafa Coşkan, Türkiye Sakatlar Derneği, Istanbul; Dr Beyhan Erçağ, Vakıflar Bölge Müdürlüğü, Istanbul; Yalova Tourist Office; Zeynep Demir and Sabahattin Türkoğlu, Yıldız Palace, Istanbul.

Photography Permissions

Dorling Kindersley would like to thank the following for their kind permission to photograph at their establishments: the General Directorate of Monuments and Museums, the Ministry of Culture, the Ministry for Religious Affairs, İstanbul Valiliği İl Kültür Müdürlüğü, İstanbul Valiliği İl Müftülüğü, the Milli Saraylar Daire Başkanlığı and Edirne Valiliği İl Müftülüğü; also the many churches, restaurants, hotels, shops, transport services, and other sights and establishments too numerous to thank individually.

Picture Credits

a = above, b = below/bottom, c = centre, f = far, l = left, r = right, t = top

The publisher would like to thank the following individuals, companies, and picture libraries for their kind permission to reproduce their photographs:

360istanbul: 204tr.

A Turızm Yayınları: 160b; Archaeological Museum 44bl, 64bl, 65cra, 66cr, 66b, 67tl, 67c; Aya Sofia from Fossart Album 76tr;Topkapı Palace 58br; **ABC Basin Ajansi A.Ş.:** 49clb, 46br, 215tr; **The Advertising Archives:** 104tr; **Adahan Istanbul Hotel:** 183tr Aisa Archivo Icongrafico, S.A., **Barcelona:** 22cb, 26c, 34tr, 35bc, 121tc, 173tr; Louvre Museum 23c; Topkapı Palace 57bl, 59cl; **AKG, London:** 33tl; Erich Lessing 32tl, Erich Lessing/Kunsthistoriches Museum, Vienna 34cb; **Alamy**

Images: Jon Arnold Images Ltd 81tl; Mark Collinson 195crb, David Crossland 194br, Jeff Greenberg 109br; Ali Kabas 193c; B. O'Kane 228tr; Justin Kase zninez 2bl; Justin Kase zsixz 231cla, 232bl, 235bc; Karl F. Schöfmann 202tl; John Stark 192cl, 193tl; **Ancient Art and Architecture Collection Ltd**: 22cr, 25tr; **Aquila Photographics:** Hanneand Jens Eriksen 171b; **Tahsın Aydoğmuş:** 4t, 19br, 23bl, 45b, 73cra, 74tr, 77bl, 80t, 88tr, 121ca, 146b, 172bl; **Jon Arnold Images:** Walter Bibikow 11tr; **Avis Budget Group:** 245cl, 245clb.**Baylo Suites:** 186bl; **Benaki Museum, Athens:** 27ca; **Bread and Butter:** 203br; **Bridgeman Art Library, London:** British Library *A Portrait of Süleyman the Magnificent* (1494–1566), Persian 34br; National Maritime Museum, London *Battle of Lepanto, 7th October, 1571,* Anonymous 29tr; Private Collection *Constantine the Great* (*c.274–337 AD, Roman Emperor 306–337AD*), gold aureus 22tl; Stapleton Collection *Ibrahim from a Series of Portraits of the Emperors of Turkey, 1808,* John Young (1755–1825) 35tl; Victoria and Albert Museum, London *Sultan Mahmud II: Procession,* Anonymous 35tc, 163cl, 163crb; © **The Trustees of the British Museum**: 163cla; **Bunk Hostel:** 185tl; 188br **Cafe Mese:** 196b; **Çalikoğlu Reklam Turızm Ve Tıcaret Ltd.**: 220br; **Jean Loup Charmet:** 31tr, 35crb; **Manuel Çıtak:** 48bl, 105cr, 143tr, 164bl; **Cok Cok Thai Restaurant and Bar:** 201br; **Bruce Coleman Collection:** 143br; **Corbis:** Lynsey Addario 177br; David Bathgate 238br; Atlantide Phototravel/Massimo Borchi 227cr; Paul Hardy 174cl; Robert Landau 237bl; Michael Nicholson 10br; Robert Harding World Imagery/Neil Farrin 8-9; Adam Woolfitt 10cla; Alison Wright 179tr; **Culinary Institute Restaurant:** 200tl; C.M Dixon Photo Resources: 64tr.

Dreamstime.com: Steve Allen 96t; Enisu 138; Alexandre Fagundes De Fagundes 12bl; Ihsan Gercelman 152; Levent Karaoglu 36, 52; Yulia Makarova 136-7; Nexus7 102; Mario Savoia 110; Softdreams 226bl; Nikolai Sorokin 50-1; Muharrem Zengin 2-3, Minyun Zhou 86.

Edition Hotels: 189tc; **ET Archive, London:** 20; Bibliotheque de L'Arsenal, Paris 26t; National Gallery 34bl; **Mary Evans Picture Library:** 144bc, 173bl; ES Collection/Vatican Library 25tl.

Fes Café: 197tr; **First Army HQ, Istanbul:** 135br. .

Getty Images: 32crb, 34cla; Gary Yeowell 190-1, 224-5; **Photographie Giraudon, Paris:** 28crb; Bibliotheque Nationale, Paris 35bl; Lauros 31bl; Topkapı Palace 28br, 29c, 30cl, 30–1, 34ca; **Ara Güler:** 25bl, 28tl, 37br, 89br, 130c, 219tr; Mosaics Museum 79c; Topkapı Palace 1, 59tr, 59b, 83tr, 97bl, 163bl; **şemsı Güner:** 45tl, 131cra, 142tr, 160tr.

Sonia Halliday Photographs: 30bc 129b; engraved by Thomas Allom, painted by Laura Lushington 25cr, 31br, 61tr; Bibliotheque Nationale, Madrid 23t; drawn by Miss Pardoe, painted by Laura Lushington 106cr; Topkapı Palace 35tr, 78br; **Robert Harding Picture Library:** Robert Francis 37cla;

Michael Jenner 1, 57br; Odyssey, Chicago/Robert Frerck 42bl, 170b; Adam Woolfitt 41clb, 93tr, 210bl; **The House Cafe:** 205br; **The House Hotel Bosphorus:** 187tr

İDO-Istanbul Sea Bus Company: 242tr, 243c, 243clb, 243tr, 244cla; **Istanbul Foundation for Culture and the Arts:** 221cb; **Istanbul Hilton:** 184tl; **Istanbul History Foundation:** 32br; **Istanbul Library:** 68br, 97cra; **Istanbul Metropolitan Municipality:** 231tr; **Istanbul Modern:** 206bl.

Gürol Kara:100cl, 117br, 148ca, 155tr, 171tl; **İzzet Kerıbar:** 5bl, 18tr, 49cra, 54ca, 130tr, 140bc, 141tl, 148clb, 175br, 175ca, 176tr, 176cl, 176b, 177tc, 179bc, 214br.

José Luczyc-Wyhowska: 218tr, 219cl/cr/bl/blc/brc/br.

Magnum Photos Ltd.: Topkapı Palace/Ara Güler 30bl, 35clb, 43b, 57tl; **Military Museum, Istanbul:** 129t.

Nar Lokanta Restaurant: 190bl, 199tr; **Nour Foundation, London:** The Nassar D. Khalili Collection of Islamic Art Ferman (MSS801) 97tr, Mahmud II (CAL 334) 97cr, Leaf (CAL 165) 97cl; Burnisher (SC1210) 97bra, Knife (SC1297) 97brb.

Dick Osseman: 177clb; **Güngör Özsoy:** 62tr, 72b, 159tl, 159cra, 172c.

Paşabahçe Glassworks: 148t; **Pera Museum:** 105cb; Pera Palace Hotel Jumeirah: 188tl; **Pictures Colour Library:** 46br, 215bl, 218cl; **Plan Tours:** 239tl; **Poseidon:** 190bl.

Shutterstock: rm 178cla; **Sixt AG:** 245cla; **Antony Souter:** 55b; **Remy Sow:** 182c; **Spectrum Colour Library:** 155br; **Star Gazete:** Murat Duzyol 227br; **The Stockmarket:** 132tl; **SuperStock:** age fotostock 70,72bl, 124tr; **Tips Images** 89tl.

Tatılya: 222b; **TAV Investment Holding Co.**: 236cla; **TCDD: - Turkish State Railways:** 237tl, 244br; **Travel Ink:** Abbie Enock 37bc; **Trip Photographic Library:** 156bc; Marc Dubin 47cra; Turkish Information Office: Ozan Sadık 47bc.

Westside Café and Bistro: 207tl; **Peter Wilson:** 58c, 77tr, 77cla, 120clb. **Erdal Yazici:** 46cla, 169bl, 171cr.

Front endpaper: Dreamstime.com: Enisu Rtc; Ihsan Gercelman Rtr; Levent Karaoglu Rbl; Mario Savoia Ltr; Nexus7 Rcr; Minyun Zhou Lcb; **SuperStock:** age fotostock Rbr.

Jacket
Front and Spine top - **4Corners:** SIME/Luca Da Ros.

Map Front Cover - **4Corners:** SIME/Luca Da Ros.

All other images © Dorling Kindersley.
For further information see: www.dkimages.com

Special Editions of DK Travel Guides

DK Travel Guides can be purchased in bulk quantities at discounted prices for use in promotions or as premiums. We are also able to offer special editions and personalized jackets, corporate imprints, and excerpts from all of our books, tailored specifically to meet your own needs.

To find out more, please contact:
in the United States **SpecialSales@dk.com**
in the UK **travelspecialsales@uk.dk.com**
in Canada DK Special Sales at **general@ tourmaline.ca**
in Australia **business.development@pearson. com.au**

Phrase Book

Pronunciation

Turkish uses a Roman alphabet. It has 29 letters: 8 vowels and 21 consonants. Letters that differ from the English alphabet are: **c**, pronounced "j" as in "jolly"; **ç**, pronounced "ch" as in "church"; **ğ**, which lengthens the preceding vowel and is not pronounced; **ı**, pronounced "uh"; **ö**, pronounced "ur" (like the sound in "further"); **ş**, pronounced "sh" as in "ship"; **ü**, pronounced "ew" as in "few".

In an Emergency

Help!	İmdat!	eem-dat
Stop!	Dur!	door
Call a doctor!	Bir doktor çağırın!	beer dok-tor chah-ruhn
Call an ambulance!	Bir ambulans çağırın!	beer am-boo-lans chah-ruhn
Call the police!	Polis çağırın!	po-lees chah-ruhn
Fire!	Yangın!	yan-guhn
Where is the nearest telephone?	En yakın telefon nerede?	en ya-kuhn teh-leh-fon neh-reh-deh
Where is the nearest hospital?	En yakın hastane nerede?	en ya-kuhn has-ta-neh neh-reh-deh

Communication Essentials

Yes	Evet	eh-vet
No	Hayır	h-'eye'-uhr
Thank you	Teşekkür ederim	teh-shek-kewr eh-deh-reem
Please	Lütfen	lewt-fen
Excuse me	Affedersiniz	af-feh-der-see-neez
Hello	Merhaba	mer-ha-ba
Goodbye	Hoşça kalın	hosh-cha ka-luhn
Good morning	Günaydın	gewn-'eye'-duhn
Good evening	İyi akşamlar	ee-yee ak-sham-lar
Morning	Sabah	sa-bah
Afternoon	Öğleden sonra	ur-leh-den son-ra
Evening	Akşam	ak-sham
Yesterday	Dün	dewn
Today	Bugün	boo-gewn
Tomorrow	Yarın	ya-ruhn
Here	Burada	boo-ra-da
There	Şurada	shoo-ra-da
Over there	Orada	o-ra-da
What?	Ne?	neh
When?	Ne zaman?	neh za-man
Why?	Neden	neh-den
Where?	Nerede	neh-reh-deh

Useful Phrases

How are you?	Nasılsınız?	na-suhl-suh-nuhz
I'm fine	İyiyim	ee-yee-yeem
Pleased to meet you	Memnun oldum	mem-noon ol-doom
See you soon	Görüşmek üzere	gur-rewsh-mek ew-zeh-reh
That's fine	Tamam	ta-mam
Where is/are ...?	... nerede?	... neh-reh-deh
How far is it to ...?	... ne kadar uzakta?	... neh ka-dar oo-zak-ta
I want to go to ...	... a/e gitmek istiyorum	... a/eh geet-mek ees-tee-yo-room
Do you speak English?	İngilizce biliyor musunuz?	een-gee-leez-jeh bee-lee-yor moo-soo-nooz?
I don't understand	Anlamıyorum	an-la-muh-yo-room
Can you help me?	Bana yardım edebilir misiniz?	ba-na yar-duhm eh-deh-bee-leer mee-see-neez?

Useful Words

big	büyük	bew-yewk
small	küçük	kew-chewk
hot	sıcak	suh-jak
cold	soğuk	soh-ook
good/well	iyi	ee-yee
bad	kötü	kur-tew
enough	yeter	yeh-ter
open	açık	a-chuhk
closed	kapalı	ka-pa-luh
left	sol	sol
right	sağ	saa
straight on	doğru	doh-roo
near	yakın	ya-kuhn

far	uzak	oo-zak
up	yukarı	yoo-ka-ruh
down	aşağı	a-shah-uh
early	erken	er-ken
late	geç	gech
entrance	giriş	gee-reesh
exit	çıkış	chuh-kuhsh
toilets	tuvaletler	too-va-let-ler
push	itiniz	ee-tee-neez
pull	çekiniz	cheh-kee-neez
more	daha fazla	da-ha faz-la
less	daha az	da-ha az
very	çok	chok

Shopping

How much is this?	Bu kaç lira?	boo kach lee-ra
I would like ...	... istiyorum	... ees-tee-yo-room
Do you have ...?	... var mı?	... var muh?
Do you take credit cards?	Kredi kartı kabul ediyor musunuz?	kreh-dee kar-tuh ka-bool eh-dee-yor moo-soo-nooz?
What time do you open/ close?	Saat kaçta açılıyor/ kapanıyor?	Sa-at kach-ta a-chuh-luh-yor/ ka-pa-nuh-yor
this one	bunu	boo-noo
that one	şunu	shoo-noo
expensive	pahalı	pa-ha-luh
cheap	ucuz	oo-jooz
size (clothes)	beden	beh-den
size (shoes)	numara	noo-ma-ra
white	beyaz	bay-yaz
black	siyah	see-yah
red	kırmızı	kuhr-muh-zuh
yellow	sarı	sa-ruh
green	yeşil	yeh-sheel
blue	mavi	ma-vee
brown	kahverengi	kah-veh-ren-gee
shop	dükkan	dewk-kan
till	kasa	ka-sa
bargaining	pazarlık	pa-zar-luhk
That's my last offer	Daha fazla veremem	da-ha faz-la veh-reh-mem

Types of Shop

antiques shop	antikacı	an-tee-ka-juh
bakery	fırın	fuh-ruhn
bank	banka	ban-ka
book shop	kitapçı	kee-tap-chuh
butcher's	kasap	ka-sap
cake shop	pastane	pas-ta-neh
chemist's/ pharmacy	eczane	ej-za-neh
fishmonger's	balıkçı	ba-luhk-chuh
greengrocer's	manav	ma-nav
grocery	bakkal	bak-kal
hairdresser's (ladies)	kuaför	kwaf-fur
(mens)	berber	ber-ber
leather shop	derici	deh-ree-jee
market/bazaar	çarşı/pazar	char-shuh/pa-zar
newsstand	gazeteci	ga-zeh-teh-jee
post office	postane	pos-ta-neh
shoe shop	ayakkabıcı	'eye'-yak-ka-buh-juh
stationer's	kırtasiyeci	kuhr-ta-see-yeh-jee
supermarket	süpermarket	sew-per-mar-ket
tailor	terzi	ter-zee
travel agency	seyahat acentesi	say-ya-hat a-jen-teh-see

Sightseeing

castle	hisar	hee-sar
church	kilise	kee-lee-seh
island	ada	a-da
mosque	cami	ja-mee
museum	müze	mew-zeh
palace	saray	sar-'eye'
park	park	park
square	meydan	may-dan
theological college	medrese	med-reh-seh
tomb	türbe	tewr-beh
tourist information office	danışma bürosu	da-nuhsh-mah bew-ro-soo
tower	kule	koo-leh
town hall	belediye sarayı	beh-leh-dee-yeh sar-'eye'-uh
Turkish bath	hamam	ha-mam

Transport

airport	**havalimanı**	ha-**va**-lee-ma-nuh
bus/coach	**otobüs**	o-to-**bewss**
bus stop	**otobüs durağı**	o-to-**bewss** doo-**ra**-uh
coach station	**otogar**	o-to-**gar**
dolmuş	**dolmuş**	dol-**moosh**
fare	**ücret**	ewj-**ret**
ferry	**vapur**	va-**poor**
sea bus	**deniz otobüsü**	deh-**neez** o-to-**bew**-sew
station	**istasyon**	ees-tas-**yon**
taxi	**taksi**	tak-**see**
ticket	**bilet**	bee-**let**
ticket office	**bilet gişesi**	bee-**let** gee-sheh-**see**
timetable	**tarife**	ta-**ree**-feh

Staying in a Hotel

Do you have a vacant room?	**Boş odanız var mı?**	bosh o-da-**nuhz var** muh?
double room	**iki kişilik bir oda**	ee-**kee** kee-shee-**leek** beer o-**da**
room with a double bed	**çift kişilik yataklı bir oda**	**cheeft** kee-shee-**leek** ya-**tak**-luh beer o-**da**
twin room	**çift yataklı bir oda**	**cheeft** ya-**tak**-luh beer o-**da**
for one person	**tek kişilik**	tek kee-shee-**leek**
room with a bath	**banyolu bir oda**	ban-yo-loo beer o-**da**
shower	**duş**	doosh
porter	**komi**	ko-**mee**
key	**anahtar**	a-nah-**tar**
room service	**oda servisi**	o-**da** ser-vee-**see**
I have a reservation	**Rezervasyonum var**	reh-zer-vas-yo-**noom** var
Does the price include breakfast?	**Fiyata kahvaltı dahil mi?**	fee-yo-**ta** kah-val-tuh da-**heel** mee?

Eating Out

A table for ... please	**... kişilik bir masa lütfen**	... kee-shee-**leek** beer ma-sa **lewt**-fen
I want to reserve a table	**Bir masa ayırtmak istiyorum**	beer ma-sa 'eye'-**uhrt**-mak ees-**tee**-yo-room
The bill please	**Hesap lütfen**	heh-**sap** lewt-fen
I am a vegetarian	**Et yemiyorum**	et yeh-**mee**-yo-room
restaurant	**lokanta**	lo-**kan**-ta
waiter	**garson**	gar-**son**
menu	**yemek listesi**	ye-**mek** lees-teh-see
fixed-price menu	**fiks menü**	feeks meh-**new**
wine list	**şarap listesi**	sha-rap lees-teh-see
breakfast	**kahvaltı**	kah-val-**tuh**
lunch	**öğle yemeği**	ur-leh yeh-meh-**ee**
dinner	**akşam yemeği**	ak-**sham** yeh-meh-**ee**
starter	**meze**	**meh**-zeh
main course	**ana yemek**	a-na yeh-**mek**
dish of the day	**günün yemeği**	gewn-**ewn** yeh-meh-**ee**
dessert	**tatlı**	tat-**luh**
rare	**az pişmiş**	**az** peesh-meesh
well done	**iyi pişmiş**	ee-**yee** peesh-meesh
glass	**bardak**	bar-**dak**
bottle	**şişe**	shee-**sheh**
knife	**bıçak**	buh-**chak**
fork	**çatal**	cha-**tal**
spoon	**kaşık**	ka-**shuhk**

Menu Decoder

badem	ba-**dem**	almond
bal	bal	honey
balık	ba-**luhk**	fish
bira	**bee**-ra	beer
bonfile	**bon**-fee-leh	fillet steak
buz	booz	ice
çay	ch-'eye'	tea
çilek	chee-**lek**	strawberry
çorba	chor-**ba**	soup
dana eti	da-**na** eh-**tee**	veal
dondurma	don-door-**ma**	ice cream
ekmek	ek-**mek**	bread
elma	el-**ma**	apple
et	et	meat
fasulye	fa-**sool**-yeh	beans
fırında	fuh-ruhn-**da**	roast
fıstık	fuhs-**tuhk**	pistachio nuts
gazoz	ga-**zoz**	fizzy drink
hurma	hoor-**ma**	dates
içki	eech-**kee**	alcohol
incir	**een**-jeer	figs

ızgara	uhz-**ga**-ra	charcoal grilled
kahve	kah-**veh**	coffee
kara biber	ka-**ra** bee-**ber**	black pepper
karışık	ka-ruh-**shuhk**	mixed
karpuz	kar-**pooz**	water melon
kavun	ka-**voon**	melon
kayısı	k-'eye'-uh-**suh**	apricots
kaymak	k-'eye'-**mak**	cream
kıyma	kuhy-**ma**	minced meat
kızartma	kuh-zart-**ma**	fried
köfte	kurf-**teh**	meatballs
kuru	koo-**roo**	dried
kuzu eti	koo-**zoo** eh-**tee**	lamb
lokum	lo-**koom**	Turkish delight
maden suyu	ma-**den** soo-**yoo**	mineral water (fizzy)
meyve suyu	may-**veh** soo-**yoo**	fruit juice
midye	**meed**-yeh	mussels
muz	mooz	banana
patlıcan	pat-luh-**jan**	aubergine
peynir	pay-**neer**	cheese
pilav	pee-**lav**	rice
piliç	pee-**leech**	roast chicken
şarap	sha-**rap**	wine
sebze	seb-**zeh**	vegetables
şeftali	shef-ta-**lee**	peach
şeker	sheh-**ker**	sugar
su	soo	water
süt	sewt	milk
sütlü	sewt-**lew**	with milk
tavuk	ta-**vook**	chicken
tereyağı	teh-**reh**-yah-uh	butter
tuz	tooz	salt
üzüm	ew-**zewm**	grapes
vişne	**veesh**-neh	sour cherry
yoğurt	yoh-**urt**	yoghurt
yumurta	yoo-moor-**ta**	egg
zeytin	zay-**teen**	olives
zeytinyağı	zay-**teen**-yah-uh	olive oil

Numbers

0	**sıfır**	**suh**-fuhr
1	**bir**	**beer**
2	**iki**	ee-**kee**
3	**üç**	ewch
4	**dört**	durt
5	**beş**	besh
6	**altı**	al-**tuh**
7	**yedi**	yeh-**dee**
8	**sekiz**	seh-**keez**
9	**dokuz**	doh-**kooz**
10	**on**	on
11	**on bir**	**on** beer
12	**on iki**	**on** ee-kee
13	**on üç**	**on** ewch
14	**on dört**	**on** durt
15	**on beş**	**on** besh
16	**on altı**	**on** al-tuh
17	**on yedi**	**on** yeh-dee
18	**on sekiz**	**on** seh-keez
19	**on dokuz**	**on** doh-kooz
20	**yirmi**	yeer-**mee**
21	**yirmi bir**	yeer-mee **beer**
30	**otuz**	o-**tooz**
40	**kırk**	kuhrk
50	**elli**	eh-**lee**
60	**altmış**	alt-**muhsh**
70	**yetmiş**	yet-**meesh**
80	**seksen**	sek-**sen**
90	**doksan**	dok-**san**
100	**yüz**	yewz
110	**yüz on**	yewz **on**
200	**iki yüz**	ee-**kee** yewz
1,000	**bin**	been
100,000	**yüz bin**	**yewz** been
1,000,000	**bir milyon**	**beer** meel-yon

Time

one minute	**bir dakika**	**beer** da-kee-ka
one hour	**bir saat**	**beer** sa-at
half an hour	**yarım saat**	ya-**ruhm** sa-at
day	**gün**	gewn
week	**hafta**	haf-**ta**
month	**ay**	'eye'
year	**yıl**	yuhl
Sunday	**pazar**	pa-**zar**
Monday	**pazartesi**	pa-**zar**-teh-see
Tuesday	**salı**	sa-**luh**
Wednesday	**çarşamba**	char-sham-**ba**
Thursday	**perşembe**	per-shem-**beh**
Friday	**cuma**	joo-**ma**
Saturday	**cumartesi**	joo-**mar**-teh-see